BULGARIA IN ANTIQUITY

An Archaeological Introduction

BULGARIA
IN ANTIQUITY

An Archaeological Introduction

R. F. HODDINOTT

ST. MARTIN'S PRESS
NEW YORK

In gratitude to
the archaeologists and others who,
whether in person or through their work,
have made this book possible

Acknowledgements

Photographs made available under the general aegis of the Bulgarian Committee for Friendship and Cultural Relations with Foreign Countries are gratefully acknowledged from the following sources:

Archaeological Museum, Sofia (Pls. 10, 11, 12, 13, 18, 28, 29, 32, 33, 42, 43, 44, 45, 46, 47, 48, 50, 51, 62, 66, 77, 82, 91, 92, 93, 98, 125, 128, 129, 130, 131, 132, 133, 134, 135, 202 by Rosa Staneva; Pls. 16, 79, 80, 175 by Peter Hlebarov)

Archaeological Museum, Plovdiv (Pls. 30, 34, 38, 39, 52, 118, 120, 126)

Archaeological Museum, Varna (Pls. 23, 24, 25, 26, 27, 89, 144, 150, 191, 196)

Razgrad Museum (Pls. 108, 109)

Silistra Museum (Pls. 88, 90)

The assistance rendered by the Directors of these Museums and their colleagues, including, in some cases, special photography for this book, is warmly appreciated. In addition, I am especially grateful to the undernamed for the following: Pl. 94 by courtesy of T. Ivanov and the Director of the Sofia Archaeological Museum; Pl. 102 (P. B. Tarashenko) by courtesy of B. Sultov and the Director of the Veliko Turnovo Museum; Pl. 103 by courtesy of G. Toncheva; Pls. 163, 164, by courtesy of V. Antonova, Director of the Shoumen Museum.

Contents

PART THREE
CHRISTIANITY AND THE BYZANTINE WITHDRAWAL

List of Plates

List of Figures

Abbreviations

Foreword

As the formation of the Bulgarian nation belongs to the Middle Ages, the title of this book is contradictory in the sense that it is concerned with the territory of Bulgaria when it had other names and was inhabited by other peoples. Unlike Britain, in Antiquity it lay close to the centre of the world of Greece, Rome, and Persia, although at the same time acting as either a key bastion or a vulnerable frontier.

In the twelve hundred years from the country's 'discovery' by Greek colonists about 600 B.C. until its conquest and settlement by the Slavs, such a situation ensured it an inescapably important role. Yet, outside Bulgaria, this is not generally reflected in archaeological literature, and on most archaeological maps of Europe Bulgaria is an almost empty space. Study of the monuments of neighbouring territories suggested to me the illusory nature of this 'empty space' and aroused a wish to see and to evaluate what it contained.

There are reasons, some of them substantial, why Bulgaria is so little known in this connection. Less than a century has passed since the country was among the more depressed provinces of the Turkish empire, of which it had been part for 500 years. Archaeology has consequently been a late starter. In the last quarter-century, the rapid progress of industrialisation and mechanised agriculture has accelerated the uncovering of new finds and sites, often of great importance. The rescue digs involved have placed a severe strain on national archaeological resources and exacerbated the problem of prompt and adequate publication. Archaeological reports are normally published in Bulgarian or, occasionally, in Russian. The Western-language summaries that usually accompany them have often been too cursory to be of use. Moreover, even readers of Bulgarian experience difficulty in gaining access to basic reports published outside the main archaeological journals.

The resulting lack of interchange of expert views has been no less a disadvantage to Bulgarian than to foreign archaeologists. This book, the result of several journeys during which almost every corner of the country, major site, and museum were visited, supported by my wife's willingness to translate many thousands of words from archaeological reports of the last 70 or 80 years, is an attempt to begin to redress this imbalance regarding the period broadly definable as Antiquity, one of several in which the sites and monuments deserve wider knowledge and critical attention. Very little of the material has hitherto appeared in a western European language, although a few journals, such as, in English, *Antiquity*, have consistently drawn attention, within the limitations of space, to outstanding discoveries. Evaluation has been sporadic and rare anywhere.

Three distinct divisions emerge, each overlapping slightly but together forming a coherent chapter of the historical development of the country. In the first part, 'Thracians and Greeks', the general settlement pattern has yet to be established by further excavation, and native written sources do not exist. The approach, concentrating on the Black Sea colonies and on a few sites and some outstanding burials in the Thracian interior, therefore differs somewhat from that of the two later sections, when the territory was an integral part of the known world and a more comprehensive picture can be drawn.

The second part, 'The Roman Presence', invites many comparisons with other Roman provinces, including Britain. For reasons of space, analogies have been confined to a very few related sites in neighbouring territories; but the descriptions, photographs, and plans should enable an interested reader to draw his own parallels.

The transition from Rome to Byzantium, which began in A.D. 330, profoundly affected the area, lying as it did between the new capital and both the western provinces and the northern barbarians; but archaeologically the dividing-line is most apparent in 378, the year of the Visigothic triumph over the emperor Valens and of the accession of his successor, Theodosius I. Here, although a few relevant earlier monuments are included, begins the period described in 'Christianity and the Byzantine Withdrawal', by the end of which the Slavicised interior was once again almost as much a *terra incognita* to the then civilised world as it had been when Greek colonists first settled on the Black Sea coast.

Because historical circumstances varied greatly in different parts of the country, archaeological sites and finds have been grouped geographically as well as in their chronological setting, but the continuity of individual sites should be easy to follow. The grouping must not, however, mislead the reader in need of an archaeological guidebook. First, it has been necessary to be selective in order to describe as comprehensively as possible and within their historical and social context monuments chosen because they are either representative or outstanding. Secondly, some of the sites no longer exist and others are inaccessible or difficult to visit, for a variety of reasons. But if the traveller in or through Bulgaria finds that this introduction tempts him to explore, even a little, he will be well rewarded. Attention has been concentrated on sites rather than – with outstanding exceptions – chance finds. Certain sites about which little is yet known have been briefly mentioned in view of their potential importance.

Place-names constitute a problem which I cannot claim to have solved. In some cases, both antique and modern names are known, sometimes only the latter; there are also sites, identified by inscriptions, in what is now the middle of nowhere. Moreover, names of settlements and of physical features were by no means constant throughout Antiquity, nor are they always undisputed. Whilst Greek was the language in which the country was first described and was later in common use, especially in the south and along the whole coast, Latin was long dominant on the Danube. This also complicates the nomenclature of gods. Artemis and Diana co-exist.

Consistency therefore seeming impossible, I have adopted the following general guidelines. Mountains and rivers are given modern, Bulgarian names, facilitating reference to modern maps (both ancient and modern names of rivers and mountains, where known, appear on the two maps included). Ancient names of sites are used where they have been identified with reasonable certainty; modern equivalents are given at the first text mention and again, if it falls later, at the first main site description. Both appear on the maps, in the site bibliography, and in the index. Unidentified sites are referred to by the nearest modern settlement or location.

Greek, Latin, and Byzantine technical terms have presented another difficulty. Over a range of twelve hundred years one man's daily diet can be another's exotic – or dubious – rarity. Where technical terms have been considered necessary, they have been briefly explained within their context when first used.

To avoid tiresome repetition of dates and the background of events, a brief Historical Outline has been included. Readers unacquainted with the period in this area may find it useful to glance at the relevant section of this Outline before reading the main text.

My four visits to Bulgaria within the last nine years – covering most of the sites described, some more than once – were planned and carried out completely independently by my wife and myself. Only once, at my request, an official guide was provided, when we visited a monument in a military zone. We are therefore especially grateful to the Directors of Museums and other archaeologists and scholars in associated disciplines who have been so generous with their time and assistance, in some cases contributing their own photographs as well as their publications. The number is too great to list, but I hope they will find Barbara's and my appreciation reflected in the dedication. They will probably also find mistakes, for which I must accept full responsibility.

I must gratefully acknowledge, too, the invaluable assistance of the Bulgarian Committee for Friendship and Cultural Relations with Foreign Countries with official introductions and permits, and the gift of many photographs of museum objects. In the same connection my warm thanks are due to the Directors of the National Archaeological Institute and Museum in Sofia. It is also a pleasure to thank the Director and staff of the Great Britain–East Europe Centre in London for their constructive advice, for the continuing contacts afforded by meetings at the Centre, and for the use of its Library.

During the research for this book we have received and would like to record our appreciation of the warmly given assistance from Librarians and their colleagues of University of London libraries, in particular, of the Institute of Archaeology, the Joint Library of the Institute of Classical Studies and the Societies for the Promotion of Hellenic and Roman Studies, the School of Slavonic and East European Studies, and the Warburg Institute. Similar thanks are due to the Library of the Victoria and Albert Museum, and also to the Reference and Lending Departments of the Chiswick District Library.

I am especially grateful to my publishers for adopting a generous attitude towards illustrations and plans which will be of particular value to the student in view of the difficulty of access to many of the publications and sites.

Bulgaria welcomes tourists and we are grateful for helpful introductions from Balkantourist in both London and Sofia. But official resources are not yet geared to provide for the wanderer. This circumstance brings its own reward in the shape of many acts of practical kindness for which my wife and I would like to thank countless strangers in the cities, towns, and villages and on the roads of Bulgaria.

My wife's role in the preparation of this book has been no less than mine. All translations from Bulgarian and Russian are her work and, both at home and abroad, research, compilation, and writing have been shared. The work has benefited greatly from our discussions and – usually – constructive criticisms of each other's share. As titular author, it is a pleasure to record my collaborator's unstinting and equal contribution and my son Geoffrey's practical help in photographic and other technical matters.

London,   R. F. H.
September 1973

PART ONE
Thracians and Greeks

1 The Land and the People

The land of Bulgaria, less than half the size of Great Britain, emerges into history as the core of a much bigger area of south-east Europe inhabited by the Thracian people. To east and west – the shores of the Black Sea and the mountainous backbone of the Balkan peninsula – the boundaries of modern Bulgaria coincide with those of ancient Thrace. To the south and south-east, a large area of Thrace bordering the Aegean, the south-east shore of the Black Sea, and the Sea of Marmara falls within modern Greece and Turkey. To the north, except for a short land frontier across the Dobroudja, Bulgaria's frontier with Romania is the Danube (Pl. 1). In early Antiquity the Danube, then known as the Istros or Ister, served as a unifying link between the Thracians living to the south and those whose territories reached into the Carpathians and the north-west hinterland of the Black Sea.

Within Bulgarian Thrace the dominating feature is the west–east mountain range known to the Greeks as the Haimos, today sometimes as the Balkan, but in Bulgaria usually called the Stara Planina, 'the Old Mountain'. Penetrated by only one river, the Iskur, the ancient Oescus, in the west, most of its passes, except in the extreme east, must have been closed during the harsher winters that then prevailed. Rising steeply from the south and descending gradually towards the Danube, tributaries of which cut steep gorges through its extensive karstic foothills, this range and not the Danube was the original dividing-line between north and south Thrace (Pl. 2).

South of the Stara Planina and protected by it from the northern winds lies the fertile Thracian plain, sometimes now called 'the market garden of Europe'. At the end of the eleventh century, according to the *Gesta Francorum*, Bohemond and his crusaders found here 'an exceeding abundance of corn and wine and nourishment for the body'. In prehistory this was one of Europe's cradles of civilisation. The Thracian plain is watered by the river Maritsa, the ancient Hebros, which empties into the Aegean. Its numerous tributaries include the Tundja, the Greek Tonzos, the upper course of which drains the Valley of Roses lying between the Stara Planina and a lower, shorter range, the Sredna Gora.

The Thracian plain is bounded on the south by another west–east belt of mountains, penetrated by the Struma, the Greek Strymon, in the extreme west, partly by the neighbouring valley of the Mesta, the Greek Nestos, and decisively in the east by the Maritsa and Tundja. Between the Struma and the Maritsa stand the deep and intricately folded massif of dense forests, high fertile valleys, plateaux, and peaks formed by the Rila, Pirin, and Rhodope ranges. In the east the Rhodopes are lower, as are the Sakar and Strandja hills which extend to the shores of the Black Sea, but they were wide and high enough to hinder communication except where the rivers opened gaps.

The central region of west Bulgaria, in effect an abutment of the spinal massif of the Balkan peninsula, comprises a series of relatively high, fertile, and well-watered mountain-ringed plains which can be termed collectively the Western uplands. The largest contains the modern capital of Bulgaria, Sofia, and has

PLATE 1 The Danube near Ratiaria

PLATE 2 The Stara Planina from the Shipka Pass

always been an important centre of communications. The Struma valley, in places no more than a narrow gorge (Pl. 3), provides a route to the Aegean and others off it lead to northern Macedonia and to the Adriatic. To the north the Iskur links the Sofia upland with the Danube valley.

The Sofia upland is also crossed by the great highway which passes from Central Europe via Belgrade and Niš and on through the Thracian plain and the Maritsa gap to the Bosphorus and Asia. Often referred to as the 'Diagonal', it has had at least seven thousand years use.

The Thracians are identified as speaking a common Indo-European language with certain regional variations of dialect. They can also be distinguished from their neighbours by customs reflected in archaeological finds made in excavation of their settlements and burials. Such knowledge of the Thracian language as exists is mostly based on place and personal names and rare, brief inscriptions using Greek characters, for there was no written Thracian language (Pl. 4). Hence the historical sources are Greek or Roman, written with varying degrees of prejudice and accuracy from Greek or Roman viewpoints and consequently needing to be treated with appropriate reserve.

A difference can be observed between the Greek attitude towards the Thracians and their eastern neighbours, the Scythians. The Greeks preferred the latter. They lived far enough away for neither party to appear a danger to the other, and the agricultural riches of the Ukraine infinitely surpassed the resources of the much smaller Thracian plain. The profits of the Scythian trade are not only shown in the size and prosperity of the neighbouring Greek colonies, but also by the immense scale, in terms of wealth and ritual slaughter, of the Scythian royal graves.

The Thracians were not only a much less attractive commercial proposition; they were unruly, unreliable, and pugnacious, and Thraco–Greek antagonism dated at least as far back as the Mycenaean period: in the *Iliad* they appear as firm allies of the Trojans against the Greeks.

Excavations in Bulgaria have invariably shown a Thracian substratum beneath the Greek coastal cities. According to Strabo, the Black Sea colony of Mesambria (Nesebur) was the 'bria' – a Thracian word for town – of a chief named Mena. It is unlikely, certainly in the case of the earlier settlements, that the Thracians yielded their homes to the Greeks without bitter fighting. Homer's description of an incident in the Trojan war could easily have been a piece of sixth- or fifth-century B.C. reporting. A Thracian captain Peiros, having first smashed the ankle of Greek Diores with a jagged stone, had despatched him with his spear. Whereupon

> Aetolian Thoas hit him in the chest with a spear, below the nipple, and the bronze point sank into the lung. Thoas came up to him, pulled the heavy weapon from his breast, and, drawing his sharp sword, struck him full in the belly. He took Peiros' life but did not get his armour. For Peiros' men, the Thracians with the topknots on their heads (Pl. 5), surrounded him. They held their long spears steady in their hands and fended Thoas off, big, strong and formidable though he was. Thoas was shaken and withdrew.[1]

While prepared to view barbarians with disdain but equanimity from a distance, the Greeks usually regarded the Thracians in the light of undesirable neighbours, as indeed they often were.

Herodotos, describing the Thracians as the most numerous of peoples after the Indians, comments on the chronic disunity which effectively prevented them from becoming the most powerful of nations. Indications of the main tribal of the Sofia upland may have been a branch of the latter, but parts of the Western uplands were also inhabited by the Celtic Skordiski. North of the Stara Planina, the Triballi lived west of the Iskur-Vit (ancient Utus) divide, to the east of which were the Getai, the name given to a large group occupying both sides of the Danube. Herodotos calls them the most valiant and just of the Thracians, possibly a reflection of the better relations between the north-west Black Sea

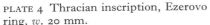

PLATE 4 Thracian inscription, Ezerovo   PLATE 5 Letnitsa, plaque, *ht.* 5·5 cm.
ring, *w.* 20 mm.

defeated such attempts, the fact that wealthy Thracians were buried with rich items from the treasure they owned when alive – rather than with inferior substitutes as was often the custom in Greek graves – has been a constant spur to the fortune-hunter. But happily some have escaped.

Tumulus burial was common to all the Thracian tribes, but the construction of the tomb and of the mound varied considerably, as did the funerary ritual. Tumuli were built singly or in groups and closely or widely spaced. A large necropolis could cover a huge area. Dimensions varied; the present height may be no guide to the original and, although less subject to change, the diameter at the base varied enormously. Some tumuli were enclosed by a low retaining wall. The mound might consist of earth, sometimes mixed with rubble or pebbles, or a dry-stone cairn might enclose the tomb and the rest of the mound be of earth.

A large tumulus might contain several burials, sometimes occurring within a fairly short time of one another. The grave itself might be a pit, perhaps roofed or lined with branches or beams, or a stone construction of varying complexity, consisting of one or more compartments. In more elaborate stone tombs a tendency towards a north–south orientation has been observed, the entrance being to the south; houses were probably built in the same way. Cremation and inhumation were practised in the same necropolis and even in the same tomb: if grave goods rightly interpret the sex of the deceased, this was not a factor in the choice. The act of cremation was carried out either at the grave or outside the mound. Herodotos gives what may be an eyewitness report of a burial on the outskirts of a Greek colony:

Referring to the ritual of Thracian tribes in the west, Herodotos writes:

> Those above the Crestonæans do as follows: each man has several wives; when therefore any of them dies, a great contest arises among the wives, and violent disputes among their friends, on this point, which of them was most loved by the husband. She who is adjudged to have been so, and is so honoured, having been extolled both by men and women, is slain on the tomb by her own nearest relative, and when slain is buried with her husband; the others deem this a great misfortune, for this is the utmost disgrace to them.[6]

The picture presented by the Greeks of Thracian religion is confused. Herodotos describes the Getai as worshipping a single god and as believing in their own immortality. The Getic god was known by several names, one being Zalmoxis, and Herodotos recounts a Getic custom:

> Every fifth year they despatch one of themselves, taken by lot, to Zalmoxis with orders to let him know on each occasion what they want. Their mode of sending him is this. Some of them who are appointed hold three javelins; whilst others, having taken up the man who is to be sent to Zalmoxis by the hands and feet, swing him round, and throw him into the air, upon the points. If he should die, being transfixed, they think the god is propitious to them; if he should not die, they blame the messenger himself, saying, that he is a bad man; and having blamed him, they despatch another, and they give him his instructions while he is yet alive.[7]

On the other hand, Herodotos refers to Thracian gods of tribes south of the Stara Planina by the names of members of the Olympic pantheon. Except for

PLATE 7 Thracian Horseman relief, *ht.* 20 cm.

their kings, who, he says, worship Hermes as their supreme and ancestral deity, only Ares, Dionysos, and Artemis are acknowledged. Unlike his remarks about the Getai, it may be suspected that this information was second-hand, for these are manifestly Hellenised versions of Thracian deities. Hermes was the son of Zeus and guide of the dead, but perhaps also reflected the taxes extorted by the Thracian kings from the Greeks, as Ares the fighting qualities of the Thracians, 'for whom to be idle is most honourable but to be a tiller of the soil most dishonourable; to live by war and rapine is most glorious'.[8] The extent to which the Greeks adopted and perhaps adapted the Thracian attributes and rites of Dionysos is unknown, but in Thrace it is probable that he was essentially a fertility god. Artemis had many aspects; Bendis was, as far as is known, the only Thracian goddess; as such, hunting was one of her attributes and in this respect, but not necessarily in others, they corresponded.

The Thracians borrowed their religious representational art as well as their alphabet from the Greeks. Thus Thracian religion was further disguised by a fundamentally Greek iconography. It was not, as far as we yet know, the Thracians but the Greeks of Odessos (Varna) who built a temple to the Getic 'Great God' and certainly the Greeks who depicted him on their coins. Artemis-Bendis, often represented with indistinguishable attributes, was another example of Greek syncretism.

An unquestionably, essentially Thracian religious figure is the Thracian Horseman or Hero, who first appeared in the Hellenistic period in the conventional iconography of a horseman riding slowly towards a goddess, and reappeared in the Roman period, when other iconographic forms were used, especially that of a hunter, usually on small relief tablets suitable for placing in a cave or other sanctuary. These icons, for such they were, often had a strong chthonic character, their votive and sometimes funerary purpose being basically consistent with a religion in which heroisation of a dead ancestor was an underlying theme. Their iconographic debt to Greece is impossible to estimate, especially since almost all known examples are relatively late in date; but association of the Thracian concept of immortality with the Thracian as well as Greek concept of heroisation is supported by the most common inscription: 'Hero'. The horseman may alternatively or additionally be identified with one of the gods, most frequently Asklepios, but often Apollo and sometimes Dionysos; sometimes there is a Thracian epithet which cannot be surely translated. The icon-like quality of the small stone reliefs has helped to preserve them. Under Christianity they were reinterpreted as representing a new 'hero', St George, and in the early years of this century on St George's Day peasants were still making pilgrimages and bringing sick people to be cured to one of Bulgaria's main Thracian Horseman sanctuaries, one identified particularly with Asklepios.

NOTES

1 Homer, *Iliad* IV, trans. Rieu, E. V., *The Iliad*, Harmondsworth, 1950, 91.
2 Xenophon, *Anabasis*, VII,4.
3 Dremsizova-Nelchinova, Ts., *Purvi Kongres na Bulgarskoto Istorichesko Drujestvo*, Sofia, 1972, I,335 ff.
4 Dremsizova, Ts. and Antonova, V., *Iz Shoumen* I,1955, 5 ff.
5 Herodotos V,8, trans. Cary, H., *Herodotus*, London, 1901, 309.
6 Herodotos V,5, ibid., 308.
7 Herodotos IV,94, ibid., 268, 269.
8 Herodotos V,6, ibid., 308.

2   The Black Sea Cities

I. APOLLONIA PONTICA

Apollonia Pontica (Sozopol) was founded by Miletos towards the end of the seventh century. Strabo says the greater part of the city occupied an offshore island, which must have been the present Sveti Kyrikos, but it extended over the Sozopol peninsula and Greeks also settled on the Atiya peninsula, a few kilometres to the north. The site was evidently chosen for its two excellent harbours – the city's emblem on coins was an anchor and a prawn – rather than trade. Its immediate hinterland was rugged and had no easy routes to the interior. The growing seaborne traffic plying the western Black Sea coast had shown the need for a port of call for revictualling and repairs between the Bosphoran harbours and such wealthy trading colonies as Histria and Olbia, established some half a century earlier farther north.

The Salmydessian coast of south-east Thrace between Apollonia and the Bosphorus had earned an evil reputation from its treacherously dangerous shores and the ferocity of the inhabitants. Aeschylus in *Prometheus Bound* describes Salmydessos as 'the rugged jaw of the sea, hostile to sailors, stepmother to ships'. Xenophon goes into more detail:

> In this part great numbers of ships sailing into the Euxine get stranded and wrecked since there are sandbanks stretching far out to sea. The Thracians who live here put up pillars to mark their own sectors of the coast, and each takes the plunder from the wrecks on his own bit of ground. They used to say that in the past, before they put up the boundary marks, great numbers of them killed each other fighting for the plunder. Round here were found numbers of couches, boxes, written books and a lot of other things of the sort that sailors carry in their wooden chests.[1]

No wonder Apollonia prospered. The colony, like others, must have had agricultural land, and good profits could be made from servicing storm-damaged shipping, supplying provisions, and providing recreation facilities for the sailors. Thence it developed as a point of transhipment and exchange of luxury goods manufactured in the Greek cities of the Aegean, notably pottery, textiles, jewellery, and wine, for raw materials such as grain, salted fish, hides, and flax from the rapidly increasing number of colonies dotted along the north-western and northern coasts of the Black Sea. Late in the sixth or during the fifth century, Apollonia successfully fostered dependent settlements in its vicinity, the most important, probably, being Anchialos (Pomorie), a valuable source of salt north of the Gulf of Bourgas.

With much coastal erosion and the picturesque tourist resort of Sozopol overlying the original city, opportunities for excavation have been small. A hoard of blunted copper arrowhead currency on the Atiya peninsula may reflect early dealings with the Asti tribe within whose territory the settlement lay,[2] and who almost certainly previously inhabited Apollonia. The earliest relics of the Greek city came to light during the dredging of the harbour in 1927. Of the substantial quantity of mostly fragmented pottery almost all the sixth-century pieces were imports from Ionia, Rhodes, and Samos. One complete and fragments of two more funerary *stelai*, or grave stones, of the same period were also recovered. All three show an enthroned female figure, a Cybele, Demeter, or other 'great goddess'. In the complete stele (Pl. 8) she appears to be resting a bowl, held in her right hand, on the arm of her seat. The primitive sculptural form is impressive; classic proportions are absent and drapery is indicated schematically. A terracotta figurine ascribed to the third quarter of the sixth century portrays a gracefully proportioned and executed version of a similar goddess. Found on the Atiya peninsula were headless fragments of a fine marble male statuette from the same period possessing a Late Archaic simplicity (Pl. 9).

After the ejection of Persia from Europe in 478 B.C., control of the Black Sea trade passed to Athens and Ionian imports dwindled to a trickle. A chance find in 1895, probably belonging to the beginning of this period, is the funerary stele of Anaxander, identified by a brief inscription at the top, showing a man leaning on his stick and gazing down at his dog, which stretches up on its hind legs to accept something from his hand (Pl. 10).[3] The subject was popular in the Greek world from the end of the sixth century, but, whilst the tall, narrow shape was in vogue during its last three decades, the strong stylistic resemblances with the stele from Orchomenos by Alxenor of Naxos in the National Museum of Athens, which is attributed to the first quarter of the fifth century, suggest the Apollonian stele was Greek work imported in the second quarter of the century. There are still traces of Late Archaic style in the rendering of the hair and drapery, but the peaceful realism and rhythmic composition bring it within the classic tradition.

Athenian commercial instincts were probably responsible for the development of trade with the hitherto neglected interior by such subsidiary colonies as Anchialos and Sladki Kladentsi, a site 3 kilometres west of Bourgas of which the antique name is unknown where two stores of commercial *amphorae*, large two-handled earthenware containers used for wine or oil, have recently been found. The success of this policy is reflected by finds of fifth-century Apollonian coins as far west as the Stara Zagora region and by the city's power to commission a colossal bronze statue of Apollo, 30 cubits (13·2 metres) in height, from the famous sculptor Kalamis. The temple of Apollo the Healer, the Milesian patron god, stood, presumably, on Sveti Kyrikos, and fifth-century architectural fragments, among them part of a frieze of rigidly profiled warriors now in the Louvre,[4] may have belonged to this sanctuary. Athenian ascendancy is also reflected in fifth- and fourth-century pottery dredged from the harbour.

Two of the city cemeteries were partially excavated between 1946 and 1949. The major site was part of a necropolis extending for at least 4 kilometres along the road running south from the city. The excavation area, known as Kalfa, is close to the shore about 2 kilometres from Sozopol and now consists of sand dunes, beneath which some 900 graves were uncovered in a strip about 150 metres long and 10 to 30 metres wide. Although the shifting nature of the dunes gave no help in dating by depth from the surface, compensation was provided by stratification; in some places as many as 11 graves occurred within a depth of 5 metres. The second was a smaller excavation; in an area about 20 metres long and between 10 and 20 metres wide about a hundred graves were found. It lay

PLATE 8 Apollonia, stele, *ht.* 98 cm.
PLATE 9 Apollonia, statuette, *ht.* 90 cm.
PLATE 10 Apollonia, Anaxander stele, *ht.* 2·40 m.

much closer to the old city, by what is now called the Morska Gradina or Marine Gardens. Burials found here began about the middle of the first half of the third century and ceased after about a hundred years. The results of both excavations have been fully published and reflect the fluctuating history of the city and lives of the citizens over several centuries.

Apollonia's first or Ionian phase is not represented at Kalfa. Graves of this period would have been nearer the city and, since sixth-century stelai have been recovered from the channel between Sozopol and Sveti Kyrikos, they may have been in land now eroded by the sea. Another cemetery may also have existed between Sozopol and the Atiya peninsula.

Chronologically the excavators divide the graves into three main phases: the first, beginning about 460 and lasting a hundred years; the second, from about 360 to 290; and the third, from about 290 to 175. Inhumation predominated throughout, only 11 cremations being noted. The skeletons normally lay stretched out on their backs, arms alongside the body, in the common Greek manner, and were oriented in no particular direction. Wooden coffins were usual, sometimes above them gabled tops consisting, in the case of adults, of four pairs of large square tiles, with similar tiles placed upright to close each end.

Only 22 stone tombs were found. Cists built of cut stone blocks, these were flat-topped and seldom much larger than the coffins. Two children's graves were built side by side with a surround-wall. The stone tombs belonged to the second phase, the earliest of them being attributed to the mid-fourth century and the majority to the late fourth or early third. Some were re-used, even into Christian times. Eleven older children were buried in *pithoi*, or large wide-bellied storage jars, and 17 babies in amphorae – these are dated to the second half of the fourth century.

Seven crouched burials were exceptions to the normal manner of inhumation; five had both arms and legs bent up to the chin, in the other two the arms were missing. They are dated to the latter part of the fourth or early third century and may perhaps have been of Thracians who retained their ancient ritual, as happened in Black Sea cities farther north, although among the Thracians generally this form of burial is typical of a much earlier period.

The 11 cases of cremation are also attributed to Thracians. These are dated to the mid-fourth century or later; the body seems usually to have been burnt elsewhere and the charred bones then placed in clay urns, exceptions being a red-figure *krater*, or deep wide-mouthed bowl for mixing wine with water, and a cylindrical stone urn with a stone lid. One adult cremation was contained in two bowls of about the same size, one upside down serving as a lid. With the much-burnt bones were eight small objects of fired grey clay of different shapes, including a spindlewhorl, a weight, a miniature bowl, a bead, and what was perhaps a primitive figurine, which alone showed traces of burning. These were probably magic objects and occur in some burials elsewhere (p. 64).

The inventories and the value of the grave goods varied from period to period, and significant differences occur between richer and poorer graves. Besides vessels for eating and drinking, the former contained toilet accessories and other luxuries; children had toys. The latter might have only one rough, locally-made pot or nothing at all. Nevertheless, the absence of architecturally outstanding graves is matched by the quality of the goods placed with the corpses. Plato

PLATE 11 Apollonia, oinochoe, *ht.* 14·5 cm. PLATE 12 Apollonia, lekythos, *ht.* 21·5 cm.

would have approved the lack of funerary ostentation shown, but the explanation may be either that the élite of the city were buried elsewhere or simply that the population basically consisted of small traders and middlemen. The relatively little jewellery found, particularly in the earlier graves, may, of course, be due to theft. About 30 stelai were recovered, still above the graves. Most bore no more than the two names of the deceased.

The intensification of trade with the Thracian interior to provide Athens with raw material she could no longer obtain from Asia Minor and the ensuing prosperity of Apollonia are reflected in the funerals of about 460 to 430. Almost all the pottery, averaging some four objects to a grave, although very occasionally reaching a score, was imported from Attica; the few exceptions were probably left over from the Persian occupation. Only one piece of Ionian ware occurs in a grave later than 430. Most of the pots were for everyday use and of little artistic merit. Nevertheless, a black-figure Attic *oinochoe*, or wine-jug, of about 470 was found in a grave of the second quarter of the fifth century. Made of fine light brown clay, it shows Artemis and Apollo against a light red rectangular ground, the remaining surface being decorated with a black glaze (Pl. 11). There were also a number of red-figure *lekythoi*, or small narrow-necked jugs for scented oils, generally showing women at their toilet or otherwise occupied in the home, like the lekythos illustrated in Pl. 12, found in a child's grave and dated to the third quarter of the fifth century. In a grave of the same date were two blue glass *aryballoi*, or globular vases; a quantity of black-glaze pottery which included four *kylikes*, or shallow two-handled wine-cups, turned upside down, evidently a ritual act; two aryballesque lekythoi; and terracotta figurines of Aphrodite, Demeter, and Silenus – two of the last, one of especially fine clay, representing him with breasts, an enlarged belly, and genitals.

The only 80 terracotta figurines discovered all belong to these three decades. Some were toys, but in certain richer tombs they were associated with a ritual hearth, where, after a funeral banquet, animal and fish bones, fruit stones, and pots were tossed on to the bonfire. The custom of breaking pots at a funeral was also a contemporary practice in the Thracian hinterland.

After 430, terracottas disappear and grave goods generally become fewer and inferior in quality, although almost all are still Attic imports. Athenian trade continued, on a reduced scale; not only did Athens have troubles, but, after the death of Sitalkes in 424, the Odrysian state, which had been favourable to Athens and had provided stable conditions for trade, began to disintegrate. Nevertheless, early fourth-century finds include a red-figure bell-krater displaying satyrs and maenads on the front and three youths on the back, which, together with a similar vase found in a Thracian tumulus in the Mezek area, is attributed by Sir J. Beazley to the Black Thyrsus painter.[5] Also from the first half, probably the second quarter, of the fourth century comes the only painted stele – a sandstone slab 1·72 metres high excluding the wedge base – found in any west Black Sea city (Fig. 1). The elaborate architectural design on the upper part incorporates a pediment

1   2   3   4

FIG. 1 Apollonia, painted stele: 1. Dark red. 2. Light blue. 3. Light brown. 4. Dark grey
FIG. 2 Apollonia, amphora-ringed tomb

occupied by a picture, probably of a siren. In the upper part of the stele is a separate area divided off by two [horizontal] red lines, in which a stag is shown, attacked by a lion. Both pictures are much damaged and their details indistinguishable. So far as one can tell, the stag is dark blue and the lion light brown. There are four vertical red lines along the slab which are perhaps the outlines of two columns. Between them at their base is a two-line inscription, illegible because of the perishable nature of the stone but no doubt the name of the deceased. Above the red horizontal lines are other traces of red ornament.[6]

The middle of the fourth century saw a revival in Apollonian prosperity, but there is some evidence of trouble in the unusual feature of a number of mass burials without grave goods. They may have been due to a natural disaster, but could have been connected with the Macedonian arrival. Apollonia entered into an alliance with Philip II, who successfully exploited Thracian disunity to reduce the Odrysai and their rivals to varying degrees of subjection. However, the archaeological evidence from the Kalfa necropolis suggests that the city's brief renewed prosperity was between the years 360 and 340 – before the peak of Macedonian power – when Athens was making fresh efforts to exploit the Thracian trade, her commerce interrupted with Egypt as well as Asia Minor. To these two decades are attributed many flamboyantly decorated 'Kerch-style' vases; these were mostly lekythoi, often aryballesque, but included other forms as well. Manufactured in Athens between 380 and 310, largely for the Scythian and Thracian export market, the polychrome colouring, extending to the use of white, blue, pink and even gilding and barbotine work, hardly conformed to Athenian taste. The subjects were preponderantly domestic scenes from the women's quarters, often including Eros. Others showed children with toys or the household dog, youths in the gymnasium, and scenes from Greek mythology with an apparent emphasis on Dionysos. A large lekythos depicting Demeter, Persephone, Triptolemos, Dionysos, and Hermes is an example of a group of vases especially associated with Apollonia.[7]

The next half-century, beginning about 340, saw the slow decline of the city. Until 320 the Kerch-style lekythoi continued to be plentiful, but thereafter all imported objects became noticeably fewer. With the ascendancy of Macedonia and Alexander's ejection of the Persians from Asia Minor, the links with Athens inevitably weakened. Amphora stamps suggest intensified trade with Heracleia Pontica during the second half of the fourth century, no doubt an attempt at diversification; but by its last quarter the regular use of ships capable of the direct north–south sea route across the Black Sea had undermined the foundations of Apollonia's economy. The city's first bronze coins were minted in 350 and soon they replaced silver ones in many graves.

Aristotle in his *Politeia* quotes Apollonia as an example of factional dispute following the admission of new settlers into a city. Whence and when these came is not specified, but during this half-century there are signs of the lowering of barriers between Greeks and Thracians. Thracian *fibulae*, or brooches, appear for the first time in the necropolis in the second half of the fourth century, as well as the fragile funerary garlands of gilded clay grapes or raspberries, rosettes, and ivy leaves that were fashionable among Greeks and Thracians alike towards the end of the century, and there is a sudden profusion of local pottery. During the whole period between 360 and 290 about a quarter of the clay vessels found in graves are local work, including painted clay imitations of the earlier alabaster or glass Egyptian-type *alabastra* (small vases for unguents or perfumes). After two centuries of importing everything but rough kitchenware, Apollonia had to fall back on its own or other local resources.

A funerary ritual unique here is attributed to this period. In a circle of 7 metres in diameter enclosing a stone-built tomb, 27 amphorae were arranged, mouths outwards, level with the roof of the tomb (Fig. 2). Inside the tomb only a grey clay pot and a fragment of a bronze *strigil*, or perspiration scraper for use by athletes and after bathing, accompanied the skeleton. Thirteen of the amphorae were fairly well preserved and, whilst without stamps, are considered to be Thasian types of the second half of the fourth or the beginning of the third century. A similar circle of amphorae was found nearby in a very early dig; another occurs round a cremation burial at Olbia.

The third stage of Apollonia's existence marked by these graves began about 290, about three-quarters of the way through the long reign of Lysimachos. The Greek colonies now served as garrison towns and at the end of the fourth century and the beginning of the third graves of soldiers, buried with their weapons, occur. Now, too, a new burial ritual appears, in which the coffined body and grave goods are placed in an immense earthen jar.

By the end of Lysimachos' reign in 281, Apollonia, politically and economically, had fallen behind the neighbouring Megarian colony of Mesambria. The Celtic invasion and occupation of much of south-eastern Thrace was a further blow. Apollonia was not captured, but a fragmentary inscription in Doric dialect found in the city is generally interpreted to mean that it had been forced to join Mesambria to seek from Antichos II Theos aid against the Celts.[9] Contemporary inscriptions from Mesambria, Kallatis (Mangalia), and Histria refer to the granting of proxeny or honorary citizenship to Apollonians, suggesting a possible exodus of some of the wealthier and more timorous.

During the final phase represented in these excavations, the Kalfa site must have been too distant from the city and the Morska Gradina cemetery came into use. From here came one of the very few carved stelai. Third-century in date and probably commemorating a warrior killed in battle,[10] it shows a young man with two spears in his left hand and his right resting on a *herm*, a quadrangular pillar, usually decorated with genitals and surmounted by a bust. The inscription below is almost entirely lost (Pl. 13). The stele was not connected with any known grave.

Many Morska Gradina graves of between the second quarter of the third and the second quarter of the second century had no grave goods at all. In a few, some imported objects, such as Megarian bowls and some gold ornaments, were found, but almost all the pottery was local. Tile-roofed graves continued. A relatively rich cremation burial may indicate the status achieved by Thracian members of the community.

The liquidation of the Celtic kingdom in 218 revived the old antagonism between Apollonia and Mesambria. According to an Apollonian inscription, of which a fragmentary copy was found at Histria, at some time in the first half of the second century Mesambria captured Anchialos and then its fleet, suddenly appearing before the walls of Apollonia, looted and profaned the temple of Apollo, although failing to take the city. The rescue of Apollonia and the defeat of Mesambria with the aid of forces from Histria is also recorded.[11] Apollonia was among the cities allied with Mithridates of Pontos against Rome in the first century, probably playing only a modest part. Fierce resistance to the Roman forces under M. Terentius Varro Lucullus in 72 B.C. is said to have brought destruction on the city and its fortifications. Pliny relates that the 'tower-like' bronze statue of Apollo by Kalamis that for four centuries had symbolised the greatness of Apollonia was shipped to Rome to adorn the Capitoline.

II. MESAMBRIA

Towards the end of the sixth or at the beginning of the fifth century the Milesian monopoly of the west Black Sea coast was broken by a Megarian settlement. Mesambria or Mesembria Pontica (Nesebur) – both names were used in antiquity – was probably a foundation of the earlier Megarian colonies of Byzantion and Chalcedon on the Sea of Marmara. Its present name has evolved with little change from that given it by the Greeks and Thracians.

North of the Gulf of Bourgas and immediately south of the last eastern spur of the Stara Planina, the colony occupied a peninsula now only 850 metres long and 300 metres wide, linked to the mainland by an isthmus so low and narrow that artificial banking was needed to make a modern road. Steep cliffs, subject to erosion, protect the north and east coasts, but on the south the land slopes gently to the sea. The situation offered easier access to the interior than Apollonia possessed, as well as fairly low and easy passes facilitating trade with the north.

The colony was probably the result of a succession of migrations from the Persian threat, which may account for a more independent economic development than that of Apollonia – one of a planned series of settlements in a time of peace. By about the middle of the fifth century economic prosperity was shown by the issue of coins. Naulochos (Roman Templum Iovis, modern Obzor), just north of the Stara Planina, was an early offshoot of Mesambria.

No major excavations have taken place in modern Nesebur, with its confined, densely populated area and its long history as a busy maritime town. But 20 relatively large-scale soundings between 1944 and 1964 have identified three distinct cultural layers prior to the Turkish period. The earliest was Thracian; it included both Bronze and Early Iron Age material, but extended over only part of the peninsula and varied from 20 centimetres to 2 metres in depth. Next, several metres thick and overlying the whole peninsula, was a Greek layer, distinguished by its pronounced yellow colour, caused by the disintegration of the mud bricks used to build houses. The third layer contained remains from the Romano-Byzantine period. Large stretches of the original Greco-Hellenistic ramparts have fallen into the sea or been otherwise destroyed, but short sectors, particularly near the isthmus, have been excavated. At the site of a necropolis which stretched several kilometres along the coast towards the south-west, there has also been some excavation, although, apart from early chance finds, these have been mostly salvage digs before refugees were housed here in the 1930s.

There is little doubt that the Greek colony was encircled by a fortified wall at an early stage. Almost all the north-eastern sector and perhaps also an acropolis

PLATE 13 Apollonia, stele frag-   PLATE 14 Mesambria, pre-Hellenistic city wall
ment, *ht.* 36 cm.

PLATE 15 Mesambria, cyma fragment, *ht.* 18 cm.

have been eroded. Some slight impression of the damage can be gained at
the site of the Sea Basilica, the north nave of which now lies at the bottom of a
sheer cliff (Pl. 189). The narrow western shore facing the mainland has been more
fortunate in suffering only from man.

Here the gateway, through which runs the road into the town, dates from the
Romano-Byzantine period, but some remains of the earliest ramparts have been
excavated nearby, following a line very close to the later walls. The lowest and
first building period is dated to the fifth or, at latest, early fourth century. With
foundations 2 metres deep, the outer façade is dry-stone walling, generally using
ashlar blocks of varying size, irregularly laid, but here and there strengthened
by hooking one block into its neighbour, or, more rarely, laid in regular courses
of unequal height. In the second building period, tentatively assigned to the
fourth century, the isodomic method was used, the courses regular and of equal
height. In the third period, stability was ensured by laying the blocks in courses
to expose long sides and ends alternately, a system to gain added strength

perhaps introduced by the end of the fourth century, but common throughout the later Hellenistic era. This substantial façade was backed by an *emplecton*, or fill, of broken stone and yellow clay like that used for the bricks of the houses. As only parts of the emplecton have survived and nothing of the inner façade, the thickness of the wall is unknown. There were also no signs of towers. A short distance east of the Byzantine north-west angle tower an early sector of the north ramparts was found. Finely jointed ashlar blocks, rectangular or trapezoidal in shape, are laid without mortar in nearly even courses, with some of the blocks hooked to the next. The emplecton contained fragments of archaic Attic pottery and this wall is regarded as another sector of the original fortifications (Pl. 14). A later repair made use of a fourth- or third-century Doric capital.

Soundings located several houses in the Greco-Hellenistic layer; the earliest, attributed to the fifth century, has still to be published. Building levels were distinguished by superimposed floors with evidence of habitation between them. Four Hellenistic houses had peristyles, probably with wooden pillars, and stood apart from their neighbours. Outside walls were coated with a plaster of fine lime and sand, with painted decoration in various colours, including Pompeian red, yellow ochre, green, and black. About a quarter of one Hellenistic house was excavated. Fragments of black-figure vases and sixth-century Chian amphorae were found beneath the floor, together with part of an inscription mentioning a sanctuary of Apollo. The excavated sector consisted of an irregularly paved and peristyled rectangular courtyard and rooms on the north and east sides. In the north wing a stone staircase with six steps making a right-angled turn descended into a cellar with stone walls 2·20 metres high. The debris of the collapsed upper parts of the house consisted of tiles, decomposed mud bricks, and fragments of stucco, painted red, blue-black, white, and in imitation of marble. There were also Mesambrian coins of the fourth to second centuries, terracottas, and ceramic fragments, including a mould for a 'Megarian' bowl. Built towards the end of the fourth century, the house was apparently reconstructed in the second. An interesting point about some of the building materials is an almost certain link with Olbia, a link also shown by decrees erected in the latter city. Fragments of fourth-century Mesambrian *cymata*, or curved architectural mouldings, bear the same stamp as is found on Olbian tiles and, on the basis of Mesambrian material, much of it unpublished, I. B. Brashinsky recognises close analogies between cymata and ornamental frontal tiles of both cities (Pl. 15).[12]

Although some building material may have been imported, Mesambria possessed its own industries, to a much greater degree, on present evidence, than Apollonia. Besides finished objects, remains of two furnaces were discovered close to the Hellenistic house. The remnants of one, together with the discovery of a 'Megarian' bowl mould in the nearby house, suggest that it was a pottery kiln. The construction of the better-preserved furnace, the quantity of slag in its vicinity, and holes in the ground suitable for melting ingots, all pointed to a metallurgical purpose.

Close to the house and furnaces was the *bothros*, or sacrificial pit, of a temple. The contents, dating from the fifth to the third centuries, included fragmentary inscriptions which indicate a sanctuary of Zeus and Hera. No early public buildings have yet been found, but epigraphic evidence shows that the chief temple was dedicated to Apollo, probably Pythian Apollo, much honoured in

PLATE 16 Mesambria, Kallikrita stele,   PLATE 17 Mesambria, stele, *ht.* 60 cm.
ht. 1 m.

PLATE 18 Mesambria, hydria, *ht.* 50 cm.   PLATE 19 Mesambria, hydria detail,
ht. 10·50 cm.

Megarian colonies and to whom was addressed a second- or third-century A.D. votive tablet of the Thracian Horseman found in the city. Dionysiac rites are attested by several inscriptions. Two, one of which had been erected in the temple of Apollo, refer to the ceremonies taking place in the city's theatre. Other inscriptions indicate special attention to the cults of Athena Sotira, Demeter, Hekate, and the Dioskouri. From the third century onwards, and especially about the first century B.C. when the presence of refugees from Egypt offers a ready explanation, there are references to Isis and Serapis.

Aspects of Mesambrian life touched upon in other, mostly fragmentary inscriptions, include a probably third-century decree declaring free entrance to the harbour in times of peace or war; a treaty with a Thracian chief, Sadalas (p. 48); praise of a person who provided grain cheaply to the Mesambrians; and a late third-century decree honouring a woman, unfortunately so fragmentary that both her name and her virtues remain unknown. It is the earliest official honour paid to a woman found on the west Black Sea coast and an unusual feature at this time in a Greek city.

The approximate site of the mainland necropolis has long been known. More than fifty years ago, I. Velkov wrote:

> Over an extent of 2 to 3 kilometres the whole area is strewn with broken stone and brick and fragments of antique pottery. In some places there are larger accumulations of such fragments and more massive stones. Antique coins are always to be found here, especially after a spell of strong wind.[13]

Large numbers of the burials were direct interments into the earth and in an area subject to constant weathering and habitation through the ages they were easily destroyed. By 1964 less than a hundred tombs had been identified, most through chance or the salvage digs of the 1930s. They were mainly inhumations of the fourth and third centuries, laid in variously oriented rectangular tombs, little larger than coffins, built of thick stone slabs smoothed on the inside but only roughly shaped on the outside; horizontally laid slabs formed the roof. Exceptions included a gabled tomb, like those at Apollonia but with two large limestone slabs balanced over the corpse instead of tiles, and double tombs, divided merely by a partition wall. Another possessed a small 'antechamber' with closed walls of three single slabs attached to the main compartment with no facility for intercommunication. Robbers had removed the grave goods, but charred embers and burnt potsherds in the 'antechamber' suggest a sacrificial purpose. Similar tombs were found in Thracian cemeteries in north-east Bulgaria. The tomb with the richest grave finds (see below) was also one of the largest (3 metres long, 1·60 metres wide, and 1·20 metres deep). The limestone blocks were more carefully dressed than usual, being smoothed inside and out.

The earliest funerary stele – that of Kallikrita – was found re-used south of Nesebur, in the village of Ravda. In spite of its damaged condition, the subject of a seated woman amusing a child with a toy and watched by a female attendant holding up an alabastron in her left hand and carrying a basket in her right, is portrayed with sympathy and dignity (Pl. 16). The Attic theme of the seated woman and her attendant, at its finest exemplified by the stele of Hegeso in the National Museum of Athens, was popular all over the Greek world. It is likely that Kallikrita's stele, undoubtedly provincial work, was carved in a Mesambrian workshop of the end-fifth or early fourth century. Three stelai bearing reliefs of a *kantharos*, or drinking cup, the earliest attributed to the second half of the fifth or beginning of the fourth century and the latest to the third, also come from the necropolis.

Another popular Attic subject was that of a teacher and his pupil (Pl. 17). Again, in this mid-third-century provincial version, stiff, a little disproportionate, and with an exaggerated zoomorphic chair leg, something of character comes through in the two personalities.

In some third-century graves, remains of clay 'fruit' garlands like those in Apollonia were found. A more appropriately Mesambrian grave find was the Megarian-type bowl; the quality of clay and workmanship of those recovered suggest local work.

Considering the extent to which the cemetery was robbed in antiquity and later, it is surprising that three bronze *hydriai*, water vessels with two horizontal and one vertical handles, have been preserved. One had served as a cremation urn; it was decorated with a bronze relief of the rape of Oreithyia by Boreas (Pl. 18). This motif was repeated on another, whilst the third showed the young Dionysos accompanied by Silenus (Pl. 19). Although sometimes used for cremations, these vessels were primarily valuable water jugs, coming within the category of expensive wedding gifts, as when Pseudo-Demosthenes refers to one 'alongside a flock of fifty sheep, with the shepherd and a serving boy'. G. Richter, analysing a group of 20 such hydriai, concluded that they originated from a single workshop in the second half of the fourth century.[14] According to her, the source may have been Attica; Chalcedon has also been suggested.[15] The discovery of three in a site so little excavated could be due to chance, but is more likely to indicate either an origin closely connected with the colony or a successful export-import policy. More than a score of bronze hydriai of other types have been found in wealthy Thracian graves in the interior.

There was probably little time lost between burial and the surreptitious removal of the richest grave goods. The construction of the stone tombs made robbery easy. As the most valuable objects were usually placed near the deceased's head, once the grave had been located or if the ceremony had been watched, it was only necessary to take up one roof stone to secure the major booty.

The large tomb mentioned above is one of the very few found intact, perhaps because of its superior construction or because it was originally covered by a tumulus. It contained the skeleton of a woman; fragments of fine gold thread all over the interior suggest that she wore or was covered by a rich textile. Besides three pots of local coarse ware and the ritual fragments of a *stamnos*, or jar for mixing wines, commonly found in these tombs, and three glass alabastra, there was a rich collection of gold jewellery, mainly of well-known Hellenistic types. There was a chain necklace with finials shaped like animal muzzles and enclosing opals, and beads from at least two others, one of glass. The finest workmanship was evident in a pair of earrings – in which one end of the hoop terminates in the foreparts of Pegasus and from the hoop is suspended a miniature amphora with elaborate filigree and granular decoration (Pl. 20). The earrings had been much worn and the wings of Pegasus were damaged; one had been repaired, not very skilfully, with a different, paler gold.

The most unusual of several rings was found on the skeleton's finger – a spiral

PLATE 20 Mesambria, ear-
ring, *diam.* 2·7 cm.

PLATE 21 Mesambria, finger-
ring, *l.* 6·1 cm.

with a fantastic beast's head with crocodile jaws at the top (Pl. 21). Three jewels, of which one amethyst remains, were inset in clumsily stylised shoulders and two more at the base of the spiral. This development of the common snake-spiral ring, an example of which was also found in Mesambria has few if any analogies in either Scythian or Thracian animal art. Also unusual was an oval brooch just over 8 centimetres across, to which was welded a bronze pin. Ornamented with a well-designed filigree decoration and inset with seven stones, it was of a type found elsewhere in this cemetery, but usually simply decorated by a mythological scene hammered on a mould without especial skill.

Near this tomb were several others, partially robbed or badly damaged, and two tumuli, suggesting that this isolated part of the cemetery was used by wealthy Thracians living in the city. The opulent grave goods, contrasting with those of Greek tombs, probably reflected not only Thracian belief in an afterlife in which one's most precious possessions would be needed, but also a belief in the power of ancestors over the living.

The use of the pale gold noted above extends to the manufacture of at least nine ornaments found in Mesambria, including the moulded oval brooches. In one case it has been suggested that, lacking the correct matrix, the craftsman combined two others to achieve the semblance of a *Nike*, or Victory. The nature of these various jewellery finds suggests the likelihood of a goldsmith's workshop in Mesambria by some time in the third century.

In spite of the mention of unpublished fragments of fine imported and local pottery among the debris of buildings and the representations of kantharoi on stelai, remarkably little ware of any artistic value is known. An exception is a red-figure bell-krater, almost identical in shape to others found in Apollonia and Odessos; it shows a young girl being conducted towards Dionysos and erotes, a dancing satyr in attendance.

Little is known of Mesambria during the Macedonian period, although it was at this time that the city replaced Apollonia as the leading Greek colony on the south-west Black Sea coast. Doubtless access to the Getic areas north of the Stara Planina was an advantage, but probably the traditional adaptability of its citizens, shown by their mutually satisfactory relations with the Thracians in the hinterland, was a basic factor.

A partially preserved decree throws some light on Mesambrian–Thracian relations. Erected originally in the temple of Apollo but being carefully housed by a Nesebur dentist when brought to the notice of archaeologists in 1949, the decree records a treaty between the city and a Thracian ruler, Sadalas.[16] A rendering of the fragment reads:

> . . . to Sadalas as soon as possible. Sadalas must be crowned with a gold wreath during the Dionysiac festivals at the theatre as a benefactor to the city. To him and his heirs will be granted citizenship – the right to represent the honour of the city; to take first place at the public games; to bring his ships in and out of the harbour of Mesambria without hindrance; to be crowned every year with a wreath of the value of fifty staters. The treasurer must write the oath and the agreement on an inscribed slab and place it in the sanctuary of Apollo near the tablets of the ancestors of Sadalas, Mopsuestis, Taroutin, Medistas and Kotys. Agreement between Sadalas and the inhabitants of Mesambria: if a Mesambrian ship is wrecked at sea off the territory of Sadalas, having delivered its cargo . . .

The names of Sadalas and his ancestors are Thracian. The courteous formula of a 'gold wreath' was a euphemism for a fairly substantial annual tribute. The inscription is adjudged 'careful work of the early Hellenistic period',[17] but in the absence of sufficient comparable local material, no more precise dating is possible on epigraphic evidence. Nor can Sadalas be identified with any certainty. It is a common Thracian name and he could have been a local Astian ruler or an Odrysian. Thus dating to a large extent depends on the period when a Thracian could have been sufficiently influential and powerful to have such relations with and receive such tribute from Mesambria. G. Mihailov considers this could only have been between the death of Lysimachos in 281 and the Celtic arrival in 278.[18] Other scholars have either minimised the power of the Celts[19] or felt that the reign of Lysimachos need not be excluded.[20] The existence of Seuthopolis, albeit some distance inland, may be cited in support of each view.

Archaeology does not record undue hardship in Mesambria in the third century. The teacher and pupil stele (Pl. 17) probably represents local work and an epitaph stylistically influenced by the *Iliad* may also suggest a degree of cultured leisure. The same necropolis continued in use.

In the second century, Mesambrian ambition led to the attacks on Anchialos and Apollonia already described. But when M. Lucullus arrived at the head of a Roman army in 72 B.C., Mesambria seems again to have adapted to circumstance. While Apollonia resisted, here there was no struggle; the next spring the city erected a decree in honour of Gaius Cornelius, commander of the Roman garrison. Fierce resistance to Burebista's Daco-Getic invasion is, however, recorded. Dio Chrysostom says that all the Greek cities south to Apollonia were captured, but judging by votive plaques to the protecting gods, Mesambria may have escaped, and certainly the city survived, perhaps little harmed, into the Roman era.

III. ODESSOS

Odessos (Varna) was founded by Miletos about 585 or 570 B.C. From the beginning, it was essentially a trading colony. Among Greek coastal cities between the Stara Planina and the Danube delta it was second in importance to Histria in the northern Dobroudja, until the latter's decline, when first place was taken by the later Doric foundation of Kallatis, also in modern Romania. Other colonies included Kruni, by some authors identified with Dionysopolis (Balchik) renamed after a statue of Dionysos had been 'miraculously' washed up on its shore, a precedent later followed by some famous Byzantine icons, and Bizone (Kavarna). Excavation and published finds of early date from these and other sites have as yet been minimal. There were also Thracian coastal settlements.

Although dredging operations or soundings showed Bronze Age life under Apollonia and Mesambria, Odessos and its immediate vicinity go back archaeologically to the Late Chalcolithic period and beyond. Lake Varna, around which many pile settlements had been built, was an inlet of the Black Sea until about the beginning of the first millennium B.C., but the silting-up of the bar still left an excellent harbour. When the Greeks arrived, the region was inhabited by the Krobyzi tribe, a branch of the Getai, with whom Milesian Histria had already established good and profitable relations. The hinterland was fertile, well forested, and rich in game.

Today, Varna is Bulgaria's third most populous city and her chief port. Even during the Roman period the walls were extended to include an area more than double the original settlement of some 13 hectares, and this involved the demolition of Greek and Hellenistic public buildings. In such circumstances, archaeology has always been severely hampered. Sufficient vestiges of the Greek curtain walls have been identified to show that they formed a basis for at least part of the Roman fortifications. Within the early walls, sites of only two pre-Hellenistic buildings have been located.

Outside, chance finds and salvage digs over the last 90 years have traced the outlines of the two main early cemeteries; both were used until the mid-first century B.C. for both cremation and inhumation burials. One stretched northeast along the old road to Dionysopolis, covering the whole 44 hectares of the modern Morska Gradina by the seashore; the other, smaller but densely packed with graves, was near the north shore of Lake Varna. Another, apparently less extensive area north of the city was also used for burials. Three other cemeteries in the neighbourhood are specifically attributed to Thracian villages, rather than the Greek city. Two had several high mounds, excavated by K. Škorpil before they disappeared beneath modern Varna; the third consisted of low mounds now transformed into vineyards.

Škorpil is an honoured name in Bulgarian archaeology. Two brothers, Hermenegild and Karel Škorpil, were idealistic Czechs who, when Bulgaria gained independence in 1879, decided to help the newly free Slav country discover, understand, and preserve its past. The elder, Hermenegild, came first, and by 1882 Bulgaria's first archaeological society was founded in Sliven, close to where so many major prehistoric tells have since been discovered. In Varna, where a similar local society was formed a little later, Karel, the greater archaeologist, took the lead in building up an archaeological museum. On countless journeys of exploration he also made many important discoveries, especially in north-east Bulgaria, where an outstanding contribution was the identification of Pliska, the first capital of the medieval Bulgarian state. No less important to science was the stimulus he gave to local appreciation of the heritage of the past and the consequent founding of civic archaeological societies and museums. This did not endear him to those archaeologists and officials whose aim was to build up a collection of 'treasures' for a national museum; to them Karel Škorpil's individualism, his interest in sites (as opposed to objects of silver and gold), and the enthusiasm with which he infected local societies seemed often obstructive. He also antagonised – and fought – developers interested in land only as marketable property, those who viewed ancient monuments as cheap quarries for building materials, and people primarily interested in selling finds abroad to the highest bidder. Škorpil's contribution to Bulgarian archaeology is incalculable and it is warming to see it now recognised. The village where he made one of his last discoveries, an Early Byzantine basilica with a fine mosaic floor, has been renamed Shkorpilovtsi; he was buried at the site of another basilica he had found, at Djanavar-tepe, near Varna. In the city itself, the Archaeological Museum, with its tradition of scientific archaeology and fine collection, is Karel Škorpil's main memorial.

The two early buildings within the city were probably cult edifices. In the first, the remains of a wall $1\frac{1}{4}$ metres thick were traced for 9 metres; on part of another wall at right-angles to it was the base of a Doric column with empty spaces for four others. This may have been the *pronaos* (porch or vestibule) of a temple. Even less was left of the second building, found below the ruins of a Hellenistic temple. It is thought to have been the *temenos*, or sacred precinct, of a temple of Demeter, the main evidence being pottery from the end of the sixth century and beginning of the fifth from three bothroi which bordered the supposed sanctuary.

The layer above this suggested temenos of Demeter provides some archaeological evidence of Hellenistic cults.[21] Here were the remains of an almost square dry-stone walled building (4·30 by 4·20 metres) with a single entrance. Potsherds attest its fourth-century construction, although there were later repairs. To the south of the sanctuary a well, an oven, a bothros with fragments of amphorae, a herm, and black-glaze ceramic were found, together with two marble votive reliefs. On one relief is a goddess with a quiver of arrows over her shoulders, a *patera*, or saucer-like dish often used for libations, in her right hand and two (?) spears in her left. A tiny male worshipper stands at one side and a dog sits below the patera at the other. The relief is dedicated to Phosphoros (the light-bearer), an epithet applied both to Artemis-Bendis and to Hekate. On the basis of the inscription this relief is dated to the third–second century[21] or to the second–first.[22] The other relief, attributed to the second century, shows a horseman advancing in a stately manner towards a standing figure.

FIG. 3 Odessos, Corinthian oinochoe, detail of decoration

Beneath is a short dedication to the 'Heros Karabazmos', a Thracian epithet
which also appears on a number of Horseman tablets found in the sanctuary
of a Thracian settlement at Galata, 11 kilometres south of Odessos.

Another syncretism was the 'Theos Megas', the Great God, probably Zalmoxis,
later known as Darzalas, who also had a temple at Histria. Depicted on coins
and represented by terracotta figurines in tombs from the fourth century onwards,
the Great God of Odessos seems to have possessed the attributes of a chthonic
fertility god. On both coins and statuettes he holds a cornucopia and a patera,
on the statuettes often wearing the ivy- or vine-leaf crown of Dionysos. Coins
of the third century in particular frequently portray him on horseback, possibly
an identification with the Thracian Hero and another pointer to the close links
between Odessos and its Getic hinterland. A first-century B.C. list of the priests
of the Great God of Odessos included a Thracian name and, during the Roman
period, games known as 'Darzaleia' were held in his honour.

The interrelations of Thraco-Odessitan cults, which appear to centre on the
Great God, are by no means clear. Their associations probably included the
Samothracian mystery cult of the Kabiri, which flourished in all the north-
western colonies as well as in the interior (p. 96). Epigraphical evidence of the
local Samothracian cult appears not only in a third- or second-century inscription
found in Odessos, but seems to be implied in one on Samothrace itself.[23]

The earliest pottery found in Odessos consists of five Corinthian vases dated
to about the first quarter of the sixth century. An early chance find and the only
Corinthian ceramic found in Bulgaria, they probably came to Odessos as articles
of trade through an Ionian intermediary. The main decoration of a trilobed
oinochoe, a band of heraldically arranged mythological winged creatures and
lions, is finely executed (Fig. 3).

Sixth-century Ionian pottery is rare and mostly in fragments; one shows a
stylised hunting scene with brown figures on a light background. Two lekythoi
are decorated with bands of black glaze on a yellow-brown background. An
unusual fragment, attributed to fifth-century Ionia, is the broken-off neck and
mouth of an amphora, decorated Janus-like on each side of the handles with the
face of a bearded satyr, the hair indicated by small stamped circles.

Of greater artistic importance is a head dated to the first half of the fifth century
(Pl. 22). The use of local marble demonstrates the existence of an Odessitan
workshop. The head, which was intended to wear a diadem or crown, may have
represented Apollo.

Isolated finds from the necropolis areas reflect dependence on Attic imports
from the beginning of the fifth century, although the earliest object found *in situ*

PLATE 23 Odessos, bell-krater, *ht.* 31 cm.

PLATE 22 Odessos, head, *ht.* 27 cm.

cannot be dated before the century's end. In two cases, a black-figure lekythos and a black-glaze *olpe*, a jug with an even rim and no spout, identical finds occur in fifth-century tumuli at Douvanli and near Stara Zagora, but such parallels do not necessarily imply an Odessitan source; similar vases were found at Apollonia and Attic pottery was then an important item of trade for all the Greek colonies.

Fourth-century finds reflect the popularity of the Kerch-style vases. One, a bell-krater, depicts on one side a horseman crowned by a Nike and watched by a seated youth holding a torch and on the other three young men, one holding a strigil; it contained partly burnt human bones (Pl. 23). The vase, dated to the middle or third quarter of the fourth century, is ascribed to the painter of two Ferrara vases whose work has also been identified at Apollonia, at Olynthos, and in south Russia.[24] Women's heads are a popular decoration on lekythoi.

There is no mention of any use of Odessos by Philip II or Alexander, although its potentialities as a base for controlling the Getai seem obvious. Both reigns in general increased the trade and prosperity of the city and its Thracian neighbours. The rule of Lysimachos was more oppressive; taxation increased and Odessos, like the other Greek cities, had to support a substantial garrison. In 313, the leading city of the region, Kallatis, led a general revolt against the Macedonian garrisons, with the hope of Odrysian and perhaps Getic support. However, although Kallatis resisted for a long time, quick action by Lysimachos achieved the speedy surrender of Odessos and Histria and ensured the allegiance of the Getai.

It is doubtful if the area north of the Stara Planina suffered much from the Celtic kingdom, but 'barbarian' pressures from the North were generally beginning to make their presence felt on this fringe of the Greek world. In

PLATE 24 Odessos, sarcophagus appliqué, *ht.* 17·5 cm.

PLATE 25 Dionysopolis, krater, *ht.* 17·5 cm.

179 B.C. the Bastarnae passed through, and Odessos was an early victim of Burebista's Daco-Getic invasion of the mid-first century. Odessos, like Mesambria, had adapted to the commercial decline of Athens and to local changes. Under the threat of Burebista, links with the resurgent Odrysian vassal kingdom of the Romans grew stronger. Although this lacked stability, it was a trading area and also a refuge for at least a few Odessitans during the Daco-Getic invasion: soon after Burebista's death, a decree acknowledged the protection given by one Sadalas.[25] Certainly not the Sadalas of the Mesambrian inscription, this one also is not clearly identified.

Funerary innovations typical of the Macedonian or Early Hellenistic era include barrel-vaulted Macedonian-type ashlar chamber tombs. Five have been identified in the vicinity of Odessos. One was found in 1932 beneath a large tumulus on which a memorial was being erected to commemorate the Polish prince 'Ladislas of Varna', who died here in battle against the invading Turks in 1444. The fourth-century B.C. tomb was conserved as part of the memorial to the fifteenth-century warrior prince. Its entrance had been destroyed and the contents looted in the distant past. A vaulted *dromos*, or passage, led into a square tomb chamber built of carefully dressed dry-stone blocks. In a similar tomb a wooden coffin had been decorated with terracotta appliqués of satyrs and maenads, like the one illustrated in Pl. 24.

A Thracian tumulus cremation near Galata contained a quantity of gold jewellery, including two finger rings, each with a woman's head in relief on the gold bezel, considered to be imported Greek work of the fourth or third century. The mound itself, one of six in the necropolis, contained numerous sherds of black-glaze ceramic. More evidence of Greek influence in the Hellenistic period came from another tumulus burial by the Dionysopolis road. This mound, 25 metres in diameter, was one of the earliest excavated by the Škorpil brothers. In it was the skeleton of a woman wearing gold earrings composed of twisted, tapering hoops with lion-head finials, a Hellenistic type which gained

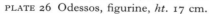

PLATE 26 Odessos, figurine, *ht.* 17 cm.   PLATE 27 Dobroudja, figurine, *ht.* 12·5 cm.

widespread popularity in Bulgaria in the fourth century; other examples were found at Mezek (p. 73) and Seuthopolis. A bronze obol for Charon lay in the dead woman's mouth.

At Dionysopolis itself, in a badly damaged ashlar tomb with two marble biers, a bronze krater, used for burning aromatic substances, was found by one of the skeletons. A ring encircling the top of the krater supported a dish-shaped sieve. The decoration, hammered in relief from a mould and well executed in the crowded Hellenistic manner, consists chiefly of scenes from Euripides' tragedy *Iphigeneia in Tauris* (Pl. 25). The krater is attributed to the fourth or third century, the tomb itself being later. However, comparison with the silver 'Chryses' kantharos in the British Museum and with fragments of a marble krater from Mahdia in the National Museum, Bardo,[26] suggests that an early second-century date may be more likely.

Third-century imports included bone plaques decorated with figures finely incised with a sharp point. They were used to decorate coffins that in shape, if one may judge from the examples found on the Taman peninsula, imitated ornate stone sarcophagi and probably came from Asia Minor. Of four such plaques found in the Galata burial containing the gold finger rings, two depicted women's heads and two Dionysiac scenes. The material shows traces of paint. Ivory panels, decorated in much the same way, were found in the Great Bliznitsa and Kul Oba burials of the Taman and the Crimea, although here attributed to the fourth century.[27]

Few stelai have been found which predate the Roman period. Then the theme of the funerary feast became immensely popular (Pl. 149), so it is interesting that it appeared here as early as the fourth or third century B.C., when its use was beginning in Attica and Asia Minor. Besides the customary composition of the dead man reclining on a bier, a seated woman, and a three-legged table bearing food, the earliest Odessitan stele includes a horse's head, a snake-entwined tree, a herm, and, being only partially preserved, probably other details, including attendants. In the Thracian lands the horse, snake, and tree were soon to be hived off to the separate iconography of the Hero Horseman, but in this early stele they are probably symbols of heroisation. Another funerary feast stele, of the third or second century B.C., is simpler; the upper part, which alone remains, shows only the man and the woman. G. Toncheva notes a gap during the first century B.C. and the first century A.D. before the theme's recurrence.[28]

A study of over 300 amphora stamps in the Varna museum provides useful evidence regarding the import of wine and olive oil to Odessos and Bizone from the main Greek production centres.[29] The first to capitalise on the decline of Athenian power and Philip II's stabilisation of Thracian affairs was Thasos, which exported amphorae of wine and oil into the Thracian interior both via the north Aegean colonies and by the Bosphoran sea route to the Black Sea colonies. This trade continued intermittently from about the middle of the fourth century until the end of the second. Rhodes, a major commercial power in the east Mediterranean, entered the market during the second half of the third century and by about 220 had almost monopolised the wine trade, a position held until the mid-second century. About the third decade of the second century, Sinope began to export olive oil to the west Black Sea coast; judging by the amphora stamps, this too was on a substantial scale. Heracleia Pontica was another big exporter, but the period and extent of its trade with Odessos are matters of some dispute. In view of the Thracian origin attributed to Dionysos, the import of wine may appear surprising, but north of the Stara Planina the climate at that period may well have been too harsh for easy viticulture. The Thracian plain in fact was the destination of large numbers of the imported amphorae. The extent to which new wine of local origin was passed off as Thasian or Rhodian by virtue of the 'label' on the amphora is, like many a similar fraud perpetrated today, unlikely ever to be known.

Opportunities to excavate Greek Odessos have been so limited that the city's ability to survive in any circumstances is the main evidence for local industry. The fifth-century head and the many reliefs, although the great majority date from the Roman period, argue convincingly in favour of a well-established tradition of stonemasonry and carving. By contrast with Apollonia and Mesambria, many terracotta figurines have been found. The remains of at least one potter's workshop, excavated at the north-east corner of the Morska Gradina necropolis, included many fragments and rejects, mostly of burnt or misshapen figurines. The local yellowish-pink clay was used, but it is hard to say if all the moulds were imported or, as seems likely, moulds were made locally to portray Odessitan subjects. The broken but lively figurine of a dancer, waving what are probably clappers in her one remaining hand, was found in this workshop (Pl. 26). Another broken statuette of a bearded man with a shrewd wrinkled face from some unrecorded spot in the Dobroudja is probably also local work of the third century (Pl. 27).

Through continuing support from the Asiatic kingdom of Pontos and close links with neighbouring Odrysian vassal kings, Odessos was able to retain a gradually diminishing independence for longer than the cities of the south. Finally, without resistance, it accepted Roman suzerainty about 27 B.C.

NOTES

1 Xenophon, *Anabasis*, VII,5, trans. Warner, R., *The Persian Expedition*, Harmonds-worth, 1949, 277–8.
2 Brashinsky, I. B., *Arh* XII/2, 1970, 11.
3 Munzova, L., IBAI XXXII, 1970, 255 ff.
4 Seure, G., *Revue archéologique* XIX, 1924, 328.
5 *ARV* II, 1432.
6 Trans. from Venedikov, I. and Velkov, V., *Apoloniya*, Sofia, 1963, 329.
7 *ARV* II, 1482.
8 Kurtz, D. C. and Boardman, J., *Greek Burial Customs*, London, 1971, 320.
9 *IGB* I, 388.
10 *IGB* I, 395 ter.
11 Pippidi, D. M. and Popescu, M., *Dacia*, Nouvelle Série, III, 1959, 235 ff.
12 Brashinsky, op. cit., 11.
13 Trans. from Velkov, I., IBAD, 1919–20, 136.
14 Richter, G. M. A., *AJA* L, 1946, 361 ff.
15 Chimbuleva, Ya., *Arh* IV/3, 1962, 38 ff.
16 *IGB* I, 307.
17 Robert, J. and L., *Bulletin épigraphique* LXVI, 1953, 38–9.
18 Mihailov, G., IBAI XIX, 1955, 149 ff.
19 Danov, H. *GSUFIF* XLVII, 1951–52, 110 ff.
20 Gulubov, I., *Iz Bourgas* I, 1950, 7 ff.
21 Toncheva, G., *Actes Ist BC*, II, 353 ff.
22 *IGB* I, 88 bis.
23 *IGB* I, 78 bis; Fraser, P. M., *The Stones of Samothrace*, London, 1960, no. 6.
24 *ARV* II, 1693–4.
25 *IGB* I, 43.
26 Webster, T. B. L., *Hellenistic Art*, London, 1966, 168–9, 189 ff.; Pls. 53, 54, and App. 12.
27 Artamonov, M. I., *Treasures from Scythian Tombs*, London, 1969, Pls. 257–62, 301–3.
28 Toncheva, G., *Arh* VI/1, 1964, 37 ff.
29 Mirchev, M., *Amphorite pechati ot muzeya vuv Varna*, Sofia, 1958.

3 The Thracian Interior before the Macedonian Conquest

I. DOLNO SAHRANE

Where burials are concerned, interest is naturally focused either on the more monumental constructions or on those especially rich in grave goods, features which highlight the degree of culture reached in an area and the extent of contact with neighbouring peoples. Yet in their relative simplicity the commoner, poorer graves of more ordinary people are archaeologically at least as important because they reflect indigenous traditions more strongly. Before turning to the major tumuli, a brief description of some graves from a small necropolis with a long existence will help to provide a degree of perspective, even if no example can be chosen which may be called representative, and a comprehensible pattern for the country has still to be traced.

Dolno Sahrane is 15 kilometres west of Kazanluk. Near Seuthopolis, it was in Odrysian territory by the Early Hellenistic period and probably before. Four tumuli excavated in the 1960s contained burials reaching back to the end of the Bronze Age and forward to medieval Christianity. One tumulus, 18 metres in diameter and less than $2\frac{1}{2}$ metres high when excavated, was erected in the sixth century B.C. for two burials; another, much older, was re-used in the sixth–fifth century for four. In all cases, the bodies were laid out flat on a bed of stones, with the grave goods beside them, then covered with another layer of stones, above which the earth mound was piled. Bronze objects from the former mound were an arc-shaped fibula, flattened at the top of the curve where it was decorated by five ribs in relief; an open-ended finger ring; and three short sections of thin, narrow spirals, possibly from a necklace. Coarse, thick-walled hand-made pots, often with tongue- or bud-shaped handles, had also been left between the layers of stones, but they had been broken beyond reconstruction. Such pots continued in use for a very long time, sometimes as cremation urns in poorer graves. The grave goods of the four burials of the sixth to fifth centuries in the latter tumulus were, in probable order of date: (i) a large clay urn with tongue-handles and a small clay cup, both hand-made; (ii) none; (iii) two large pots both beyond reconstruction, but one of coarse hand-made ware with tongue-handles, the other wheel-made, of finer clay and amphora-like in shape; (iv) a slightly curved iron knife and an iron arc-shaped fibula.

The latest of the four tumuli excavated was constructed about the end of the fifth or the beginning of the fourth century and used only for cremation. It was enclosed by a rough stone retaining wall, 34 metres in diameter. A round hearth, slightly above ground level, was found in the centre of the mound, piled with greasy black ashes and embers. The act of cremation was thorough; the charred remains were then inserted into an amphora (Pl. 28), the neck of which was thrust into another amphora with its neck broken off, and turned upside down before being buried. Fragments of a third amphora were also found, stuck into the mouth of the first. It was impossible to tell from the remains if more than one person had been cremated. The grave goods included two arc-shaped iron fibulae and a small iron knife. All the pottery was local and, with one possible exception, wheel-made. The influence of Greek models was pronounced, especially in the amphorae, although the only two cups that could be reconstructed, both with twin handles rising above the mouth (Pl. 29), as well as the fragments of a similar type of jug and another cup, demonstrated the strength of earlier Thracian traditions. Apart from the grave goods, five pithoi were found in the east and south parts of the mound; their contents, if any, are not known.

The sex of the skeletons could not be ascertained, but the presence of knives usually signified a male burial.

II. DOUVANLI

In the neighbourhood of Douvanli, a village in the Thracian plain about 25 kilometres north of Plovdiv, a large necropolis containing the richest tumulus burials in Bulgaria was excavated in the late 1920s and early thirties. Out of some 30 tumuli excavated, six contained burials of outstanding interest, all oriented more or less east–west. The table below gives some basic details of each, sex having been determined according to grave goods, arms and armour indicating a man, normally feminine jewellery and toilet accessories a woman.

Tumulus	Approximate date	Burial method	Sex	Diameter	Height when excavated
Moushovitsa	end sixth or early fifth century B.C.	inhumation	woman	32 metres	4 metres
Koukouva	early fifth century	unknown	woman	80 metres	10 metres
Lozarska	early fifth century	cremation	unknown	50 metres	8 metres
Golyama	mid-fifth century	cremation	man	45 metres	7 metres
Arabadjiska	second half of fifth century	inhumation	woman	30 metres	2·70 metres
Bashova	end fifth or early fourth century	cremation	man	35 metres	6 metres

All mounds had been under the plough and where, as at Koukouva tumulus, traces of a retaining wall were found, many stones had been removed for building material or to facilitate cultivation.

The Moushovitsa tumulus

The skeleton, armless, lay on its back in a possibly timber-lined pit grave about 3½ metres long and 2 metres wide, in the exact centre of a mound formed by alternating layers of black earth and local soil. The grave goods, as at Mesambria, almost all by the head, were those of a lady of high rank and included some fine gold jewellery.

A large gold *pectoral*, or ornamental breast plaque, with stylised birds round the edges, embossed using a single punch, had remained *in situ* (Pl. 30). Through

PLATE 28 Dolno Sahrane, amphora-urn, *ht.* 40 cm.
PLATE 29 Dolno Sahrane, cup, *ht.* 8·5 cm.

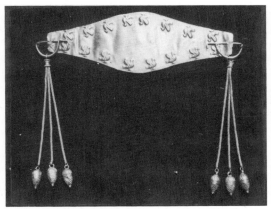

PLATE 30 Douvanli, pectoral, *w.* 25·9 cm.
PLATE 31 Douvanli, neck-amphora, *ht.* 42·2 cm.

holes at each end were attached plain arc-shaped fibulae from which three stylised bud pendants were suspended by cord-chains, all items being made of pure gold. Gold or, less frequently, silver pectorals were a usual feature of noble Thracian burials, both male and female – in inhumations placed where they had obviously been worn in life – during a period from about the turn of the sixth-fifth centuries until the middle or second half of the fourth. They varied considerably in size and shape, but were invariably longer horizontally than their vertical width; ornamentation also varied, but was usually embossed; holes at the horizontal ends enabled them to be attached to a garment.

Round the neck was a gold necklace with 20 hollow globular pendants or *bullae*. They were decorated with filigree rosettes and granulated borders, and suspended by broad loops, a type with analogies in Etruscan jewellery.[1] Another necklace, or part of the first, lay behind her head; it consisted of 19 little biconical gold beads. Two massive splayed spiral earrings had been attached to her ears; each weighed over 26 grams. In shape they resembled an omega, with finials of closely granulated pyramids. Ten tapered hoop earrings, nine with their lower halves identically decorated with filigree and granulation, lay beside the head.

Other grave goods included a bronze hydria, which was lidded by a silver *phiale mesomphalos* – a shallow bowl with a central *omphalos* or boss. This type of dish, considered to have some ritual significance, had both Greek and Persian variants and was common in rich Thracian graves before the Hellenistic period. D. E. Strong considers the Moushovitsa phiale, relatively deep and with its embossed, pear-shaped ornament, 'may not be Greek'.[2] There was also a large black-figure neck-amphora, portraying on one side Theseus fighting Procrustes (Pl. 31) and on the other Dionysos with a satyr and maenad. The amphora is ascribed to the Troilos painter, a Late Archaic vase painter who normally worked in red-figure.[3] The toilet accessories were a bronze hand mirror, three miniature Egyptian glass oinochoai, and seven alabastra. A terracotta bust, 11·5 centimetres high, of a dignified female wearing earrings, was perhaps a portrait of a deity. There were also several household vessels of high quality.

North of the head was a strange medley of 42 tiny objects, among them triangular pieces of agate, bronze finger rings, larger rings of amber, iron, and clay, coloured glass beads, clay balls, and Mediterranean seashells – *Cardium*, *Murex*, and *Cypraea*. A possible meaning for this and a similar collection from the Arabadjiska tumulus is suggested on p. 64.

Antedating the Persian invasion, the burial in the Moushovitsa tumulus is a testimony to the cultural impact of Greece on the Thracian aristocracy.

The Koukouva tumulus

The Koukouva or Koukova tumulus, the largest in the necropolis, was partly planted with trees, partly used for grazing, and partly as a vineyard until 1925,

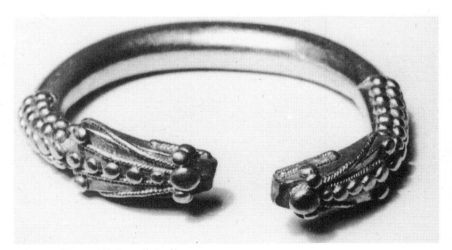

PLATE 32 Douvanli, bracelet, *diam.* 9 cm.

when a peasant irrigating vines struck what he immediately saw to be a tomb of dressed limestone blocks. In haste to get at the treasure, he and his friends flung out the earth which had fallen in through the broken roof, and with it pottery and other objects which were smashed or lost. Two days later, when the news reached the Plovdiv museum, not only had all the gold and silver disappeared, but even the floor stones. Intense activity by officials and archaeologists succeeded in tracing some of the grave goods, but almost certainly there had been many more. Even so, the total weight of gold recovered was over 1¼ kilograms. The objects clearly suggested a female burial, although no human remains survived.

Some of the gold jewellery was very like that at Moushovitsa. Part of a necklace had similar globular pendants; there was an almost identical pair of 'omega' earrings and seven of tapering hoops, with both filigree and granulated decoration. There was also a pectoral, similar in shape and size, but without any fibulae or pendants it may once have possessed, and decorated with an overall repoussé pattern. New items included a torque of twisted gold wire, weighing 349 grams, and a pair of open-ended solid bracelets with stylised snake-head finials carrying heavy granulation (Pl. 32) and two finger rings with pointed oval bezels, one with a cock engraved in intaglio. One fish and fragments of others in sheet gold – there had originally been as many as sixteen – are not jewellery in the accepted sense; there are Scythian analogies and they probably had some religious significance, showing the dead woman to have been a priestess.

By good fortune, a superb silver-gilt amphora (Pl. 33) was saved. Its shoulders and bulge were decorated with a double row of lotus flowers and palmettes, below which was vertical channelling. The handles were in the form of fantastic beasts with lion heads and manes and ibex horns (broken off on one side). Wings were indicated in relief on one handle; on the other they were outstretched to form a spout. N. K. Sandars has described the amphora as 'absolutely typical of the unlocalised Achaemenian court style'.[4]

There was a silver phiale mesomphalos as at Moushovitsa, but with a larger boss and a fluted body, five bronze vessels including two hydriai, a bronze mirror, and an iron tripod. An alabastron and five pottery kylikes, one black-figure, the other four identical and coated with black-glaze, were also traced.

At Koukouva Greek and oriental influences appear together; the amphora may be a direct legacy of the Persian occupation.

The Lozarska tumulus

In the Lozarska tumulus a stone sarcophagus, carved from a single block and with a monolithic lid, was found 4 metres south-east of centre and 4 metres above ground level. The pressure of the earth mound had caused some damage. The contents were very different from those of the other major burials. Inside were burnt bones but no ashes, so that cremation must have taken place elsewhere. The main feature was a wooden bed with a curved headrest and four turned legs of a design current in Greece in the fifth and fourth centuries B.C.[5] There were holes in the remaining bed-frame for cords or some form of webbing, and pieces of a red cloth on the bed. The only grave offering was a late black-figure Attic lekythos with a rather crude palmette decoration. The Greek influence is paramount here.

The Golyama tumulus

Here the tomb, at ground level in the centre of the mound, was built of dressed white sandstone blocks, almost all more than a metre long, and on three sides was enclosed by a second row. Six large transverse pedimented blocks formed the roof. The inner dimensions were those of a large sarcophagus (2·33 metres long by 1·08 metres wide by 1·11 metres high).

The cremation burial of a man was undisturbed. A pile of burnt bones had been placed in the middle of the floor, on top of them two gold pectorals and a gold ring, with a little earth and fine embers. The whole was covered by a carmine red cloth, probably with a light brown woven pattern and tiny gold sequins sewn to it, but on exposure to the air the textile crumbled to dust.

The smaller pectoral, 17½ centimetres across, was somewhat similar in shape to those at Moushovitsa and Koukouva, except that the lower edge was more like an obtuse angle than a curve, whilst the upper had a rounded indentation in the middle, perhaps to fit some kind of collar, unless it was to be worn just below the neck. Hemispherical bosses were punched across its breadth and round the edges, where they were linked by tangental pitted lines. The larger pectoral was roughly boat-shaped, 38½ centimetres across and with a much deeper indentation in the centre of the upper edge. The overall punched decoration of rosettes, open flowers, bosses of various sizes, made up a roughly symmetrical pattern possessing a primitive barbaric splendour. The variety of shape and decoration of these pectorals is very great – a fine example of the same period at the Ashmolean Museum in Oxford from a male burial in a tumulus at Dulboki, between Stara Zagora and Nova Zagora, is wider and rather more symmetrically decorated than the larger one at Golyama. The grave finds from Dulboki are a unique collection outside the Thracian regions and give an excellent idea of a rich Thracian burial of this time.

The pointed oval bezel of the gold finger ring had an intaglio figure of a naked rider on a galloping horse, saddleless but with bridle and reins. Engraved

PLATE 33 Douvanli, amphora, *ht.* 27 cm.
PLATE 34 Douvanli, kantharos, *ht.* 25·5 cm.

PLATE 35 Douvanli, appliqué, *diam.* 9 cm.
PLATE 36 Douvanli, appliqué, *w.* 6·4 cm.

in Greek letters round the bezel was the name ΣΚΥΘΟΔΟΚΟ, Skythodokos being no doubt the name of the owner.

In Golyama, for the first time at Douvanli, the grave goods included engraved and gilded silver vessels, a Greek fashion beginning about 450 B.C., to which date are assigned two stemmed kantharoi found here.[6] Both were identical in shape and in displaying satyr's heads between the curve of the handle and the rim. Apart from this, one was quite plain. The other (Pl. 34) had finely gilded scenes on the body of the vase – on one side a girl offering a fawn to Dionysos and on the other a satyr and maenad. Eight silver-gilt appliqués were found in a position suggesting they had been attached to a disintegrated jerkin. On either side of a Gorgon head (Pl. 35) was a Nike driving a quadriga (Pl. 36); five lion heads were arranged symmetrically below.

Between the appliqués and a fine bronze hydria had been a leather helmet. All that remained were the bronze cheek and neck guards, and elaborate appliqués with palmette and spiral decoration. Close to the ashes lay a curved iron sword of the single-edged slightly curved Thracian type, 82 centimetres long (Fig. 4), a fragment of ivory decoration remaining on the handle, two iron spearheads, and part, perhaps, of an iron belt. The only pottery noted was a damaged late black-figure lekythos, found outside the tomb.

The Arabadjiska tumulus

In the south-western part of the mound, a shallow pit had been dug (4·20 metres long, 3·0 metres wide, and only 20 centimetres deep) and within this a smaller and deeper pit (2·50 metres long, 1·45 metres wide, and 35 centimetres deep). The latter, lined and roofed with beams, contained an undisturbed female inhumation.

The skeleton, lying on its back, as at Moushovitsa, was adorned with gold

FIG. 4 Douvanli, Golyama tumulus, Thracian sword, *l.* 82 cm.

jewellery of broadly the same type as in the earlier female graves. The pectoral on the breast, alike in shape, was only about two-thirds the size, and in decoration closely resembled the smaller one in the Golyama burial. The necklace was composed of 17 hollow globules with filigree and granulated decoration, but here hung by little tubes and the earlier loops generally replaced by similarly decorated beads, which, minus pendants, also formed the back of the necklace. Two twisted 'omega' spiral earrings lay beside the head, with granulated decoration below as well as on the pyramidal finials. There were also six boat-shaped earrings decorated with fine filigree; the thin wire of the hoop passed through the hollow interior of the 'boat'.

On the skeleton's left hand was a gold ring like the 'rider' ring from the Golyama burial, but less finely executed and the Greek lettering is now indecipherable. Other grave goods included a plain silver flask and silver sieve, an Attic red-figure hydria with a domestic scene, and a black-glazed kylix. A bronze hand mirror and an alabastron were the only toilet accessories found.

In the north-west corner of the pit was a neatly laid out collection of 50 small objects. They included some miniature stone axes identifiable as Late Chalcolithic or Early Bronze Age artefacts; partially pierced clay spindlewhorls, looking like rejects from some prehistoric workshop; sling-stones or, perhaps, pebbles; a bronze horse frontal ornament of a common Thracian type (see p. 76); knobs of coloured glass and stones or fragments of fired clay in different shapes; and *Cardium* and *Murex* shells.

The collections here and in the Moushovitsa burial are not unique in Bulgaria. Comparable, if smaller, collections have been noted in graves as far north as Oryahovo on the Danube, at Vratsa (p. 79), and as far south as Apollonia (p. 36), as well as in the north-east. V. Mikov has suggested an explanation based on an ethnographical analogy, a 'healing ceremony' at which he was present in Sofia in the 1930s, for people suffering from headache caused by bewitchment or the evil eye. The witch, he said, prepared a bowl of water, throwing into it such fired clay objects as cubes, balls, and rings. Watching the ripples and bubbles, she mumbled unintelligible words. Then the remaining objects were inserted, including a stone ball, a *Murex* shell, and lastly a *Cardium* shell, with which she scooped up some of the liquid and then poured it back, muttering: 'Mother of God' and 'Christ'. Prayers followed, then one by one the witch took the objects out and rolled them about. Finally, the sick person dipped the right-hand fingers into the water, moistened eyes and forehead, and drank a mouthful. Powder scraped from miniature stone axeheads and mixed with water was said to relieve chest pains; the cure for typhus was 'heavy' stones in water drunk by the sufferer.[7]

If the Sofia witch had been repeating a ceremony – demoted to a superstition – which two and a half millennia earlier had been the prerogative of a royal Thracian priestess, it is not the only example of such continuity found in Bulgaria.

The Bashova tumulus

Early in the excavation a sacrificial pit was found in the centre of the mound, 2 metres below the surface; there were no signs of burning, only local potsherds and an Attic red-figure *pelike*, or twin-handled wine jar, depicting two women

PLATE 37 Douvanli, phiale mesomphalos, *diam.* 20·5 cm.
PLATE 38 Douvanli, kylix, *diam.* 13 cm.

sacrificing at an altar. The grave itself was a roughly rectangular pit (about 3 metres long, 2 metres wide, and 1·70 metres deep) in which a stone tomb (2·10–2·20 metres long by 1·10 metres wide) had been built, roofed by thick wooden beams which had rotted and collapsed.

The ashes of the dead man lay on a silver phiale mesomphalos.[8] This had as its principal decoration four chariots galloping either in procession or in a race round the inside of the bowl (Pl. 37). The chariots, each with their four horses, charioteer, and accompanying armed warrior, were particularly finely engraved and then gilded. In each, the horses and human beings were individually portrayed. The warriors wore different armour and carried different insignia on their shields. One gripped the chariot rail, as if terrified; another leant excitedly forward to grasp the reins, to the consternation of his charioteer. The dish, which probably dates to the last decades of the fifth century,[9] has the word ΔΑΔΑΛΕΜΕ prominently engraved on the outer side. Also appearing on three other silver objects, this could be an invocation or the name of the owner.

One of the other inscribed vessels is a kylix, on the shallow inner base of which is engraved, equally finely but with tender delicacy, a wreath-encircled scene of a goddess (? Selene) riding over the sea (Pl. 38). The third inscribed object is a fluted horn *rhyton*, a vessel from which wine was drunk from a spout at the bottom, terminating in the foreparts of a horse and with a lotus and palmette band round the rim. Although the horn rhyton was a drinking vessel of Persian origin and was popular among Scyths as well as Thracians, there seems little doubt that this specimen, like the kylix and the phiale, was the work of a highly skilled Greek silversmith. The fourth inscribed item was a simple silver jug with a fluted body.

The customary gold pectoral was found together with the remains of armour. It was small (13·8 centimetres across), but proportionately wider than those in the other Douvanli burials, and was also unusual in being decorated by the figure of a semi-stylised lion.

Of the armour, a bronze corslet, badly damaged, with separate front and back, was simply decorated with linear curves emphasising the major muscles. This is a typical example of fine Greek work of the fifth–fourth centuries.[10] Lying underneath it were found the remains of what had probably been an iron helmet and a broad iron belt, as at Golyama, both too decayed for reconstruction. Weapons had included a curved iron sword, again recalling Golyama; a short straight dagger of which part of the scabbard remained; 40 bronze triple-edged arrowheads; and fragments of two iron spearheads of the long leaf-shaped type with strongly emphasised vertical ribs.

As usual, there was a bronze hydria, this one with a decoration below the vertical handle of open tracery enclosing a Silenus mask, beneath which hung a large palmette and above two heraldically opposed lions. Also of bronze were a plain *situla*, or bucket-shaped vessel, with twin mobile handles, and a low vase with flat horizontal shoulders, both closely resembling finds at Mezek (Fig. 6), a jug, and a shallow two-handled bowl.

The pottery consisted of two Attic red-figure hydriai and a black-glaze jug

FIG. 5 Douvanli, Bashova tumulus, hydria detail, 'theoxeny'   PLATE 39 Douvanli, hydria, *ht*. 45·5 cm.

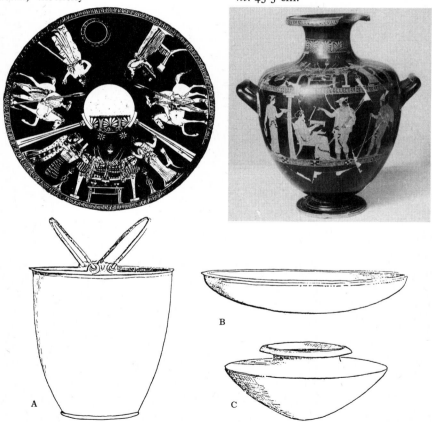

FIG. 6 Mezek, bronze grave goods: A – *ht*. 20 cm.; B – *diam*. 32 cm.; C – *ht*. 15 cm.

identical in shape and decoration to the inscribed silver jug. The larger hydria (Fig. 5 and Pl. 39), a fine example, is ascribed to the Kadmos painter.[11] The scene on the shoulder is rare. Two worshippers, a man playing a *kithera* and a woman with raised hands, stand at either side of a sumptuous empty couch, before which a table is spread for a feast. Two pillars enclose this scene; behind them two men advance, each carrying two spears and leading a horse; behind again are an old man leaning on a stick and a woman carrying a dish. The worshippers by the couch wear crowns and are richly dressed, probably a priest and priestess, and the two men with horses may be the Dioskouri. The scene has been interpreted as the theoxeny – a feast offered to a deity – of the Dioskouri.

Five of these six graves contained objects of outstanding archaeological and artistic interest. The sixth, the purely Greek Lozarska, is an enigma in a Thracian tumulus. The gold pectorals, of local workmanship, with the possible exception of the Bashova lion, are an essentially Thracian feature, which, although found in Thrace before the Persian occupation, probably stemmed from Persian origins. The dead of both sexes were honoured equally. On one hand there is the sumptuous feminine jewellery, on the other the magnificent plate and the accoutrements, many of them iron and therefore badly corroded, of the men.

The importance of hydriai, already observed at Mesambria and shared by the Greeks in their homeland as well as other peoples, notably the Greek-influenced Trebenište culture of Macedonia, is evident. They must surely be symbolic of water, accorded universal reverence as essential to life in all primitive religions. There is some evidence that hydriai were associated with Orphic beliefs in the afterlife,[12] but no assessment is yet possible of the extent to which Thracian religion was permeated by Orphism as interpreted by the Greeks.

There are grounds for thinking that two, if not all three, of the women were priestesses; a collection of 'magic' objects would not have survived the rape of Koukouva. The men must have been primarily warrior leaders. For them all to have amassed objects of such richness and superb quality is a strong argument in favour of royalty.

Problems arise in trying to assign the Douvanli necropolis to a particular tribe. There is no historical evidence for an Odrysian presence so far up the Maritsa basin in the early part of the fifth century. Thus the Moushovitsa and probably the Koukouva and Lozarska tumuli antedated the foundation of the Odrysian state unless it had been already created under the Persians as a means through which they could control the territory. The other main contenders are the Bessi, normally associated with the highlands of the central and western Rhodopes. Nevertheless, one of their main centres, Bessapara, is believed to have been situated near Pazardjik, west of Plovdiv on the edge of the Thracian plain. Logically, therefore, Douvanli could be the necropolis of their rulers, strange as it seems to have chosen open country rather than one of the wild mountainous plateaux of the Rhodopes. In the highest range of these mountains, according to Herodotos, a sanctuary of Dionysos existed from which a Bessi priestess delivered oracles – perhaps using her collection of 'magic' objects. Nevertheless, the fighting qualities of the Bessi (or Satrai, as Herodotos calls the group to which they belonged[13]) were such that no Thracian tribe would

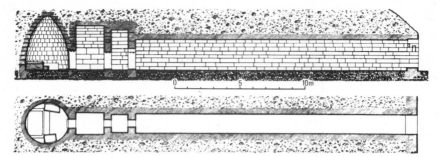

FIG. 7 Mezek, Mal-tepe tomb

PLATE 40 Mezek, Mal-tepe dromos

PLATE 41 Mezek, Mal-tepe tholos, detail

lightly have undertaken the violation of their royal graves. The balance of such evidence as exists seems to give them Douvanli.

III. MEZEK

Almost on the Turkish frontier, the village of Mezek is about 8 kilometres west of Svilengrad, where the Maritsa creates its gap between the eastern Rhodopes and the Sakar hills. Some 25 kilometres eastward is Turkish Edirne (Roman Hadrianopolis and Thracian Uskudama), an Odrysian tribal centre strategically placed at the junction of the Maritsa and the Tundja, with access downstream to the Aegean Greek colony of Ainos. Around Mezek and extending into Turkey is a large and widely scattered necropolis with several groups of tumuli, nearly all of which were plundered in Antiquity – a Roman lamp in one tomb tells its own story. A direct link with Uskudama is possible, but surface and chance finds, particularly from a flat-topped hill where remains of a medieval fortress still dominate the region, show the existence close to Mezek of an important Iron Age settlement, which prospered especially in the fifth and fourth centuries B.C. This lead has still to be followed up, but at least two other Thracian forts guarding the area have been located.

Mal-tepe (*Imanyarska tumulus*)

This tumulus is usually known by its Turkish name, meaning 'hill of the treasure', although the Bulgarian 'mound of the treasure-hunter' is equally appropriate. The largest mound of the whole necropolis, its diameter is about 90 metres and its present height about 14 metres.

Early this century, peasants poking round the foot of the mound stumbled on the life-size bronze statue of a wild boar. The size and weight – 177 kilograms – made it embarrassingly difficult to sell with the circumspection necessary for maximum profit. But a leg, broken off in antiquity, was found nearby. Following a familiar tradition, the peasants sent the single limb to Plovdiv, hoping to stimulate a large offer for the whole body. But the secret was not kept. Mezek was then in Turkey, where the authorities, once alerted, halted negotiations, although some years elapsed before the boar was surrendered to the Archaeological Museum of Istanbul. A Turkish excavation had reached only the retaining wall when the First World War ended operations; post-war territorial changes transferred Mezek to Bulgaria.

Quiet fossicking by the peasantry continued. In the early 1930s three men unearthed part of a bronze candelabrum, also at the foot of the mound. The next day they came on the tomb entrance, but it was a dark and frightening hole. The superstitious and thoroughly scared trio returned to the village for physical and moral support. They returned with a team which, headed by the mayor and teacher and equipped with lanterns, entered the tomb. Unfortunately, although archaeologists came quickly and traced many of the grave goods, the tomb had already been cleared, except for two under-floor burials. The position of the grave goods could only be doubtfully ascertained by questioning the peasants who removed them. The tomb appeared also to have been disturbed in Antiquity. None of the bones, said to include those of horses, had been kept, except for one horse's tooth.

The retaining wall had long been used as a quarry. Originally it was about 5 metres thick, faced with huge flagstones, also used to close the entrance. Outside the latter were the remains of a carelessly constructed building of unknown dimensions, containing in its debris the burnt bones of a large animal, possibly a horse. This structure was outside the retaining wall and thus must have remained visible.

The entrance, on the north-east, was built of horizontally laid ashlar blocks, the upper three stepped and topped by two blocks meeting in the centre. This led to a dromos, similarly corbelled but with the overhanging ends of the blocks trimmed to form an even surface (Pl. 40). The dromos, $21\frac{1}{2}$ metres long and rising to a height of over $2\frac{1}{2}$ metres, is impressive in its proportions and perfect dry-stone masonry. After two rectangular antechambers, massive bronze double doors of a similar type and decoration to those of marble or bronze found in Macedonian tombs, opened into the *tholos* or beehive-shaped tomb, 3·30 metres in diameter and 4·30 metres high in the centre (Fig. 7). The consummate craftsmanship and consequent preservation of the tholos were such that the excavator could not tell if the dry-stone walls had been strengthened by iron cramps (Pl. 41). In execution and design – its simplicity (now) unmarred by any sign of plaster or painting – the tomb has an abstract and aesthetically satisfying beauty.

In spite of resemblances between Mal-tepe and the very much larger 'Treasury of Atreus' at Mycenae, there can be no direct relationship. The tradition of such tombs continued and sixth- to fourth-century examples occur as near to Thrace as Asia Minor, Thessaly, and the north Black Sea coast. Mal-tepe and other tholos tombs near Mezek and east of Edirne are probably most closely related to those of the fifth to mid-third centuries in the Kerch and Taman peninsulas which were built by Greek architects for the indigenous ruling class. B. Filov, on the evidence of the finds, considers it unlikely that Mal-tepe was constructed before the first half of the fourth century, an opinion which is generally accepted and which agrees with the dating of Scythian tombs of a similar type. A doubt must, however, remain. Historically the fifth century, when Odrysian power was at its height and when, as at Douvanli, Thracian rulers possessed great wealth and were open to influences from many directions, cannot be ruled out. Nor, on the other hand, can the late fourth century, the date to which the earliest finds are attributed and which is supported by the Macedonian-type doors.

The furniture does not attain the standard of the architecture. A large mono-lithic sarcophagus opposite the entrance obviously belonged to the original burial and suggests an inhumation. The tomb and antechambers have two stone-paved floors and the sarcophagus stands on the lower, earlier one. A smaller, lower block in front was perhaps a podium for sitting beside the sarcophagus or, more probably, for offerings. Two casket-urns at each end of the podium are rec-tangular except where one side is curved to fit the wall, but they differ in size and crowd and destroy the symmetrical harmony of the chamber. Both had been thoroughly rifled, but in size and shape suggest cremation burials.

Nothing was found between the main chamber's two floors, but a second, quite undisturbed burial phase was discovered between those of the two antechambers, although only 5 centimetres separated the levels. Each contained a single crema-tion; judging by the jewellery, both were female. Both had a silver coin of Alexander the Great, providing a *terminus post quem* for this phase; the other finds were dated to the last quarter of the fourth century.

The grave goods from the tomb chamber were, in the main, found scattered outside or obtained by purchase, and must have been only a small proportion of the original total from the three burials. Various little gold appliqués were recovered. A pair 3·4 centimetres high and about half as wide, ornamented with highly stylised and skilfully hammered plant motifs, seem almost to be vegetal counterparts of the stylised animal appliqués found elsewhere in Mezek, at Vratsa (p. 76), and many other Bulgarian sites. There were also several rosettes and two rectangular appliqués with filigree work framing a cornelian and a large number of gold beads.

Fragments of two iron swords, one spear, and a bronze helmet indicated at least one male burial. According to the Douvanli pattern, the two cremations would have been male and the main inhumation burial female, but Douvanli is by no means typical. Here in Mal-tepe are a group of three more or less con-temporary mixed burials, and two subsequent (female) cremations.

The bronze objects, all of excellent quality and workmanship, are dated by the excavator to the latter part of the fourth or early third century. Of particular note is the candelabrum, pieces of which were found inside as well as outside the tomb, enabling a partial reconstruction. A tripod terminating in curved lion legs bore a long stem, from the top of which two hooks probably carried lamps on chains. Above them was poised a dancing faun, holding up a cup shaped like a large open flower (Pl. 42). The vigorous realism of the carefully executed figure is especially noticeable in his diabolically mischievous face. The diadem above his horns and animal ears is of a distinctive *kalathiskos* or basket type, apparently formed from overlapping leaves.

PLATE 42 Mezek, candelabrum statuette, *ht.* 34·5 cm.

PLATE 43 Mezek, collar detail, overall *w.* 29 cm.

Bronze vessels included a situla with twin mobile handles below which were palmette decorations so elaborate as to suggest stylised faces of satyrs. A plainer cauldron had a single handle with a ring for hanging it over a fire. Jugs of various shapes, including an *askos*, an asymmetrical vessel with its mouth off-centre and a single handle, were beautifully proportioned and ornamented at the handle base. A round lion-head appliqué, a ring in its mouth, was found by the door and almost certainly decorated it. The only surviving examples of pottery, three amphorae, two of them Thasian and one locally made, cannot certainly be linked with the other finds.

The under-floor burial in the inner antechamber was the richer of the two. The grave goods included a gold bead necklace from which hung by a broad ring a filigree-decorated pendant like a more elaborate version of the Douvanli bullae (p. 59), and a gold wire chain necklace with lion-head finials. There were also five gold lion-head earrings like others at Galata, near Varna, and Seutho-polis, and objects resembling fish scales. More finds were a glass alabastron, coloured glass beads and numerous ones of clay, clay grapes, and gilded clay objects with heads like raspberries recalling the wreaths found in Apollonian graves (p. 39) and elsewhere, a broken silver needle, and several spindlewhorls. The grave goods in the outer antechamber were somewhat similar but generally less costly. Neither approach the wealth of the Douvanli female burials.

Other finds have features which are not pure Greek or Thraco-Greek. These include an elaborate lunula-shaped iron collar which, although highly orna-mental, was also a very serviceable piece of armour (Pl. 43). The upper surface was plated with silver on which traces of gilding remained. A series of concentric bands of different relief motifs began with lion heads on the vertically raised neck-guard. Then came rows of highly stylised palmettes, tiny human heads, a broad vegetal band with continuous symmetrically spiralling tendrils springing from a central female bust, an almond-shaped motif, and, lastly, another row of human heads. Filov points out that although all the motifs are Greek and fulfil the most exacting technical requirements, by treating them without apparent relation to meaning or size, an abstract and 'barbaric' effect quite contrary to the canons of Greek art is produced. He draws comparisons with fourth-century B.C. Celtic art, notably the Amfreville helmet; nevertheless he classes the collar with Thracian pectorals and suggests that it was made in a Black Sea or Aegean colony, possibly Amphipolis.

L. Ognenova-Marinova and I. Venedikov relate the collar to fragments from two tumuli near Vurbitsa and Yankovo, both on the north slopes of the eastern Stara Planina. The Yankovo find was also connected with a circular stone tomb chamber, although only the base row of stones has survived. Both fragments appear very like the Mal-tepe collar in shape and incorporate the spiralling tendril motif in almost identical fashion. These authors attribute the non-Greek features of the three pieces to oriental influences.[14] P. Jacobsthal, on the other hand, has suggested southern Italy as a possible origin for the Mal-tepe collar.[15]

There was also a group of small bronze objects, some with stylised human heads of a type that Jacobsthal has identified as metal parts of a Celtic chariot.[16] The question thus arises of a third burial phase during the Celtic occupation in the third century B.C. The Celts were accustomed to tumulus burials and Mezek lay well within the estimated boundaries of their kingdom; one so magnificent and with a clearly indicated entrance might have proved irresistible.

The bronze boar may perhaps provide support for the theory of a Celtic phase. This animal had a chthonic significance for both Thracians and Celts, but no other Thracian tumulus is known to have been associated with a wild boar, other than by a boar's tooth among the grave goods or boars' bones among those of other animals consumed during ritual feasting. In Celtic areas, apart from boar figurines, an actual boar burial in a stone tomb with grave goods has been excavated at Sopron-Bécsidomb in Hungary and burials of wild boar were associated with two chariot graves in the Champagne area of France – in one case the ritual knife remaining in the carcase.[17] At Mal-tepe the original site of the boar is unknown. The animal is realistically though roughly modelled. There is an impression of bristly fur with no suggestion of muscle or bone, but behind the boar's right ear is a spear wound from which fall three drops of blood.

The collar is superior work and doubtfully Greek. There is a likelihood of the boar being made by or for the Celts; the chariot parts are Celtic. We still know almost nothing about the Celtic kingdom in Thrace, but if the collar is Celtic, it reflects the Persian influence on Celtic art in which Thrace and its art played an intermediary role.

Other Mezek tumuli

Near Mal-tepe, on a hill called Kurt-kale, another tholos tomb was found in a tumulus only 30 metres in diameter and six high when investigated. The tomb had been thoroughly looted in Antiquity and there remained only some horse bones in a bowl and amphora fragments. Entered from the south, the tomb had no dromos and only one antechamber preceded the beehive-shaped tomb chamber, its base diameter just over $3\frac{1}{2}$ metres and height nearly the same (Fig. 8). The antechamber was roofed by a corbelled vault of four layers, each comprising four stone blocks laid across the corners of the row below. The construction of the tomb was characterised by the same meticulous workmanship that marks Mal-tepe. The stone blocks were carefully rusticated except for a smooth narrow strip round the edges and, again, no plaster or paint was discernible. The floors had been dug up by the robbers and no tomb furniture had survived.

Remnants of another ashlar tomb were found in the smallest tumulus of the necropolis. Ploughing had greatly reduced its size and most of the stones had been removed, but in one corner two or three rows of regularly laid blocks remained from what had been a simple rectangular tomb, oriented east–west and measuring 6·26 by 2·80 metres. The stones were carefully smoothed and squared except that three outer faces remained rough and uneven. The east-façade-wall was squared inside and out. The tomb was destroyed in Antiquity and the mound re-used for a second burial. However, the first still contained a human skull, a small iron axehead, an iron arrowhead, a blue glass bead, a small coarse greyish-black pot, other pieces of local grey and red pottery, fragments of a Greek black-glazed vase, and one of a small red-figure vase. The last, according to the excavator, suggested a fourth-century *terminus ante quem* for the tomb.

Some interesting grave goods were found by chance just outside the village. Any tumulus or cairn that had existed had been completely eroded and no re-

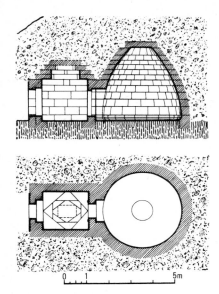

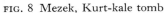

FIG. 8 Mezek, Kurt-kale tomb

PLATE 44 Vratsa, bridle appliqué,
l. 10 cm.

mains of any form of tomb were found; the burial thus appears either to have
been straight into the earth or else in a wooden coffin or lined pit now completely
perished. The offerings included a deep silver mesomphalos phiale with a ribbed
bowl showing Achaemenid influences.[18] and four silver harness appliqués, one a
frontal with a lion head erect above two horned animal heads, the others flat
side-pieces, each portraying three stylised panther or lioness heads. These latter
have a general resemblance to examples in the fourth-century second burial at
Vratsa (Pls. 44, 46, 47) and contemporary finds elsewhere in Bulgaria, Romania,
and south Russia. Among bronze objects were a damaged situla, a biconical
jug, a shallow dish, and a shallow flat-shouldered pot (Fig. 6), all grave goods
represented at other sites. Some iron fragments were probably the remains of
scale armour, and sherds were found of imported pottery.

The Selska tumulus, second largest in the whole necropolis, was just north of
the village. It had a diameter of 80 to 85 metres and was a little under 13 metres
high. Although almost entirely excavated, no signs of a primary burial were
found. Instead, at ground level in the centre of the tumulus a wooden post
$1\frac{1}{2}$ metres high, remnants of which had survived, had been erected and a cairn
of small pebbles piled around. Above this was a small mound of black earth
followed by a layer of larger stones and then another of black earth. On top of
this, layers of soils of various colours had continued to be laid, at least until the
twentieth-century height of the tumulus was reached. The soil, unlike the earth
used for the other mounds, contained very few potsherds, suggesting an early
date, perhaps before the period with which this book is concerned. Possibly the
Selska mound was either a cenotaph or a ritual burial of an ancestral deity.

IV. VRATSA

The town of Vratsa lies on the northern edge of the Stara Planina almost due north of Sofia, with which it is linked by the Iskur gorge and relatively easy passes. In the pre-Roman era it fell within the territory of the Triballi, a tribe always outside the Odrysian sphere.

In 1965, workmen digging foundations for a new building in the town centre penetrated a mound known as the 'Mogilanska mogila' and came on a mass of rough stones and rubble, indicating a grave. An immediate salvage dig showed the excavation to be of such importance that work was still continuing when I visited the site in 1969. Preliminary publications of the finds, however, permit some account to be given of a series of major burials of added interest because of their geographical situation.

Three burials were discovered in the mound, which had a stone and rubble base varying in height from 60 centimetres to 1·30 metres. The first, built of uncut stones at the original ground level, was circular, with a diameter of 9½ metres. Looted and almost entirely destroyed at a very early date, no indication of the roofing survived. Some human bones were found inside, and just outside a red-figure Kerch-style *skyphos*, a deep stemless cup with two horizontal handles. Other pots included a glossy grey Thracian cup, in shape between a skyphos and a kylix. The red-figure skyphos provides a *terminus ante quem* of about 380 B.C. and, taking the later burials into consideration, this one probably dates to early in the second quarter of the fourth century.

Later in the same century, the mound above the round chamber was levelled, a second tomb built in the southern part of the tumulus, and the mound heap re-formed. This was the tomb found in 1965. The complex, 12 metres long inside and four wide, consisted of two east–west oriented rectangular rooms, the main tomb chamber and an anteroom, connected by a short passage. The walls were formed by irregular dry-stone layers, with other stones heaped round them. The floor was of stamped clay and the roof had been of wooden beams nailed together.

Near the entrance to the antechamber were the remains of a four-wheeled chariot. The skeletons of two horses, yoked to it for their ritual slaughter, lay where they had fallen, the iron bits still in their mouths. The chariot, the earliest found in Bulgaria, seems to have been a heavy vehicle with iron-rimmed wheels and other iron parts. Beyond it lay the skeleton of a riding horse, its bit made of silver and its harness decorated with 20 silver appliqués, 11 of them on the bridle. The discovery of the last was especially important as it showed for the first time the position of the appliqués – which are a common feature in Thracian burials.

A frontal occupied the centre of the horse's forehead – an erect animal head, in this case of a fantastic beast (Pl. 46). It had been made by hammering silver sheet on to a mould, the details being worked with a chisel. The neck was holed to take the bridle strap or cord. The other bridle appliqués were in five pairs, all examples of highly stylised animal art, flat and carved in low relief. One pair showed a lion attacking a horned animal (Pl. 44); the rest were cut-out animal heads, usually three, sometimes accompanied by one or more other animals, encircled round a central boss and enclosed within a border (Pl. 47). Shallow silver rings were soldered to the backs to attach them to the harness. These

PLATE 45 Vratsa, wreath, *diam.* 24 cm.

PLATE 46 Vratsa, bridle frontal, *ht.* 3 cm.
PLATE 47 Vratsa, bridle appliqué, *diam.* 8·5 cm.

appliqués reflect a fundamental difference between Thracian and Scythian stylisation in their general rejection of distorted posture. All the other nine silver appliqués from the harness were virtually identical female heads, flat at the back, where there was a bronze ring, and clumsily moulded. No reconstructions of the chariot or horse harness have yet been published.

Also in the antechamber, near the riding horse, lay the contorted skeleton of a young woman, aged about 24. The head of the iron spear that had killed her was still between her ribs. She is thought to have been a slave, since the only other object by the body was an iron fibula – no doubt a dress fastening – near the shoulder. Eighteen iron spearheads were found nearby.

PLATE 49 Vratsa, vessels – 'fircone' vase, *ht.* 14 cm.

PLATE 48 Vratsa, greave detail, overall *ht.* 46 cm.

PLATE 50 Vratsa, phiale, *diam.* 10 cm., detail

PLATE 51 Vratsa, earring, *ht.* 7·5 cm.

The main tomb chamber contained a double burial, a man aged about 30 and a woman about 18.[19] The man's grave goods lay on his right. Much of the armour was badly damaged by the collapse of the roof, but a magnificent silver greave survived almost unscathed (Pl. 48). The knee-guard consisted of an ivy-crowned 'Medusa' head. Serpents and fantastic reptilian beasts emerge from her tresses; two others, one winged, the other clawed by a bird, decorate the shin-guard. Selective gilding of the monsters and the head, including horizontal bands across one side of the face, heightens the effect of the skilfully worked decorative motifs. A pair of greaves from a Thracian grave at Agighiol in the Romanian Dobroudja is very similiar and may have come from the same workshop, although they lack the creative vitality of the Vratsa find.

There was also a badly smashed bronze helmet, fragments of a curved iron sword in a scabbard, of knives or daggers, and of a quiver with 80 bronze arrowheads, some with parts of wooden shafts. Beyond the arms and armour were bronze and silver vessels, the former including two *situlae* and a hydria, the latter a small handleless flask, the lower conical part entirely covered by overlapping scales to give the impression of a fir-cone (Pl. 49), a scarcely bigger jug with gilt fluting on the shoulder and the handle terminating in a palmette, and five phialai. One of these last, of the Greek type and with fine radial fluting, has soldered to the centre a medallion of a female head in profile, framed in bands of leaf ornament (Pl. 50). The others, plain and of the mesomphalos type, all bore the pricked words ΚΟΤΥΟΣ ΕΤΒΕΟΥ. Kotys is a common Thracian name, borne by several kings and occurring in other inscriptions on phialai; the second word still awaits clear interpretation.

The female skeleton lay on the left of the male. Like the slave woman, she had been killed – or had committed suicide. The knife which pierced the left breast had not been withdrawn and the position of the bones suggests that she was left as she fell. A fine laurel wreath of gold, weighing just over 200 grams, was still round the skull (Pl. 45); and by the ears were a pair of elaborate, exquisitely worked gold earrings of the disc and boat type first introduced about 360 B.C.[20] From a concave disc worked in filigree and granulation hung an intricately decorated boat, bearing a sphinx, from which bud pendants had been suspended by tiny chains. Both disc and boat were adorned with rosettes (Pl. 51). Earrings of this general type have been found in the Thracian Chersonese, in south Russia, and at Eretria. A bronze hand mirror lay by the left hand, and gold hair pins were also found. Forty tiny gold rosettes and palmettes strewn about the head and neck had probably ornamented a veil. Round the neck was a glass-bead necklace with a multicoloured pendant, a satyr-like head with beard and bulging eyes – perhaps an amulet. Little clay figurines and other objects nearby recall the collections at Douvanli.

This tomb provides interesting archaeological support for Herodotos' account of the ritual sacrifice of the favourite wife (p. 30). Although Vratsa is far from the areas he knew, the custom is one he describes as belonging to the unidentified Thracians who lived beyond the land of the Krestonians, whose territory lay north of the Chalkidiki peninsula. As the grave goods include Greek imports, it is possible that Herodotos was told of such a ceremony by a trader who had visited the Triballi. This double burial probably took place about the middle of the fourth century.

The third Vratsa burial is believed to have been a double inhumation, although the tomb was looted and the bones scattered. Again consisting of two rectangular chambers, together measuring 13½ by 6 metres, it was outside the original retaining wall of the mound. A horse's skeleton, lacking head and neck bones, with some plain silver and bronze harness appliqués but no bridle ornaments, lay in the antechamber. Grave goods left behind included ten much-oxydised bronze plaques, a rotted leather quiver with 73 bronze three-edged arrowheads, and two small iron knives. A bronze fibula and a ring with a bird carved on its bezel could have belonged to a man or a woman; possibly feminine belongings were a tiny gold bird, a gold pendant, and fired clay objects – balls and other shapes, anthromorphic figurines, miniature boots and vases – again suggesting magical practices. There was also a flat-handled silver jug, 8 centimetres high, with a vertically channelled spherical body like that from the Bashova tumulus, and another little jug of gold, 9 centimetres high, with a handle composed of a 'Herakles' or reef knot. The shoulders have a band of linked palmettes, below which two quadrigas, each with single drivers, are placed back to back. In front the leading horses are on either side of a giant palmette. These figures show a combination of naturalism and primitive stylisation which suggest local work, comparable with some plaques found at Letnitsa, further east along the northern edge of the Stara Planina, and of approximately the same period (Pl. 5).

Fragments of Attic black-glaze pottery helped to date the tomb to about the middle of the second half of the fourth century. Full publication of the Vratsa tumulus will add greatly to archaeological knowledge of antique Thrace.

NOTES

1 Higgins, R. A. *Greek and Roman Jewellery*, London, 1961, 141.
2 Strong, D. E., *Greek and Roman Gold and Silver Plate*, London, 1966, 77.
3 *ABV* 400.
4 Sandars, N. K., *Antiquity* XLV, 1971, 108.
5 Richter, G. M. A., *The Furniture of the Greeks, Etruscans and Romans*, London, 1966, 56.
6 Strong, op. cit., 78–9.
7 Mikov, V., *Izsled Dechev*, 668–9.
8 This follows B. Filov, but I. Velkov's excavation report (IBAI VI, 1930–31) does not mention that the phiale contained ashes.
9 Strong, op. cit., 80.
10 Snodgrass, A. M., *Arms and Armour of the Greeks*, London, 1967, 92.
11 *ARV* 1643.
12 Kurtz, D. C. and Boardman, J., *Greek Burial Customs*, London, 1971, 210.
13 Herodotos VII, 111.
14 Ognenova-Marinova, L., *Actes 1st BC*, II, 397 ff.; Venedikov, I., IBAI XXXI, 1969, 5 ff.
15 Jacobsthal, P., *Prähistorischer Zeitschrift* XXV, 1934, 86, n. 28.
16 Jacobsthal, P., *Early Celtic Art*, Oxford, 1944, 151–2, Cat. nos. 164, 176.
17 Joffroy, R. and Bretz-Mahler, D., *Gallia* XVII, 1955, 5 ff.
18 Strong, op. cit., 100 ff.
19 Nikolov, B., *Obzor* II, 1970, 79.
20 Higgins, op. cit., 123.

4 Macedonian and Hellenistic Influences

Philippopolis (Plovdiv), on a group of hills, overlooking the river Maritsa, occupies the most commanding position of the whole Thracian plain. The Yasa-tepe tell on its outskirts flourished in the Late Neolithic and Chalcolithic periods. Resettlement began nearby at the end of the Bronze Age on Nebet-tepe, one of three hills linked by a precipitous ridge. Stratigraphic excavation and pottery finds here have shown a gradual expansion which appears to have accelerated considerably between the sixth and fourth centuries when, according to Ammianus Marcellinus, the site was known as Eumolpias. The necropolis of the pre-Roman city has not been discovered, although one tumulus of the fifth–fourth and one of the third century have been excavated. The first, on top of Yasa-tepe, was a simple cremation burial; a second nearby was revealed by the chance find of a fine third-century grey Thracian kantharos (Pl. 52).

A monumental tomb, dated to the late fourth or early third century, lies across the river to the north. The entrance, of two upright monoliths surmounted by an even more massive third, led into a flat-roofed ashlar antechamber, $1\frac{1}{2}$ metres square. The tomb chamber, 2·45 metres wide and 2·20 metres long, was similarly constructed, except for a domed ceiling, formed, like the ante-chamber at Kurt-kale, of three rows of stone blocks laid diagonally across the corners of those below. The chamber had been painted, and there are sculptured fragments of a Macedonian-type bier with stone imitations of turned wooden legs. The tomb had been thoroughly robbed, leaving only a late fourth-century coin and fragments of a gilded clay 'raspberry' wreath.

The settlement's increased prosperity was undoubtedly due to Greek trade. Strategically placed at a naturally defensible crossroads, with access by the Maritsa to the Aegean, it stood on the 'Diagonal' route between Europe and Asia and at the junction of others leading south-west through the Rhodope and Pirin mountains to the Mesta and Struma valleys, north over the Stara Planina to the Danube, and north-east via Beroe (Stara Zagora) and Kabyle (near Yambol) to the Black Sea cities of Mesambria, Anchialos, and Apollonia.

Following his conquest of Thrace, Philip II established a Macedonian con-tingent on and around the three linked hills – Nebet-tepe, Djambaz-tepe, and Taksim-tepe – and renamed the 'city' after himself. These hills have remained the city's core, and for much of Antiquity its citadel, although the urban boun-daries soon extended to include three others – Djendem-tepe, Sahat-tepe, and Bounardjik-tepe. The Greeks might call it maliciously 'Poneropolis' – the 'city of criminals' – but Philip's name has stuck. Thracians either used the Greek form or a Thracian version, 'Pulpudeva'. The Slav name was 'Pupuldin', the Turkish 'Filibe', and the present 'Plovdiv' derives through medieval Slavo-Bulgar variants of the Thracian version. The Romans renamed it 'Trimontium', but Philippopolis continued to be used.

PLATE 52 Philippopolis, kantharos, *ht.* 12 cm.

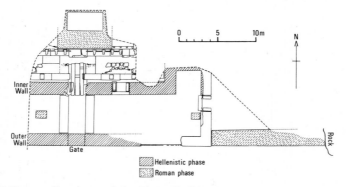

FIG. 9 Philippopolis, gate and double wall, Djambaz-tepe

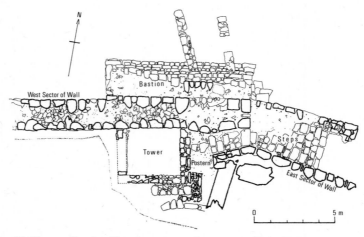

FIG. 10 Philippopolis, fortifications at north postern, Nebet-tepe

Yet, on present archaeological evidence, neither Philip nor Alexander appear to have been responsible for the Hellenistic fortifications of the city described in 1868 by A. Dumont. 'On voit à Philippopolis', he writes,

les vestiges d'une enceinte pélasgique. Ces fragments des murs sont au sommet d'une colline très escarpée de trois côtés, la colline de Nebet-tepe, une des trois acropoles qui donnèrent autrefois son nom à la ville de Trimontium . . . Toutefois l'histoire . . . et plus encore la manière primitive dont les murailles sont construites, nous prouvent qu'elles appartiennent à la haute antiquité. Les pierres, de grandes dimensions, ne sont pas taillées; elles ont la forme des polygones irreguliers et sont assorties sans ciment, de manière à ne laisser entre elles aucun interstice. Ces restes de murs, au nombre de trois, sont situés sur le côté de l'acropole qui regarde la Maritza. Le plus septentrional mesure 6 metres de long sur deux environ de haut; les deux autres, qu'on voit à l'est, offrent à peu près les mêmes dimensions.[1]

The excavator of the Hellenistic wall of Nebet-tepe, L. Botousharova, states: 'One can trace it along high parts of the north slopes of Nebet-tepe and on the ridge of the peak it passes over a paved area of a settlement strewn with pottery of the second half of the fourth century'. Of the buildings inside the walls, she says: 'We have reason to think that the Thracian settlement did not evolve quickly into a real Hellenistic city. In the second half of the fourth century, Philippopolis must have been a small settlement; no street paving or big buildings have been found.'[2] It seems that in the Macedonian period the function of Philippopolis may have been military rather than administrative. The surviving walls are, in general, situated on the steeper slopes which, in the time of Philip, might have been considered relatively secure without the massive defences which have now been exposed. The easier slopes have been inhabited for over two thousand years; any trace of Macedonian or Thracian fortification here would long ago have been destroyed.

Stretches of Hellenistic wall have been discovered on both Nebet-tepe and Djambaz-tepe. On the latter, sectors of two parallel walls, 5 metres apart and facing south, were found with a vaulted entrance in the outer leading by an unroofed corridor to a gate in the inner (Fig. 9). Both walls, varying from a little under to a little over 2 metres thick, were faced on both sides with irregular, roughly cut blocks of local syenite and light grey mortar, with an emplecton of broken stone mixed with mortar. The outer gateway, 2·20 metres wide, was arched by nine trapezoidal sandstone blocks rising to 3 metres at the keystone. The inner gateway was similarly vaulted, except that the blocks forming the vault projected well over 2 metres inside, in the opinion of the excavators to support a floor connected with the defences.[3]

On the north edge of Nebet-tepe the Hellenistic fortifications excavated were: two sectors of curtain walling; a bastion; an internal tower; and a flight of steps climbing to a postern gate (Fig. 10). The western sector of the curtain wall began at a sheer rock face and, mostly laid directly on the rock surface (Pl. 53), ran in a straight line east–north-east for about 33 metres, passing outside the postern to end at the top of the steps. Its eastern end, for a length of 9·20 metres. had walls 2·10–2·40 metres thick and was protected by the bastion; over the remaining length the thickness was a constant 2 metres. An emplecton of tightly

PLATE 53 Philippopolis, Hellenistic wall   PLATE 54 Philippopolis, Hellenistic wall with bastion

PLATE 55 Philippopolis, Hellenistic postern entrance

packed stone was slightly reinforced by mortar towards the outside. The inner face was laid without mortar and the large stones were unworked. On the exterior, the outer faces had mostly been roughly shaped and laid on beds of light grey mortar, also used to plaster over the joins, in the interstices of which pieces of tile and flat stones were wedged. Occasionally, larger and better-finished blocks are noticeable. Seemingly at random, the wall had been strengthened by inserting the facing stones as 'headers' lengthways into the emplecton.

The stepped bastion was about 3 metres deep at its base, built directly on top of soil against an already strengthened wall (Pl. 54). Behind was the postern gate and the internal tower. Traces of two parallel walls extended from the bastion down the north slope as though remaining from an earlier entrance to the fortress.

Continuing without a break east of this western sector of curtain wall was the retaining wall of the staircase (Pl. 55). Eight stone steps, laid without mortar, separated it from the eastern sector of the curtain wall, which was faced in a similar manner but set further back than the western. For a distance of about $2\frac{1}{2}$ metres before the top step, the curtain wall bent to create a platform some 80 centimetres wide in front of the postern gate. The inner part of the wall and its continuation east to another sheer rock face was rebuilt in the Roman or Early Byzantine period (Pl. 176).

The almost square tower – 3 by $3\frac{1}{2}$ metres, with walls about 70 centimetres thick using light grey mortar – stood behind the bastion commanding the approach to the postern. It was entered from the south. Beneath the south-east corner, a 20- to 40-centimetre layer of earth containing black-glazed sherds was found above a pavement of river stones, thus providing a fourth–third-century *terminus post quem* for this building. L. Botousharova advances this date to the end of the third century on the ground that the light grey mortar was not used earlier, and she considers these fortifications to date between the third and the first centuries.[4] Lysimachos, therefore, seems the most likely ruler to have initiated these defences, although his work may have been heavily damaged, by either the Celts or the Thracians, and then reconstructed by the latter sometime before or after the Macedonian occupation of the city in 183 B.C.

II. THE PANAGYURISHTE TREASURE

Diodorus Siculus tells a possibly apocryphal story about Lysimachos when captured by the Getai in 293 B.C., but set free by their king Dromichaites after being offered a symbolic banquet, aimed to secure the peaceful continuance of Getic rule over the Danubian territories. The banquet was prepared to show two ways of life. The Getai sat on straw, ate humble food off wooden boards, and drank from horn or wooden cups. Lysimachos and his fellow Macedonians (their captured goods being used for the purpose) were seated on draped couches before a silver table bearing a magnificent feast with wine poured into gold and silver cups. The story ends in Lysimachos' assent to Dromichaites' pointed suggestion that the Macedonian way of life in their own land was preferable to that of the Getai and a consequential 'live and let live' agreement.[5] Whether true or not, the episode reflects a conception of Macedonian luxury which is vividly represented in a collective find made in 1949 near the town of Panagyurishte

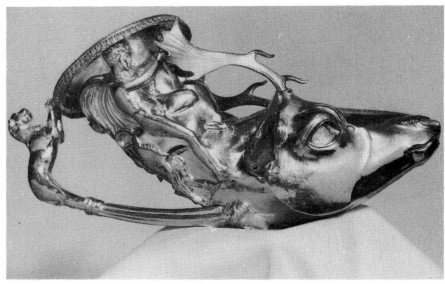

PLATE 56 Panagyurishte
treasure, rhyton

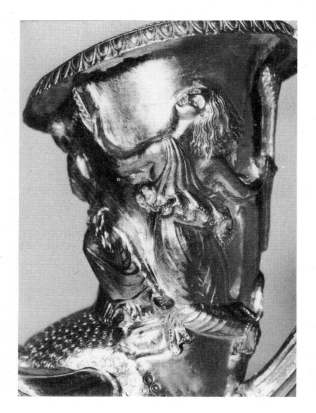

PLATE 57 Panagyurishte
treasure, rhyton

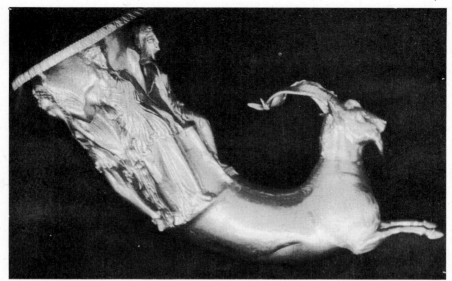

PLATE 58 Panagyurishte treasure, rhyton

and now in the Plovdiv Archaeological Museum. The find consisted of a gold hoard of nine elaborately decorated gold vessels, weighing a total of 6·10 kilograms.

Seven were rhyta, three of them in the form of animal heads, one horn-shaped but ending in the foreparts of a goat, and three vases in the form of erect female heads. In addition, there was an amphora-rhyton with two drinking spouts enabling it to be used simultaneously by two persons, and a large phiale mesomphalos. All were of pure gold, formed by being hammered on to moulds which produced repoussé relief decoration, with details etched by a chisel. The work of more than one craftsman and, in all likelihood, more than one workshop, the objects were probably assembled over a period of time.

The three animal-head rhyta, all with handles, form one contemporary group. Two have stag heads with branching antlers (Pl. 56) and the third a ram's head with well-flattened horns, the drinking spout being in the animal's lower lip. The upper part is decorated in high relief with figures from Greek mythology, usually named. The handles are in the form of a lion, placing its forepaws on the rim of the vase and standing on a fluted column, terminating at the base with a female head. One of the two stag-head rhyta, 13½ centimetres high and weighing 674·6 grams, depicts the Judgement of Paris, although Paris is called here Alexander. The other, 13 centimetres high and weighing 689 grams, shows Herakles capturing the Arkadian stag and Theseus fighting the Marathon bull, scenes not identified by name. The composition of the second rhyton is symmetrical and, unlike the first, with its elaborately draped figures, Herakles wears only a lionskin and Theseus a *chlamys*, or short cloak. The ram's-head rhyton shows Dionysos and a maenad, Eriope, both seated, with an unnamed dancing maenad on either side (Pl. 57).

The horn-rhyton, 14 centimetres high and weighing 439·05 grams, is slimmer, handleless, and more gracefully proportioned than the head-rhyta (Pl. 58) although lacking the classical restraint of the earlier example at Douvanli. The drinking spout is between the goat's forelegs. Above is Hera, enthroned, with Artemis and Apollo, each holding a bow, on either side. At the back is a Nike. All four figures are named.

Two of the three female-head rhyta – usually thought to represent Amazons – are almost identical, although from different moulds. They are $21\frac{1}{2}$ and $22\frac{1}{2}$ centimetres high and weigh 460·75 and 466·75 grams respectively. The tall concave neck of the vase is mounted on thick tresses of hair, caught up, behind, by a star-studded veil which is tied in front with a bow. The base of the woman's columnar neck is encircled by a necklace with pendants, a lion head in the centre having its mouth as the spout. The much smaller neck of the third vase – $20\frac{1}{2}$ centimetres high and weighing 387·3 grams – springs from a helmet decorated with two griffons. The curly hair, unconfined, falls freely round the helmet to the base of the vase. It has a similar lion-head spout, and all three vases have handles very like those of the animal-head rhyta, except that a winged sphinx replaces the lions and palmettes the female faces.

The largest object in the treasure is the amphora-rhyton. Twenty-nine centimetres high, it weighs just under 1·70 kilograms (Pl. 60). Comparison with the silver-gilt amphora from the Koukouva tumulus at Douvanli is interesting. The form and proportions of the neck are different; that of the Panagyurishte amphora is taller and the concave profile, with its exaggerated lip resembling those of the female-head rhyta, reflects a stylistic debasement. But there are many resemblances: the plain neck, the shape of the body, and the handles, except that centaurs have here replaced the fantastic beasts and there is no spout. The shoulder again has the customary lotus and palmette bands, repoussé work in fairly high relief, although much lower than that of the scene below, which is an entirely new departure.

Below one handle a double door is slightly ajar to reveal the head and forearms of a terrified old man. Five warriors approach, four brandishing swords, the fifth sounding a horn. The foremost is already hammering at the door. All loom considerably larger than the old man and are even taller than the doorway. (I. Venedikov suggests this may be intended to show perspective.) Each is naked except for a chlamys, and heavily muscled. Four are bearded, the fifth, much younger, is clean-shaven. The faces of the four swordsmen express tense ferocity. This scene occupies most of the space, but between the back of the trumpeter and the door is an apparently unconnected scene of an old and a young man, leaning on knobbed sticks and conversing calmly. No identifications are given and the scenes have been variously interpreted, perhaps the most likely being episodes from the *Seven Against Thebes*.

On the base of the vase the mouths of negro heads provide two spouts. Since the rhyton is held aloft when drinking, the bottom is also decorated. The infant Herakles is fighting two snakes; with him is a bearded old man, wearing an ivy-leaf crown and drunkenly holding a kantharos to one of the spouts (Pl. 61).

The phiale mesomphalos, 25 centimetres in diameter and $3\frac{1}{2}$ centimetres high, and weighing 845·7 grams, is made from a gold lacking the reddish tinge apparent in the other vases (Pl. 59). Its massive plain rim encloses three concentric rows of 24 individual negro heads in high repoussé relief, palmettes filling the

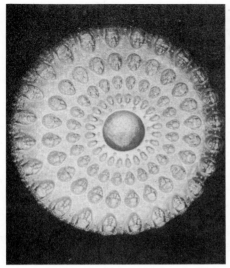

PLATE 59 Panagyurishte treasure, phiale mesomphalos

PLATE 60 Panagyurishte treasure, amphora-rhyton

PLATE 61 Panagyurishte treasure, amphora-rhyton, detail of base

intervening spaces. The heads gradually decrease in size as they approach the omphalos, ringed by 24 acorns. A possible clue to its origin is provided by two weight stamps, one expressed, like that on the amphora-rhyton, in terms of Persian darics, the other in Greek drachmai. The Persian unit used was the gold daric (or its Greek equivalent, the stater) of Lampsakos on the Asian shore of the Dardanelles, a city whose coins were slightly heavier than normal, usually weighing about 8·44 grams. Since the mark signifies 100, this would represent approximately the weight of the phiale measured by this unit. The Greek drachma, on the other hand, was a silver unit which replaced the gold daric as the standard of currency in Asia Minor soon after the death of Alexander the Great. Although this type of phiale is known from the late fifth century, it is a reasonable assumption that the Panagyurishte example came from a Hellenistic city of Asia Minor, probably Lampsakos, shortly before or about the time of the death of Alexander in 323. Possibly the original or a later purchaser may have insisted on its being re-stamped according to the new standard, not necessarily in Asia Minor. Alternatively, it may have been made several decades earlier and been stamped for the first time in Lampsakos in the twenties of the fourth century.

The name of Hera on the horn-rhyton is written in Ionic dialect, whilst in the scene of the Judgement of Paris (or Alexander) on a stag-head rhyton it appears in Attic dialect, but as the figure bears no resemblance to portraits of Alexander, this only suggests that the inscription was added at a time when Attic had superseded Ionic in Asia Minor, and merely provides a *terminus ante quem* for this group of rhyta. The substitution of Alexander for Paris reflects adulation of the former, but is unlikely to have been made in his lifetime. Oriental influences are strongly apparent in the amphora-rhyton. They can also be traced in the flowing and elaborately detailed apparel of most of the figures on the rhyta.

Regarded as a whole, the impression given by the treasure is of extravagant, even barbaric flamboyance. The element of Hellenistic 'baroque', expressing an exuberant triumph that ruptures the boundaries of taste to spread into gluttony, nevertheless retains a certain aesthetic validity and occasionally reaches standards of superb craftsmanship. The era of Alexander the Great represented a break-away from the petty despotisms and quarrels of the Greek city-states. It was a vision of a new world and artistically such a concept went to people's heads, as later in Europe the Counter-Reformation committed extravagances and excesses when freed from the unnatural restraints imposed by those fulfilling an historic necessity for reform.

With the possible exception of the phiale, the hoard may be dated variously to about the last quarter of the fourth century and the first quarter of the third. How it was assembled is unknown, as are the dates of the different objects. The trite uninspired nature of some of the figures may be due to inferior work-manship or to later degeneracy. Probably about the end of this period it was buried – almost certainly to preserve it from an enemy – near a Thracian settle-ment of local importance and prosperity in the Sredna Gora foothills.

Venedikov writes that the treasure was 'produced not in a country with ancient Greek traditions of art, but somewhere in the Hellenistic East which had not yet rid itself completely of its Persian tradition'. Certainly not made for Greeks, the obvious candidates are Macedonians or Thracians. The former are the more likely – the irresistible conquerors and liberators – although the twin spouts of the amphora-rhyton smack of the Thraco-Scyth. It is necessary to remember that the gold artefacts found in Macedonia and Thrace must represent only a minute proportion of what then existed. So much gold did not have to belong to Alexander or Lysimachos. Made for or assembled by a Macedonian, it may have passed to a wealthy Thracian, someone likely to appreciate a good drinking set, especially a gold one. Whoever hid the treasure, the Celtic invasion of about 279 or the subsequent establishment of the Celtic kingdom was probably the reason. The evidence of the labourers who dug it up suggests careful burial, carried out by either a local chief or a military leader facing disaster with little time to spare. A fleeing general is usually suggested, but perhaps the local chief of this secluded hill-land, which contains tumuli and the remains of several fortresses, is more likely. It is difficult to discern any religious purpose for the vessels, although they might possibly have been offerings to some sanctuary.

III. BRANICHEVO

Philip II's annexation of Thrace probably had little direct effect on the countryside outside the path of military operations. A group of Getic tumuli near Branichevo, 60 kilometres north of Shoumen on the road to Silistra – though like the Dolno Sahrane graves, not to be considered typical – illustrates the burial practices of a small group of simple Thracians at this time.

Eleven tumuli were excavated. In the four smallest, 5 or 6 metres in diameter and $\frac{1}{3}$ metre or less high, destruction had been severe and finds were minimal. Three others were 6 to 8 metres across; they were scarcely higher than the destroyed group, but contained burials, as did another three with diameters of 12 to 15 metres and about 1 metre high. By contrast, one mound was 41 to 44 metres across and over $4\frac{1}{2}$ metres high. All had originally been higher and perhaps wider. The disparity in size between the one large tumulus (another large one was not excavated) and the rest was reflected in the grave goods. These also dated the whole group to between the middle of the fourth and the beginning of the third centuries B.C.

Burial was without exception by cremation, but in only one case did this take place within the tumulus area. Here the corpses of a man and a woman, with their clothes and appropriate equipment or ornament, were burnt on a pyre which was fierce and prolonged, judging by the thick layer of black ash and embers, the baked earth below, and the remains of the bones. Fragments of little jugs suggested the addition of libations and a feast was indicated by numerous scorched bones of calves, sheep, goats, pigs, and fish as well as amphora fragments in the earth of this and the other mounds. Afterwards, the man's bones, mixed with those of animals, were placed in one urn and the woman's similarly mixed in another. In the man's urn were also two curved iron knives; in the woman's three spindlewhorls, three beads, and a silver coin of Apollonia. The simple tongue-handled urns were placed in a pit beside the pyre with three small jugs and a cup made of coarse local ware arranged round them; two better-quality bowls, turned upside down, lidded the urns. The whole was covered by an earth mound.

It is interesting to see in this simple burial another apparent corroboration of the description by Herodotos of Thracian funeral rites and to find that the

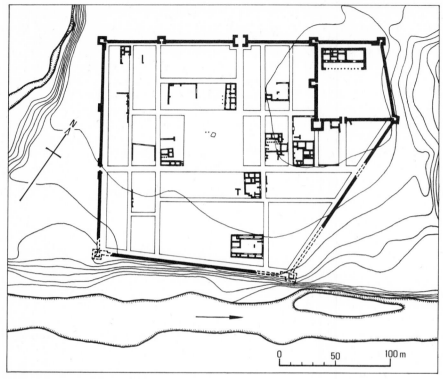

FIG. 11 Seuthopolis, city plan

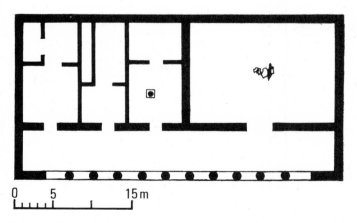

FIG. 12 Seuthopolis, palace-temple

Getai may also have killed and buried the wife simultaneously with the husband (p. 30). The presence of the pyre is the main difference between this and the other small tumuli. In one, a bowl, lidded by another, contained the burnt bones of a child; in two, there was only one bowl containing bones, but whether of one or two persons could not be ascertained. In another tumulus, human bones were distributed among five bowls, two of them lidded; one bowl also contained three knives, a second a short sword and a wild boar's tooth, and a third five spindlewhorls. As all the bowls were small, the largest only 17 centimetres high, 29 centimetres across at the rim, and 12 centimetres at the base, this probably also represented a 'husband and wife' cremation. Another mound covered at least four separate interments, perhaps members of the same family.

The large tumulus was clearly erected for the local chief. Inside was a rough, more or less rectangular, tomb, constructed of river stones mortared with clay. A few bones had been put into an amphora, together with a gold pendant. Two other amphorae stood in a corner and grave goods of various kinds were placed on the floor. Armour consisted of a bronze helmet with short nose and cheek guards and a substantial rear neck guard, and numerous pieces of an iron hauberk. The latter was made of strips, some decorated with small bosses within embossed circles, linked by tiny rings; it appeared to have been decorated by a small snake made from silver wire. The only weapons were three broken iron spearheads. A bronze appliqué composed of three horses' heads symmetrically arranged round a circular boss and two silver bell-like pendants were probably bridle ornaments of symbolic significance, as no horse bones were found. As well as the two amphorae, provision for eating and drinking included a twin-handled bronze situla, much damaged and undecorated except for two incised lines below the rim and a simple palmette between the twin handle rings; and a small silver phiale, not quite 7 centimetres high, of the common Achaemenid type, with a flat base. The lower half had an overall decoration of repoussé lozenges, the concave upper half was plain but had inscribed on opposite sides: THPHC and ΑΜΑΤΟΚΟΥΓΑΔΡΥ. A clay kantharos was a local copy of a Greek model.

IH

The chief's wife was buried separately in a peculiar fashion for this period and place. A shaft, later filled with broken stones, was sunk and from the bottom of its western side a hole, measuring approximately a cubic metre, was hollowed out, then packed with burnt bones, grave goods, and earth. Apart from a single black-glazed clay bowl on a ring base and a bronze hand mirror, all the offerings were ornaments, among them a round bronze clasp and a bronze arc-shaped fibula, a silver pendant and several appliqués, including one of gold leaf with a rosette motif similar to that on the clasp.

The settlement linked to the necropolis evidently had a short life. It may have been annihilated through natural or human causes, the clan may have temporarily exhausted the soil and moved on, or may simply have emigrated to a safer or more profitable position. We know it only through its dead.

IV. SEUTHOPOLIS

The construction of the Georgi Dimitrov dam near Koprinka, a village 4 kilometres west of Kazanluk in the Valley of Roses, unexpectedly opened an

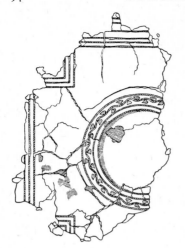

FIG. 13 Seuthopolis, hearth-altar   PLATE 62 Coin of Seuthes (III)

unknown chapter of Thracian history. A seven-year salvage dig, begun in 1948, brought to light the remains of a carefully planned and fortified city of the fourth–third century B.C. Unrecorded in the sources, an inscription found in the sixth year of the work identified it as Seuthopolis – the city of Seuthes. The site, now under the waters of the dam, awaits its full publication; thus conclusions based on the brief, although authoritative, information available in some general articles and preliminary studies are necessarily tentative.

Seuthopolis stood on a low terrace of the Sredna Gora inside a sharp bend of the river Tundja, which, running 4 to 5 metres below the site, gave further protection by its confluence here with a small tributary (Fig. 11). The fortifications, forming an irregular pentagon, used these natural advantages so that only the north-west wall occupied an exposed position. The walls were about 2 metres thick, except on the south-west where, the ground falling steeply to the river, they were a little less. Foundations of two rows of large stones carried a mud-brick structure reinforced by a wooden framework, fastened by long iron nails found in large quantities. Roughly square towers, three-quarter projecting, occupied the four main angles. Three partly projecting towers reinforced the fifth corner and the north-west wall. A gateway, probably double, in the centre of this wall was defended by a half-projecting rectangular tower. Another entrance in the east wall seems only to have required reinforcement by bastions.

The area enclosed was small, no more than about 5 hectares. The greater part consisted of streets and buildings laid out on a normal Hellenistic grid plan, but in the northern corner, which was also the highest point, was a citadel, possibly a fortified residence (*tyrsis*) or a temple complex, separated from the rest of the city by towers and a curtain wall fully as powerful as the outer defences. The principal structure in this citadel was rectangular and stood near the north-west wall. It consisted of a large hall, 18 metres long and 12 metres wide, occupying the north-east end, and three subdivided rooms (Fig. 12). Four doorways opened from them on to a colonnaded portico which ran the whole 41 metres length of the building and faced a large rectangular courtyard, paved with pebbles, leading to a fortified gateway. The usual Hellenistic construction of mud brick on stone foundations had been embellished by imported terracotta antefixes and other architectural ornaments. A Doric capital and the bottom drum of a granite column found in the courtyard may have come from either the colonnade or the monumental gateway. Fragments of painted stucco, with wax added to the paint to give a glossy finish, and stone fragments from the interior of the great hall suggest a black-tinted stone plinth round the base of the walls and a dado imitating polychrome marble slabs. The upper parts were Pompeian red and the ceiling white. A clay hearth altar occupied a central position, and another was found in the middle of the next room. The base of a staircase was discovered in one room.

The citadel area excepted, a road ran right round the inside of the city walls. From the north-west and south-west gates two streets, 6 metres wide and paved with pebbles, led into the agora, which was relatively large – 46 by 48 metres. Narrower, similarly paved streets ran parallel to the two main ones and divided the city into building blocks of varying sizes. Nor were the excavated houses uniform. Some were built round a peristyled courtyard; others had their main rooms shielded by a southern portico with wooden columns on stone bases facing a more or less open courtyard. The foundations were of broken stone and clay; the mud-brick superstructure sometimes had a wooden framework; the roofs were tiled. In one house the remains of stairs were found. Most houses had a hearth altar in the main room. Like those in the inner fortress, they were usually decorated with incised geometric and vegetal ornamentation (Fig. 13).

Although the city was small, the houses were spaciously planned, usually extending from one street to the next. Two or three might make up a whole block, and an area of 300–350 square metres was common; the largest house covered 500 square metres. Water came from wells, and a drainage system took the domestic waste through stone channels, clay pipes, or curved tiles to drains – usually laid along the middle of the streets – which, utilising the gradient, emptied through spouts in the curtain wall into the river.

Bones of domestic animals, several iron ploughshares, and blades resembling pruning knives indicated a farming economy. There was plenty of wheel-made local grey and red pottery. Imported ware included Thasian amphorae and a great deal of Attic black-glazed pottery. Terracotta figurines were also popular, possibly originating from Odessos or the Dobroudja colonies.

Eight hundred of the 1,300 antique coins found were issues of Seuthes. Their ten bronze denominations indicate an advanced money economy. As considerable numbers have also been found, singly and in hoards, along the upper reaches of the Tundja, Seuthes' kingdom was apparently concentrated in the present Valley of Roses. T. Gerasimov has noted two types of coins.[6] One carries his name and a horseman on the reverse and the head of Zeus on the obverse, in the manner of Philip II's coins. The other is broadly similar, but the face of Zeus, though still bearded and with flowing, laurel-crowned locks, is far more individual (Pl. 62). Gerasimov suggests this is a portrait of Seuthes. The supposed portraits vary considerably, but the head illustrated certainly fits a ruler with Seuthes' remarkable powers of survival over a period of exceptional danger and strife. Plainly present, too, is the craftiness of one capable of correlating his own image with that of the king of the gods in a manner to appeal to Thracian loyalties and religious ideas without open offence to his probably nominal Macedonian suzerain; the coins might merely be Thracian imitations of Philip's issues. Gerasimov's interesting suggestion is supported by the publication so far of only a few coins and the mint has not been identified; there is no reason to suppose it was Seuthopolis.

The inscription identifying Seuthopolis was a decree carved on a marble slab found in the room next to the great hall of the citadel. The greater part of the Greek text, which was intact, is still unpublished, although translations into Bulgarian, Russian, and Latin have appeared.[7] The decree appears to record a solemn undertaking by one Berenike and her four sons – Ebrizelmes, Teres, Satakos, and Sadalas – consequent upon an act of Seuthes whilst he was in good health. Two other persons are concerned, Spartokos and Epimenes, one by name Thracian and the other probably a Macedonian. The presumption is that Berenike – a Macedonian name – was either the widow or the wife of and regent for an aged or ill Seuthes. The details of the undertaking are obscure, but it is expressly stated that the decree is to be carved on stone slabs to be set up at Kabyle, in the Phosphorion – probably a temple of Artemis and Hekate – and in the agora, and at Seuthopolis, in the temple of the Great Gods and in the sanctuary of Dionysos by the agora.

As a fragmentary inscription in the Seuthopolis agora mentions a Thracian priest of Dionysos, it is generally assumed that the temple of the Great Gods – usually the Samothracian Kabiri – was the great hall in the inner fortress. It is the earliest indication of the Kabiri cult in the Thracian interior. One passage in the decree may mean that the sanctuary was controlled by Berenike and her sons and that Epimenes had taken refuge there, as was the custom on Samothrace. If, as is thought, the citadel enclosed both the temple of the Great Gods and the royal residence, priestly functions on the part of the royal house would be implied, as Herodotos says was the practice among the Bessi. Such functions could accord with an identification of Seuthes with Zeus on coins. Berenike's name appears alone in the conventional ending as the person especially responsible for ensuring the undertaking is kept, giving rare epigraphic support for the archaeological evidence of the princely graves on the status of women among the Thracians.

Seuthes – the third Thracian king known of this name – is first mentioned in written sources as rising against the Macedonians in 325, when Alexander was embroiled in Asia. In 323, there was an indecisive battle between Seuthes and Lysimachos. Ten years later, Seuthes agreed to support a league of Black Sea cities against Lysimachos (p. 52), but on the latter's unexpectedly speedy arrival Seuthes changed sides. However, when Lysimachos had to return south with part of his army to deal with an invasion by Antigonos, Seuthes joined the latter and ambushed Lysimachos on his way across the Stara Planina. A hard battle ended in victory for Lysimachos. Seuthes then drops out of the historical record, although coins issued by Lysimachos on or after 306 were overstruck with his name. Whether this Seuthes was one or more persons is impossible to say, but, usually identified for convenience as Seuthes III, it is now evident that he (or they) tried valiantly and constructively to revive the Odrysian kingdom and made good headway against heavy odds.

The life of the city was brief. There had been some kind of forerunner in the inner fortress area, where coins of Philip II were found with local pottery below a thin layer of ash. The new city was probably built in the last two decades of the fourth century under Greek architects, perhaps from a Black Sea city – a surmise only, because, for all we know, a time may have come when Seuthes received substantial aid from Lysimachos. Besides the coins of Seuthes, others in the ruins date from the reign of Alexander the Great to that of Demetrios II (239–229). Numerous burnt bricks and fragments of battering rams indicate that at some stage – the mid-third century is proposed – the city was besieged, sacked, and put to the flames. A later and humbler resettlement perished after a few decades, then the Tundja flooded the area, covering it with sand and gravel. Deserted for some 1,400 years, when a small medieval village established itself here, the site of Seuthopolis has now been submerged once more beneath the Tundja's waters.

V. TUMULI OF SEUTHOPOLIS AND THE KAZANLUK REGION

Three large tumuli near Koprinka and Seuthopolis were also excavated before being submerged by the waters of the dam. In the first, Koprinka No. 1, the cremated remains and grave goods of a Thracian woman lay at the base of a small cairn over which the earth mound had been heaped. Her gold jewellery included a necklace of 36 hollow spherical beads, half of them decorated with filigree forming a double spiral, and a pair of the lion-head hoop earrings popular in the Hellenistic period. Bronze vessels included a fine oinochoe, the base of the handle adorned with the relief head of a young satyr, and a situla with twin handles, below them a stylised ivy leaf. There was also a Greek aryballesque lekythos and other imported pottery, a clay lamp, and the terracotta statuette of a young girl.

Koprinka tumuli Nos. 2 and 3 contained inhumation burials. In No. 2, a passage almost 3 metres long led through a rectangular antechamber, measuring about $2\frac{3}{4}$ by 2 metres, into a tholos chamber about 5 metres in diameter. In tumulus No. 3 (Fig. 14) the tomb was smaller and had no dromos. Unlike the stone-built tholos tombs at Mezek and elsewhere, the Koprinka pair belong to a very small group, all near Kazanluk, built of fired bricks shaped in special moulds. Those used for the antechambers were rectangular, those in the circular tomb chamber were segments of the circle with appropriately curved inner and outer ends. Although the Koprinka tombs were destroyed to near ground level, bricks from the dome were easily distinguished by the slant-cut face of their inner sides, producing, like the corbelled stone slabs at Mal-tepe, a smooth, even surface. Since only one thickness of brick was used, the structure was strengthened by a 'jacket' of rough stones mortared with clay before the earth mould was raised.

Two other brick-built vaulted tombs have been excavated, one in Kazanluk itself, the other 13 kilometres farther east, at Muglish. Both are larger than the Koprinka tombs, Muglish, as yet unpublished, being the largest of all; both have painted interiors. A third, much-damaged tomb with signs of paintings has been found at Krun, 6 kilometres north of Kazanluk, but at the time of writing no details of it are available.

Tumulus No. 2 at Koprinka contained two secondary inhumations; both were in rectangular brick graves, roofed by stone slabs and just big enough for, in one case, a male with an iron spear and strigil and, in the other, a female whose few grave goods included a gold necklace and fibulae. The bricks used, as well as those in a similar grave on the edge of the dam, were not new but, as is clear from their shapes, came from the destroyed domed tombs.

The available evidence points to a late fourth- or early third-century date for all the graves, probably with no great lapse of time between the three types. Although this was the high period of prosperity for Seuthopolis, within the city the use of fired brick was extremely limited and, in almost all cases, the bricks were re-used. Only mud brick seems to have been employed in the buildings. Suddenly therefore, for a very brief period, it appears that well-fired bricks of good quality were manufactured in a highly skilled and sophisticated manner exclusively to construct domed tombs. Then, apparently no less suddenly, this brickmaking ceased, although the old bricks were used for new tombs of a quite different type – one that corresponded to a cist grave – and for utilitarian purposes in the city. The origin of the craftsmen with the skill not only of brickmaking but of building circular domed chambers is, as is their fate, an unsolved mystery. Perhaps a consequential benefit of Seuthes' relationship with Antigonos was a visit from Greco-Syrian craftsmen who took their secret with them when they departed or died. But there is no evidence to support such an origin. It can only be said that the importance of the burial ritual to the Thracians is again emphasised.

The first brick tholos tomb was found in 1944 in Kazanluk. Its fortuitous excavators were troops digging an air-raid shelter in what was thought to be a natural hillock, 7 metres high and 40 metres in diameter. The soldiers, fortunately tunnelling from the south, soon came upon and burst through a rough masonry wall to find the entrance to a narrow room that was blocked at its north end by a large rectangular granite slab. Knocking this down, they came into a circular chamber decorated with curious paintings. At this point archaeologists took over the 'air-raid shelter' and began an attempt to conserve a splendid and unique example of Greco-Thracian tomb painting.

The tomb (Fig. 15) consisted of a now much-destroyed, roughly constructed outer chamber, probably unroofed. This led into a rectangular brick-built antechamber or dromos – its precise function is unclear – with a 'gabled' ceiling formed by overlapping slant-cut bricks. The brick-built, beehive-shaped chamber into which this opened had a diameter of 2·65 metres and reached a height of 3·25 metres. The top was slightly truncated by a massive square capstone, the lower part of which was carved to form a round 'stopper'. As at Koprinka, the bricks were specially tailored to give a smooth and rounded inner surface, and the tomb was reinforced by a 'jacket' of broken stones mortared with clay.

Like the rest, the tomb had been looted in Antiquity, although here the structure had been undisturbed. The few remaining objects included human bones, identified as belonging to two persons, one a woman. Perished wood and nails suggested a coffin or coffins. A rusted iron spearhead, pieces of a curved knife, and an iron bit from a horse's bridle, as well as broken horse bones (in the outermost chamber), are evidence of a male burial, but there was nothing to tell

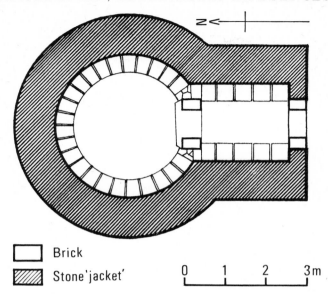

Brick

Stone 'jacket'

0   1   2   3m

FIG. 14 Koprinka, tumulus no. 3

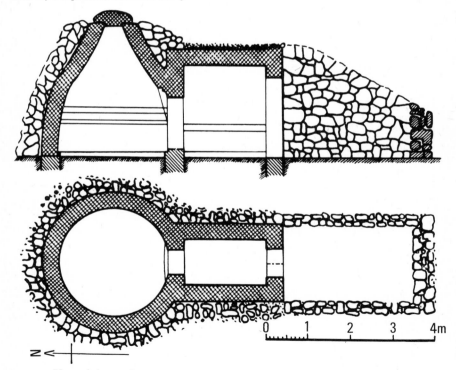

0   1   2   3   4m

FIG. 15 Kazanluk, tomb

whether the two had been buried at the same time. A hundred and forty tiny sequin-like gold appliqués, 1·2–1·6 millimetres across, must have come from some perished textile. Small gilded clay rosettes and vessels, almost all broken, of Thracian and Greek ware, among them a clay oinochoe and amphora, also a gilded silver jug, were found scattered about, some in the entrance chamber, by which were two sacrificial hearths.

The whole interior of the brick antechamber and tholos was painted inside and this has miraculously survived almost intact. Working with four colours, white, black, red, and yellow, the artists used tempera and encaustic, the latter given a mirror-like sheen by adding wax and marble dust. Even the entrance chamber had been plastered and coated with stucco to conceal its roughness. The floors of both inner rooms were Pompeian red. The walls imitate marble revetment, black orthostats enclosed by narrower bands of white in the ante-chamber, the reverse in the tholos. In both cases a wide red band covers the beginning of the curve of the vault. Above this, in the antechamber, a band with tendrils emerging schematically from a central stem runs along the walls, enclosed in narrower bands of architectural motifs. Finally, reaching to the top of the vault, a horizontal panel on each side depicts a battle scene. Although the order of battle is formal, two foot-soldiers meeting in single combat in the centre with cavalry and other foot-soldiers advancing behind them, the movements are lively and realistic, and in dress and accoutrements the four armies are individually characterised. V. Mikov has suggested that the forces at the southern end on both sides are Thracian. This is almost certainly so on the east wall, but less sure on the west.

The upper decoration of the circular chamber, consistent with the proportions of the tomb as a whole, starts at a higher level than that of the antechamber. First is a band of alternating *bucrania*, or garlanded ox-skulls (later ox-heads), and rosettes. Above this is the principal zone (Pl. 65). Opposite the doorway a man is seated on a multicoloured cushioned bench, before him a rectangular three-legged table bearing various foods. He wears a short-sleeved *chiton*, or tunic, and a brown mantle, and on his head is a laurel crown, painted yellow-gold. His right hand holds a cup, his left reaches out to clasp the right forearm of a woman seated on a throne beside him while she rests her hand on his.

The man, the enthroned woman, and a woman offering him a bowl of fruit. including pomegranates, food of the dead, form the centrepiece of a scene which encircles the dome. Whereas he looks towards his seated partner, she gazes downwards and raises her left hand to support her chin. Her dark, carefully arranged hair is half covered by a long semi-transparent white veil, drawn back to disclose earrings and falling across her lap over the arm of the chair (Pl. 64). She wears a long white chiton, under a brown *himation*, a loose garment, with a lower edging of white. The throne is a splendid, ornate example of Early Hellenistic furniture.[8] The high back is intricately decorated, the legs carefully turned and painted, the arms supported by sphinxes or griffons.

The woman bearing the pomegranates is also nobly, but more simply, dressed. Her height, her head reaching the architectural zone above, designates her as a main participant in the rite. Like the enthroned woman, her expression is of dignified sorrow; with bowed head she is gazing at the face of the man.

The rest of the zone is taken up by an attendant retinue. Behind the standing

PLATE 63 Kazanluk tomb, detail   PLATE 64 Kazanluk tomb, detail

woman a male servant carries an oinochoe and a cup like that held by the man; two women follow, playing long pipes; behind, two saddle horses are accompanied by a groom and a warrior. On the left of the seated woman a female servant brings two boxes, the larger – a coffer – held shoulder high, the smaller by its handle. Behind, another woman carries a blue cloth, possibly a folded veil; then a groom (Pl. 63) leads four horses harnessed to a chariot. These horses back against the saddle horses to complete the circle. For all characters the convention is observed that men have dark and women fair skins.

In the top zone, separated from the main one by three bands of architectural motifs and one of animal heads and lotus flowers, three chariots, each drawn by two horses, are being driven at full gallop round the capstone. Their frenzy contrasts vividly with the calm of the scene below. A similar chariot motif occurs on the painted representation of a vase in the Muglish tomb.

Although the composition must have been the inspiration of a single artist, master craftsmen painted the most important parts, assistants did the rest. Even at best, the execution of the individual figures does not reach the highest standards of Early Hellenistic art. On the other hand, the ensemble ranks as a masterpiece of this or any period. Designed in perfect relationship to the peculiar beehive shape of the tomb, it achieves a three-dimensional quality whereby the people portrayed inhabit the burial chamber and participate in a sacred rite, one moment of which is brilliantly preserved. The dignity and serenity of a ritual once associated with the passing of the dead to another life still envelop and awe the spectator. No two-dimensional pictures can convey this, but unfortunately, despite all efforts, contact with the air is gradually causing the paintings to

deteriorate, and lest they fade and crumble admission is stringently controlled.

The main scene is usually interpreted as indicating that this is the tomb of a princely husband and wife. The evidence of male and female burials in the tholos chamber supports this view, but it is wise to keep an open mind. The perfection of the composition within its unusual architectural frame leaves little doubt that the construction and decoration of the brick tombs were closely interconnected. Both architects and artists are with reason assumed to be of Greek origin from somewhere in the Hellenistic world. Thus the Kazanluk tomb presents a Thracian religious concept at least partially visualised in terms of Greek religious art – it is related to funerary feast stelai – but too little is known about the former to isolate its elements in this Thraco-Greek synthesis. Was the seated woman, as Herodotos describes and as happened at Vratsa, a favourite wife buried to accompany her husband? Or was she a royal priestess who in Douvanli, a century earlier, would have been given separate burial? Or was she, perhaps through east Greek influences, a Persephone-type goddess to whom the dead prince or king came after death – as in the early Thracian Horseman reliefs of Odessos? And to what extent did the scene reflect the prominent part played by women such as Berenike in the history of Seuthopolis? Another question without an answer from the limited evidence of a single tomb is how much the pervading atmosphere – restrained sorrow combined with serene dignity – represents a Thracian funerary concept or was the contribution of the foreign artists.

The Kazanluk tomb is generally dated, like those at Koprinka, to the late fourth or early third century, although on minor stylistic points D. P. Dimitrov has recently proposed the second quarter of the third century.[9] But the brick construction clearly links it with the Koprinka and Muglish tombs. Until there is a clue to the antecedents of this remarkable group and pending the full publication of Seuthopolis, the likelihood of a link between the tombs and the peak period of the only nearby city of which we know must remain a possibility; although further exploration of the area may bring to light another 'city', perhaps at Kazanluk itself, with greater claim to being the brickworkers' centre.

VI. KABYLE

The site of Kabyle, mentioned in the Seuthopolis decree (p. 96), was identified almost a century ago by K. Jiriček and the Škorpil brothers as a terrace dominated by an acropolis-like hill near Yambol (Pl. 67). Some 100 kilometres east of Seuthopolis, it lies on an earlier course of the river Tundja, now a kilometre away, just about half-way between that city and the Black Sea coast.

Polemically referred to by Demosthenes as one of Philip II's 'miserable dens', Kabyle was probably one of the Thracian centres where, like Philippopolis, Philip settled a Macedonian colony. Although long uninhabited, it has been left untouched until now, except for a salvage dig of one relatively undistinguished Late Hellenistic tumulus. The present excavations, begun in June 1972, must yield a rich reward. From unknown origins, Kabyle existed until its destruction by the Visigoths in A.D. 378, when the survivors may have moved to Diampolis (Yambol). Between the main centres of the Thracian plain and the south-western Black Sea cities, connected by river with the Aegean and over easy passes

PLATE 65 Kazanluk tomb, detail

of the Stara Planina with Odessos and the Greek cities farther north as well as the Danube, the site had exceptional economic and strategic advantages. That it profited by these is shown by the Seuthopolis inscription and by its issue of silver and bronze coins in the third or second century B.C. Kabyle may also have minted coins in the second half of the third century for the Celtic king Kavaros, perhaps as a form of tribute.[10] The city was occupied by the Roman expedition of 72 B.C. and was probably later renamed Diospolis.

VII. BEROE AND ITS VICINITY

Another centre with naturally advantageous communications, Beroe (Stara Zagora) could hardly fail to be important. Although the present city stands on a Roman foundation, officially entitled Augusta Trajana but more generally known as Beroe, it replaced an older settlement of this name in the neighbourhood, possibly on the river Bedechka, a kilometre from Stara Zagora. Here within a tiny area 'as much imported black-glaze pottery as was found in the whole of Seuthopolis'[11] was discovered by chance, almost all in small fragments. Although unpublished, pieces have been tentatively dated to the fifth to second centuries B.C. All that we have of Thracian Beroe therefore – the name suggests that in the fourth century it was another of Philip II's colonies – is a probable rubbish dump. While this is in itself valuable, a planned search of the immediate neighbourhood may uncover another major pre-Roman settlement.

The presence nearby of two rich tumulus burials, both cremations and dated by their contents to about the first century B.C. or a little later, suggests that Beroe survived the Celtic invasion without undue harm, and its Roman successor dates only from the second century A.D. The grave goods show that both burials were male. In one, a large bronze or copper cauldron contained objects of Thracian and imported origin, in this case not Greece but Italy. There was a silver vase of the 'Boscoreale' type and a silver sieve inscribed in Latin that it had been made for Rufius by Sextus Maetennius. In addition, besides fragments of Thracian scale armour, other armour, arms, and harness, there were four silver-gilt *phalerae*, or plaques, embossed in high relief, which can hardly be other than purely Thracian work.

At the time of writing, only one phalera has been published (Pl. 66); another has survived whole, but one or both of the others suffered severe damage in the crematory fire. The central figures of the published phalera – 17·8 centimetres across – may be Herakles and the Nemean lion. If so, while the execution is skilful, the myth, which was similarly represented on a fourth-century phalera found near Panagyurishte, had little significance for the craftsman, such is the tameness of the protagonists. The six beasts formally arranged round this scene show he was more at home with myths of another kind. Four are griffons, eagle-headed at the top, lion-headed at the bottom. Those between could be canine or feline. Their collars are perhaps a symbolic device or indicate their use for hunting. It is doubtful, in view of their evident ferocity, that they are domestic animals. The other undamaged phalera, only very slightly smaller, is probably a companion piece; it had no human figure and the fantastic beasts differ in kind and arrangement.

While these are the first phalerae of their kind found in Bulgaria, examples

PLATE 66 Beroe, phalera   PLATE 67 Kabyle (1969)

very similar in decoration, workmanship, and size are known outside the country. Two, unfortunately of unknown origin, are in the Bibliothèque Nationale, Paris; another came from a peat bog in Helden, Holland, and 13 were found with other objects in an urn on the island of Sark early in the eighteenth century. Although the Sark hoard was later lost, excellent drawings recently came to light and have been fully discussed by D. F. Allen, the phalerae being related to the other examples, including those from Stara Zagora.[12] Allen concludes that all are likely to have originated in Thrace, those in the west having in the first place been used by Thracian auxiliaries of the Roman armies. Comparing them with earlier metalwork, it is not difficult to recognise the Thracian tradition of animal art.

These phalerae, so much larger than the harness appliqués from earlier Thracian graves, must have been differently used. One might have been attached to a horse's chest harness, but they are more likely to have decorated the saddle cloth or the horse's flanks. It is also possible that Thracian nobles wore them on coats of mail or ceremonial attire, a c. first-century B.C. form of pectoral.

The other tumulus burial was similarly a warrior's grave. With the ashes was a gold ring, probably Greek in origin; a kneeling archer with a plumed helmet drawing his bow was carved on the red stone of the bezel. There were also remains of a bronze helmet, spearheads, and an iron double-edged sword with an ornate silver open-work scabbard which, according to its Greek inscription, was made by Seuthes of Paiagara. The site of Paiagara is unknown, but the scabbard is evidence of the skill of a Thracian silversmith who worked there and additional proof of Thracian craftsmanship in this unsettled period.

VIII. CHERTIGRAD

While cities and rulers adjusted with varying success to the Roman presence, in the conqueror's eyes the peasantry were simply a source of military manpower. Tacitus[13] writes of the last struggle for independence of one group of 'Thracian tribesmen, who, on their mountain peaks lived uncivilised and proportionately bold' and 'refused to tolerate the military levies and to devote the whole of their ablebodied manhood to the Roman service'. Instead 'they pointed to their strongholds perched upon the crags, and to the parents and wives placed in them for refuge, and threatened a war intricate, arduous, and bloody'.

Tacitus refers to events which took place in A.D. 26. Such a stronghold, one of many still to be found in the less accessible mountain regions, is Chertigrad, now being excavated. It stands on a peak about 1,300 metres above sea level on the northern slopes of the Stara Planina, in the region of the upper Vit, about two hours on foot from the nearest village and only accessible from the south-west. This approach was defended by a dry-stone wall, about 2·20 metres wide, faced on both sides with well-laid local stone with a filling of small stones, a substantial barrier. As no material had been taken away for re-use, the original height could be estimated – 3 to 3½ metres. There were two building phases, both using the same method. A rectangular platform, 2·40 by 1·40 metres, built into the inside of the wall, defended a narrow entrance between its south end and the cliff edge. Approached by a natural ramp below the wall, this entrance was apparently closed when necessary by improvised means.

About 15 single-roomed buildings stood in small groups inside the walls, one near the entrance probably serving a defensive purpose. The largest, 5·80 by 8·60 metres, with three sides of well-laid dry stone walling and a fourth of rough stone and mud construction, was perhaps some kind of public building. On the east cliff, an artificially cut niche was found, oriented to receive the sun's first rays and almost certainly created for a religious purpose.

Finds which could help to date the fortress have so far been meagre. Pending completion of the excavations, it seems that it was in existence in the Hellenistic period, continued under the Roman, with a place in the later imperial defence strategy, and was finally abandoned in the second half of the sixth century A.D.

V. Velkov rightly points out that the fortress is typical of the background against which Tacitus describes a last stand against the Romans and the ending of the old order – or disorder – and the beginning of the new.

In A.D. 26, Poppaeus Sabinus, with a Roman legion from Moesia and Thracian auxiliaries in the service of a client-king, moved against some Thracian tribesmen

. . . concentrated in the wooded gorges. A few, more daring, showed themselves on the open hills, but were driven from them without difficulty, when the Roman commander advanced in battle-order, though cover was so near that little barbarian blood was spilt. Then, after fortifying a camp on the spot, Sabinus . . . made himself master of a narrow mountain-ridge running without a break to the nearest tribal fortress, which was held by a considerable force of armed men and irregulars. Simultaneously, he sent a picked body of archers to deal with the bolder spirits who, true to the national custom, were gambolling with songs and war-dances in front of the rampart. The bowmen, so long as they operated at long range, inflicted many wounds with impunity; on advancing closer, they were thrown into disorder by an unlooked-for sally . . .

. . . The camp was then moved a stage nearer the adversary; and the Thracians . . . [Roman auxiliaries] were left in charge of the earlier lines. They had licence to ravage, burn, and plunder, so long as . . . the night [was] spent safely and wakefully behind entrenchments. At first, the rule was kept: then . . . they began to leave their posts for some wild orgy, or lay tumbled in drunken slumber. The enemy, therefore, who had information of their laxity, arranged two columns, by one of which the raiders were to be attacked, while another band demonstrated against the Roman encampment; not with any hope of capture, but in order that, amid the shouting and the missiles, every man engrossed by his own danger might be deaf to the echoes of the other conflict. Darkness, moreover, was chosen for the blow, so as to intensify the panic. The attempt on the earthworks of the legions was, however, easily repelled: the Thracian auxiliaries, a few of whom were lying along their lines, while the majority were straggling outside, lost their nerve . . . and were cut down all the more ruthlessly because they were branded as renegades and traitors . . .

On the following day, Sabinus paraded his army in the plain, in the hope that the barbarians, elated by the night's success might venture battle. As they showed no signs of descending from their stronghold . . . he began their investment, with the help of the fortified posts . . .; then drew a continuous fosse and breastwork, with a circumference of four miles; and lastly, step by step, contracted and tightened his lines of circumvallation, so as to cut off the supplies of water and forage; while an embankment began to rise, from which stones, spears, and firebrands could be showered on the no longer distant enemy. But nothing told on the defence so much as thirst, since the one spring remaining had to serve the whole great multitude of combatants and non-combatants. At the same time, horses and cattle . . . were dying for lack of fodder; side by side with them lay the bodies of men, victims of wounds or thirst, and the whole place was an abomination of rotting blood, stench, and infection.

To the confusion was added the last calamity, discord; some proposing surrender, some to fall on each other and die; while there were those, again, who commended, not unavenged destruction, but a last sortie . . . The younger fighting men were divided between Tarsa and Turesis . . . Tarsa, crying out for a quick despatch, a quietus to hope and fear alike, gave the example by plunging his weapon into his breast . . . Turesis and his followers waited for the night: a fact of which the Roman commander was not ignorant . . . Night was falling, with a storm of rain; and the wild shouting on the enemy's side, alternating as it did with deathly stillnesses, had begun to perplex the besiegers, when Sabinus made a tour of his lines and urged the men [not] to be misled . . . every man should attend to his duties without budging from his post or expending javelins on an illusory mark.

Meanwhile, the barbarians, speeding down in their bands, now battered the palisades with hand-flung stones, stakes pointed in the fire, and oak-boughs hewn from the tree; now filled the moats with brushwood, hurdles, and lifeless bodies; while a few, with bridges and ladders . . . advanced against the turrets, clutching them, tearing them down, and struggling hand to hand with the defenders. The troops, in return, struck them down with spears, dashed them back with their shield-bosses, hurled on them siege-javelins and piles of massive stone. On each side were incentives enough to courage: on ours, the hope that victory was won, and the more flagrant ignominy which would attend a defeat; on theirs, the fact that they were striking the last blow for deliverance – many with their wives and mothers close at hand and their lamentations sounding in their ears. Night, screening the audacity of some, the panic of others; blows dealt at random, wounds unforeseen; the impossibility of distinguishing friend from foe; cries echoed back from the mountain ravines, and so coming apparently from the rear – all this had produced such general confusion that the Romans abandoned some of their positions as forced. Yet actually none but a handful of the enemy made their way through; while the remainder, with their bravest either dead or disabled, were at the approach of daylight pushed back to their stronghold on the height, where surrender at last became compulsory.[14]

Further operations were soon suspended by the 'premature and stern winter of the Haemus range'. Poppaeus Sabinus received a triumph, and 20 years later Thracia was formally constituted a Roman province.

NOTES

1 Dumont, A., *Mélanges d'archéologie et d'épigraphie*, Paris, 1892, 196.
2 Botousharova, L., *Arh* VII/3, 1965, 3.
3 Botousharova, L. and Kolarova, V., *God Plovdiv* VII, 1971, 75 ff.
4 Botousharova, L., *God Plovdiv* V, 1963, 77 ff.
5 Diodorus Siculus, XXI, 12.
6 Gerasimov, T., *IBAI* XIX, 1955, 123 ff.
7 *IGB* III/2, 1731.
8 Richter, G. M. A., *The Furniture of the Greeks, Etruscans and Romans*, London, 1966, 22, Fig. 79.
9 Dimitrov, D. P., *Arh* VIII/2, 1966, 1 ff.
10 Gerasimov, T., *IBAI* XXII, 1959, 111 f.
11 Nikolov, D., *Arh* IX/4, 1967, 33.
12 Allen, D. F., *Archaeologia* CIII, 1971, 1 ff.
13 Tacitus, *Annals*, Bk. IV, XLVI, trans. Jackson, J., London, 1963, 83, 84.
14 Ibid., Bk. IV, XLVII–LI, 85–93.

PART TWO
The Roman Presence

I. RATIARIA AND THE NORTH-WEST

The establishment of permanent Roman camps along the Danube, extending from Pannonia into, first, what is now north-west Bulgaria and gradually reaching to the Black Sea coast, arose from the need to set up a viable line of defence against the Daco-Getic threat to Macedonia. While a measure of control had been attained over the Thracian tribes south of the Danube, those north of it – in present-day Romania – remained aggressively independent under the military leadership and influence of the Dacians based in the mountainous regions of southern Transylvania. Thus, instead of to the partially Hellenised interior, it was to the lesser-known north-west and south banks of the Danube that Roman organisation was first introduced and followed by a policy of Romanisation to replace the existing Thracian structure.

Ratiaria

Ratiaria (Archar), one of the oldest and to become one of the wealthiest Roman cities on the lower Danube (Pl. 1), was described by Dio Cassius as strongly fortified when Crassus campaigned against the Triballi and other Moesian tribes in 29 B.C. It grew rapidly in the first century A.D. and received the title of Colonia Ulpia Trajana following the conquest of Dacia. Predominantly although by no means exclusively settled by Romans and others of Italic descent – civilians as well as soldiers – the city was the focal point for the Romanisation of the surrounding territory. The name is generally considered of Latin origin and survives to some degree in that of the modern village of Archar.

Ratiaria's commercial potentialities, as inscriptions show, also drew traders from Asia Minor. Besides serving as a port and point of transhipment enabling Danubian traffic to avoid the dangerous 'Iron Gates', it was the northern terminus of the shortest land route from Lissus (Lesh) on the Adriatic, and hence from Italy, to the lower Danube. In addition to its garrison, Ratiaria was a headquarters of the Danube fleet, at least from the time of Aurelian, who made it the chief city of the new province of Dacia Ripensis after the evacuation of trans-Danubian Dacia. Among its industries was one of the five imperial munition factories in the Balkan peninsula.

Today the site, on either side of the little Archar river, is covered by fields and vineyards, the village of the same name, and, on a low hill, the hamlet of Turska Mahala, where the citadel probably stood. Excavations undertaken within the last 20 years or so are reported to have located a necropolis, an aqueduct, and the beginning of the road to Bononia (Vidin), and to have shown that the city expanded westward after becoming a provincial capital, but the work has not yet reached publication stage. Surface finds have yielded many inscriptions and other objects. Essentially Roman and typical of many found along the Danube in its shape and carefully carved formal decoration of ivy and vine is a mid-second-century stele erected by a lady of probable Greek origin in memory of her Roman husband and her 'dulcissima' and 'pientissima'

PLATE 68 Ratiaria, stele   PLATE 69 Ratiaria, Mercury, sarcophagus detail

18-year-old daughter[1] (Pl. 68). Other funerary intrusions into this land of tumulus burials are the locally carved sarcophagi. One – also of the Antonine period – has on one short side a relief of Hermes-Mercury, here no doubt intended as the herald of the dead but also suggestive of the commercial acumen and statecraft of Ratiaria (Pl. 69). Yet on two other approximately contemporary sarcophagi, both very alike, a small framed uninscribed relief of the Thracian Horseman appears as the centrepiece of otherwise elaborate conventional ornamentation, an illustration of the headway made even here by this Thracian cult in the second century.

A dedication to Porobonus, a god of Celtic origin, has also been discovered, one of only three known in east Europe, the others at Abritus (Razgrad) and Olbia in south Russia. Worship of the Roman pantheon is naturally well represented, notably of Jupiter and Juno – portrayed together in a chariot on one relief – Pluto, Proserpina, Ceres, and Hercules. Mithras is a prominent second-third-century addition. An unusual marble statuette of Hercules was found recently by an Archar farmer when building a pigsty. The muscular but pensive hero is seated, his chin resting against his right hand, his club dangling against his left knee (Pl. 70), a fascinating, coincidental mid-second-century intermediary between the 'Thinker' statuette of the Neolithic Hamangia culture of the Dobroudja and Rodin's *Penseur*.

Bononia

About 10 kilometres upstream from Ratiaria and within its territory was Bononia (Vidin), a station of secondary importance during the Roman period.

The name is equivalent to Bologna and Boulogne and the site may have been a Celtic settlement before the Roman arrival, when a cavalry detachment was stationed here. Bononia's remains now lie below a busy modern town and the medieval and Turkish fortress of Baba Vida on the bank of the Danube. In the latter area soundings have uncovered fortifications of the second half of the third century, when the evacuation of Dacia must have increased its military importance. The best-preserved part was a polygonal north-east angle tower, a powerful structure enclosing an area 13 metres across, of which walls up to 2 metres high and nearly 3½ metres thick were found. A public bath with its heating system and a drainage network carrying waste into the Danube, dating from about the same period, have also been identified.

PLATE 70 Ratiaria, Hercules, statuette, *ht.* 41 cm.

PLATE 71 Bononia, head, *ht.* 37 cm.

A recent chance find near the fortress was the fine bronze head of a young man, stylistically associated with the reign of Trajan (Pl. 71). Such work is likely to have come from or through Ratiaria.

Castra Martis

A station on the road leading west from Ratiaria to Naissus (Niš) and the Adriatic has been identified some 24 kilometres south-west of Vidin. This is Castra Martis (Kula), where a short sector of wall has been uncovered. In the main square of the little town are substantial remains of a small square fort – its sides 34 metres long – built to protect the north-east angle of Castra Martis. One of the four round angle towers – still, with later repairs, 16 metres high – has given the town its Bulgarian name, 'kula' meaning 'tower'. The three other towers, walls and inner buildings including the garrison commander's quarters, barracks, and a craft workshop have been excavated (Pl. 72), and the structure dated to the late third or early fourth century. Unlike the walls which, so far as one can tell, were of stone only, the towers were of roughly dressed stone,

PLATE 72 Castra Martis, Kula fort

bonded with irregularly spaced layers of three brick courses. The single entrance, flanked by guardrooms, was in the south wall.

Montana

Excavation – halted by the First World War and only resumed in 1968 – is now uncovering the most renowned Roman sanctuary in this corner of Bulgaria, the temple of Diana and Apollo at Montana (Mihailovgrad, formerly Ferdinand). By 161–63, if not before, Montana, situated where the Marcianopolis (Reka Devnya)–Nicopolis-ad-Istrum (near Nikyup)–Melta (Lovech) road bridged the Ogosta on its way to join the Ratiaria–Naissus highway, had achieved the status of Municipium Montanensis. Fortifications, including a great U-shaped angle tower measuring 24 by 18 metres, were, it seems, constructed about the middle of the third century and lasted until the late fifth or early sixth.

The temple of Diana and Apollo, on the evidence of many Latin inscriptions, was already in existence in the second century and occupied the site of an earlier Thracian sanctuary – a great spring at the foot of the rocky hill on which the fortress stood. It is believed to have survived destruction until the fifth century.

The 1915 excavations uncovered a niche hollowed out of the cliff by the spring, intended for a statue of Diana. An altar dedicated to her stood in front of it; nearby was another to Silvanus. Three statuettes of the goddess were found among the ruins as well as broken pieces of others of Silvanus, Apollo, Hygieia, and a Thracian Horseman relief with part of a Greek inscription – a rarity in Montana where Latin was commonly used. Many fragments of altars and votive tablets to Greco-Roman deities, mostly Diana and Apollo, were used as building material in the town. Worship of the huntress goddess seems to have been especially widespread in this region; another sanctuary is known to have existed at Almus (Lom). In view of the Thracian origins of the sanctuary, the find of a Thracian Horseman relief almost certainly reflects syncretism with Apollo, just as Bendis with Diana-Artemis. With such continuity in the ancient world, it is hardly surprising that an altar consecrated to Diana and Apollo was discovered beneath the altar table of a Mihailovgrad church.

Other cult objects from Montana include a find of 11 small clay plaques depicting religious motifs or gods, usually framed in *aediculae*, or pillared niches[2]. The superficial resemblance to the Abritus collection of bronze plaques (pp. 164 ff) is very striking, but the Montana group are much cruder and entirely devoid of oriental influences. Exceptions to the normal pantheon here are Epona standing between two foals – a Celtic influence possibly connected with the Cohors II Gallorum stationed in the province under Trajan – and a Thracian Horseman.

II. OESCUS AND ITS VICINITY

Oescus

Oescus (near Gigen) shared with Novae (near Svishtov) the main burden of defending the central region of the lower Danube. Established in the early years of the first century A.D. as the headquarters of Legio V Macedonica, it replaced an earlier Triballi settlement; Ptolemaeus refers to it as Oescus Triballorum. The site was a low plateau with steep slopes on the north and north-west, some 5 kilometres from the Danube and its confluence with the Iskur, the ancient Oescus. Like Ratiaria, it was an important centre of Romanisation and attracted a considerable civil population. Identified by Count Marsigli in the eighteenth century, Oescus was first excavated in 1905–6, the main purposes being apparently a search for works of art and the location of the forum. A large area was uncovered to little scientific purpose, no results being published and no records left. The ruins were then abandoned until 1941–43, when an Italian team excavated a large building outside the city walls. Excavations by Bulgarian archaeologists in 1947–52 and again more recently have thrown much new light on the antique city and it is encouraging to know that work is being continued.

The oldest stone fortifications probably belonged either to the end of the first century, after the Dacian invasions of 85–86, or to the beginning of the second, before the departure of Legio V Macedonica (of which the future emperor Hadrian was a tribune) in 106 as a result of the conquest of Dacia. Massive walls, some 3 metres thick but, except by the gate, apparently without bastions or towers, enclosed a roughly pentagonal area of about 18 hectares. A ditch about 15 metres wide gave added protection. The city expanded rapidly in spite of the loss of its military importance, but with the legion's return on the evacuation of Dacia in 271–75, Oescus again became a major fortress of the *limes*. The city had suffered severely at the hands of the Goths in the middle of the third century. The original wall was repaired and a new one built to enclose a further 10 hectares on the long east side. Faced on the outer side with well-cut stones, it was strengthened at intervals by horseshoe-shaped towers and, at the sharp north-east angle, by a round projecting one. Flanking towers protected the north and east gates. Temples as well as houses were demolished to make room for the wall, but many large buildings were left outside, as well as the dwellings of those without citizenship. The plan of the fortified area now resembled the end view of a gabled house, the ground floor of which was represented by the third-century addition.

Within the city there was the usual grid of intersecting north–south and east–west streets. Paved with large stone slabs, some showing wheel-ruts, these were from 3½ to 7 metres wide, the main ones being colonnaded. Beneath them ran water-supply and drainage systems, the former in clay and lead pipes. Wells provided a reserve, but the main water-supplies came by aqueducts, one 20 kilometres long. In a shorter aqueduct from a spring near Gigen, well-fired clay pipes were found, with tile-covered openings at intervals for cleaning and unblocking.

South of the probable location of the forum stood one of the city's major buildings, the temple of Fortuna, a complex extending over an area 29 metres wide and some 50 metres long. The temple was entered from the south through a Corinthian-style portico bearing a long dedicatory inscription to the effect that the temple was erected by leading citizens in the reign of Commodus, whose name was chiselled out following his generally welcome assassination. The portico opened into a peristyled courtyard, also in Corinthian style, at the northern end of which stood the sanctuary. Along the sides of the temple, rooms with mosaic-paved floors are thought to have been used for commercial purposes by the guild who built it.[3] Destruction at the end of the fourth century, probably either by the Visigoths or by local Christians, was complete and it is likely that the present desolate scene of heaps of massive broken columns, bases, Ionic and Corinthian capitals, architraves, and battered fragments of pediment has changed little in 1,600 years – except for a space cleared to build a church in the twelfth century. The architraves from the colonnade – with their motifs of bucrania, garlands, masks, animals, dolphins, eagles, snakes, and the wine barrel, like other sculptures in the same area are the work of skilled and talented craftsmen (Pls. 73–75). Matching them is a panel of the coffered ceiling of the portico (Pl. 76).

Sculpture appears to have continued to be a flourishing industry in Oescus until the disastrous Visigothic wars of the late fourth century. Among the more interesting finds in the neighbourhood is a fine sandstone head, found in a nearby village and probably looted from the city (Pl. 77). Stylistically dated to the end of the third century, it is believed to be a portrait of Diocletian. Others, within roundels, may be either architectural fragments or funerary reliefs (Pl. 78).

On the other side of the street, south of the temple of Fortuna, was an even larger structure; 72 metres long, it occupied a whole block or *insula*, and was reconstructed several times. The entrance was again from the south. On the east

PLATE 73 Oescus, Temple of Fortuna, architraves

PLATE 74 Oescus, Temple of Fortuna, architrave detail

PLATE 75 Oescus, Temple of Fortuna, architrave detail

PLATE 76 Oescus, Temple of Fortuna, ceiling detail

PLATE 77 Oescus, head of Diocletian, *ht.* 29 cm.

PLATE 78 Oescus, roundel fragment

side some 15 rooms were uncovered, most with hypocausts using *pillae*, or small brick piers. More heating came from warm air circulating between the walls and their marble revetment. An apsed room, 27 metres long and 12 metres wide, was a ceremonial hall. In a room near the entrance, 7·20 metres long by 6·60 wide, was a mosaic floor of literary as well as archaeological interest. A black and white chequered border frames a tripartite coloured picture, the two outer sections being narrow rectangles. On one side, two fighting cocks are separated by a formal garland and a tree; top and bottom are missing. The other side, showing different fishes in a river, is realistic and asymmetrical. The square middle section inscribes an octagon, with a boar, a lion, a bear, and a (now lost) bull in the corners, representing the seasons. In the octagon are four actors, three wearing comic masks. Part of the scene is lost, but above the heads a Greek inscription reads 'Menander's Achaians' (Pls. 79, 80).

Menander is known to have written over a hundred comedies, but this find, probably dating to the first half of the third century A.D., added another, then

PLATE 79 Oescus, mosaic floor detail

unsuspected. A since discovered papyrus[4] listing some titles of Menander's plays has included 'The Achaians or the Peloponnesians', almost certainly the same play. T. Ivanov, who discovered the mosaic, suggests that the scene depicts the quarrel between Agamemnon and Achilles, with Nestor attempting vainly to mediate and Patroklos, without a mask, standing behind; he relates it to scenes in the House of Aion at Antioch, also linked to comedies by Menander. This Trojan war interpretation has been queried, largely on the grounds that all the surviving comedies are based on contemporary – fourth-century B.C. – themes, not on mythological subjects, although this need not necessarily exclude a parody of Homeric heroes. The only Roman mosaic known in northern Bulgaria, its high, if provincial, quality confirms the impression created by the sculptured fragments of the prosperity and even luxury of Oescus.

To the east of this building were the public baths. Built in the second century by the then east wall, they were reconstructed after the extension of the city and covered an area of 700 square metres. The baths have not been published in detail, but it is known that they followed the common Roman pattern; the

PLATE 80 Oescus, mosaic floor detail

floors and walls were revetted by slabs of white, grey, and pink marble. Across the road to the north was a row of shops.

The 1941–43 excavations uncovered a large complex of unknown purpose occupying some 3,500 square metres outside the walls, immediately south of the original south-east corner (Fig. 16; Pl. 81). On the west side, two apsed rooms, one with three side-chambers, enclosed two rectangular ones. In the centre, a large hall was partitioned into four areas by three pairs of walls which projected from the long sides towards the centre. North of this hall were two other rooms, one apsed, and on the east side is a plain rectangular hall. Whilst the outside walls were solid structures, the foundations of the inner ones were threaded by a system of vaulted corridors, averaging a height of $1\frac{1}{2}$ metres and a width of half a metre, reached by a flight of six steps next to the northern apse. Along most of the internal walls, clay pipes, 15 centimetres in diameter, rose vertically at irregular intervals from the vaults of these corridors to penetrate the middle of the walls.

Such intra-mural corridors are not without parallel in Bulgaria, occurring, for instance, in the baths at Odessos and a building in Serdica (Sofia). Yet in Oescus, although the general plan is not inconsistent with that of a bath, one already existed and the siting of the various entrances makes this unlikely. Also, there were no hypocausts or other evidence of baths, although A. Frova writes that this might possibly be due to later destruction, particularly of the floors. The corridors could not have been parts of a drainage system as, in an already notably damp environment, they would merely have held water. The predominant use of stone, which does not conserve heat as well as brick, would have been unsuited to a heating system. Frova consequently concludes that the corridors were for ventilation.

It must have been an important building. The surviving walls consisted of three courses of brick between a lower section of roughly cut stones and upper layers of ashlar with a rubble filling. Marble revetment slabs of many different colours were imported, perhaps from as far afield as the Greek mainland, the Cyclades, and Egypt. Architectural fragments, including white marble cornices, Corinthian capitals, hexagonal and octagonal floor tiles, emphasised the luxury of this unusual building. On the evidence of coins and of structural comparisons, Frova dates it to the first half of the third century, that is to say before the first Gothic invasions.

Graves, mostly unpublished, were found in all directions round the city, the main cemetery being along the road to Novae (near Svishtov). Inhumation was the most common burial custom and the graves varied from the elaborately carved sarcophagi of the rich to interments straight into the earth. The Triballi in the territory of Oescus continued, like the Thracians elsewhere, to construct tumuli when they were rich enough to do so.

Victories over the Goths by Constantine the Great increased the prosperity of Oescus, but he is especially associated with the city through his bridge across the Danube to connect Oescus with the fortress of Sucidava (Corabia) on the north bank. The importance of this area in trans-Danubian communications as well as defensive strategy is emphasised by the existence of another, unexcavated bridge about 18 kilometres west of Oescus between the fort of Valeriana (Dolni, Vadin) and Orlea on the Romanian bank, built under Domitian. In July 328,

PLATE 81 Oescus, extra-mural complex

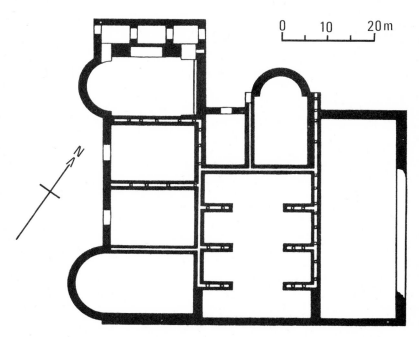

FIG. 16 Oescus, extra-mural complex

Constantine visited Oescus to inaugurate the bridge which, spanning 2,400 metres, was the longest bridge in Antiquity. Its life must have been short; possibly it was burnt down, for in 367 Valens had to cross elsewhere by means of a bridge of boats. But the substructure remained. Marsigli, in his *Description du Danube* of 1744, wrote that in the summer of 1691 the water level fell so low that gigantic piers were visible. He mistakenly referred to them as wooden. F. Kanitz described a similar occurrence in 1871. Early in the last century, a Romanian fisherman hauled up a copper crampon, causing a new legend of a gleaming Constantinian bridge of copper to oust all other local traditions.

Romanian archaeologists have found the ruins of three massive stone piers, sunk in the bed of the Danube.[5] Nearly equidistant from one another, with a longer span to the south bank, they were 33 metres long and 19 metres wide, with tapered ends identical to those of Trajan's bridge near the 'Iron Gates'. It is assumed that the superstructure was wooden, with fortified masonry towers at each end; the northern one has been excavated, but not the southern. These remains are a reminder that in the time of Constantine the concept of *Dacia restituta* was more than a dream, although one never to be realised. Oescus itself was to fade into oblivion, perhaps destroyed by the Visigoths or, at latest, by the Huns.

Inscriptions confirm close links between Ad Putea (Riben), a station on the north–south road near the crossing of the river Vit, the ancient Utus, with Oescus and Legio V Macedonica. Paradoxically, its most important find to date is the marble statuette of a 'peaceful satyr' (Pl. 82), a lazily smiling boy, naked except for a panther skin. Similar to one from Hadrian's villa at Tivoli and another from the Palatine, it is considered, like the Eros from Nicopolis-ad-Istrum (Pl. 98), to be a second-century copy of a statue by Praxiteles.

South-east of Oescus, at Kreta on the river Vit, was the quarry from which came the stone for building the city. Here in an artificial cave was a Mithraeum in which a large relief was found *in situ*. The plaque, 92 centimetres long and 60 centimetres high, depicting the usual scene of Mithras slaying the bull, stood in a niche on a pedestal, among a number of votive altars.

III. NIKOPOL

A little farther east, past the confluence of the Osum, the ancient Asamus, with the Danube and about half-way between Oescus and Novae, stands Nikopol, where soundings have recently established a stratigraphy to the pre-Roman period. So far its chief claim to fame is a Roman funerary inscription, the elegy of Aelia by her husband, one Fronto, imperial *dispensator* in Moesia Inferior, which is addressed to the 'queen of the great realm of Dis'.[6] First he prays for the everlasting peace of his precious love, so that her bones at least may rest in honour, for she deserves much praise, and that Proserpina should bid her dwell in the Elysian fields and bind her hair with myrtle and her temples with blossom. He then eulogises his wife:

> . . . Once the spirit of my home [*Lar*], my hope, my only life; she who wished only as I wished and expressed no desire contrary to mine; with no secrets hidden from me; not lacking in the household arts nor unskilled at the loom;

PLATE 82 Ad Putea, statuette, *ht.* 80 cm.

frugal in domestic management but lavish in marital love; without me taking pleasure neither in food nor in the Bacchic rite; admirable in advice; wise of mind; renowned for her good name . . .

Fronto ends by praying that her monument may be cherished for eternity, by future owners of new and different races, so that in a kindly climate, with the dewy rosebud or the pleasant amaranthus, it shall each year be put in order.

The site of Aelia's burial is unknown; Fronto was probably stationed at Oescus, or perhaps at Novae, in the latter half of the second century. The fine marble slab, a stele or perhaps the front of a sarcophagus, on which her elegy is inscribed is still in excellent condition – the centrepiece of Nikopol's public fountain, built at latest by the end of the seventeenth century when Nikopol was a Turkish fortress. In this way at least part of her husband's prayer has been fulfilled.

IV. NOVAE

Novae (Stuklen, 4 kilometres east of Svishtov) occupies a low, uneven plateau bordered on the north by the Danube and on the east by a little tributary, the Dermen. Like Oescus, earlier the site of a Thracian settlement, from A.D. 46 to A.D. 69 Novae was garrisoned by Legio VIII Augusta. Thereafter it was the headquarters of Legio I Italica for as long as a semblance of Roman military organisation persisted in this vulnerable area. An important road station, Novae also controlled one of the easier Danube crossings. The concentration of two legionary headquarters on this short riparian stretch of about 90 kilometres showed recognition of its strategic importance, apparently better understood by the Romans than by their Turkish successors, for at Novae the Russian army effected an easy crossing into Bulgaria in 1877 to bring the country independence. At the end of the second century, the area was also politically prominent. Septimius Severus owed his throne to the support of the Danubian legions, among which Legio I Italica played an important part.

Although long used as a local quarry, major excavations began here only in 1960, providing a marked contrast with Oescus. Since that date a Bulgarian team has taken the eastern sector and a Polish the western. A fortified area of about 26 hectares has been traced, the approximate extent of the walled town from the end of the third century until the early seventh. The north, west, and south curtain walls have second-century or earlier foundations, but the original east wall was abandoned when the city expanded in this direction. The basically rectangular plan was, as usual, adapted to gain the maximum advantage from the terrain, a bend in the south wall giving, in the third or fourth century, if not before, a slightly pentagonal trace. The north wall, only partially excavated, ran for just over 500 metres along the Danube, here pursuing an almost straight course. The west – and most accessible – side, about 480 metres long and incorporating a monumental gateway, joined the north and south walls at right-angles. The south wall, with a centrally sited gate, ran straight for rather over half its total length of 650 metres, then turned slightly northward. The east wall, about 420 metres long, was roughly arc-shaped.

In spite of several building phases, the line of the western defences remained unchanged throughout Novae's existence. The first wall, of uncertain date,

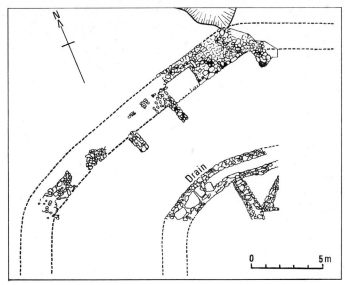

FIG. 17 Novae, north-west angle, first phase

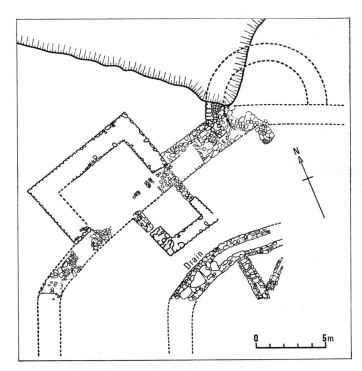

FIG. 18 Novae, north-west angle, third phase

consisted of loose stones piled up and covered with earth. Probably as early as the second half of the first century, this was replaced by a masonry wall, remains of which were found at the north-west corner with, inside, a drain of the same period running roughly parallel. The angle here was rounded off by a flat arc 20 metres long and seemingly strengthened by an internal square tower (Fig. 17). This early wall continued along the Danube, although since little of it has been excavated, its later evolution is unknown. Traces were also found near the west gate. A second stage of the north-west angle occurred when it was destroyed but rebuilt following the same plan. At a third stage, probably during the late third or early fourth century, the wall was reconstructed and strengthened with a rectangular external tower at the middle of the arc. Where the arc joined the north wall there was apparently an external semicircular tower, but its chronological relationship to the other is not clear (Fig. 18). Evidence of several building periods in the inside drain perhaps also indicates enemy penetration. Novae was besieged by the Goths in the mid-third century and was only saved by the appearance of a relief force.

So far the west gate is the most vivid reminder of Novae's former importance (Fig. 19). It stands just north of the point where the present road breaches the city wall, well within the northern half of the walled area. Preliminary work has established the full width of the gateway as 10·60 metres, thus by far the largest known in Moesia Inferior. At the excavated southern end the terminal wall was constructed of large carefully jointed ashlar with a rusticated facing. Below ground level, encased in the foundations of the wall was a vaulted passage, over a metre high and half a metre wide (Pl. 83). This may have been a concealed exit for a surprise night attack on besieging forces, but small enough to defend without difficulty against an attempted entry. The gate is thought to have been constructed in the second century or, at the very latest, the first half of the third, and to have been destroyed and rebuilt during the fourth, to which period are attributed the two external gate towers. As elsewhere, the gate provided evidence of several attacks and repairs.

A well-built horseshoe-shaped angle tower, projecting nearly 10 metres from the south-west corner, can hardly be earlier than the late third or early fourth century. The trapezoidal interior gave the walls a thickness varying from 3·20 to 4·50 metres (Fig. 20). The lower part was faced with large well-cut limestone blocks, the mortared joins strengthened with iron cramps. The obviously later upper levels were of *opus mixtum* (stone strengthened at intervals with bonding courses of brick), and the masonry was faced with smaller, more roughly cut stones and unusually poor mortar (Pl. 152).

At least nine towers have been identified in the east sector; five, all external, in the excavated part of the east wall south of the present road were either square or rectangular. Going from north to south, tower 1 was built above two earlier constructions, the first late Hellenistic or early Roman, the second incorporating a stone pavement which extended beyond the interior floor and foundations of the wall. In the tower, mid-fourth-century coins, none later than Valentinian I, suggest it may have been built in the reign of Constantine the Great and then destroyed by the Visigoths. Thereupon its military significance ceased; a later dividing wall probably converted it into a dwelling.

The fourth and largest tower on this wall defended the south-east angle

(Fig. 21). It projected about 8 metres and had an exterior width of about 11 metres. Two distinct building periods have been identified, both within the fourth century (Pl. 84).

Those between the angle tower and the south gate were more varied. Beyond a smaller, square version of the first four was a rectangular tower, no. VI (Fig. 22), which, standing in a slight re-entrant, projected inside as well as, to a greater extent, outside. Another, referred to as no. VIII, was a U-shaped structure linking two unaligned sections of the curtain wall (Fig. 23). Rather surprisingly, it seems relatively weak, with walls only 1 metre thick at the peak of the curve and just over $1\frac{1}{2}$ metres at the sides. This compares with the curtain wall's thickness of 2·80 metres. The tower bore marks of considerable damage and was rebuilt several times. An adjacent U-shaped external tower had walls about 2·60 metres thick at the sides and nearly 3 metres at the middle.

The curtain wall and towers on the east side of the town appear to have been built after the Gothic wars of the third quarter of the third century and before those of the Visigoths in 376–82. With many repairs and reconstructions, some of which were put into effect before the end of the fourth century, it seems likely to have remained more or less the east line of defence until the beginning of the seventh century. But its relationship to the original east wall has still to be resolved.

Within the walls excavations are bringing to light parts of large buildings, houses and streets, one of which clearly displays two levels, with porticoes, shops and workshops, and many minor finds. Co-ordinated soundings were made by the two teams in 1971 to locate the forum.

V. IATRUS

Iatrus or Iatrum (Krivina) lies on the right bank of the Yantra – in Antiquity the Iatrus, from a Thracian word believed to mean a swift, turbulent river – close to its entry into the Danube, about 16 kilometres east of Novae. Unlike cities such as Ratiaria and Oescus, Roman Iatrus was a fort without significant administrative functions or civilian population on the highway between Novae and Durostorum (Silistra). K. Škorpil traced the walls in the early 1900s and found a Latin inscription of the first half of the second century. Joint excavation by Bulgarian and East German archaeologists, begun in 1958, shows that it was a *castellum*, a small fortified centre, of strategic importance in the fourth century, when the fortifications uncovered were constructed. A re-used altar dated to the second or third century and dedicated to the 'invincible god' Mithras by one Marcus Ulpius Modianus of Legio I Italica links it with Novae. Unfortunately, the Yantra, which once guarded the western walls, has since eroded them, together with an unknown proportion of the castellum, through which it now flows. Flood waters of the Danube have similarly destroyed the north-western part, leaving an irregular lozenge-shaped plateau, 300 metres long with a maximum width of 100 metres (Fig. 24).

The curtain wall was a massive structure about $3\frac{1}{2}$ metres thick, faced on the outside with large rusticated ashlar blocks, the interior dimensions diminishing slightly to avoid mortar being visible on the outside. The western end emerges now from the edge of the cliff which drops down to the Yantra's present course and first runs without towers at a right-angle to the river, a steep slope to the south denying easy access. After a slight bend, a long straight stretch follows, with external horseshoe-shaped angle towers at each end (nos. 1 and 7). A large rectangular tower in the middle (no. 4) had two U-shaped ones on either side of it. From tower 7 the wall turned at a near right-angle to make a deep re-entrant which incorporated the gateway and was reinforced by U-towers. It terminated in the horseshoe-shaped angle tower 11. The wall then turned sharply to the west, now to disappear into the sector eroded by the Danube.

The walls of the U-shaped and angle towers were 3 metres thick and projected about 9 metres from the curtain wall. The rectangular tower, no. 4, was even more substantial; 30½ metres long and 15 metres deep, it projected 9½ metres beyond the wall and nearly 2½ metres inside it. Within the tower, four great rectangular stone piers, 1·77 by 1·19 metres, standing on 2-metre deep foundations, were aligned along the axis, evidently to support an upper storey capable of carrying artillery such as *ballistae* and supplies of stone balls. The tower must have given powerful protection to the relatively easy south-eastern approach to the fort. Similar rectangular structures appear in castella in the Dobroudja, notably at Capidava and, without piers, at Tropaeum Trajani.

Little is left today of the only surviving gate. Facing south-east, between but not architecturally linked with towers 8 and 9, it was double and recessed so that its exterior face lay flush with the wall (Fig. 25). The outer gate, 4 metres across, a portcullis, operated between grooves running down the jambs. A space, the *propugnaculum*, 5½ metres square, separated it from the inner door, which consisted of two pivoted wings. Inside, two gravel-laid streets, both *decumani*, east–west streets, have been uncovered; one of these was colonnaded (Pl. 85).

One excavated building extended parallel with the wall from its present western end for a distance of 62½ metres, including the first angle tower. It replaced earlier Roman constructions about which little could be ascertained (Fig. 26). The outer wall was formed by the curtain wall. The inner, 12 metres away and, like the two short ends, 1¼ metres thick, was of opus mixtum, with remains of only one layer of bricks just discernible. Following the pattern of the rectangular tower, nine piers and pilasters at each end lined its axis. The piers, the majority 1·50–1·60 by 1·80–1·90 metres, were built of finely jointed ashlar, joined by iron cramps and decorated with simple shapes in relief (Pls. 86, 87). Traces of vaulting confirm that they supported an upper storey. This building, later than the curtain wall, must have had some complementary military purpose, such as a storehouse; apart from backing on to the wall, tower 1 could only be entered from it. Like tower 4, artillery could be carried on the upper storey. The careful workmanship of the piers – the facing of the walls has been completely lost – and traces of a tiled floor have close parallels in the walls and towers of Tropaeum Trajani.

Foundations and parts of walls of one other building of the same period, a large rectangular structure 39 metres long and 14 metres wide, were excavated just north of the building described above. Its walls, 1·20 metres thick, were of opus mixtum, using bands of four courses of bricks. A stylobate to carry piers or columns down the centre indicates an upper storey. Below the building were earlier constructions, including walls of stone and mud and, still lower, a male inhumation burial without grave goods.

In a nearby sector, soundings revealed rather confused evidence of two early building periods. Both were Roman and here, too, were the remains of two stone and mud walls. The first was like the earliest constructions found at Serdica and Abritus, as well as those below the rectangular building, and may date to the first century A.D. At the second level were floors of stone with white mortar. T. Ivanov suggests that the earlier was destroyed during the mid-third-century Gothic invasion; and that the second existed between the end of the third or the beginning of the fourth – it may have been contemporary with the walls – and the late fourth century, when the site was prepared for a Christian basilica (p. 245).

Coin finds, analogies with other Balkan sites, and structural features suggest the walls were built during the period of refortification of the Danube *limes* by Licinius, Galerius, and Constantine the Great. The long building attached to the wall at the western end was added during the second half of the fourth century or, at latest, the beginning of the fifth. The other rectangular building also belonged to the second half of the fourth century, probably prior to the Visigothic invasions of 376–82.

VI. TRANSMARISCA

West of Durostorum, the castellum of Transmarisca (Toutrakan) occupied the strategic site of an earlier Thracian settlement opposite the confluence of the Danube and the (Romanian) river Argeş – the Mariscus of Antiquity. Existing from the second century, the earliest parts of the stone fortifications now being excavated are thought more likely to belong to the late third century, when the fort was garrisoned by detachments of Legio XI Claudia. This connection with Durostorum, which was to continue to be the legion's headquarters until the sixth century, is confirmed by the find of stamped bricks.

A late third-century inscription honouring Diocletian for his victories over the barbarians, his restoration of peace to the land, and his erection of the *praesidium*, or fortress, of Transmarisca may mean that the original fortifications had been destroyed by the Goths and that those now being uncovered are the work of Diocletian. Almost identical inscriptions have been found at Sexaginta Prista (Rousse) and Durostorum.

The importance attained by Transmarisca in the fourth century is shown by Valens' choice of it as a base from which to build a pontoon bridge across the Danube to pursue his campaign against the Visigoths.

VII. DUROSTORUM

Durostorum (Silistra) replaced a Getic *oppidum*, a fortified hilltop settlement, probably conquered by the Romans early in the first century A.D. To the north, a wide marshy sector of the Danube, extending almost to the delta, protected the Dobroudja. Troesmis (in modern Romania) defended its northern end, Durostorum its southern, and, of greater importance from the point of view of

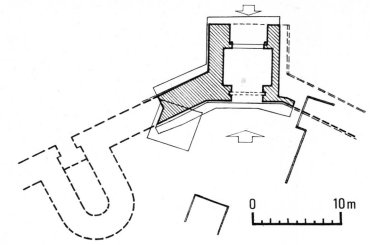

FIG. 25 Iatrus, gate

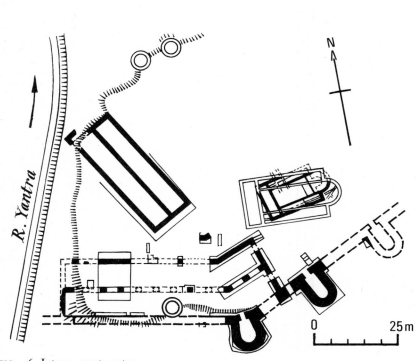

FIG. 26 Iatrus, west sector

PLATE 85 Iatrus, street excavation   PLATE 86 Iatrus, pier detail

PLATE 87 Iatrus, pier

PLATE 88 Durostorum, helmet-mask,
ht. 25·3 cm.

PLATE 89 Silistra district, Athena, head,
ht. 33 cm.

PLATE 90 Silistra district, Mithraic
relief

imperial defence, the approach to Marcianopolis, Odessos, and easy passes of
the Stara Planina to the south.

Following the First Dacian war of 101–2, during which Decebalus had crossed
the Danube near Durostorum to invade Moesia Inferior, the city became the
headquarters of Legio XI Claudia and remained so until the legions were replaced
by *foederati*. At the same time, Legio V Macedonica was temporarily transferred
to Troesmis. Hadrian visited Durostorum in 123–24 and a flourishing settlement
soon grew up – the *canabae Aeliae* – round the legionary headquarters, to
become a major centre for the Romanisation of this part of Moesia Inferior. The
settlers were mainly veterans of Italic and Western origin – some from Ratiaria
and Oescus but many from Spain, Gaul, Germany, and Britain. Cohors II
Flavia Britonum was stationed temporarily here. By the third quarter of the
second century, Durostorum had become a *municipium*, a city granted considerable civic autonomy, and, with the departure of Legio V Macedonica to Dacia,
Durostorum was left the sole legionary headquarters on the Danube east of
Novae.

Many Getai still lived outside the town – and occupied lowly positions within it. Some degree of integration is shown by the funerary monument of a legionary, he and his wife apparently of Italic origin but their sons all bearing Getic names, including Decebalus. Some of the hinterland had been settled by members of the warlike Bessi tribe, transported from the Rhodopes and here given favoured status. Besides normal legionary cults, notably Mithraism, an altar was erected by a group of soldiers to the 'Heros Suregetes', a probable reference to the Thracian Hero – of whom there is more evidence in the country-side – the epithet being similar to one used at Bessapara (near Pazardjik).

The area suffered severely from a combined invasion of the Karps, Goths, and Sarmatians in 238. A votive tablet from an inhabitant of Durostorum thanks the gods for preserving him from captivity, a fate clearly met by many others. An official inscription thanked Aurelian for his work of reconstruction. Nevertheless, for the next hundred years the Danube defences in the neighbourhood remained vulnerable to the northern tribes lured by the wealth of the coastal cities, notwithstanding an attempt at pacification and political-religious penetration by means of Christian missionary activity in the middle decades of the fourth century.

Durostorum must have played a part in Valens' campaign against the Goths – he was there in the autumn of 367 – but after his defeat and death, although the fortified town survived, disaster overcame the countryside.

The existence of the modern frontier city of Silistra and erosion by the Danube have until recently prevented much excavation of the site, the earliest fortifica-tions so far discovered being some Early Byzantine foundations of the fortress wall. There are some chance finds, such as a bronze helmet-mask[7] (Pl. 88) attributed to the first or second century, a probably third-century marble head broken from a statue of Athena (Pl. 89), a Mithraic relief in lively local style (Pl. 90). But although the main archaeological remains of Roman Durostorum are hidden, its name is famous in Christian hagiography for the martyrs, chiefly of Legio XI Claudia, who suffered for their faith under Diocletian and Galerius.

The story of the best-known soldier martyr here, St Dasius, is linked with the troops' custom of celebrating the Roman feast of the Saturnalia. Lots were drawn, the winner designated 'king' and allowed a month's 'reign' of unbridled licence, then put to death as a sacrifice to Cronus. In 304, the lot fell to Dasius, a Christian legionary. Knowing he could not escape death, Dasius rejected his Saturnalian role, was thrown into prison, and killed.[8] After the general adoption of Christianity, a cult of St Dasius developed, centred on the shrine containing his relics. Later, perhaps in the second half of the sixth century, the barbarian danger grew so great that the relics were transferred for safety to the cathedral of Ancona. Here they lay in a sarcophagus inscribed in Byzantine Greek with his name and the city of his martyrdom, to be rediscovered in 1908.

A second legionary martyr was Julius, whose story is touching both for the stubbornness with which a veteran of seven campaigns and 27 years' unblem-ished service refused to sacrifice to the pagan gods and for the well-meaning attempts of the prefect to devise a face-saving formula to satisfy Julius' conscience and yet comply with the letter of the law.

If you think it a sin, [the prefect said], let me take the blame. I am the one who is forcing you, so that you may not give the impression of having

PLATE 91 Durostorum, tomb painting detail

consented voluntarily. Afterwards, you can go home in peace, you will pick up your ten-year bonus and no one will ever trouble you again.[9]

All his persuasions were of no avail. Julius insisted on being beheaded.

Nevertheless, a painted pagan tomb is the most important surviving monument of the fourth century in Durostorum. The almost completely preserved painted decoration covers both walls and ceiling of an ordinary Roman masonry tomb chamber, aligned east–west and measuring 3·30 by 2·60 metres, with a shallow brick-built vault rising to a height of 2·30 metres in the centre. The entrance is in the middle of the east wall.

Round the walls, a series of rectangular panels a little over 1 metre high and 1 metre wide and enclosed by tile-red borders contain lively portraits of a man, his wife, and their household. Within the light background of the panels, a second rectangle, outlined in dark green, sets off each figure. The master and his wife occupy a joint, wider panel, facing the entrance (Pl. 91). They stand with heads turned towards each other, but whilst she gazes at her husband, he looks into the distance, obviously preoccupied. He carries a scroll; she rests one hand on his shoulder and holds a rose in the other. The heads are unnaturally large, possibly a conventional indication of their rank or status. He wears a long tunic with full-length sleeves and decorated cuffs under a loose mantle fastened by a fibula at the shoulder. A white kerchief hides almost all the wife's brown hair. She, too, wears a long tunic, over which is a white dalmatic splashed with grey and an embroidered ochre and red *clavus* or vertical stripe.

Maidservants are advancing in the panels on either side; one carries a jug and a long-handled dish, the other a drape; next, on the side-walls, are two more, one holding up a mirror and another bearing three jars in a special holder, perhaps for her mistress's toilet (Pl. 92). The last wears a bead or pearl circlet in her hair, rings in her ears, and two bangles on each wrist – and the smug expression of a favourite. Next, a youth carries over his shoulder a pair of tights, complete with belt, one hand holding a pair of shoes by their laces (Pl. 93). Like the other menservants, his dress is a short, long-sleeved, belted tunic, reaching to just over the knee. Behind him a boy is carrying and adjusting the folds of a mantle; his hair down to his shoulders probably indicates a Gothic slave. On the opposite wall are two more youths, both wearing torques, one holding a napkin and the other carrying a heavy ornamental belt. On either side of the door, narrower panels each enclose an ornate candelabrum, the candles alight and wax spilling down their sides. Above, a painted band gives a rather crude impression of beams projecting from a building into a courtyard, the central court of a modest Roman villa.

In the west lunette, above the beams, two peacocks drink from a vase, against a floral background. This symbol of immortality is so common in early Christian iconography that the tomb was at first considered Christian, an idea supported by the orientation as well as, no doubt, by the hagiographical reputation of Durostorum. In the east lunette, the scene is repeated with smaller birds, perhaps doves. The vault is covered by a network of tiny panels enclosing rural motifs – flowers, fruit, palm trees, birds, animals, and hunters – no two the same.

The paintings in the tomb, probably built in the second half of the fourth century and apparently never used, are unusually interesting, although naturally provincial in style. Clearly commissioned by the two prospective occupants, it presents a delightful picture of the bourgeois Roman citizen at home in this

PLATE 92 Durostorum, tomb painting detail

PLATE 93 Durostorum, tomb painting detail

corner of the empire. By comparison with those in the Kazanluk tomb of some six hundred years earlier (Pls. 63–5), the paintings lack any note of mourning. Superficially the scene is similar, but here death is shown as a perpetuation of the pleasanter aspects of life. Only the lunettes carry reminders of immortality, but it is an afterlife in which ordinary people continue in their appropriate earthly station. The roughly contemporary saints' heads from the fourth-century church at Tsar Krum (Pls. 163, 164) present as great a contrast in their spirituality as do the dignity and solemnity of the Thracians of Kazanluk.

However, Christianity developed strongly in fourth-century Durostorum, reinforced by the teaching of the Arian Gothic translator of the Bible, Ulfilas, one of whose pupils, Auxentius, a leading protagonist of Arianism, became bishop of the city in 380. Meanwhile the martyrdom had happened in 362 of another famous local saint, Aemilianus, during Julian's brief persecution. Julian's representative, Capitolinus, was appointed to enforce the revival of the old cults. During a huge banquet to celebrate his achievements, Aemilianus entered an unattended pagan temple, smashed the idols with a hammer, upset altars and candlesticks, spilt the libatory wine, and departed unseen. The furious Capitolinus ordered an inquiry, punishment of the temple guards, and the immediate apprehension of the culprit. No time was lost in arresting an innocent peasant passing by and dragging him to the praetorium to be executed. This demonstration of zeal was upset by Aemilianus' confession of responsibility. His bold replies to Capitolinus' questions enraged the envoy, who ordered him to be thrown to the ground and beaten. When Aemilianus admitted he was the son of a prefect, Capitolinus imposed a heavy fine on the father who had brought his son up so badly, and sentenced the latter to be burnt alive. But the flames, respecting his body, devoured the soldiers instead. Aemilianus then made the sign of the cross, commended his soul to God, and expired in peace. The story achieved much fame in succeeding centuries and, as can be seen, did not lose in the telling as it became part of the Christian tradition of Moesia.[10]

NOTES

1 Gerov, B., *Romanizmut* III, no. 186.
2 Velkov, I., *IBAI* XIV, 1940–42, 183 ff.
3 NAC, *Arh* XIII/4, 1971, 78.
4 *Pap. Ox.* XXVII 2462, discussed in Charitonidis, S., Kahil, L., and Ginouvès, R., *Les mosaïques de la maison de Ménandre à Mytilène*, Berne, 1970, 98–9.
5 Tudor, D., *Sucidava; une cité daco-romaine et byzantine en Dacie*, Brussels, 1965, 74 ff.
6 *CIL* III Supp. 7436.
7 Venedikov, I., *Eirene* I, 1950, 143 ff.
8 *Analecta Bollandiana* XVI, 1897, 5 ff.; Zeiller, J., *Les origines chrétiennes dans les provinces danubiennes de l'empire romaine*, Paris, 1918, 110 ff.
9 Musurillo, H., *The Acts of the Christian Martyrs*, Oxford, 1972, 263.
10 *Analecta Bollandiana* XXXI, 1912, 260 ff.

6 The Northern Foothills (I)

Nicopolis-ad-Istrum

Nicopolis-ad-Istrum, 18 kilometres north of Veliko (Great) Turnovo, was identified in the last century by F. Kanitz who, studying Roman ruins still known locally as 'Stari' or 'Old' Nikyup near the present village of Nikyup, found the base of a statue erected in 203 by the council and assembly of Nicopolis-ad-Istrum to Julia Domna, wife of Septimius Severus. The resulting official treasure hunt produced many finds, but the site, like Oescus, was left in disorder and unrecorded. Recent research and limited excavation have established some major features, but these can only be regarded as a beginning of an enormous but rewarding task.

Nicopolis-ad-Istrum – Trajan's 'city of victory on the Danube', founded in 102 in celebration of the Danubian battle which brought the First Dacian war to a victorious conclusion – was probably the emperor's first foundation in Thracia, then extending some way north of the Stara Planina. The main purpose was restoration of the economy of a fertile area devastated by the Dacian invasions of 85–86 and 101–2.

The chosen site was an important crossroads. Three roads led north to the Danube, two apparently to Novae, the other to Sexaginta Prista; two ran south over the Stara Planina, one over the Shipka pass to Philippopolis and the other more easterly to Augusta Trajana–Beroe. The city also stood on the road roughly parallel with the Danube which linked Marcianopolis and Odessos with the west, joining the Oescus–Philippopolis road at Melta and, farther west, the highway connecting Ratiaria with Lissus on the Adriatic. Only the city's vulnerability under the impact of later invasions caused the inhabitants to move a short distance south to Turnovo, a stronghold which later developed into the capital of the second Bulgarian kingdom and is one of Bulgaria's leading cities today.

Nicopolis, as its name implies, was neither a 'colonia' nor a 'municipium', but founded as a Hellenistic city. Romanisation was a costly business and generally considered unnecessary in Hellenised lands except for overriding reasons of military necessity. The Danube *limes* was one such exception and behind it the main objective was to achieve stability as economically as possible, with a sufficient prosperity to subsidise the empire and its armies. So, with Roman encouragement, once more a wave of Greek – or Hellenised – immigrants arrived from Asia Minor and also from Syria, and found opportunities for their skills and commercial acumen that would have been the envy of the founders of the Black Sea colonies. With all the advantages of its situation, Nicopolis prospered rapidly during the second century, stimulating industries such as the ceramic factories at Hotnitsa and Butovo and *emporia*, or official rural marketing centres, such as at Butovo and Discoduratera (Gostilitsa). Many of the wealthier citizens were landowners and had country villas. Inscriptions show that often the proprietors were Roman or Romanised – Novae was only some 50 kilometres

PLATE 94 Nicopolis-ad-Istrum, aerial view

away – and although the city's official language was Greek, the educated citizens were almost certainly bilingual.

The city was on a low plateau, sloping steeply on three sides either to a gully or to the river Rositsa. With the north-east corner cut off to conform with the terrain, the area enclosed was pentagonal rather than rectangular, 450 metres long on the west side and 505 metres long on the south, on which side the curtain wall partly coincided with the north wall of a smaller, irregularly shaped fort, the towers of which projected into the city proper. At first glance this suggests an earlier castellum, but an aerial photograph (Pl. 94) reveals a much more complicated situation.[1] The 'fort', besides rounded angle towers, apparently had others – U-shaped or semi-circular, rectangular, possibly triangular, and even pentagonal, thus suggesting various dates from the end of the third or fourth century into the Byzantine period.

The city's curtain walls also lack homogeneity. Except at the angles, no towers or bastions are discernible on the south side. Along the west wall it is possible to make out one U-shaped tower and another in the form of a horseshoe; there may be others. In the western half of the north wall, two semicircular towers are visible; at the join with the eastern half, an external rounded angle tower is less clear. The east wall is again different; it is strengthened by two circular half or three-quarter projecting towers; the northern angle tower seems to be external and rounded, but the site of a southern one is occupied by the angle tower of the 'fort'. Pending excavations, none of the main fortifications of Nicopolis can be regarded as earlier than the second century, whilst those of the southern 'fort' may perhaps date to the end of the fourth or the fifth century.

The city had two gateways, one on the north, the other on the west. Starting from the former, the *cardo maximus*, or main north–south street, continued past the east side of the forum to the annexed 'fort'. The *decumanus maximus*, running from the west gate along a line slightly south of the east–west axis, led into a large central area comprising several public buildings and the forum (Fig. 27). The streets, paved with large stone slabs, irregularly laid, probably to minimise earthquake damage, covered the drainage system (Pl. 95).

The space enclosed by the inner portico of the forum was 42 metres square, paved with huge, well-cut stone slabs. The colonnaded portico stood three steps higher; its Ionic bases, monolithic columns, capitals, and architraves were carved from limestone from the nearby Hotnitsa quarries. Rows of shops on the east and south porticoes probably had frontages to streets five or six steps below. The north side is unclear. Finds included two parallel rows of large square bases, with a row of smaller ones between.

The main entrance to the forum was on the west, where the decumanus maximus stopped at a *propylaeum*, or monumental entrance, of four great Corinthian columns, 8 metres high, a coffered ceiling and a richly decorated architrave (Pl. 96). The Greek inscription on the last shows it was erected by the city in 145 in honour of Antoninus Pius, Marcus Aurelius, and his wife, Faustina the Younger.[2] The propylaeum led to a narrow peristyled courtyard, from which, between two rooms, access was obtained to the forum's western portico.

North of this courtyard was the *bouleuterion*, or council chamber, with a frontage of $15\frac{1}{4}$ metres on the forum portico. Its walls were lined with stone seats and many fragments of inscriptions recording civic decrees and pedestals of statues were found among the ruins.

On the south side of the courtyard the *odeon*, a rectangular, roofed theatre, had a 26-metre frontage on the forum. The *scena* occupied the south side; in front, tiers of seats rose round a semicircular *orchestra*, the lower benches being stone and the upper, probably, of wood, in all sufficient to accommodate some three or four hundred spectators. The front seats were high, giving protection to spectators of gladiatorial combats and displays involving wild beasts. Rooms under the upper tiers were probably shops, those on the western side profiting from facing on to the forum portico.

The plan and architectural style of the forum and the conventionalised representations of public buildings and city gates on coins reflect the dominant influence of Hellenistic Asia Minor. This is supported by the many Greek inscriptions, altars to oriental gods, and architectural fragments littering the central area. In some cases these bear such 'signatures' of the master masons as a lizard (Pl. 97) or a dog. There must have been masons' guilds, just as inscriptions show that there were guilds of woodcarvers, leather-workers, and fullers, again on an Eastern pattern. Nicaea, Nicomedia, and Antioch in Syria are the only towns mentioned as origins of the settlers, but the many Greek names and gods displayed on coins and mentioned in votive inscriptions, such as Priapus, said to have been brought from Bithynia, Sabazius, the associated cult of Magna Mater, Serapis, Mithras, and others, as well as those of the Greco-Roman pantheon, are additional evidence of oriental immigration. The city may also owe to this influx a fine white marble statue of Eros (Pl. 98), believed to be

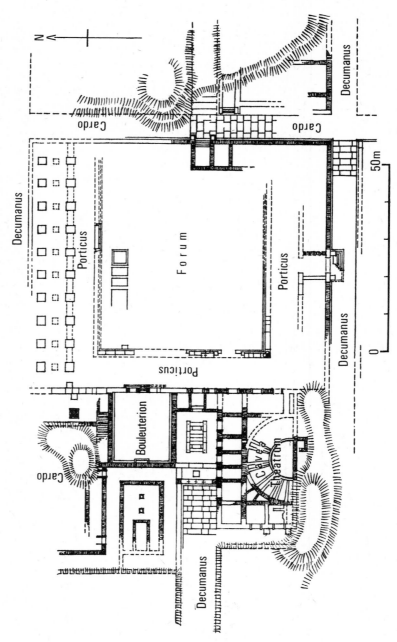

FIG. 27 Nicopolis-ad-Istrum, reconstruction of city centre

PLATE 95 Nicopolis-ad-Istrum, decumanus maximus

PLATE 96 Nicopolis-ad-Istrum, building inscription, detail

PLATE 97 Nicopolis-ad-Istrum, architectural detail

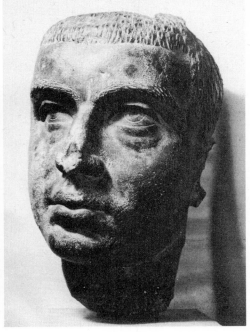

PLATE 98 Nicopolis-ad-Istrum, Eros, headless statue, *ht.* 1·40 cm.

PLATE 99 Nicopolis-ad-Istrum district, head of Gordian III, *ht.* 38 cm.

a mid-second-century copy of that carved by Praxiteles for the city of Parion and now known only from its coins.

Huge quantities of coins were issued during the period of prosperity. Subjects represented naturally included Nike, and also Haimos, the personification of the Stara Planina, shown as a young hunter, half-reclining on a rock but holding a spear; in front of the rock is a bear, sometimes attacking a stag by the tree behind it. According to the coins, temples were dedicated to deities including Zeus, Apollo, Artemis, Concordia, and Fortuna.

Early in his reign Septimius Severus transferred Nicopolis and its surrounding territory from Thracia to Moesia, which greatly increased the city's economic opportunities. His subsequent visit in 202 enabled the citizens to demonstrate their gratitude; the celebrations included a gift to the emperor of 700,000 *denarii* and the many finds of inscriptions and bases of statues of him and his family testify to his popularity. The first third of the third century saw the peak period of Nicopolis' prosperity. The earliest serious breach of the Danubian defences of Moesia Inferior occurred during the reign of Gordian III. Aptly, in the circumstances, the bronze head of a statue of this emperor (Pl. 99) was found in the bed of the river Yantra some 10 kilometres to the north, possibly where it had been dumped by a retreating looter.

In 250, the Goths, having failed to take Novae, invested Nicopolis, but suffered a severe defeat. The event establishes the existence by this period of the city walls. Further confirmation comes in Nicopolis' survival during the Gothic rampages of the next 20 years, culminating in another unsuccessful siege in 270. Aurelian's withdrawal from Dacia added the loss of a valuable market to the economic distress caused by the Gothic devastation. It also brought the barbarian threat closer. Minting ceased abruptly about 250 and buildings begun in happier times remained unfinished. The great pediment (Pl. 100) appears never to have been erected.

The peace along the *limes* imposed by Galerius and Constantine was a welcome respite; it could not revive the prosperity of the past, but a certain degree of recovery about this time is indicated by the erection of a brick and stone building occupying a large area, beginning 16 metres inside the north wall near the cardo maximus (Pl. 101). The plan, the evidence of hypocausts, and the debris of toilet articles, lamps, and glass vessels which littered one of the rooms suggest a public bath.

About 346, Bishop Ulfilas and his Visigothic Christian followers were given sanctuary and settled peacefully in the neighbourhood of Nicopolis. The Visigothic invaders of 376–82 were another matter. According to Ammianus Marcellinus, the fortified cities held out, but the countryside was devastated and depopulated. For a city so dependent on commerce, the effect on its economy must have been disastrous, even if the majority of its inhabitants survived to come to terms with the new, largely Gothic rural population.

Hotnitsa

Excavations at Hotnitsa, some 10 kilometres south of Nicopolis, show that besides being the main quarry for the city, it was an important centre for the manufacture of pottery and was probably an emporium. By 1969, 17 kilns were located, and finds of bronze statuettes and other objects reflect its share in the second- and early third-century prosperity.

Butovo

Even more important for ceramic production was present-day Butovo. Situated on the original border between Thracia and Moesia and on or near the Nicopolis–Novae and Nicopolis–Melta highways, Butovo was also the site of an important emporium, probably to be identified with Emporium Piretensium. Founded in the second century as a fortified trading post, the remains of defence walls, foundations of large buildings, and existence of re-used architectural fragments are evidence of a prosperous evolution. Successful trading and the excellence of the local clay led to the creation of production industries. Both stonemasons' and potters' quarters have been excavated. This development seems either to have been instigated by or to have attracted immigrant potters from Asia Minor, who, working alongside Thracian craftsmen, were able to turn out pottery with decorative motifs produced nowhere else in Bulgaria, although some influence appears in the Hotnitsa work. By the end of the second century imports were almost entirely superseded and Butovo factories were supplying both Novae and Nicopolis.

There were four main decorative techniques: barbotine, stamped impressions, incised drawing, and the application of clay relief figurines to a soft clay surface.

PLATE 100 Nicopolis-ad-Istrum, pediment

PLATE 101 Nicopolis-ad-Istrum, public building

PLATE 102 Butovo pottery, platter handle

Numerous moulds were found, and bowls, plates, and lamps, their surfaces crammed with naturalistic plant and animal ornament interspersed with geometric and various stylised designs (Pl. 102). Children's toys – miniature clay horses, goats, cocks – and figurines were found in the debris, as well as votive tablets, including one of Orpheus surrounded by the wild beasts.

Butovo's fate after the middle of the third century is unknown. Perhaps damaged or evacuated in the first Gothic invasions, some commercial advantages may also have been lost as a result of Aurelian's and Diocletian's administrative changes. Few of the finds yet brought to light are likely to be post-third century.

Discoduratera

Discoduratera (Gostilitsa) lies on the upper reaches of the Yantra, 32 kilometres south-west of Nicopolis-ad-Istrum and about 16 kilometres north of modern Gabrovo. It was founded, probably about the middle of the second century, as an emporium of the territory of Augusta Trajana and stood at the junction of the highway from this city over the Shipka pass to Novae and a road from Nicopolis and Hotnitsa. Less exposed than Butovo, Discoduratera escaped the first Gothic invasions, although it was probably badly damaged in the last quarter of the fourth century. The surviving fortifications belong to the end-fourth to sixth centuries.

There is no evidence of auxiliary industries, as at Butovo, but the emporium was a convenient overnight halt before or after crossing the Stara Planina. An inscription proves its existence in the reign of Marcus Aurelius, although it may have been settled earlier. Except for a few coins from local mints, the

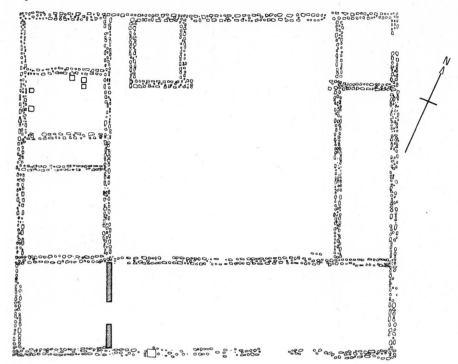

FIG. 28 Prisovo, villa rustica

earliest found were silver of the first half of the third century; they were the only silver ones – from the mid-third century onwards all were copper. Bronze or copper coins of Nicopolis, Marcianopolis, and Pautalia (Kyustendil) occurred at the mid-third-century building level, all minted under Septimius Severus and Caracalla but evidently brought again into circulation by a currency crisis due to Gothic disruption of the local economy.

Above, more coins were found, dating to the reign of Aurelian, and his successors continued to be relatively well represented until the reign of Jovian. With renewed Gothic invasions came another gap – until Theodosius I – from which only a few coins of the Western emperors Gratian and Valentinian II have been found. Thus the pattern of coin finds reflects the effect of the invasions on the local economy; doubtless greater care was taken in hard times.

Although Nicopolis and its territory were transferred to Moesia about the end of the second century, an inscription shows that Discoduratera remained under Augusta Trajana, probably until the reign of Aurelian when it, too, came under the administration of Nicopolis.

Inscriptions and coins have yielded most information about Discoduratera, but a building of the third or fourth century excavated in the north-east part of the walled settlement has also produced items of interest. It consisted of an

L-shaped group of rooms enclosing in its angle a peristyled courtyard and with two small rooms projecting on the south-west side (Fig. 61). The monolithic columns were 2·15 metres high, carved from limestone, like their bases and Ionic capitals. This building did not outlast the fourth century. Soundings showed that earlier Roman structures lay below; and re-used materials in Early Byzantine constructions included dressed stone and even parts of bronze statues. Among second- and third-century debris near the gateway were votive plaques to Zeus and Artemis and bronze statuettes of Dionysos and Herakles, as well as fragments of good-quality pottery.

Prisovo

A modest *villa rustica*, here a farmhouse not a manor, at Prisovo, near Turnovo, gives some idea of the life of a working farmer as distinct from that of a wealthy landowner. On a hill near a small tributary of the Yantra, the site remained unknown beneath trees and scrub until mechanical ploughing made it agriculturally viable. Following the discovery of archaeological material, thanks to a watchful local schoolmaster, a rescue dig took place in 1961.

Stone foundations were found of a rectangular building, $22\frac{1}{2}$ by 24 metres (Fig. 28). It had been a single-storeyed wooden structure, fastened with iron nails and then plastered with clay that, baked in the fire in which the villa perished, retained the imprint of the beams. The roof was tiled. In the south-west corner, finds of Thracian ceramic and a coin of Alexander confirmed other evidence of an earlier Thracian settlement.

Rooms of various sizes were grouped round a central courtyard; in several cases, objects found *in situ* indicated their purpose. On the south, the largest room, divided by a stone wall from the courtyard, served as a kind of barn; it contained iron agricultural implements and harness ornaments, such as two bronze bells. There was a doorway in the south wall and another, $1\frac{1}{2}$ metres wide, in a wood and mud-brick wall at its western end. An iron-bound wooden door led from the corner room to the next along the west side; both these had traces of plaster decoration in red, black, and white, the only rooms so ornamented. The many finds, chiefly of pots, suggested that the neighbouring small, narrow room was a storeroom. In the next along the west side, square brick paving on a mortared foundation was found on top of clay hypocaust pipes.

On the north side, a narrow corridor separated the north-west corner room and its neighbour, between which and the north-east corner room, with a doorway in the east wall, was a portico, shown by the remains of wooden beams from the eaves and of two wooden pillars, the base of one of which remained. Another long rectangular room, of undetermined use, occupied the middle of the east wall. It is considered that the roof sloped towards the inner courtyard and projected sufficiently to provide a rustic peristyle borne on wooden columns. There were probably other farm buildings in the vicinity. A lime pit was found about 9 metres north of the villa and 75 metres north a well, whence no doubt water was fetched in a bucket of which the iron handle was found.

There was a great deal of pottery, all wheel-made but clearly divided into rough kitchenware and finer vessels. The source of some of the latter, including lamps and other vessels with relief and incised decoration, was probably Butovo and dated to the first half of the third century. The owner possessed such items as bone spoons and a comb, as well as a useful collection of iron farm implements with whetstones and other accessories. The only luxury object found, if one excepts some of the finer ceramic, was a tiny glass gem engraved with a single-masted ship in full sail. It is easy to imagine that the farm belonged to a Thracian veteran of the Roman navy.

No inscriptions were found and the 17 Roman coins (seven of them minted in Nicopolis-ad-Istrum and Marcianopolis) were issues ranging from Commodus to Ottalicia, wife of Philip the Arab. The excavator dates the villa to the end of the second or the beginning of the third century. Razed in a fierce conflagration, there can be little doubt that this modest farmhouse was one of many similar victims of the mid-third-century Gothic terror.

II. MARCIANOPOLIS

In north-east Bulgaria the largest and most important city was Marcianopolis (Reka Devnya), founded by Trajan just within the borders of Thracia and named after his sister Marciana. Situated on the Devnya springs less than 30 kilometres from Odessos, which remained in Moesia, the new foundation demonstrated the emperor's reluctance to increase the power of the old, essentially Greek city; although he probably disliked but found it impolitic to destroy its autonomy.

Marcianopolis was a strategic communications centre – the convergence of a road network running from the lower reaches of the Danube and the Dobroudja, crossing the Stara Planina to the south, and coming eastwards from Melta via Nicopolis-ad-Istrum to reach the Black Sea at Odessos. The little existing evidence suggests that Marcianopolis, like Nicopolis, was organised on the pattern of a Hellenistic city, with many settlers of Greek, especially east Greek, origin, its Hellenistic character strengthened by contact with the coastal colonies. As one city served as a rear headquarters for Novae, so did the other for Durostorum. The fortified area is estimated at about 70 hectares, whilst Odessos, no mean city, had only 43 hectares. Like other cities, Marcianopolis reached a peak of prosperity under the Severi, when it was transferred from Thracia to become the capital of Moesia Inferior.

Valiant resistance led by Maximus, a philosopher and citizen, withstood a Gothic siege in A.D. 248. The gravity of the danger and the extent of the previous prosperity are illustrated by a hoard of two jars containing over 100,000 silver coins, dating variously from Mark Antony to Decius. Angered over Marciano-polis, the Goths took revenge on the countryside, with disastrous effect on the economy. The city ceased to issue coins. Recruitment of local Thracians into the imperial army – especially Legio XI Claudia at Durostorum – already begun in the second century, was accelerated by the general impoverishment; in the third century many also served in the praetorian guard in Rome. When these Romanised Thracians achieved veteran status, they tended to settle in or near the city and with freed slaves, ex-gladiators, and the like, gradually diluted the original population of predominantly Hellenised immigrants from Asia Minor. On the evidence of funerary and votive monuments and reliefs, B. Gerov points out that the municipal aristocracy may have included as many Romanised indigenous families as those of obvious Greek stock.[3]

Marcianopolis in the late 360s was a focal centre for the war against the Goths

PLATE 103 Marcianopolis, amphitheatre

and was Valens' temporary seat of government for about four years. This access of importance was not entirely beneficial to the countryside – a visitor to the city wrote that the soldiers were bandits who fought the local peasantry rather than the Goths. When in 376 the starving Visigoths were allowed by Valens to cross the Danube, probably via Durostorum, to settle in Moesia, the officials in charge of the resettlement were so avaricious the Goths were forced to sell their children and themselves into slavery in return for dogs to eat. Rising in desperation, and joined at some stage by Ostrogoths and Huns, they moved on Marcianopolis, where were the main Roman forces in the vicinity. Two fierce battles took place near the city. The first, in 376, was a Gothic victory; in the second, the following year, huge losses were suffered on both sides with no clear result and the remnants of the Roman army retreated behind the city walls, which were to remain intact for another 70 years.

There has been relatively little excavation of Roman Marcianopolis. The fortress appears on a coin as roughly square, with 14 towers and a vaulted gateway. On the south, sections of excavated wall reach a height of 3 or 4 metres; faced with large, smoothly dressed stones, joined by iron cramps and a mortar mixed with finely crushed tile, the wall here was nearly 2½ metres thick.

Traces of what were probably baths have been found; outside the walls, necropolises have been located. The remains of a two-storeyed peristyled villa were only 500 metres away. The main monument fully excavated is the amphitheatre, so far unique in Bulgaria (Pl. 103). Little but foundations remain to show the customary oval plan, with vaulted entrances on the north-west–south-east axis and the usual tiers of seats: one fragment bore the name 'Alexander'. A third-century funerary stele commemorating a gladiator named Narcissus

PLATE 104 Abritus, identifying inscription

shows him armed with a hauberk, a short sword, a rectangular shield, and kneeguards. Marcianopolis must have provided recreation for troops from Durostorum and other stations on the Danube; the amphitheatre, probably built in the second half of the third century, was an appropriate attraction.

Besides the existence of an imperial munitions factory which probably obtained iron ore from state-owned mines in the Strandja and perhaps the Rhodopes, the industries of the city are unknown, although they must have been many.

Coins, inscriptions, and votive reliefs show the variety of gods worshipped by the inhabitants. Coins provide evidence of the erection of temples to Zeus, Serapis, Apollo, Cybele-Urania, and the imperial cults. Altars and reliefs add Dionysos, Asklepios, Hygieia, Telesphoros, Hermes, and the Thracian Horseman. In the same way as some of the pagan cults, Christianity arrived early from the East, probably from Bithynia, and Marcianopolis, too, had its martyrs.

III. ABRITUS

Archaeology began at Abritus, or Abrittus (Razgrad), in the 1880s, when a local school inspector in natural history, A. Yavashov, helped by his friend the indefatigable Karel Škorpil, made preliminary soundings on the 'Hissarluk', a low hill outside the town. As early as 1887, only 8 years after Bulgaria became independent, he held an exhibition of finds in the local school. Forty years later, roadworks uncovered the north-west angle tower of a Roman fortress and he was still there to excavate and preserve it.

It is sad that Yavashov died unaware of the identity of 'his' city. Abritus was believed to be farther north-east until 1953, when a rescue dig unearthed a second-century altar with an inscription saying: Dedicated to Hercules for the health of Antoninus Pius and Lucius the veterans, Roman citizens and settlers in the canabae in Abritus have erected [an altar] (Pl. 104). Further confirmation came from other inscriptions and finds showing that Cohors II Lucensium was stationed at Abritus in the second century. A third-century inscription at Aquileia commemorates a centurion of Legio I Claudia born in the castellum of the 'Abritani' – another name used for Abritus.

Abritus is historically linked with the battle nearby in which Decius lost his life in 251. Pursuing the Goths on their way home from the sack of Philippopolis, he forced them to join battle. The tide flowed strongly in favour of the Romans until dusk, when Decius was misdirected into a swamp where he was thrown from his horse and engulfed. The consequent defeat of the Romans and the shameful terms accepted by their general, Trebonianus Gallus, suggest the probability that a mist of treachery as well as swamp surrounded the emperor's death. Torrential summer storms are a feature of the local climate and fully capable of converting dry land into a morass. I have seen the Beli Lom river flowing so strongly *above* a bridge here that even trucks were unable to cross it.

The sources which describe the other fortifications of this period make no mention of Abritus. Some defences may be assumed, but their nature and extent are still unknown. The excavated walls, enclosing about 10 hectares and built like those of Iatrus and Tropaeum Trajani, date to the end of the third or the early fourth century (Fig. 29). Situated on a low plateau, this fortress was basically rectangular with the east side curving where the ground falls steeply to the river Beli Lom, which also bordered the north defences. Elsewhere a moat afforded additional protection. Preserved in places up to 2 metres high and 2·40 metres thick except at the towers and gates where they were stronger, the curtain walls were faced with smooth rectangular stone blocks, larger on the outside than the inside, as at Iatrus, and with a filling of stone, mortar, and brick rubble. In some sectors, opus mixtum was found with three or four courses of brick in each band. The city – having now outgrown its earlier status of castellum – had three gates and 31 projecting towers. Because of the steep slope and river, the east wall had no gate and only one tower. Fan-shaped angle towers defended each corner. The spacing of the 20 U-towers, each on a socle of carefully rusticated ashlar and extending about 10 metres from the curtain wall, varied according to the vulnerability of the sector. Thus the south wall needed the strongest defences. Between the west angle tower and the central gate were two pairs of U-towers on each side of a massive rectangular tower; inside this two masonry piers supported an upper storey, probably for a ballista, as at Tropaeum Trajani and Capidava in the Dobroudja and the even larger structure at Iatrus. East of the gate, in a re-entrant of the wall, came first a U-shaped, then another,

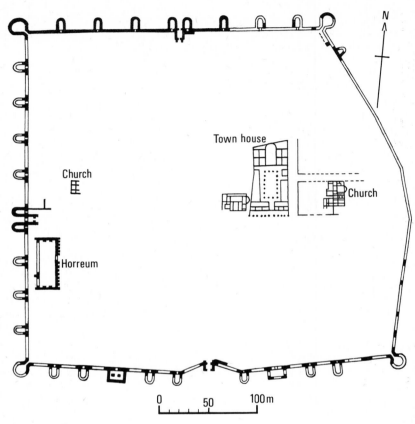

N

Town house

Church

Church

Horreum

0   50   100 m

FIG. 29 Abritus, city plan

rectangular tower. After this two more U-towers were separated by a stretch of uninterrupted curtain wall from the south-east angle tower. The walls are estimated to have been originally 10 metres high, crenellated and roofed with wooden beams and tiles.

The carefully constructed north gate, flanked by U-towers (Pl. 105; Fig. 30), had a portcullis and inner wing gates with an intervening propugnaculum, containing the probable remains of a decorative niche in one wall. The west gate, similar in plan, showed evidence of hasty building, for a stonemason's stock of funerary stelai were used as well as normal blocks; ready carved, the spaces for the prospective purchasers' inscriptions were blank. Unfinished stelai and some with inscriptions were also built into the socles of several towers.

The situation of the south gate in a re-entrant of the wall was not dictated by the terrain, its purpose was purely defensive. The flanking towers were at the beginning of the re-entrant, not integrated with the gate like those on the north

PLATE 105 Abritus, north gate

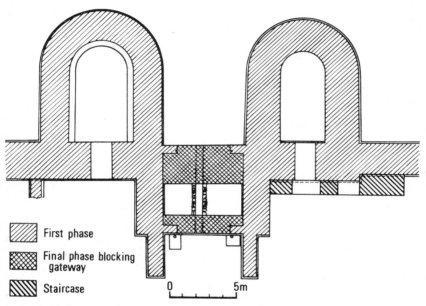

First phase

Final phase blocking gateway

Staircase

0   5m

FIG. 30 Abritus, north gate

and west sides. However, unlike the Iatrus gate, the propugnaculum and outer portcullis projected 5·60 metres beyond the curtain wall as well as inside it (Fig. 31). On a stone facing the propugnaculum the Greek letter alpha was carefully carved. There were similar stones in five towers. 'A' may have stood for Abritus; more likely it was a master mason's mark, corresponding to the lizard or dog at Nicopolis. Clay water-pipes running below the floor of this gate and west of the south-east angle tower brought water from springs at Poroishte, about 5 kilometres away.

Two large buildings stood parallel to the walls on either side of the gravelled street inside the west gate. The southern one was a *horreum*, or granary, 56 metres long by 22 metres wide, contemporary with the gate and planned so that country carts delivering loads had no need to pass farther into the city.

The forum has not been excavated, but its whereabouts are clear from the position of the gates. East of it the town house of a leading citizen has been

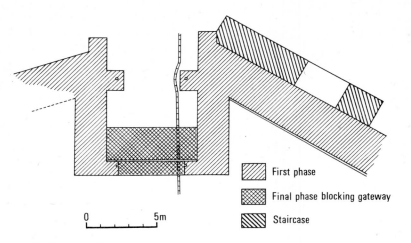

First phase

Final phase blocking gateway

Staircase

0 _____ 5m

FIG. 31 Abritus, south gate

PLATE 106 Abritus, town house

uncovered (Pl. 106; Fig. 32). Its large rectangular paved courtyard was enclosed
by a peristyle of re-used monolithic white marble columns with Ionic capitals,
their total height, including the bases and stylobates, about 5 metres. A single
long room on the west side was balanced by one large and one small on the east,
separated by an entrance from a street. The southern and main entrance was
through a string of shops, probably belonging to the establishment, behind the
colonnade of the decumanus maximus. The private quarters were on the north,

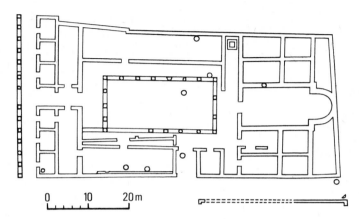

FIG. 32 Abritus, town house

PLATE 107 Gorotsvet, villa rustica

four rooms on either side of a big rectangular apsed hall, with traces of painting
on the remains of the walls.

The town house belongs to the fourth-century revival of Abritus. Remains of
second-century buildings were found beneath it and the Ionic columns and
capitals come from this period. No evidence of enemy destruction was observed
at the lower level, thus implying that these buildings did not suffer after the
Gothic victory over Decius.

PLATE 108 Abritus, Herakles, plaque, *ht.* 16 cm.

PLATE 109 Abritus, Cybele, plaque, *ht.* 19 cm.

The prosperity of the region in the late second and early third centuries is illustrated by a recently discovered villa rustica at Gorotsvet, south-west of Razgrad. This spacious structure with living accommodation and work rooms has a smaller version of the Abritus Ionic peristyled courtyard (Pl. 107). This villa could hardly have escaped the fury of the Goths.

Graves have been found outside the Abritus walls in all directions. Yavashov pioneered their recording and the collection of contents for the museum. Although the unidentified Thracian settlement known from a Greek inscription re-used in the floor of an Abritus church[4] has not been found, large tumuli of the Roman period, some containing the cremated smaller bones of the dead in an urn, testify to the continued habitation of the neighbourhood by rich as well as

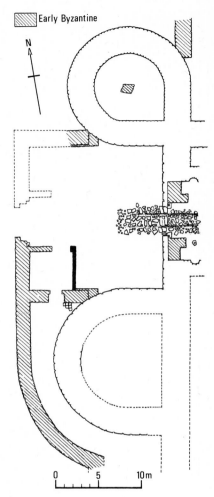

FIG. 33 Voivoda, north-west sector

poor Thracians. Roman burials followed a normal pattern. A rescue operation
in the southern cemetery has recently recorded several hundred poor interments
of the second to the fourth centuries.

In 1921, labourers in a vineyard outside Razgrad dug up 26 bronze votive
plaques, most of them portraying deities. Differing in size and shape, none
measured more than 25 by 20 centimetres; most were rectangular, sometimes
an aedicula with a gabled roof and columns framed the figure of a Greco-
Roman or, more rarely, an oriental deity. Artemis and Herakles are thus shown
on two plaques; another has Zeus and Hera side by side in individual aediculae
(Pl. 108). Oriental cults are represented more variously. In three cases the central

PLATE 110 Voivoda, angle tówer

figure is a horseman, Sabazios, carrying a horn of plenty and surrounded by other symbolic motifs. Seven depict a female-bust – Cybele-Anahita-Ishtar – with long hair falling over her shoulders and on her head an elaborate crown, a *murus coronalis* (Pl. 109). If forearms are shown, they are raised with outstretched palms in the pose which Christian iconography terms *orans*, or praying. A single example of the Eastern goddess Mâ is shown in a manner to identify her with Roman Bellona.

Even when subjects are similar, iconographic variations are often considerable. The craftsmanship also varies, but the skill behind many, irrespective of subject, suggests a local workshop where, about the second century, plaques of very high quality or cheaper, clumsier types could be bought, according to the purchaser's means and preferred cult. Such plaques were not uncommon at this time; in Bulgaria, clay versions were found at Montana (p. 116). G. Katsarov considered that the Razgrad find indicated a nearby sanctuary.[5] In the absence of excavation and in view of the variety of cults, it is also possible that the plaques formed a trader's stock, although it is tempting to associate them with the unidentified *Ara Decii* (Altar of Decius), where the emperor made many sacrifices on the night before the fatal battle.

IV. VOIVODA

An important fortified centre, first reconnoitred by K. Škorpil some 70 years ago, lies near the village of Voivoda, 23 kilometres north-east of Shoumen and 10 kilometres north of Pliska, the first capital of the medieval Bulgarian state. About half-way between Marcianopolis and Abritus, the road from Marcian-opolis probably forked either here or at Shoumen to Durostorum and to Sexaginta Prista. Soundings in the ruins, and coins of Aurelian, show that the settlement existed in the late third century, when – or in the early fourth – its walls were built.

New excavations show that Škorpil's original rough plan, based on surface evidence, needs revision. The fort was an irregular pentagon, enclosing an area of about 10 hectares. Parts of the north and west curtain walls have been traced,

PLATE 111 Madara, villa rustica

and excavations have uncovered a fan-shaped north-west angle tower, an external U-shaped tower in the west wall, and, between them, a gateway (Fig. 33). The angle tower was a massive structure, its diameter 13·60 metres and the thickness of its walls 3·05 metres. The socle carried an ashlar layer, above which were five rows of smaller, more roughly cut stones, surmounted by the remains of a brick bonding course. Smaller stone blocks with carefully dressed faces lined the inside; the fill consisted of broken stones and mortar with brick fragments. A square pier in the middle of the tower to support an upper storey is thought to be a slightly later addition (Pl. 110).

The neighbouring tower along the west wall was even more massive and was unusual in that, although U-shaped, its width was greater than its projection. The gateway between did not project outside the line of the walls and at the time of the preliminary publication the excavation of the inner part was not complete. The outer gate consisted of two pivoted wings and small vaulted side-chambers branched north and south from the propugnaculum. Although not the main gate, it showed signs of considerable use.

Part of the north wall has also been excavated, revealing a second side-gate and three towers, two said to be the largest of the Roman or Early Byzantine periods yet found in Bulgaria, a fact which stresses the strategic importance of the fortress.[6]

In one of these large towers was a hoard of *tegulae*, or flat roofing tiles, stamped DULES. In all, over a thousand bricks and tiles bearing the names of Dules, Dionysos, and others, presumably their manufacturers, have been found in the excavations of the last few years. Besides a fortress, Voivoda seems to have been a major centre for brickmaking.

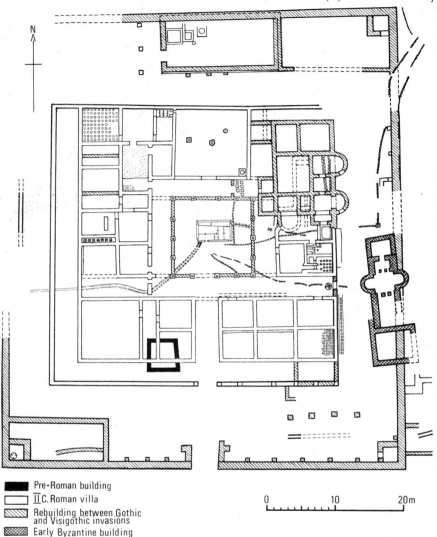

Pre-Roman building
IIC. Roman villa
Rebuilding between Gothic and Visigothic invasions
Early Byzantine building

0   10   20m

FIG. 34 Madara, pars urbana of villa rustica

V. MADARA

South of the road from Marcianopolis to Abritus the great cliffs of Madara shelter the ruins of a large villa rustica (Pl. 111) which, on the basis of fragmentary inscriptions, Ts. Dremtsizova suggests was imperial property. Certainly it controlled wealthy agricultural land and must have employed a large labour force. Built about the mid-second century on earlier foundations, the villa was sacked a century later, no doubt during the Gothic invasion. Rebuilt, it flourished until about 376 when it fell victim to the Visigoths who, according to Ammianus Marcellinus, destroyed all the villae rusticae of the region.[7]

The *pars urbana*, or residence in which the interior arrangements corresponded to a town house, of the second-century villa was square, enclosed by walls about 40 metres long, with an inside promenade on the west and south (Fig. 34). A southern entrance led past two blocks of rooms into a peristyled courtyard, in its centre a shallow paved pool supplied with piped water from outside. The southern portico continued to a gate in the east wall. North of the courtyard, opening on to the portico, was the largest of the 40-odd rooms, probably the reception hall. The rooms on the west side appear to have been purely residential; some had hypocausts. Rebuilding to a different plan had largely effaced those in the north-east sector, but the presence of a furnace just outside the rebuilt area suggests the possibility of private baths. A large baths was also excavated east of the pars urbana.

The *pars rustica*, or farm buildings, lay in several groups north of the villa; these flimsier structures, often altered and rebuilt, are hard to date. Besides shelter for animals, there were barns for storing grain. A more substantial out-building only a few metres north of the villa served for wine-making. The wine presses have survived, and some *dolia*, large jars used for storage.

After the first sack, most of the villa seems to have been rebuilt on the original plan. The radical alteration of the north-east part has similarities in its plan to the early third-century extramural building at Oescus (Fig. 16). In both cases the purpose is unknown, although for sound reasons the excavators of both dismiss the possibility of baths. At Madara, a group of rooms including a furnace, between the east gate and the new building, are believed to have continued to function as baths during the second period. It seems possible that the triple-apsed building in the north-east corner may belong to a later phase of the first period rather than the second or post-Goth period.

During the second building period the villa and the building with the wine press and store were enclosed by rectangular walls between 60 and 65 metres long, with a southern gateway opposite the villa's main entrance. This wall was later reinforced by internal square angle towers and buttresses. Another ominous portent was the apparent cessation of viticulture shown by the conversion of the large outbuilding into a granary. But none of these measures availed against the Visigothic fury.

NOTES

1 I am indebted to Professor T. Ivanov for the aerial view of Nicopolis (Pl. 94) which represents the plan of the city walls more accurately and in greater detail than the plan first published in *IBAI* V, 1928–29.
2 *IGB* II, 604.
3 Gerov, B., *Romanizmut* III, 115.
4 *IGB* II, 743.
5 Kazarow, G., *Archäologischer Anzeiger* (*Jahrbuchs des deutschen archäologischen Instituts*), XXXVII, 1922, 186 ff.
6 NAC, *Arh* XIII/4, 1971, 76.
7 Amm. Marc. XXXI, 12, 4.

7 Serdica and the West (1)

1. SERDICA AND ITS TERRITORY

Originally a Thracian settlement named from the local Serdi tribe, Serdica (Sofia) became the centre of a *strategia*, an administrative district, of Thracia in A.D. 46. Sixty years later, its key situation as a communications centre as well as its economic potentialities received recognition from Trajan, who raised it to civic status, with his family name *Ulpia* as a prefix to its title. Urban development on Hellenistic lines as in the rest of Thracia was intensified under Hadrian and his successors. Doubly protected by the Danube *limes* and the Stara Planina, it seems that walls were not considered necessary; with the Dacian conquest danger from the north became even more remote.

The Costoboki shattered this illusion in 170. Crossing the Danube, sweeping through Moesia and Thracia and southward to Athens, they devastated the countryside and damaged several cities on their path, probably including Serdica. Marcus Aurelius' decision to fortify the city was a direct result and his work was completed under Commodus.

The area enclosed by these walls was some 15 or 16 hectares, by no means the entire city. Oriented north–south, it was basically rectangular, but without the north-west corner, where the land was marshy. The north wall was slightly arc-shaped, perhaps to incorporate an existing bath complex or water-supply (Fig. 35). In the most fully excavated east sector, the wall crossed paved streets and foundations of buildings, others remaining outside. Frequently and extensively restored, the original curtain wall is thought to have been built of brick on an ashlar socle, rusticated on the outer side. It was 2·15 metres thick, except on the south, where it was at least 2·60 metres. Probably the wall was about 8 metres high; the round angle towers and the semicircular projecting ones which strengthened it at intervals were 2 metres or so higher (Fig. 36). The north and east gates have been excavated. By imaginative town planning, the City Council and the archaeological service have preserved the east gateway in its sixth-century aspect in a pedestrian underpass beneath the Boulevard Dondoukov (Pl. 165).

Evidence of burning about the mid-third century suggests some damage from the Gothic invasion, but recovery was rapid. By the fourth century the city had grown so much in size and importance – it had become the capital of the new province of Dacia Mediterranea – that the wall was extended. An area north of the original fortress and three to four times its size was enclosed, the old and new sections being linked in the vicinity of the old north gate, presenting the shape of an angular, top-heavy figure '8'. Those parts of the new wall which have been studied were ashlar with a filling of mortar and smaller river stones; it was 2·85 metres thick. A large octagonal tower projected from the north-west angle and a large round one from the north-east; others, both round and rectangular, projected at intervals along the straight stretches. About the same time, a fortified outpost or barbican seems to have been built outside the east gate. The resemblance of the new walls to those of Abritus, Iatrus, and Dobroudjan

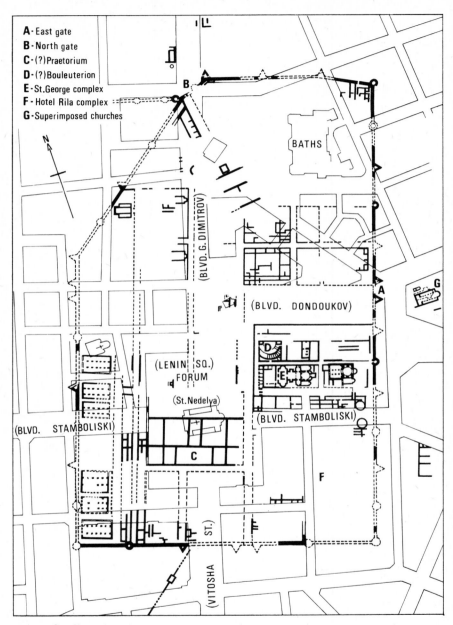

A· East gate
B· North gate
C· (?)Praetorium
D· (?)Bouleuterion
E· St.George complex
F· Hotel Rila complex
G· Superimposed churches

FIG. 35 Serdica, city plan

FIG. 36 Serdica, reconstruction of angle tower, first phase

fortresses suggests the expansion was due either to Galerius or, more probably, to Constantine, who for a time made his headquarters here and even considered it as a possible site for the new imperial capital. In 343 the city, poised almost on the boundary of the Eastern and Western halves of the empire, was chosen as the seat of a Church Council intended to heal the Arian breach, which had political as well as religious aspects. But the two sides could not even be brought to sit together and, although the Council's canons were important for the Roman Church, it was ecumenically disastrous.

The Roman plan of the city has lasted with remarkably little change. Sofia has been superimposed on Serdica. The streets in the centre run parallel to and occasionally above those built by Rome. The forum, already subject to modifications in the Roman period, is now a little larger; it has been renamed Lenin Square but has not been moved. Instead of passing through the east gate to Philippopolis, the modern traveller drives over it to Plovdiv. But for the railway station, the Boulevard Georgi Dimitrov, passing above the original north gate, would still be the direct route to the Iskur gorge and the Danube. In such circumstances, chances for excavation have had to be taken as they came and only very gradually is a picture of Roman Serdica being pieced together.

From the centre of the new pedestrian underpass it is possible to walk through the east gate and for a short distance along the decumanus maximus. This street – the *via principalis* – originally 16 metres wide and probably colonnaded, continued north of the forum, possibly to another gate in the neighbourhood of Trapezitsa street. From the north gate, the cardo maximus, 12 metres wide, joined the via principalis at the forum.

Damage during the Second World War gave an opportunity for excavation in

PLATE 112 Serdica, 'St George' rotunda

the eastern part of Serdica, both north of the via principalis near the TSUM department store and south of it in the area of the Hotel Balkan. Although the Roman street network changed very little, there were several building phases, not necessarily related to historical events or to developments in adjoining insulae.

The forum was 26 metres wide, but its length varied; there were changes in the third century at both ends, but only limited excavations have been possible. The east side was investigated during the construction of the Hotel Balkan and neighbouring buildings in the 1950s. This sector, presumably porticoed, now lies under the front rooms of the hotel and extends south to the Boulevard Stamboliski and north to TSUM. On the west side were found remains of a large and ornate two-storeyed building with a porticoed façade of the Severan period.

South of the forum, a large public building has been partially excavated as opportunity offered over the last 80 years. About 115 metres long from east to west and about 45 metres wide, it extended well beyond the west side of the forum. Today its remains lie partly under the church of St Nedelya and the south end of Lenin Square. The walls, 2½ metres thick and built of broken stone with bonding layers of brick, incorporated vaulted corridors, reminiscent of the extramural building at Oescus; they were 2 metres high and 65 centimetres wide, with air vents at intervals of 6 and 4 metres. The plan, as known, could be that of a public baths and has similarities with the second-century one at Odessos (Fig. 53). Baths fed by natural springs existed in the north-east sector in the second century, but the growth of the city may have called for others, or for one more modern; it has not been possible to excavate the earlier. This large building is dated by S. Bobchev to the third century, a time of general expansion

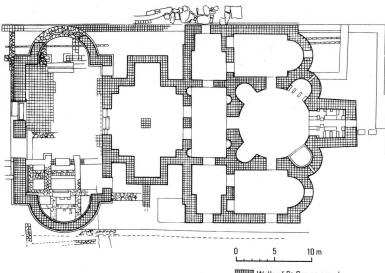

FIG. 37 Serdica, 'St George' complex

0   5   10 m

▦ Walls of St.George complex

when reasons for erecting monumental edifices are not always logical. Nevertheless, conclusive evidence for baths is lacking, and, especially in view of its
prominent situation, a more generally accepted theory is that this was the
praetorium, or residence of the governor.

Between the forum and the east wall, the width of an insula south of the via
principalis, four insulae occupied the greater part of what is now a large block
with the Hotel Balkan at its western end. During the construction of the hotel
the western sectors of the two insulae facing on to the forum were excavated and
recorded. In the northern, the earliest remains discovered belonged to an almost
square building, probably of the second century. This was rebuilt, it is thought
in the second half of the third century, along similar lines, but either by the end
of that century or early in the fourth a reconstruction included tiers of stone seats
rising from a semicircular orchestra on its north side. On the basis of the earlier
plan and the position on the forum, the excavators considered the building was
the city bouleuterion, given an amphitheatrical 'new look' when Serdica became
the capital of a province, rather than an odeon.[1] In the absence of supporting
epigraphic or other evidence, this theory cannot be regarded as proven.

Much of the southern insula was, as it still is, an open space containing
Sofia's oldest standing monument, the 'church of St George'. The rescue
excavations to its west, however, uncovered three building phases. The first
seems to have consisted of shops fronting the forum and the streets leading to it.
The second was a reconstruction of the first on a slightly different plan. The third
was the construction of what is usually termed the St George complex, of which
the present church was only the eastern part (Pl. 112).

The shopping precinct was replaced by an open courtyard, about 28 metres
wide and 20 metres deep, which extended from the forum to the entrance of a

new building. Aligned on an east–west axis, this stretched back about 45 metres and was a maximum of 27 metres wide. First, double portals led through a large outer hall, apsed on the north and south, and down three steps into a narrower, inner hall with corresponding square apses. From here another double entrance opened into a rectangular tripartite antechamber with doors into the present rotunda and, through its side compartments, into two rectangular apsed chambers flanking the rotunda and opening into it. This last had a large square eastern apse and four U-shaped apses (Fig. 37).

Minor details apart, the plan of the complex is quite symmetrical, except for the outer hall. Not only is this out of alignment, but its floor was higher, although it lacked the hypocaust-like system of small brick piers beneath the floors in the rest of the building.[2] The natural assumption that it was a later addition is contradicted by the excavators who state categorically that they were unable to detect any structural joints in the parts that survived, and who found beneath its floor a coin of Valentinian I, emperor of the West from 364 to 375.[3]

The date and purpose of the building – which are interrelated – have long been the subject of controversy, still unresolved and accentuated by the fact that the complex with its courtyard has occupied this central position for over 1,500 years, so that, earlier buildings apart, it has had many later building phases and several excavations, archaeological and destructive. If the complex is accepted as a whole and dated after Valentinian I, it could have had a Christian purpose, but the overall plan resembles no known type of church or ancillary building, such as a baptistery, of the late fourth or early fifth century. It is now generally considered that, as suggested by P. Karasimeonov, the 'hypocaust' was a precaution against the excessive damp of this quarter rather than for heating, thus disposing of an earlier hypothesis of baths.

If the possibility that the coin was dropped during a repair to the floor of the outer hall is admitted, the early fourth century is the most likely date for the complex. This is favoured by other archaeologists concerned with the excavations, who suggest that it was built as a *martyrium* for the tomb or relics of an anonymous early saint.[4] However, the likelihood is small that Christianity would have achieved so prominent a site by this time, especially for a saint so undistinguished as to have remained quite unknown.

Less attention has been given to such possible purposes as a mausoleum or as a *heroon* or shrine to the pagan patron-protector of the city, who could later have been translated into St George, the national patron saint, sometimes associated in a healing context with the Thracian Horseman. A tradition of a 'holy spring of the church' was still alive in 1940, when excavations in progress were visited by a peasant from a remote village seeking a cure for his blindness. The workmen gave him water from the fountain supplied by the city mains, with which he returned home – to be cured, it must be hoped, by his faith. Yet neither of these possibilities adequately explains the architectural arrangement.

Only a building of exceptional importance would have possessed the open court linking it to the forum, and this court must itself have fulfilled some special function, probably of a ceremonial nature. It would be consonant with a purpose as yet ignored: that the whole complex was erected as an imperial reception hall of the Constantinian period. Space was available for the deployment of guards or attendants in the courtyard and for attendants and officials in the side-rooms, while the emperor could have appeared from the square east room to greet envoys and other persons to be honoured in the rotunda. The two eastern apses in the rotunda contained pools, but originally these may have been fountains.

The tradition of such imperial reception halls is a long one, ranging from Nero's *Domus Aurea* to the mid-sixth-century *Chrysotriklinos* in Constantinople. A recently excavated octagonal building belonging to the Tetrarchic palace in Thessalonica is likely to have served such a function and at the Constantinian villa at Mediana outside Naissus a smaller but basically similar structure has been uncovered.

South-east of the 'St George' complex, in the vicinity of the Hotel Rila, new excavations are revealing a large complex with a peristyled courtyard enclosed by rooms, including octagonal and circular chambers, some decorated with mosaic. Hypocausts and water-pipes of lead and tile have also been found. When published, this building, believed by the excavators to have been constructed as a residence for Constantine, should be a notable addition to knowledge of Roman Serdica.

North of the via principalis, the construction of TSUM in the 1950s uncovered architectural fragments of the second-third centuries suggesting the existence of a spring or fountain enclosed in a hexagonal structure in a courtyard. A pre-Roman cult of Apollo the Healer existed in the city and a coin of Serdica shows the god beside such a fountain. Outside the east gate, a life-size bronze head of Apollo, still retaining traces of gilding, was found during building work (Pl. 113). Ascribed to the second century, but after some earlier Greek model, this fine head may well have come from one of his shrines.

Another important early cult was that of Zeus-Jupiter identified with Serapis-Helios, and later transformed into the state cult of Capitoline Jupiter. A three-naved building of the late third or early fourth century in the north-west part of the city has been identified on architectural grounds as a Mithraeum, but no ritual objects remained *in situ* to provide clinching evidence.

What, in Roman eyes, was the lighter side of life in Serdica appears on a fragment of a slab showing circus scenes (Pl. 114). It is carved in low relief and was found among the ruins of the 'praetorium'.[5] The presentation of the various incidents all together does not exclude their being separate 'turns' which could have taken place in an odeon. In the centre, on a garlanded platform, four men in dog-head masks act a scene with a performing animal. There are fights between bulls and bears, between a bear and a crocodile (possibly, it has been suggested, a wooden model) accompanied by an armed man, a bear attacking a man whose arms and hands appear protected. Elsewhere a bear is mauling a naked woman. On the extreme left, a tower is carved in lower relief. Two men clashing cymbals stand on the first storey; on the second Serapis, with sceptre and patera, is enthroned between two lions; on the third, an almost naked female, perhaps Aphrodite, may be holding a mirror and a comb. Except for the crocodile, the figures are skilfully depicted with gusto and savage realism. The portrayal of pagan gods dates this relief to the third or at latest fourth century.

Country estates grew up around Serdica, which offered a ready market for their industrial as well as agricultural products. Half a dozen villae rusticae have been identified in the environs of Sofia, although it is doubtful if any enjoyed the

PLATE 113 Serdica, Apollo, head, *ht.* 38 cm.

continuity found at Madara. Perhaps one of the earliest was an L-shaped building enclosing a courtyard, open on the north and east, at Gara Iskur, not far from the Philippopolis road (Fig. 38). Construction was mostly of local stone and white mortar, but brick was also used. Little pilasters projected at regular intervals along the outer side of the south wing, perhaps to support some kind of portico.

The south wing probably contained the living quarters and the west the farm buildings. At the east end of the south wing a series of little rooms, some semi-circular and all smoothly plastered, were probably baths, the two little rooms annexed to the north side serving perhaps for heating water and for cooking. No finds were reported, but the open plan suggests an early and peaceful date – and also an early end, perhaps during the third-century Gothic raids.

In the fertile territory of Serdica the inhabitants remained largely Thracian;

PLATE 114 Serdica, circus scenes, *w.* 77 cm.

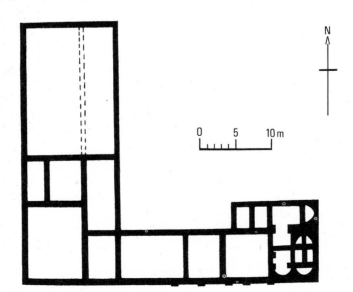

FIG. 38 Gara Iskur, villa rustica

there were many primitive sanctuaries to the Thracian Horseman; Zeus and Hera and Asklepios were also revered. According to the scanty archaeological information available, any new settlement in the Roman period was concentrated near the road stations along the main highways.

Travelling south-west along the 'Diagonal', on the present frontier with Yugoslavia, Balanstra (Kalotino) had an organisation of army veterans to defend the pass. The *mansio*, or overnight stop, of Meldia was identified at the end of the last century near Dragoman. On a hill north of Meldia were a sanctuary and cave dedicated to Sabazios; votive inscriptions were re-used in a church built on top of the shrine. On the eastern side of Serdica the settlement pattern continued, with a string of para-military settlements along the Ihtiman pass. Similarly the region of the Iskur gorge was dotted with road forts, later used for refuge during barbarian invasions.

II. PAUTALIA AND ITS TERRITORY

Pautalia

Pautalia (Kyustendil), probably formerly the chief settlement of the Dentheletai, stands at the western edge of the largest and most fertile 'pole' or upland plain of the upper Struma valley. The encircling mountains are rich in pasture and in silver, copper, and iron ores; remains of mining galleries have been found in the mountainsides, and there was gold in the hills and in the river sands. The Struma carves a southward route to eastern Macedonia and the Aegean. Westward, the road from Serdica continued over the easier mountain passes to Stobi and thence to Thessalonica or to the Adriatic.

The gods also blessed Pautalia with warm, healing springs. Their temperature

PLATE 115 Pautalia, coin depicting Hissarluk

reached as high as 75° Centigrade and the aqueducts which have been traced may have been a main source of much-needed cold water. The grateful population built temples by the springs at the foot of the 'Hissarluk', a steep abutment of the Osogovska Planina rising acropolis-like behind the city. Coins issued under Caracalla show temples on its sides and summit (Pl. 115). Here, under a ruined church – in which a pagan altar was re-used, probably as a column-base – were the remains of a sanctuary which must have occupied the prominent position on the heights shown on the coins. Votive inscriptions to Greco-Roman gods were found nearby.

Coins minted in Pautalia from 139 to 217 and inscriptions of the late second and early third centuries using the prefix 'Ulpia' show it was one of Trajan's foundations. One inscription of 135,[6] referring to a basilica built under Hadrian and probably the administrative centre of the town, has the earliest known mention of the name Pautalia. The city was organised on Hellenistic lines, Greek remained the administrative, commercial, and cultural language and Roman influence seems to have been generally less than in more strategically situated Serdica. Despite a Hellenistic influx from Macedonia and the south and, as the city grew in prosperity, to a lesser extent from Asia Minor, a (now lost) inscription of the second century[7] suggests that the administration was then virtually in Thracian hands, however much Hellenised or Romanised.

Another sign of Thracian continuity is the discovery of two buried chariots within the confines of modern Kyustendil. One is unpublished. The other, found in a specially dug trench, was a four-wheeled chariot with a suspended chassis, decorated with ornamental nails and other metalwork as well as bronze busts and statuettes of Greek mythological subjects. More unusual ornaments were five round harness plaques, flat but inset with concentric and sometimes chequered bands of yellow, green, red, and blue enamel. The small salvage dig that alone was possible prevented any search for the front of the chariot and possible horse skeletons, but the burial is thought to have been associated with a tumulus which, according to local knowledge, had existed some 50 metres away. The chariot was of a type dated to the Roman period and found in a number of places west and south of the Stara Planina. On the grounds of the clumsy expressionless bronzes, the chariot is attributed to the end of the second or beginning of the third century, by which time local industry would be sufficiently developed to produce such ornaments.

Like neighbouring Serdica, Pautalia is now a busy city where opportunities for excavation are limited. But work still in progress has shown that the city walls, although frequently repaired later, were likewise the work of Marcus Aurelius in the latter half of the second century. Parts of the early east, north, and west walls have been uncovered, including a rectangular tower, and the east gate excavated. Some paved streets have been traced inside the city.

Appropriately, the two buildings of the Roman period partially uncovered are baths, more or less contemporary and both oriented north-east to south-west. In one, discovered in 1962 during digging for a new water main, parts of six rooms were explored. A *frigidarium*, for the cold bath, on the north-east side had a floor in *opus sectile*, a pattern of variously shaped marble slabs. Less than half an octagonal room could be excavated. Apparently a *tepidarium*, a warm room, on its south-east side an apse-like niche, doubtless repeated on one or

PLATE 116 Pautalia, vaulted hypocausts

more of the other sides, accommodated a pool, thought to be for individual therapy.

The other baths excavated were a small sector of a monumental edifice, usually linked with the great Pautalian shrine, the Asklepieion. The fame of this was widespread. Votive inscriptions at the great Asklepieion of Epidauros included one dedicated to the Pautalian god. Again, little work was possible, but the five rooms partially conserved as an extension of the museum are on a much larger scale than those of the other baths. One room, probably occupying the eastern corner, was nearly 20 metres long and $11\frac{1}{2}$ metres wide. It had a thick floor of mortared stones and crushed brick to eliminate rising damp. In an adjoining room clay pipes were found with a combination of square and round brick pillae. In another, levelled summits of parallel rows of brick arches springing from low brick piers supported series of brick vaults aligned at right-angles to the openings below (Pl. 116). On these the *suspensura*, or floor, was laid. The reason for a vaulted hypocaust alongside the other type is not clear, but possibly hot water was used for heating here instead of air.

The opus mixtum construction of the walls consisted of uncut stones with bonding layers of four courses of brick, but miscellaneous fragmentary finds suggest a rich decoration, with marble floor and wall revetment slabs, fine Corinthian and other capitals, fluted pilasters, multicoloured mosaics, iridescent window-glass, and marble statues, now unidentifiable. Of a collective find of 61 silver coins on the floor of the room with both round and square hypocaust

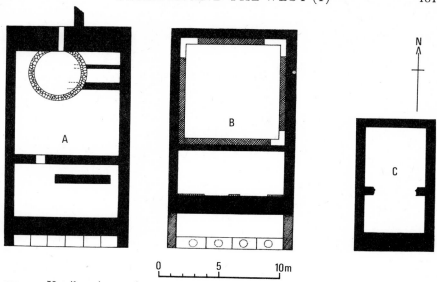

FIG. 39 Kopilovtsi, temples

piers, one of Antoninus Pius and 48 of Gordian III were identified. The dating of this and the other baths is not certain, but the coins of Gordian suggest the latter part of the third century, when Pautalia was a flourishing city in the new province of Dacia Mediterranea.

Aspects of the city's cult of Asklepios, often in conjunction with Hygieia and Telesphoros, are manifold. A ritual marble egg has been found; this symbol also appeared on coins, with or without Asklepios, as did a serpent, coiled and sometimes haloed. A collection of iron knives from the general area of the Asklepieion may well have been used for sacrifices. Just over fifty years ago, I. Ivanov described a custom 'observed until recently in Kyustendil' of throwing knives into the hot springs after using them to sacrifice a cock.[8]

The religious orientation of the Pautalians was overwhelmingly Greco-Roman. Cybele and Serapis, for instance, appear only on single coins. Zeus and Hera came into prominence later than Asklepios perhaps, but inscriptions show that a college of 13 or 14 priests was probably dedicated to the service of Jupiter, Juno, and Minerva and to the imperial cult. Women participated in the priesthood; one inscription records the erection by a priestess of a statue to herself and another shows that a husband and wife were jointly engaged in priestly duties.

A sanctuary especially sacred to Zeus and Hera was established some 5 kilometres from Pautalia, near the present village of Kopilovtsi. This was an extension of the Pautalian religious complex and used by its citizens. The remains of three temples were found, side by side, 3 to 5 metres apart (Fig. 39). Each was subdivided, the northern, roughly square compartment being the larger. The southern end of the middle temple was porticoed and its north room was later 'lined' with an inner wall.

The temples were very thoroughly and deliberately destroyed. Of the architectural decoration, two massive plain granite capitals were found intact; otherwise only a small piece of a huge marble Corinthian capital and a few fragments of pillars remain. Heads of Zeus and Hera, their faces badly battered, and two hands, survive from two colossal statues. All around were broken votive tablets. Most depicted Zeus and Hera, but Dionysos, Herakles, Hermes, the triple Hekate, and the Thracian Horseman were also represented. Finely made needles and pins of bone, bronze, and silver, the ornamental lead frames of hand mirrors, clay lamps, and other objects, among them many iron knife blades and spearheads, were either offerings or otherwise connected with the rites. Coin finds, ranging from Claudius II to Arcadius, indicate the long life of the sanctuary and its especial popularity during most of the third and fourth centuries, even after the acceptance of Christianity, no doubt its ultimate destroyer.

The territory of Pautalia

The territory of Pautalia was extensive. Archaeology, although sporadic, has demonstrated the same general continuity and an even more marked absence of Romanisation than existed in the city, providing a strong contrast to the situation on and behind the Danube *limes*. Among the cults of the countryside the most popular was that of the Thracian Horseman, of whom many small local sanctuaries were found, often associated with Zeus, Hera, Asklepios, Athena, Dionysos, and other Greek gods. A single example of a Mithraeum occurs 15 kilometres from Pautalia at an unidentified emporium at Tavalichevo, where veterans had perhaps settled, and occasional Mithraic votive reliefs have been found.

Three early villas have been located. One at Kadin Most, excavated at the beginning of this century, at a crossing of the Struma 13 kilometres from Pautalia, was associated with other settlement buildings and a necropolis, of which ten mounds were excavated. One contained three brick vaults, dated by coins from the mid-first century A.D. to the mid-fourth. The excavations showed a long Thracian cultural continuity, including chariot burial, antedating the Roman period and continuing into the late fourth century, when the large villa was destroyed, probably by the Visigoths. Another villa at Kralev Dol, southeast of Pernik, has been dated by finds of large quantities of Roman pottery to the end of the second century. From a third, north of Pernik, at Meshtitsa, came a fine second-century bronze statuette of Athena.

The Roman presence was of course felt. Within the territory of Pautalia were the Krakra stronghold at Pernik, a road fort of growing importance on the highway to Serdica, and Germania (Sapareva Banya). The latter commanded a gap between the Vitosha and Rila mountains and thus the road linking the upper Struma valley with the Thracian plain; inscriptions show it to have been a *vicus*, or rural community, garrisoned by the auxiliary Cohors Lucensium at the end of the second century. The earliest walls, ascribed to the late third century, were carefully built of broken stone, rubble, and mortar and enclosed an area 180 metres long by 140 metres wide; today their maximum height is only 70 centimetres. The buildings inside the settlement were separated by a network of narrow passages with an unusual south-east–north-west orientation, presumably so that the houses, shaded in winter mornings by the Rila peaks, could enjoy the afternoon sun. The site had (and still has) warm mineral springs, so naturally the healing gods were especially venerated; among chance finds of votive tablets, Asklepios, Hygieia and Telesphoros, the Three Nymphs, and the Thracian Horseman figure prominently.

On the southern edge of the territory was the village of Scaptopara (now a suburb of Blagoevgrad), famous for an inscription of A.D. 238 found in a vineyard outside the town in 1868 but since lost.[9] The long Greek inscription contains a plea to Gordian III from the inhabitants of Scaptopara, with a detailed description of their situation and difficulties.

The village had previously been happy and self-supporting, with enough land in the fertile Struma valley for cornfields, vineyards, and orchards and enough mountain pasture for grazing cattle. But two Roman miles away (at the modern village of Strumsko) were warm mineral springs associated with a cult and here an important fair had grown up which took place several times a year. The chief occasion was a 15-day event after the harvest, when cattle and agricultural produce were exchanged for manufactured goods brought by traders thought to have come from all over western Thrace and eastern Macedonia. Furthermore, Scaptopara lay between two unnamed Roman garrisons, one almost certainly Germania, the other unidentified.

The villagers were mainly free Thracians and included some army veterans. They paid a variety of heavy dues to the state and to distant Pautalia, including, for some, a land tax, and possibly also a sales tax. But their geographical position made intolerable a further obligation then commonly imposed: that of providing free board and lodging to civil servants, military personnel, and anyone visiting the area on a legal mission. The nearness of the two garrisons and the popularity of the fair and the springs meant that the peasants were so frequently compelled to give hospitality to all who found some pretext for being in this agreeable neighbourhood that, from being self-supporting, they were rapidly becoming destitute. Numbers had already abandoned their homes and lands. As Oliver Goldsmith, in *The Deserted Village*, wrote:

> Ill fares the land, to hast'ning ills a prey,
> Where wealth accumulates and men decay;
> Princes and lords may flourish or may fade;
> A breath can make them, as a breath has made;
> But a bold peasantry, their country's pride,
> When once destroyed, can never be supplied.

In the case of Scaptopara, after complaints to Pautalia had proved unavailing, the remaining 'bold peasantry' addressed a petition to their emperor, threatening that they, too, would be forced to depart, an act which, they were careful to point out, would also mean a loss to the exchequer.

The fair was later concentrated in Blagoevgrad itself – the Turkish name of the town meaning 'fair' – and continued to be held until about the end of the nineteenth century.

III. SANDANSKI

Sandanski – its ancient name is disputed – controlled the southern opening of the Struma gorge and was strategically and commercially the main city of the middle Struma region. Within the north-eastern boundary of Roman Macedonia it was uniquely placed for trade between the two provinces. Inscriptions demonstrate how much Sandanski's prosperity depended on this function. The earliest, carved in Greek on a funerary tablet re-used as a paving stone in a church, is dated to 121 and commemorates one Marcus Herennius Rufus, a veteran and *beneficiarius* of Legio I Italica.[10] Herennius joined the legion on its formation in A.D. 67, when recruitment was confined to persons of Italic origin; the name appears in some other Macedonian inscriptions and B. Gerov suggests he may have come from Philippi.[11] By 69, the legion was established at Novae, in which neighbourhood Herennius must have spent the rest of his 25 years' service. He then retired to Sandanski and, dying at the ripe age of 75, was survived by his Thracian wife, a freed slave.

The main event in Sandanski's calendar was an annual three-day fair, attested by several inscriptions. Locally, cattle were raised on the rich hill pastures. Silver

PLATE 117 Sandanski district, portrait fragment

probably came from the mines of Mount Pangaeus and was worked by craftsmen in Sandanski, who also used locally mined iron. Merchants from the north brought slaves; the importance of the Struma route for this traffic is endorsed by an inscription at Amphipolis. One wonders if during his army service Herennius built up a useful Danubian connection in the slave trade and thus provided for a comfortable retirement as well as finding a wife.

Sandanski's wealthiest period was the century between the reigns of Antoninus Pius, who increased the status of the city, and Gordian III. The agora was built under Caracalla. Thereafter decline set in. Possibly the defeat of the Goths by Claudius temporarily flooded the slave market.

The outline of the Roman city is completely covered by modern Sandanski; so little of the walls has been uncovered that they can only be dated sometime between the second and fourth centuries. An inscription refers to a temple erected to the *Tyche*, or Fortune, of the city. The cult of Artemis-Bendis was widespread in the middle Struma valley – more popular even than that of the Thracian Horseman – but it is likely that shrines to both existed. There were at least two mineral baths and D. Dechev suggests that the annual fair, like that near Scaptopara, was related to the cult of the healing gods, Asklepios, Hygieia, and Telesphoros, a cult here subsequently transferred to the Christian doctors Cosmas and Damian, still patron saints of the main church.[12] Sandanski itself was formerly called 'Sveti Vrach', which in Bulgarian means 'Holy Healer'.

The rural prosperity of the area in the Roman period is attested by large numbers of carved funerary monuments from the surrounding villages – relief portraits of the deceased with his or her family being the most common form of decoration. They are executed in varying degrees of rustic realism and only occasionally attain the dignity of this fine fragment from near Sandanski (Pl. 117).

IV. THE UPPER MESTA VALLEY

From the archaeological viewpoint, the western Rhodopes and the Pirin are an undeveloped region. In the Roman period, the area was mainly inhabited by survivors of the fiercely independent Bessi and other tribes. The remoter parts, so far as is known, seem scarcely touched by Roman influence or authority. That, except in the broader plains, the Romans chose to build their roads along the mountain ridges rather than in the narrow, densely forested valleys emphasises the tenuous nature of their control. Their main concern seems to have been the maintenance of strategic lines of communication, such as links between the Thracian plain and the Aegean. This must have necessitated chains of road forts, few of which have been located and none excavated.

The epithet 'Ulpia' shows that Nicopolis-ad-Nestum (the village of Zagrade, near Gotse Delchev) was another of Trajan's foundations. Situated very near the river Mesta, the ancient Nestos, it controlled two highways. One came via Drama from the Via Egnatia and the Aegean coast and continued north; the other, coming from the Struma valley, crossed the Pirin range near the modern Greco-Bulgarian border and continued north-east to Philippopolis. The northern terminus of the Mesta road was probably met by another route, which crossed the Pirin from near Blagoevgrad and thence onwards to Philippopolis.

Nicopolis-ad-Nestum has still to be studied. Until recently the substantial ruins seen by many nineteenth-century travellers were a local quarry. Chance finds of votive tablets and inscriptions demonstrate the worship of Artemis, Zeus and Hera, Dionysos, and the Thracian Horseman, a general pattern not dissimilar from that of the middle Struma valley. In spite of the relative nearness of the Roman colony at Philippi, the surviving inscriptions, all in Greek, contain only one Roman name. It was the centre of an area rich in minerals, including gold, silver, and iron ore, and mining galleries of the Hellenistic period almost certainly continued in use.

That remoteness was not total isolation is shown by a hoard of silver coins – from Nerva to Decius – at Kochan in the upper Mesta valley. Its burial was no doubt due to the invasion of a Gothic group, a similar hoard being found at Velingrad. Nicopolis may have been damaged during these Gothic raids, being too remote for help to reach it in time. Certainly the road to Philippopolis was repaired under Constantine and again under Theodosius I. It grew in strategic importance as the insecurity of the Thracian plain increased.

NOTES

1 Ivanov, T. and Bobchev, S., *Serdika I*, 1964, 17 ff.
2 Karasimeonov, P., *GNM* VII, 1942, 189 ff.
3 Ivanov and Bobchev, op. cit., 33 ff.
4 Venedikov, I. and Petrov, T., *Serdika I*, 1964, 77 ff.
5 Velkov, I., *IBAI* I, 1921–22, 20 ff.
6 *IGB* IV, 2057.
7 *IGB* IV, 2074.
8 Ivanov, I., *IBAD* VII, 1919–20, 73.
9 *IGB* IV, 2236.
10 *IGB* IV, 2270.
11 Gerov, B., *Prouchvaniya*, 51, n. 3.
12 Dechev, D., *IBAI* XIII, 1939, 190 ff.

8 The Thracian Plain (1)

Philippopolis

When the Romans annexed Thracia, Philippopolis (Plovdiv) still occupied the site of Philip II's chief centre in Thrace, the ridge of three closely grouped hills, Nebet-tepe, Djambaz-tepe, and Taksim-tepe, overlooking the river Maritsa. The Hellenistic walls surrounding it were repaired, for it was a ready-made strongpoint commanding one of the peninsula's main road junctions. The Romans renamed it Trimontium, but Philippopolis remained, like the Greek language, in general use. A degree of autonomy was also retained and under Domitian the city began to issue coins.

One of the earliest finds from the Roman period is a 'head-mask' from a mid-first-century Thracian tumulus (Pl. 118). Compared with the probably later helmet-masks from Durostorum (Pl. 88) and Chatalka (Pl. 139), this represents a different tradition. The face is of beaten silver and less idealised than the others. The rest of the head, worked to represent hair, not a helmet, is iron, with a silver laurel wreath.

Trajan's promotion of a city-based economy in Thrace, vigorously pursued by his successors during the next 100 years, caused the city to grow in importance and to expand far beyond the immediate vicinity of the 'Trimontium'. But the Costoboki invasion of 170 sent tremors through the *pax Romana* and its attendant prosperity. A new wall enclosing a far greater area was constructed in the reign of Marcus Aurelius; a bilingual inscription[1], probably placed above the new east gate of the road to Hadrianopolis, commemorated it.

The line of this wall lies under buildings and streets, and has been hard to trace. D. Tsonchev first established the presence of a wall outside the original 'Trimontium' fortifications in the shape of an irregular polygon. East and south, the line was based on excavation; on the north-west it was largely hypothetical (Fig. 41). The short south-west stretch taking in the Sahat-tepe hill appears on a coin of Marcus Aurelius minted in Philippopolis and is further supported by the existence of a third- to fourth-century cemetery just outside. Examination of different sectors resulted in various datings, but apparent inconsistencies seem to have been resolved by the recent excavation of parts of a 250-metre stretch of undeniably second-century wall, similar to the north-east sector and the east gate, much farther south than Tsonchev's line, which clearly represented a contraction of the city after the disastrous invasions of the fifth century. Accepting Tsonchev's hypothetical north-west line, the walls of Marcus Aurelius comprised a circuit of almost $3\frac{1}{2}$ kilometres, enclosing 78 or 79 hectares. This is about five times the contemporary fortified area of Serdica and impressive evidence of the city's wealth and importance.

The foundations of the second-century south wall consisted of roughly shaped stones of medium size, mortared together, supporting a wall 2·10 metres thick. The outer face of a section $2\frac{1}{2}$ metres high had three rows of rusticated ashlar, up to $2\frac{1}{2}$ metres long, clamped together and laid as 'headers' at irregular

PLATE 118 Philippopolis, head-mask, *ht*. 30 cm.

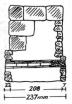

FIG. 40 Philippopolis, 2nd-century south wall: outer face and section

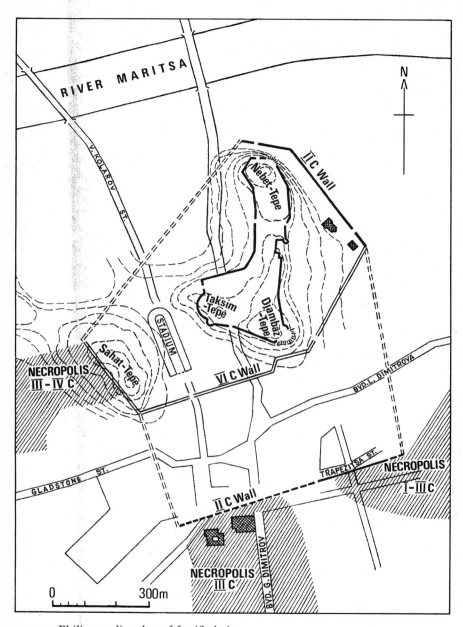

FIG. 41 Philippopolis, plan of fortified city

intervals (Fig. 40). The inner face consisted of rows of smaller roughly cut stones; between was a rubble and mortar filling. No towers were found.

The fortification of Philippopolis by Marcus Aurelius may have been a precautionary measure and not due to Costoboki destruction. In any event, soon afterwards the city reached a peak of prosperity under Septimius Severus, who conferred on it the title of *metropolis* in 196 and revisited it in 202. A coin of the former date, showing Dionysos enthroned in an aedicula, suggests the erection of a temple to the god, an hypothesis supported by several votive plaques found to the south of the 'Trimontium'. Caracalla was also specially honoured: Apollo was the city's patron and there were Pythian games for this emperor's visit in 214, when a special issue gave him the title of Alexander, thus equating him with the great conqueror. Four years later, a visit by Elagabalus, who awarded the city the honorific title of *neokoros*, or guardian of the imperial cult, was again the occasion for special games.

This prosperity was not to last. In A.D. 250, having failed before Novae and Nicopolis-ad-Istrum, the invading Goths crossed the Stara Planina, defeating on their way a Roman army led by Decius. After a siege, Philippopolis surrendered, probably through treachery from within, and for the first time the Goths obtained unrestricted possession of a wealthy city. The booty was immense; the victims, whether slaughtered or enslaved, were said to number a hundred thousand, no doubt an exaggeration but implying a substantial proportion of the inhabitants. Returning home, the Goths defeated and slew Decius outside Abritus (p. 157) and were then allowed to recross the Danube with their captives and other loot.

For some 15 years, although the pickings must have been small, Philippopolis lay open to raids. The last attack, in 267, was followed by repairs to the defences by Gallienus, commemorated in inscriptions as the city's protector and benefactor. The second-century circuit of walls seems to have been retained. Economic recovery was gradual, but the chief city of Thracia could not be allowed to decay. Diocletian stayed in the city in 293 and 295. His administrative reorganisation made it the capital of the new diocese of Thracia as well as of the smaller province bearing the same name. In the first half of the fourth century it was well on the way to regaining its earlier importance and affluence. An historical illustration is the part played by Philippopolis in relation to the Council of Serdica in 343, at which time the city's bishop, Euthymius, was an Arian. Here some 80 Eastern opponents of Athanasius met prior to the Council to organise their opposition, and again afterwards.

Some 20 years later, Philippopolis took an independent line and was a prominent supporter of Procopius, a kinsman of Julian, against Valens, refusing to admit the latter's general into the city. Although, after the defeat of Procopius, Philippopolis was retaken, punished, and garrisoned with troops picked by Valens, this last measure probably helped to preserve it in the wars that followed – ironically so, since Procopius' revolt had also been backed by the Visigoths and their heavy losses led on to the later struggle in which Valens was killed and so much of the land laid waste (Pl. 119).

Opportunities for excavation in Philippopolis have been minimal and only very recently has the forum been located. Inside the second-century walls, one important building was the stadium, built in the first half of the second century

PLATE 119 Head of Valens, lifesize

PLATE 120 Philippopolis, coin, temple of Apollo
FIG. 42 Philippopolis, medallion: temple of Apollo

as part of the city's extensive development under Hadrian to replace an earlier, more modest structure. Measuring overall 250 by 70 metres, the site – now hidden under modern Plovdiv and roughly aligned with Vasil Kolarov street – was between Taksim-tepe and Sahat-tepe, enabling the slopes of both hills to be used for seating some 25,000 to 30,000 spectators. The entrance, at the southern end, was an ornate two-storeyed edifice with Corinthian marble columns, aediculae, and five arched doorways between piers with relief herms. Curved architraves carried the common Roman motifs of bucrania linked by garlands and interspersed with masks and rosettes.

South of the stadium remains of public baths have been partially excavated. The original second-century building was adorned with marble and with floor mosaics; it may have suffered in the mid-third-century sack, for a new and larger baths complex was built early in the fourth century, its floor level only 60 centimetres above the old one. Nine rooms at the second level were excavated. The plan followed the usual Roman pattern; the decoration was probably very rich, judging by the many shades and colours of glass tesserae from wall mosaics, as well as by the natural colours of the stone floor mosaics, laid in formal geometric and vegetal patterns. This second phase did not outlast the fourth century. Another baths, also with wall mosaic but mainly with marble revetment, was found near the foot of Djambaz-tepe. Its first phase was contemporary with the rebuilding of the baths near the stadium, but it was to survive for a much longer period.

On Djambaz-tepe, behind the Hellenistic gateway in the double wall linked by a narrow corridor (p. 83; Fig. 9), remains of a monumental and richly sculptured portico were found, dated to the latter part of the second century.

PLATE 121 Philippopolis, section of frieze, *ht.* 1·08 m.

The stylobate of the outer colonnade bore columns with marble Corinthian capitals and a carved architrave. Behind this, another stylobate carried pilasters attached to an unexplored building with two entrances, the main one roughly corresponding to the axis of the vaulted corridor.

The city's main temple of Apollo was outside the walls, on another of Philippopolis' hills, Djendem-tepe. A coin of Caracalla shows its wooded slopes, a temple at the foot, half-way up a statue of Apollo standing naked on a column, holding a bow and a patera, and on the summit the temple. Beneath its pediment, between four columns, stood a similar statue of the god and at the side of the temple one of the Thracian Horseman stood on a pedestal. Another building with four columns was at a slightly lower level (Pl. 120). Medallions commemorating the visit of Elagabalus show both the temple and cult statue (Fig. 42) and the emperor and Apollo together holding the model of a temple – seemingly a different one – thus signifying the association of the Apollonian and imperial cults. A statue of Elagabalus was found in the ruins of the Djendem-tepe temple, which was destroyed under Christianity and replaced by a church.

The cult of Asklepios was only less widespread than that of Apollo, both being often identified with the Thracian Horseman. An Asklepieion is the probable origin of a marble frieze showing, in high relief, eight health deities. From left to right are Iaso, goddess of health – her name today the popular Greek word of greeting – Panacea, daughter of Asklepios, the small hooded Telesphoros, Asklepios with his serpent-entwined rod, Hygieia, Epione, wife of Asklepios, and, finally, his sons, Mahaon and Podaleirios, doctors to the Greeks in the Trojan war (Pl. 121). On stylistic and iconographic grounds the frieze is dated to the first half of the third century.

Worship of Zeus is also well attested but, judging from finds, Artemis-Bendis

PLATE 122 Philippopolis, stele

had a comparatively small following. The Thracian Horseman represents the
Hero himself as well as Apollo and Asklepios; a sanctuary to him was found on
top of the great prehistoric tell of Yasa-tepe. A second-century stele, a chance
find in Plovdiv, depicting a funerary feast in which the Roman spirit has effectively ousted the Greek, has a Pegasus in each of its stylised acroteria and two
Horsemen in a lower zone (Pl. 122). In the early fourth century a painting of the
funerary feast – again with six figures – was used to decorate a tomb outside the
city's southern wall.

The streets and houses of Roman Philippopolis are almost unknown, but south
of the city wall, a rescue dig in 1960 uncovered parts of one north–south and
three east–west streets with drains under the irregularly shaped flagstones. Six

rooms of a large house on the widest street were excavated (in the area now the garden restaurant of the Hotel Trimontium). In spite of massive stone foundations over 2 metres deep, possibly part of some earlier, more solid structure, the building was relatively flimsy, with a wooden framework containing lath and plaster or mud bricks. In another house was a peristyled courtyard with wooden columns on stone bases. Coin finds date this extramural quarter from the late first century to half-way through the third, when it was destroyed by the Goths.

The residential district of Philippopolis stretched some way beyond Marcus Aurelius' walls into the flat land between the city's outlying hills. Only to the north was the land useless, due to the marshes and flood waters of the Maritsa. Beyond the suburbs, south-west, south, and south-east, were the three main Roman necropolises, the earliest graves found being to the south, near the road to Kuklen, where one of the city aqueducts began. Many tombs, usually brick-built but sometimes ashlar joined with iron cramps, are dated by coins to the reigns of Antoninus Pius and Marcus Aurelius. Towards the end of the Antonine period tiles began to be used to cover the inhumation burials.

Although there are written indications that Hellenised or Romanised Thracians continued to play a part in the life of the city, archaeological evidence is lacking, except in the cults and in the tumuli. North of the Maritsa, the neighbourhood of the domed fourth-century Hellenistic tomb (p. 81) continued in use as a Thracian necropolis in the early Roman period. Two tumuli with incineration burials have been dated to the second or early third century A.D. Thracian tumuli of the Roman period were also found in the old south necropolis on the Kuklen road.

The Gothic sack no doubt included wholesale tomb robbery, for which there was ample time before the city fell. At the same time the suburbs outside the walls, including the one partly excavated, were razed. Depopulation and shock left neither immediate need nor resources for rebuilding. The ruins, within easy reach of the walls, became an obvious place to bury the dead. For about a century after the sack the main areas in use appear to have been just outside the south wall and on the western slopes of Sahat-tepe.

Peroushtitsa and Kurtovo Konare

In the fertile countryside, the larger settlements were generally either road stations, sometimes also serving as emporia, or Thracian villages mainly subsisting on agriculture. Except for fragments of defence walls many times rebuilt, the chief remains are often of sanctuaries, more solidly constructed than the houses and even after destruction more likely to leave recognisable traces of their original purpose.

Peroushtitsa, 15 kilometres south-west of Philippopolis, was evidently a wealthy and Hellenised site of the first category. A life-size polished marble head of a young man, dated to the first half of the third century, is one of the finer examples found in the Thracian plain (Pl. 123). A hole drilled in the hair above the forehead is for the attachment of a chaplet. Near the ruins of the 'Red Church' is a great spring, and close by were found votive tablets to the Thracian Horseman, Cybele, Hera, the Dioskouri, and the Greek gods. There were also marble statuettes of Asklepios, Hygieia, and Telesphoros and fragments of statues. The evidence here suggests a rich community and an appropriately

PLATE 123 Peroushtitsa, head, *ht.* 26 cm.　　PLATE 124 Kurtovo Konare, Mithraic relief, *ht.* 51 cm.

elaborate sanctuary. The general prosperity of the neighbourhood is endorsed by the find at Kurtovo Konare, some 6 kilometres distant, of an intricately carved marble Mithraic relief (Pl. 124), perhaps set up by a Bessi veteran.

Burdapa and Batkoun

The excavation of two shrines farther up the Maritsa proved especially rewarding. The first, on the left bank of the river near the village of Ognyanovo (formerly Saladinovo), some 30 kilometres from Plovdiv and 10 kilometres from Pazardjik, is identified by inscriptions as the nymphaeum of the vicus of Burdapa and dated to the second–third century. Excavated in 1896, two parallel walls about 6 metres long were found, no doubt the long walls of the usual rectangular structure. There was no architectural decoration, but V. Dobrusky found 95 small votive relief tablets depicting the Three Nymphs; there were also a few fragments dedicated to the Thracian Horseman and one inscription suggesting an identification with Bendis-Artemis. Many little clay lamps and toilet articles were also found. The few coins were mainly from local mints of the third century.

The nymphaea which are known to have been associated with springs and the baths of cities in Bulgaria have not yet been fully studied. Thus the cult of the Nymphs, here widespread, is chiefly known through small votive tablets. Invariably a trio, the Nymphs are sometimes associated with other deities, and are carved from local stone with varying skill. Often they appear by themselves, generally in three iconographical versions. In one, standing side by side, each is decorously dressed in a long chiton. In another, the three are quite naked, except possibly for a headdress; the central Nymph, her arms embracing her companions – although a hand reaches towards a round object held by one – presents her back, although twisting her head to look over her shoulder. The third Nymph usually holds a mirror in her hand. Water gushes from two urns in the

PLATE 125 Burdapa, Three Nymphs, plaque, *ht.* 24 cm.

PLATE 126 Batkoun, statuette fragment, *ht.* 22 cm.

lower corners (Pl. 125). In the third and least common version, the Nymphs, naked and presented frontally, perform a spirited dance, whirling scarves over their heads. All three types are represented at Burdapa.

The other sanctuary, some 15 kilometres farther west by a spring near the village of Batkoun, was a second- to fourth-century Asklepieion, with nearly 200 Greek and few Latin inscriptions, chiefly on altars and relief tablets of Asklepios – shown alone or with Hygieia and Telesphoros – and sometimes identified with the Thracian Horseman. Statues, statuettes, and tablets without inscriptions numbered over 100. In contrast to many local reliefs, the marble torso of a statuette (Pl. 126) assigned to the second century may well have been imported; the splendid plasticity of the folds of the himation emphasises the smooth body and makes full use of the fine marble. A small head of Asklepios is ascribed to the following century. Carved in a coarser-grained marble, this may be local work, although the masterly combination of dignified repose in the features with the animation in the slightly concave pupils of the eyes shows a master's hand. Whilst Burdapa is purely local and Thracian, Batkoun reflects a wider world.

II. HISSAR

Hissar, 40 kilometres north of Plovdiv, possesses the best-preserved Early Byzantine walls in Bulgaria, yet strangely little is known of its early history. In the Roman period it seems primarily to have been a health resort for the wealthier inhabitants of Philippopolis, but although the mineral springs which have made the present town a leading Bulgarian spa were used in the Hellenistic period, there is no archaeological evidence to connect it with the nearby princely necropolis of Douvanli. No identifying inscriptions have been found, and the historical sources offer a choice of possibilities – Augustae, Sevastopolis, and

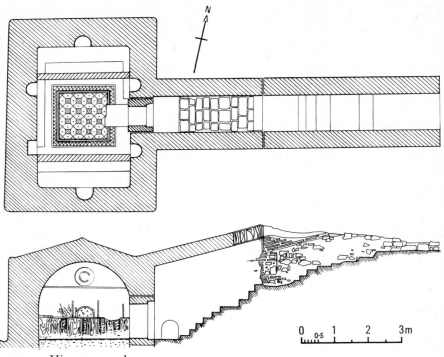

FIG. 43 Hissar, mausoleum

Diocletianopolis. There is considerable evidence to support the last, but this still leaves the earlier name unknown and it is generally called by the Turkish and Bulgarian name of Hissar, meaning fortress.

There has been little excavation of the first phase of the city walls, which seem to have provided the foundations for those visible today. They enclosed a roughly quadrilateral area of about 30 hectares, protected on the east, west, and south by streams, their banks steep and beds quite wide. Only on the north was access easy; this was defended, perhaps from an early period, by a double wall, and by a ditch which also enclosed the east and part of the south walls (Fig. 86). The earlier gates and towers that have been located were often at approximately the same sites as the later ones, the towers being square and projecting externally from the walls. Opinions differ whether these walls were built about the end of the second century, destroyed by the Goths who sacked Philippopolis in 250, and rebuilt with some modifications towards the end of the century – or whether they were built soon after the Goths had demonstrated the vulnerability of a hitherto peaceful area. Pending fuller excavation, the later date for the original construction seems more probable and would also accord with the name of Diocletianopolis. There is general agreement that the walls were badly damaged by the Visigoths in the third quarter of the fourth century.

Excavation of two baths, one in the western half of the walled city, the other beyond the east wall in the locality known as Momina Banya, has also been limited since both are in use today. A Turkish establishment covers part of the former, but excavation in the 1930s suggests there was a complex on customary Roman lines, including two large stepped pools and two small ones, apparently for individual treatment. The complex occupied an area about 45 metres long and 35 metres wide. The opus mixtum construction, revetted with marble, was dated to the second half of the fourth century. Water was piped from a spring outside the west gate, but in the hot mineral springs above which the baths were built and which heated its rooms, coins were found ranging from Philip II of Macedon to Valens. Visigothic destruction is thus probable; some clumsy repairs were impossible to date. Fourteen votive tablets to the Three Nymphs were built into the wall of a nymphaeum – and chance finds elsewhere in the town testify to the cult of Asklepios, Hygieia, and Telesphoros.

There has been even less opportunity to examine the Roman remains at the Momina Banya. They are thought to have been similar to, although rather smaller than, those inside the walls. A building inscription of about 303 mentioning the Tetrarchy probably refers to the baths, but its exact provenance is unknown.

More evidence of fourth-century prosperity comes from the cemeteries lining the roads outside the walls. Of five identified, none has been systematically excavated, but the largest stretched for about half a kilometre from the south gate. The earliest graves here are ascribed to the third century, but the majority date from the fourth to the sixth. Several brick-vaulted family tombs have been found, but the most interesting is a fourth-century mausoleum about 300 metres south-west of the town. The tomb was entirely underground. There was no trace of a mound. A now partly destroyed dromos, probably originally brick-vaulted, led to a staircase descending to a rectangular vaulted chamber with six niches in the walls and two funerary beds (Fig. 43). Remains of wall painting, including stylised rosettes, are still visible; on one bed is a painted imitation of drapery. The floor of this chamber is paved with a mosaic in two shades of red, black, and white; it has a regular geometric linear pattern enclosed by a wide border, the whole strongly reminiscent of a *kilim*, or non-pile type of rug woven in many parts of the Balkan peninsula as well as the East. The beds are oriented east–west, but the grave was throughly looted centuries ago and it is impossible to say whether it was pagan or Christian.

Hissar is remarkable among Roman towns in Bulgaria in possessing, according to present archaeological evidence – and no other exists – a first real flowering in the fourth century.

III. BEROE – AUGUSTA TRAJANA AND ITS VICINITY

Beroe–Augusta Trajana

East of Philippopolis, at the foot of the Sredna Gora in the north of the Thracian plain, Augusta Trajana (Stara Zagora) replaced Thraco-Hellenistic Beroe. The two sites were so close that both names were used for the Roman city until, in late Antiquity, Augusta Trajana dropped out of use. The new city administered a wide area, extending over the northern slopes of the Stara Planina and south to the east Rhodope foothills. Doubtless Trajan considered it wise for Philippopolis, with its long traditions of autonomy and power, not to enjoy unrivalled supremacy in the Thracian plain.

The virtual destruction of Stara Zagora in the liberation war of 1877–78 uncovered parts of the city wall, originally constructed under Marcus Aurelius in his fortification programme for Thracia. More was found when a theatre was built in 1911 and a plan of the Roman city established which later research has augmented but not substantially changed. Irregular in shape, the walls enclosed an area of 48·5 hectares, thus inferior in size to Philippopolis and Marcianopolis, but much larger than, for instance, Serdica or Nicopolis-ad-Istrum.

The transfer of Nicopolis-ad-Istrum from Thracia to Moesia by Septimius Severus diminished the influence and ultimate prosperity of Beroe–Augusta Trajana, but in the contemporary atmosphere of economic expansion, the immediate impact was probably small. Coins struck in the city between the reigns of Marcus Aurelius and Gallienus circulated all over Thracia and Moesia Inferior until the mid-third-century Gothic invasions. Under Diocletian's administrative reforms, all territory north of the Stara Planina, including the emporium of Discoduratera (p. 151), became part of Moesia Secunda. This territorial loss was partly offset by the increasing importance of the city's site which, however, increased its liability to attacks and, together with the administrative changes, may largely account for the unusual lack of expansion beyond the early walls. Probably another reason was that Beroe–Augusta Trajana owed its wealth more to its vast and fertile territory in the Thracian plain than to any industrial, military, or political prominence; so far as the last is concerned, it was chosen as Pope Liberius' place of exile when, in 355, he refused to excommunicate Athanasius. But, while flimsy ephemeral dwellings must have existed in the early years for those whose status did not permit them to live inside, no permanent expansion was apparently needed for craft, commercial, or other quarters. Instead there seems only to have been an outdoor market for country produce south-west of the walls, where a large paved area was found with a big drainage channel under it but no trace of any superstructure. The scene here must have been very much like the daily or weekly markets of today. Apart from this, in the course of time, cemeteries, not suburbs, bordered the walls, extending in no particular date order towards a ring of Thracian settlements 3 or 4 kilometres away.

The second-century wall was 2·60 metres thick and faced with regular rows of small tufa blocks. Bastions, 1·60 metres square, projected internally at 8-metre intervals. Later, probably during the mid-third-century Gothic danger, the spaces between the bastions were filled in, making the walls 4·20 metres thick. The city did not suffer the fate of Philippopolis, although the territory was devastated and Decius, unexpectedly attacked nearby in 250, was obliged to flee with the survivors of his army to Oescus.

A projecting square tower constructionally linked to the curtain wall was found on the south side in 1911; its sides measured 6·30 metres. A similar one was found 50 metres away in 1950 and two others since. The south gate has been excavated; the site dates from the building of the first wall, but the present structure to the Early Byzantine period.

Despite its irregular shape, the city plan followed the usual grid pattern, which remained unchanged from the second to the sixth centuries. The later streets were laid on the earlier ones and made use of the original water-supply. Most of the drainage channels had to be hollowed laboriously out of the rock on which Augusta Trajana was built and had their exits through vaulted openings in the curtain wall. The water came from springs north of the city and, apparently dispensing with any central storage point, reached the citizens' individual clay pipes from the street mains simply by force of gravity.

The earliest streets were carefully paved with large, irregularly shaped flag-stones. The cardo maximus had a pavement of long narrow slabs on either side, as did another street, 6·20 metres wide, which may have been the decumanus maximus. Chances to excavate buildings have been limited. Decorative reliefs suggesting a theatre and stylistically dated to the time of Hadrian have been found, but not its site. One street cuts through the remains of a huge unidentified building dating to about the end of the second or early third century. Sculptural fragments include oval marble columns and a large frieze of oak leaves in high relief. Some glass mosaic tesserae were also found.

A rescue operation is gradually uncovering another monumental building covering some 7,000 square metres. The south rooms so far explored have brick hypocausts and this complex, dated by the excavators to the reign of Commodus, may well be the city baths. An amphitheatrical construction, stone paved and with stone benches, backing on to the south wing of the building, is also being excavated.[2] Of the temple to Zeus-Sabazios, restored on the occasion of Septimius Severus' visit in 202, no trace has been found except the first lines of a com-memorative inscription.[3] A Latin inscription from below the present market hall is likewise the only evidence for the construction of an Augustaeum in 223 by legionary veterans.

The Constantinian period, when a statue of the emperor was erected, was one of prosperity. A large, probably residential building (excavated during the construction of the opera house) at the corner of the cardo maximus and the probable decumanus maximus was built in the first half of the fourth century, although later substantially reconstructed (Fig. 98). To the first phase are attributed the outer walls, surviving up to a height of $1\frac{1}{2}$ metres, built of opus mixtum with bonding courses of five layers of bricks, and a fine floor mosaic, carefully laid on a mortared rubble base in an almost square room with sides of about $9\frac{1}{2}$ metres. The tiny tesserae of marble and other stones, tile, and glass, were white, black, grey, yellow, red, blue, brown, and green in a wide variety of shades. Although somewhat damaged by later rubbish pits, the composition is reasonably clear. Four zones surrounded a central field or *emblema*, the first three were purely geometric, the last had octagons with a corded border and a white ground containing different animals, a hare, deer, dog, and so on. The central field was unequally divided into a narrower section with vines enclosing deer and ducks facing a large hydria, and an almost square section in which was a brick-paved octagon. Triangular areas outside the octagon were filled with fishes, ducks, and nereids, and an almost totally destroyed Greek inscription. Opposite the probable main entrance was another mosaic inscription of which only 'Καλος' is left. In an adjoining room the remains of a stove and a handmill suggest that the room with the mosaic floor could have been the dining room; the central octagon no doubt contained a pool or fountain. Excavation of the street at the same level produced coins from Alexander Severus to Constantine. This town house, like the one at Abritus, probably bordered the not yet identified forum and was an official residence, damaged but not destroyed in the fourth-century Visigothic raids.

Starazagorski Mineralni Bani

Besides the baths in the city, yet to be firmly identified, there were others in the rural surroundings of Starazagorski Mineralni Bani some 15 kilometres to the west, where warm mineral springs emerge in a deep cleft of the Sredna Gora's southern slopes (Pl. 127). The baths used today were built in the eighteenth century by the Turks with many of the Roman materials, but the healing attributes of water in the locality have not been confined to the springs. D. Tsonchev writes that a double trough, probably a Thracian or Roman wine-press, hollowed in the rock of the hill above the baths was locally known as late as the 1930s as 'the Virgin's Trough' and, when filled with rainwater, was visited by sick peasants seeking a miraculous cure.

Only a brief note and a plan of the Roman baths have been published. The complex consisted of 12 rooms covering an area of 2,500 square metres (Fig. 44). According to the building inscription published by D. Nikolov[4] (Fig. 45), the baths and adjoining nymphaeum (not yet excavated) were erected about 163 in honour of the Nymphs and for the citizens of Augusta Trajana at the personal expense of Ulpius Hieronymus. Born in Bithynian Nicomedia, he may have

PLATE 127   Starazagorski Mineralni Bani, Roman baths

been one of the immigrants encouraged by Hadrian to promote the urbanisation of Thracia. By the reign of Marcus Aurelius he had made a fortune, achieved the rank of chief priest, and married; his wife, also a Roman citizen, is described as a priestess. It seems clear that the baths and nymphaeum were built for her to preside over and thus achieve promotion, an example of marital co-operation in professional life capable of various interpretations.

The springs were so hot that no artificial heating system was needed. The chief supply point, built above the main spring, was a square vaulted under-ground shaft, the vaults supported by small brick piers; pipes brought cold water from outside. The decoration (much of it mentioned in the inscription) included

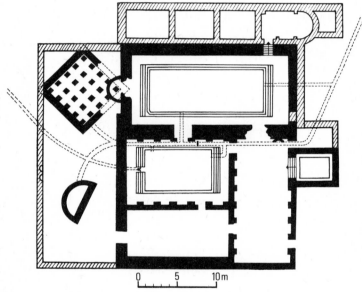

FIG. 44 Starazagorski Mineralni Bani, Roman baths

FIG. 45 Starazagorski Mineralni Bani, building inscription

PLATE 128 Augusta Trajana, head, *ht.* 26 cm.

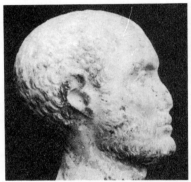

PLATE 129 Augusta Trajana, head, *ht.* 27 cm.

PLATE 130 Augusta Trajana district, head, *ht.* 19 cm.

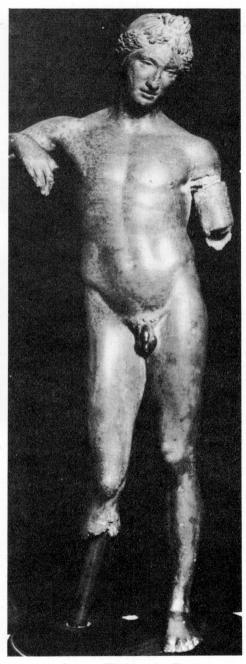

PLATE 131 Augusta Trajana, Apollo, statuette, *ht.* 50·5 cm.

PLATE 132 Augusta Trajana, Thracian Horseman plaque, *ht*. 20 cm.

marble revetment, floor mosaics, statues, and reliefs. Reconstruction was necessary from time to time. A fragment of a dedicatory inscription to Alexander Severus was re-used in the Early Byzantine period. But coins and other finds suggest that, with brief interruptions, the baths remained in use for a thousand years.

The construction of fine public baths so far from the city suggests not only stability but affluence. Although this has not yet been demonstrated architecturally within the walls, it is reflected in sculptural finds. The portrait heads from life-size marble statues (Pls. 128–30), a bronze statuette of Apollo (Pl. 131), and a marble relief of the Thracian Horseman (Pl. 132) illustrate both the standard of art and the population blend in this Hellenised Roman city of Thracia.

Arzus and Pizus

Urban wealth was balanced in the countryside by rich Thracian estates. Finds in the city cemeteries are no richer than those from rural tumuli built by those

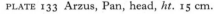

PLATE 133 Arzus, Pan, head, *ht.* 15 cm.   PLATE 134 Trite Mogili, Zeus, statuette
detail (overall *ht.* 17 cm.)

who, no doubt also possessing town houses, drew their wealth chiefly from
agriculture, gloriously symbolised by a head of Pan (Pl. 133) found in the ruins
of Arzus (near Kalugerovo) in the south. Arzus was a station on the 'Diagonal';
12 Roman miles west along the road lay the emporium of Pizus (near Dimi-
trievo), made famous by a long inscription which not only records its foundation
– in 202 – by Septimius Severus but sets out in detail the conditions in which
the new market was established.[5] The names of each of the 171 chosen settlers
and the nine villages from which they were drawn were listed. The terms of
reference of the local administration, its relationship with the officials of Beroe-
Augusta Trajana, and the emporium's special privileges, particularly its immuni-
ties concerning the supply of corn and draught animals and exemptions from
military charges and exactions, were all carefully drawn up and inscribed on a
stone tablet which good fortune has preserved. The potential prosperity of
Pizus makes an interesting contrast with the plight described in the petition of
Scaptopara.

Trite Mogili, Mogilovo, and Krun

Chariot burials provide more archaeological evidence of Thracian rural wealth.
At Trite Mogili, about 4 kilometres north-east of Stara Zagora, the necropolis of
an unexplored settlement from which came a fine bronze statuette of Zeus
(Pl. 134) contains three large tumuli, about 200 metres apart, which gave the
modern village its name. In 1960, between two of the mounds, the skeletons of
ten horses, together with five chariots broken into pieces, were discovered in a
trench 10½ metres long by 5 metres wide and less than 2 metres deep. In spite of
their damaged condition, some idea was gained of the original form of the

PLATE 135 Trite Mogili, chariot reconstruction

chariots. One was two-wheeled, presumably for sport or war. The others were
four-wheeled, one at least of the simple cart type still sometimes used in rural
areas. The metal parts of a four-wheeled travelling chariot were found *in situ*
and a reconstruction was attempted (Pl. 135). Both the box of the cart and its
seats had been elaborately decorated with bronze statuettes and silver reliefs of a
variety of Greco-Roman deities and mythological scenes, probably local work.
Yokes and harness were also much adorned and, in all, over a hundred bronze
objects were found. This chariot must have been the 'state coach' of its owner.
The trench contained many bronze and copper vessels, strigils, and a double-
edged, Sarmatian-type sword, objects normally placed near the remains of the
dead, instead of 60 metres from the base of the nearest known tumulus. The
horses' skeletons were of the same size and general type as those of today and
aged between three and seven years. The finds have been only briefly published,

PLATE 136 Mogilovo, Amazon, appliqué, *w.* 21·5 cm.

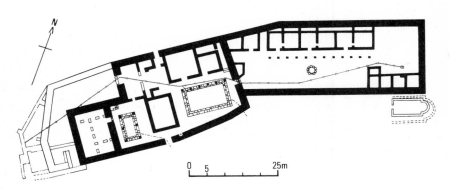

FIG. 46 Chatalka, pars urbana of villa rustica

but the chariots are dated on stylistic grounds, especially of the metal finds, to the latter half of the second century.

Similarly dated are some much finer bronze ornaments from the remains of another, less well-preserved chariot, found at Mogilovo, south-west of the city. These include a striking statuette of an Amazon, no doubt Hippolyta, dying on horseback, probably an imported copy of a statue, and a well-executed bust of Herakles or rather, it is thought, of Commodus with Heraklean traits (Pl. 136).

North of Beroe – Augusta Trajana and of the Thracian plain, inscriptions indicate that the mid-second-century defences included such key points as the main pass over the Stara Planina, the Shipka (Pl. 2). A little way south of the

Shipka road station about 70 fragments of statues and reliefs were found in a walnut grove near the village of Krun – the remains of a sanctuary to the Thracian Horseman and Apollo which was patronised by the garrison as well as the peasantry during the second half of the second century and the beginning of the third. Its monuments had been as systematically destroyed as those at Kopilovtsi, outside Pautalia.

IV. CHATALKA

The villa rustica at Chatalka, 18 kilometres south-west of Stara Zagora, was the estate of a wealthy Thracian. Although the extent of the property is unknown, judging by the various groups of buildings it was quite large and included the sheltered valleys of two streams, the Mogilovska and the Chatalka, descending from the Sredna Gora. The gentle slopes were probably as fertile then as now, covered with vineyards, orchards, and vegetable gardens but destined to be submerged by a hydro-electric project when the extensive salvage dig still in progress has been completed.

The pars urbana, covering an area of 4,500 square metres, occupied the two upper terraces of a small plateau 30 metres above the confluence of the two streams, their steep, almost vertical banks providing natural defences (Fig. 46). The proprietor's living quarters occupied the western sector of the complex, which was enclosed by a 2-metre-thick wall, faced with ashlar, with a rubble and mortar filling. Besides posterns in the north and south walls, a larger gate, wide enough for carts, in a re-entrant at the north-west corner led into a small yard with a little guard lodge.

The accommodation in this sector was divided into two wings, each with its own courtyard containing an ashlar-lined *impluvium*, or pool. The smaller, western courtyard had a peristyle with a stylobate and the remains of six limestone Doric columns (Pl. 137). In a large room beyond were remains of stairs to an upper storey; it has been suggested that these were the women's quarters. Another large room on the opposite side of the courtyard might have been the kitchen, serving both wings. East of it was the second and larger court-yard, constructed like the first but with columns only on the north, perhaps forming a portico in front of the main rooms, which were faced with well-cut,

PLATE 137 Chatalka villa, west courtyard

PLATE 138 Chatalka villa, east courtyard

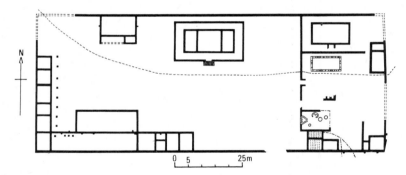

FIG. 47 Chatalka, villa rustica, complex with pottery workshop

rusticated limestone blocks (Pl. 138). Building techniques and materials suggest the villa was built as early as the first century when Hellenistic methods had not yet been superseded. By the south-west corner, beyond the 'women's quarters', many apparently deliberately broken fragments of votive tablets, mostly dedicated to the Thracian Horseman, lay in a destroyed house shrine. There were no indications of a heating system; the owners must either have used simpler forms or passed the winter in the city.

The eastern sector of the pars urbana occupied a slightly lower terrace; here were a small baths, a well, and staff quarters, faced with a wooden colonnade on stone bases. The type of construction was similar, except in the baths, where fired brick was used for the usual *apodyterium*, or dressing room, *frigidarium*, *tepidarium*, and *caldarium*, or room containing the hot bath, the last with a hypocaust and next to the *praefurnium*, or furnace. The lower parts of several dolia for water storage were found.

The pars urbana yielded 230 coins ranging from the first to the fifth centuries, further evidence for a first-century building date. Two Roman phases have been identified, the first lasting until a total destruction, probably by the Goths, in the mid-third century. Rebuilding followed quickly on similar lines, but using more fired brick. This phase lasted until the Visigothic wars.

A few metres west, across a little gully, was a second walled complex, a regular rectangle enclosing an area of 7,500 square metres (Fig. 47). Here, on stone foundations, the superstructure was of wattle and plaster. The smaller, eastern section, occupying about a quarter of the whole, contained a pottery, an open pool, and living accommodation. The pottery had a large workshop with three ditches or pits for emulsifying and purifying clay, two small kilns, and two heated rooms for shaping and drying, next to the praefurnium. Three channels supplied the large amount of water needed. It is estimated that a pottery of this size would have functioned all the year round on a commercial basis, not merely to serve the needs of the estate. The rest of the complex was a large yard lined with stables, other farm buildings, and living quarters for the workmen.

On the right bank of the Mogilovska stream was a separate baths with seven rooms, three with hypocausts, and a vestibule with a geometric-patterned stone mosaic floor. The building technique relates this to the first phase, and the excavator suggests that when the pars urbana acquired its own baths, these were turned over to the staff, but the reverse seems equally likely, given their respective sizes and sites.

A kilometre away, on the left bank of the Chatalka stream, another complex combines flimsy farm buildings with a masonry baths which included three apsed rooms with hypocausts below (Fig. 48). As stones from the villa were used to restore the complex, it is considered part of the Chatalka estate, but the

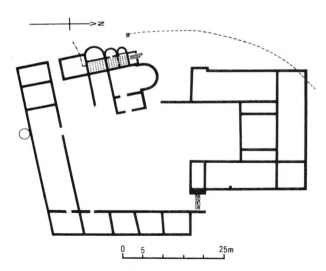

0   5   25m

FIG. 48 Chatalka, outlying building with apsed baths

180 coins here date from the first to the third centuries and it may first have belonged to another landowner who did not survive the Goths.

Seven large tumuli near the pars urbana are proof of Thracian ownership. The closest – and largest – was over 20 metres high with a base diameter of 80 metres. At ground level in the centre of the mound was a large rectangular pit, once roofed with beams, in which a narrow trench contained cremated remains, together with ash, embers, and a large quantity of nuts and almonds. The plan of the tomb is thus very like that of the earlier Arabadjiska tumulus (p. 63), and the many and rich grave finds, not yet fully published, also indicate a female burial. The abundant gold jewellery included a necklace, earrings, finger rings, pendants, and a wreath of oak leaves. The necklace was composed alternately of red bezel-set gems, some of those surviving being engraved with female heads or the figure of Fortuna, and of stout sheet-gold plaques, pierced in the lace-like *opus interrasile* technique. The earrings had granulated ornament on their lower curves and a long hook for insertion into the ear. The jewellery in general is attributable to the first century A.D. Feminine accessories also included combs, a hand mirror, and even what the excavators suggest was pink toilet powder. Various larger objects, including a candelabrum and bronze and clay vessels, stood outside the trench, where was also the imprint of a big wooden chair.

Ten metres above this burial was found a marble chest with another cremation burial, presumably male because of the predominantly warlike nature of the grave goods. These were unfortunately damaged, but most of a Roman bronze helmet-mask has survived (Pl. 139), not unlike that from Durostorum (Pl. 88), but with flowing curls below the helmet. Other parts of the armour are comparable with Sarmatian finds and may have been trophies of warfare in Scythia. Another 10 metres higher, a little below the present surface of the mound, another cremation burial was found. With less rich grave goods than the other, it also belonged to a warrior.

On the basis of imported grave goods from Italy and the Greek East, the female burial has been dated to the mid-first century, the second to its end, and the last to the early second century.

The other tumuli averaged only 10 metres in height; almost all contained single cremation burials of both sexes, dated to the first and second centuries, one perhaps to the early third. By this time large tumuli had ceased to be the custom, probably a result of increasing foreign influence, although the reforms of Septimius Severus also made it less easy to empanel the labour force required.

A more distant cemetery with low tumuli was also partly excavated. This is thought to have been used by the villa servants or the inhabitants of some local dependent settlement.

V. THE EASTERN RHODOPES

Haskovo Mineralni Bani

A tangle of hills and valleys making up the eastern end of the Rhodope mountains slope down to the right bank of the Maritsa as it leaves the Thracian plain. Partly controlled from Beroe-Augusta Trajana and partly from Hadrianopolis, this region, relatively densely populated during the Roman and Early

PLATE 139 Chatalka, helmet-mask, *ht.* 23 cm.

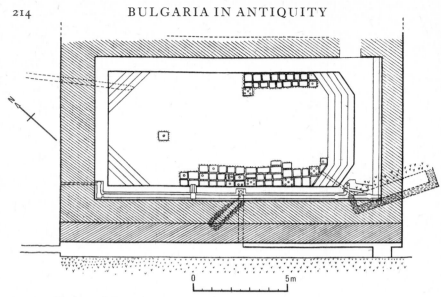

FIG. 49 Haskovo Mineralni Bani, a pool

PLATE 140 Sveti Duh

Byzantine periods, has been little studied. Baths and a hill fort which were part of a settlement have been identified 20 kilometres west of Haskovo on the left bank of the Banska, a tributary of the Maritsa. In a rescue dig in 1936 at the Mineralni Bani of Haskovo, four groups of mineral springs up to 150 metres apart showed signs of Roman use; there were also the remains of buildings, but much destruction had been caused by invaders, road construction, and the building of the modern spa.

One rectangular pool was comparatively well preserved, although the outer buildings were barely visible and excavation was impossible. Brick steps at the south-eastern end and across the north and west corners provided access (Fig. 49). The walls of the 1·40-metre-deep pool were of broken stone faced with ashlar, their very substantial nature suggesting a vaulted roof. Although the walls went down to bedrock, below the floor of the pool a metre-thick porous layer of rubble and mortar blanketed the powerful flow of the hot spring, the temperature of which was lowered by cold water from elsewhere, before being filtered upwards through holes in the floor slabs of the pool. An efficient if primitive form of water tap regulated the cold flow as required. Besides such small objects as bronze fibulae and glass bracelets, many bronze and copper coins dating from the second half of the third century to the early sixth were found in the outflow channel.

A second group of almost completely destroyed rooms probably included a similar pool, but a third was preserved up to $1\frac{1}{2}$ metres high; many fragments were also found of the piping which had brought cold water from the rock fissures. The two adjoining pools in this complex were smaller than the one described above, each about 7 metres long and $4\frac{1}{2}$ metres wide.

A coin of the Thracian vassal-king Rhoemetalkes (11 B.C. to A.D. 12) in the last group of springs is the earliest archaeological evidence of their use although, again mainly on numismatic grounds, the bath complexes are thought to have been built during the second century and the first half of the third. The spring with the Thracian coin may have been part of a nymphaeum for fragments of votive tablets to the Nymphs, Artemis, and Silenus were found in the surrounding ruins.

Sveti Duh

'There is almost no peak or high hill in the Eastern Rhodopes where survey does not reveal the remains of fortifications.'[6] Sited to be visible from one another, the purpose of the fortresses was to protect the 'Diagonal' and other important routes along the Maritsa tributaries. On the hill of Sveti Duh (the Holy Spirit), which rises steeply behind the Haskovo Mineralni Bani, is a fort probably representative of many others, and now in process of excavation. It was one of a chain running from the highest peak in the area, the Aida or Mechkovets, to Dimitrovgrad on the Maritsa. From Sveti Duh it would be easy to signal to the neighbouring forts at Aida and Tatarevo (Pl. 140).

The fortress wall, 2 metres thick, built of large rusticated stone blocks with a filling of broken stone, enclosed an almost circular area nearly 40 metres in diameter on top of the hill. Two stretches of wall, the rampart walk reached by wooden stairs, the holes for which are still visible, and two projecting square towers have been cleared. The curtain wall was prolonged to form one side of an

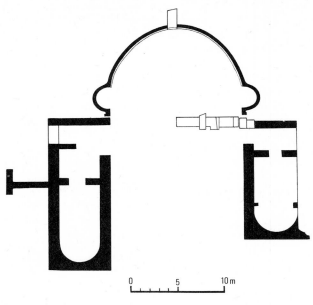

FIG. 50 Kasnakovo, nymphaeum

internally projecting tower, which is about 7·70 metres square inside and contains a layer of debris covered by heaps of roof tiles. This first phase is provisionally dated to the second or early third century. Destroyed by the Goths about 250, the curtain wall was rebuilt soon afterwards, using opus mixtum and red mortar.

Kasnakovo

Not far from Klokotnitsa, above which stands another fort in the same chain as Sveti Duh, are ruins which include a cliff sanctuary near the village of Kasnakovo. They were discovered by peasants at the end of the last century, looking for the source of the excellent spring water which, since it had been named by the Turks 'the well of the unbeliever', they hoped would have some sacred value for themselves, as Bulgarian Christians. On finding the springs, they built a little chapel from stones lying around. Nearly fifty years later archaeological excavation uncovered the pagan sanctuary. It was centred on an apsidal support wall against the cliff from which gushed three springs, one at either end of the curve and the third emerging from a vaulted niche almost in its centre (Fig. 50). On the carefully dressed stone arch framing the vault, a now much deteriorated Greek inscription dedicated the spring to the Nymphs and to Aphrodite from the builders of the nymphaeum, a Romanised Thracian and his wife.[7]

A low stone wall and ceremonial entrance probably joined the ends of the curved wall enclosing the springs. Extending at right-angles on either side were

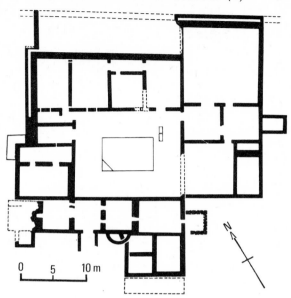

FIG. 51 Armira, pars urbana of villa rustica

two rectangular apsed buildings. The eastern, nearly 18 metres long and 7 metres wide, contained the remains of an ornamental brick cornice and some elaborately carved marble architectural fragments. The western, which was shorter, had the remains of a floor mosaic. Both must have been related to the cult.

The building inscription has been dated to the second century and the buildings, on the basis of the architectural fragments, to the end of the third, the difference being possibly due to successive building phases. The springs continued in use for a long time, the support wall being repaired when necessary with fragments of a marble architrave and other stones from nearby buildings as yet unexcavated.

Armira

Armira, 4 kilometres south-west of Ivailovgrad and named after a small tributary of the Arda, is the site of a large villa rustica. The important city of Hadrianopolis (Edirne, in Turkey) on the 'Diagonal' at the confluence of the Maritsa and Tundja and just beyond that of the Maritsa and Arda, is an easy 40 kilometres away. The villa's rich and essentially urban decoration creates a vivid impression, as unexpected, in its simpler manner, as that given by the imperial villa of Piazza Armerina in Sicily, lost likewise in a sunny sheltered valley.

Excavation here is still continuing. The latest published information gives the area of the pars urbana as 2,200 square metres; what were probably labourers' quarters, ancillary farm buildings, and other work rooms have been traced nearby. The main building stood on land sloping down to the river; it had

PLATE 141 Armira villa, Artemis sur-
prised bathing, mosaic detail

PLATE 142 Armira villa, portrait, mosaic
detail

required levelling. The north walls – the best preserved – were found standing
to a height of up to 1·80 metres; about half a metre thick, they were built of
dressed stone and white mortar. Three building phases were noted, all apparently
within the first 60 years of the second century. The first was relatively modest,
the next two, although single-storeyed, were much larger and more grandiose.
Figure 51 shows the plan of probably most, if not all, of the third phase which,
according to the preliminary reports, added the rooms east of the courtyard to
the structure of the second phase. Over 20 rooms were then arranged round a
large peristyled courtyard, with a central impluvium. Vast quantities of nails
and roof tiles were scattered over the floors and in three of the northern rooms
pieces of window-glass were found. Two praefurnia heated many of the rooms
by means of hypocausts using brick piers and clay pipes or, in some cases,
intra-mural ducts. A double wall had been built along the north-west sides of the
building and along the north side of the large *triclinium*, or dining room, in the
east corner, perhaps partly to prevent subsidence and partly for ventilation.

The courtyard and seven rooms were laid with mosaic, originally covering
an area of 450 square metres of which 260 square metres were found *in situ*.
Heaps of broken marble sculptural decoration lay in most rooms. Walls not
revetted with marble had coloured plaster. The excavator has described the
probable appearance of the courtyard. Stylobates *in situ* showed that the colonnade ran near the edge of the pool and consisted of 14 spirally fluted columns,
one at each corner, three on the longer sides and two on the shorter. Intercolumnar slabs were linked by herms, each wearing a different expression and
one, at least, being Janus-headed. The architrave was carved with acanthus
leaves, Gorgon heads, and Ionic mouldings, and was smoothly polished behind.
The four walls enclosing the courtyard had a pilastered revetment imitating a

colonnade. Their socle was preserved along the whole north side and, in places, the carved base. The pilasters, to be correct pseudo-pilasters, also had profiled bases, vertical fluting, and decorated capitals; 16 capitals were found intact and fragments of another ten. No two are the same, and the motifs, imposed on various types of stylised acanthus, include a lifelike snail, eagles, a bee, a satyr's head, a Gorgon head, and two little dolphins. Between the pilasters were large marble slabs, some incised with geometric or *trompe l'oeil* designs, others with borders of ivy leaves. A few retained traces of red colouring. The floor was laid in an interlacing geometric mosaic pattern, except in the southern part where wide white bands also contained vegetal motifs. One of the east rooms, with similar marble pseudo-pilasters, had the remains of an opus sectile pavement.

The floor mosaics mostly consisted of white and greyish-blue stone tesserae; occasionally more colours were used, but so rarely that the overall effect is hardly changed. The floors remained in use for a long time and many tesserae are very worn. Mosaicists could not have been available for repairs, since marble slabs were used to fill gaps.

One of the north-east rooms has the best-preserved and some of the most interesting mosaics. The floor is divided into three zones, a central square flanked by two rectangles. The larger areas in the central zone contain a series of framed mythological scenes, many concerned with Dionysos or Artemis. The figures are executed in graphic outline, neither portrait-like nor highly stylised, but more in the manner of bold pen and ink drawings (Pl. 141). The smaller areas contain theatrical masks, panthers, female heads, a little bird, an ivy leaf, and so on. At the base of the square is a fine male portrait, assumed to be the owner of the villa (Pl. 142). The smaller, carefully chosen, tesserae portray a noble, gentle face in masterly fashion. It is curiously placed in the upper part of an otherwise empty panel, perhaps designed for an inscription or for a pendant portrait of the wife, for some, perhaps domestic, reason omitted. Panels on either side contain full-length portraits of naked infants, surely his sons. Although the heads are disproportionately large, the figures are realistically and not very sympathetically rendered. One cannot mistake them for *erotes*.

The mosaic floor of the triclinium included a central zone depicting Medusa, surrounded by the four Seasons and the four Winds and by heads of maenads and satyrs. Belonging to the villa's third phase, this mosaic differs in the use of white and red as basic colours and a large number of others for the details. The room had painted walls, of which only tiny multicoloured fragments remained above the marble socle.

The purpose of the other rooms is hard to define. Strangely, pottery, usually the commonest find in houses, was extremely scanty and consisted mainly of coarse third- and fourth-century local ware. Coins, also few, ranged from the second to the fourth centuries. The owners may have had time to remove the more valuable objects, but the scarcity of kitchenware is odd. Perhaps the villa was very thoroughly looted before it was set on fire, and possibly unexcavated servants' quarters may provide a partial answer. Nevertheless, the limited evidence of the pottery and coins, when associated with the signs of wear and tear on the structure, points to continuous peaceful residence over about 250 years. Such conditions, so different from those obtaining farther north, are historically possible. But the Visigothic invasion of 376–82 was accompanied by widespread devastation in the eastern Rhodopes and Ammianus Marcellinus specifically refers to the destruction of villas in the vicinity of Hadrianopolis, after Valens was defeated near the city in 378.[8] Archaeological evidence shows that this villa was gutted by fire and abandoned. For a time parts of the burnt-out skeleton remained standing, to collapse by degrees. Thus some fragments of the marble revetment were found immediately above the mosaic floors; others fell upon an intervening layer of soil.

Provisionally, the first modest structure has been dated to the end of Trajan's reign or the very beginning of Hadrian's. The second was built ten to twenty years later under Hadrian; on stylistic grounds much of the sculpture is assigned to this phase, including the revetment capitals and herms, as well as the mosaic portraits. The third, the north-east wing, followed quickly, as is shown by the identical style of the acanthus leaves of its pseudo-pilasters and those of the peristyle. This, then, would have belonged to the reign of Antoninus Pius.

Pending the completion and full publication of the excavations, this dating seems to accord with the historical background. The growth of Hadrianopolis out of Thracian Uskudama was rapid. The city minted coins until the reign of Gordian and was the chief city of the province of Haemimontus from the reign of Diocletian. There would have been many rich villae rusticae in the environs. The surroundings of the Armira villa have long been vineyards and the only tumulus excavated – with a base diameter of 40 metres but now only $2\frac{1}{4}$ metres high – yielded no relevant evidence, although it stood only 250 metres away at the top of the slope. Perhaps Armira was not, like Chatalka, a Thracian manor, but the private residence or hunting lodge of some high official from Hadrianopolis, a provincial dignitary's version of imperial Piazza Armerina.

NOTES

1 *IGB* III/1, 878.
2 *BASEE* II, 1971, 45.
3 *IGB* III/2, 1588.
4 Nikolov, D., *Arh* X/1, 1968, 43 ff.
5 *IGB* III/2, 1690.
6 Aladjov, D., in *Rodopski Sbornik* II, Sofia, 1969, 252.
7 *IGB* III/2, 1714.
8 Amm. Marc. XXXI, 6, 2.

I. THE SOUTHERN CITIES

Writing in A.D. 9 of his voyage of exile to Tomi (Constanța in Romania), Ovid prays for his ship:

> . . . may she steer her way along the Thynnian bays; and thence impelled past the city of Apollo, may she pass on her course the walls of Anchialos. Thence may she pass the harbours of Mesembria and Odessus and the towers, Bacchus, that are called after thy name.[1]

If the Salmydessian coast with its Thynì inhabitants had not entirely lost its evil reputation, the Greek cities were accommodating themselves to Rome; but although both Apollonia and Mesambria were minting coins again by the time of Trajan, their economy and influence had suffered. In the first centuries of Roman rule, both seem largely to have been bypassed, although it has been suggested that the Hellenistic walls of Mesambria were repaired in the reign of Marcus Aurelius and again soon afterwards.

No doubt to counterbalance Greek influence, Vespasian founded a colony of veterans from Legio VIII Augusta (then at Novae) at Deultum (Debelt) on the eastern north–south road. Although the city prospered, there is little archaeological evidence yet to support its history. Mid-third-century coins of Deultum show a beehive, probably symbolising a main item in a largely agricultural economy, although the safeguarding of the highway from Hadrianopolis to Marcianopolis must have given it and other inland settlements a military and strategic importance, which was to grow when Hadrianopolis became a gateway to the new capital.

The Romans also encouraged the development of Anchialos (Pomorie), hitherto a minor trading station but which was issuing coins under Domitian. Trajan named it Ulpia Anchialos and enlarged the territory under its administrative control. Besides serving to offset the economic power of Mesambria and its founder-city, Apollonia, the considerable salt-beds south of the city must have been an important commercial factor. The baths of Anchialos, Aquae Calidae (Burgaski Mineralni Bani), were on the site of a Thracian village some 20 kilometres inland from the city. Here was a famous sanctuary of the Three Nymphs, in whose honour games were held under Septimius Severus, Caracalla, and Geta, although only a few chance finds, including votive tablets with the same iconography as represented at Burdapa, are known. When Anchialos was captured by the Goths in 270,

> . . . they are said to have stayed for many days, enjoying the baths of hot springs situated about twelve miles from the city . . . There they gush from the depths of their fiery source and among the innumerable hot springs of the world they are particularly famous and efficacious to heal the sick.[2]

Excavation of Anchialos began in 1969. In 1970, the excavator reported the identification of the decumanus maximus, paved with large stone slabs, and

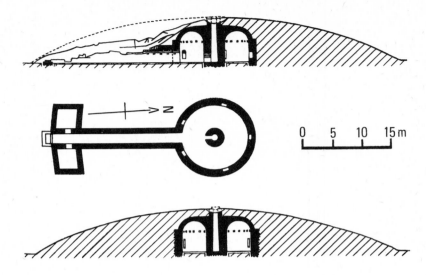

FIG. 52 Anchialos, mausoleum

on its south side the excavation of part of a pentagonal building with a peristyled inner courtyard. An aqueduct had been traced to Bryastovets, some 20 kilometres away to the north-west.[3] As this is one of the few coastal sites not completely overbuilt, excavations may be fruitful. Coins and written sources suggest strong fortifications, and inscriptions are evidence for bronze statues of Caracalla and Alexander Severus. The many and varied types struck almost without interruption during the second century and first part of the third contrast with the few and spasmodic types emanating from Mesambria.

Five kilometres west of Anchialos is its only published archaeological monument, a large, late Thraco-Roman tumulus mausoleum just off the main road from Bourgas to Nesebur (Fig. 52). A 22-metre-long dromos with opus mixtum walls and brick vaulting was flanked at the entrance by two side-chambers, now outside the remains of the mound; but their slightly trapezoid shape was no doubt planned in accordance with its original periphery. The dromos led directly into the circular tomb chamber, a spacious brick-vaulted ring-corridor, its centre a hollow pillar from which spring the inner curves of the vault (Pl. 143). The general proportions and skilful vaulting, in fact, create the impression of a circular domed chamber. The central pillar had two openings – opposite the dromos and at the top. There had been a wooden spiral staircase inside; it is impossible now to determine the relationship between the top of the pillar and that of the mound, but its purpose seems likely to have been ventilation. Five arched niches were arranged symmetrically round the outer wall of the ring-corridor; all varied in width and height.

The tomb is difficult to date. It has been assigned to between the second half of the second century and the end of the fourth,[4] and to the fourth century.[5] As has been seen, large Thracian tumuli persisted until the early third century.

PLATE 143 Anchialos, tomb chamber

Thrace had a tradition of 'false' or corbelled domed tombs with long dromoi, as at Mezek (p. 40) and Kazanluk (p. 98). The brick parallel with the latter springs at once to mind, although it is difficult to sustain. A 'genuine' dome, such as those appearing in Roman mausolea, could not have borne the immense weight of earth forming a rich Thracian's tumulus. Hence the original solution of the central pillar supporting a wide ring-vault that produced the illusion of a domed chamber, probably under quite a low mound. This tomb may represent some imported tradition adopted and adapted by Thracians at Anchialos. Etruscan parallels have been suggested, but to be valid it is necessary to reconcile the wide discrepancy in dates.

Where the Stara Planina meets the sea was the town of Aristaeum (Emona) referred to by Pliny. The trading station of Naulochos (Obzor), 10 kilometres to the north, was renamed Templum Iovis by the Romans. Both these are archaeologically unexplored.

II. ODESSOS AND THE NORTH

For Odessos (Varna), the picture during the Roman period was very different from that of her southern counterparts. Although Trajan's foundation of Marcianopolis was only 23 kilometres away and the junction of almost all the important highways, the two cities proved to be complementary. With the growing

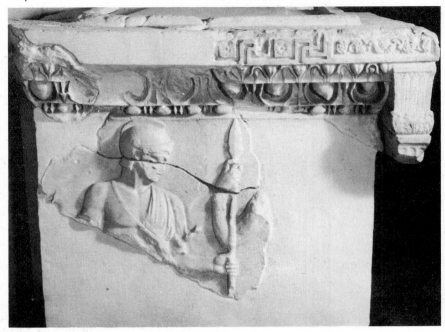

PLATE 144 Odessos, sarcophagus fragment

importance of the lower Danube, the port of Odessos, especially during the
second century and the first half of the third, enjoyed a boom, serving as a main
channel for the Romanisation of the north, while the old links with other Black
Sea cities, especially those to the north, with Asia Minor and the whole Aegean
world, were maintained and intensified. Like all Moesia Inferior, the economy
of Odessos declined sharply with the mid-third-century Gothic invasions, and
the increased emphasis on Marcianopolis as a military centre may well have
curtailed her neighbour's prosperity. The fourth century was probably a period
of relative poverty until the Visigothic invasions brought the value of a northern
port into prominence – the imperial navy's control over the sea-lanes rendering
them safer than the inland road network. The harbour is likely to have been
repaired by Valens, who used it during his military expedition to the lower
Danube.

Sectors of the second-century Roman wall found here and there under
modern Varna bear witness to the increase in the size of the city under Roman
rule. It is estimated that the fortifications enclosed an area of about 43 hectares.
Numerous inscriptions show that a number of the new inhabitants were
Thracian, but many came from Asia Minor. These immigrants were culturally
Hellenised, some were of Hellenic stock, so that Odessos remained essentially a
Greek city, with Romans and Romanised inhabitants in a very small minority.

Part of a sarcophagus slab from the early period ranks among the city's finest
reliefs (Pl. 144). Broken in antiquity and re-used in pieces, its original location
is unknown. The reassembled fragments show that at the top was an intricate

PLATE 145 Odessos, head, *ht.* 31 cm.

carved decoration and that the side slab had an elegant pilaster with acanthus and other vegetal motifs. Of the scene depicted the upper part only of a youth remains. Wearing a sleeveless chiton and helmet, he is accepting a tall spear with his left hand from a figure of whom only a hand and arm remain. The pose is frontal, but the head appears in profile. The scene is interpreted as a detail of the hiding of Achilles on Skyros. There is little doubt that the sarcophagus was imported, either from Asia Minor or, as has recently been suggested by analogy with one found in Athens, from Attica.[6] Stylistically dated to the first half of the second century, it is an eloquent reminder of the continuing Hellenism of the city.

    But Roman art and architecture also made their contribution to the city's cultural history. An example is the beautiful second-century head (Pl. 145) of a young woman. Proud yet gentle, the modelling of the face is still impressive,

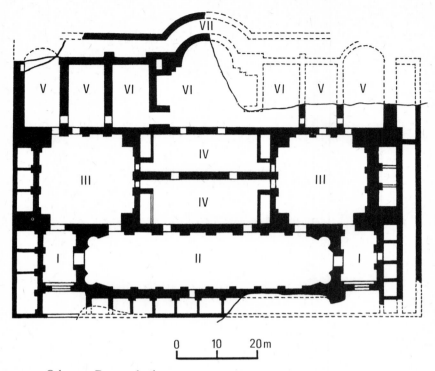

FIG. 53 Odessos, Roman baths

despite damage to nose and chin. And the major excavated archaeological site of any period is a large, luxurious Roman baths, the best preserved yet found in Bulgaria.

The complex occupied about 7,000 square metres. In the centre of the modern city, part of the site is still built on, but the work accomplished and the typical Roman arrangement have enabled the excavator to reconstruct the plan of the whole (Fig. 53). A general division into two symmetrical parts perhaps provided for the separation of men and women, but intercommunicating doors made the complex a single unit.

The walls survive to a height of from $2\frac{1}{2}$ to 18 metres and are from 1·60 to 2·40 metres thick (Pl. 146). Well-cut stone usually alternates with bands of brick, but some walls are built entirely of brick, as well as all apses, niches, and pilasters. Parts at least of all the brick doorways survive, many still retaining their monolithic ashlar jambs and lintels supported by a brick framework (Pl. 147). Large quantities of white marble fragments show that the walls of rooms and pools were revetted with marble slabs; floors were marble and the *apodyteria* floors probably had large central areas of *opus Alexandrinum*. Capitals, architraves, and statue-pilasters were also part of the rich interior decoration.

Two monumental entrances on the north led in each case to a *vestibulum* (I) with access to a spacious *palaestra* (II) between them, used for athletic

PLATE 146 Odessos, Roman baths

PLATE 147 Odessos baths, tepidarium doorways

PLATE 148 Odessos baths, hypocausts

exercises, sports, recitations, lectures, or as a general meeting-place. Each *vestibulum* also led to a large square *apodyterium* (III). In the north-west corner of the western *apodyterium* one of the massive square piers which supported the roof still stands to a height of 18 metres. The roof, vaulted and perhaps in places domed, was of light tufa blocks.

Each *apodyterium* had a wide entrance to the *palaestra* and two much narrower ones to the two *frigidaria* (IV), parallel rooms with *piscinae* at either end. The warm rooms were in a row on the south side. First, entered from an *apodyterium* were – at either end of the building – what were probably two *tepidaria* (V), not completely excavated, then a central tripartite *caldarium* (VI). Along its sides were additional thick brick walls, no doubt to retain the heat, their wings and the apse forming perhaps a *sudatorium,* or sweating room. From the north of the *caldarium* were two entrances to the south *frigidaria*. A vaulted gallery ran along the whole south wall, enclosing the *praefurnium* – usually underground, but here, owing to the uneven terrain, almost at ground level.

The praefurnium linked all the hypocaust systems below the floors of the warm rooms, which were also heated by hot air rising up ducts in the walls behind the marble revetment. Below the suspensura the hypocaust installation consisted of vertical clay pipes half a metre apart, with little columns of square bricks round the walls (Pl. 148). Wide vaulted passages circulated warm air from room to room, under the thresholds or the partition walls.

The drainage system is well preserved, a symmetrical arrangement of vaulted channels with a total length of some 300 metres. The channels were either contrived within or close by the foundations, but, where necessary, free-standing constructions intersected the substructure of the halls to drain away the large quantities of dirty water produced by such an installation.

The baths were built on the ruins of earlier buildings – the depth of the foundations has not yet been established. Coins from the drains date from the reign of Antoninus Pius up to and including that of Claudius II. It is thus likely that the baths were built soon after the middle of the second century, a period which coincides with the construction in 157 by the then legate for Moesia Inferior of a new aqueduct to meet the needs of the expanding population. An altar dedicated by the same legate was found with other material relating to the worship of Asklepios and Hygieia, in the north-western corner of the baths, suggesting a nearby and probably associated Asklepieion. Asklepios and Hygieia are only known on coins of Odessos in the reign of Gordian III when, according to the evidence of the drains, the baths were still in use. Other finds briefly reported include many coins from the period after the reign of Constantine, together with pottery, lamps, and other everyday objects of the fourth century and later, so it is not possible to say when the baths were abandoned. Probably disuse and decay came gradually after the Gothic invasions. Later, little houses were built inside or round the walls, profiting from their solid construction. These may have collapsed gradually or as the result of a calamity, such as the violent earthquake of 544 when, according to Theophanes, the sea rushed in over 4 miles of land. In the course of centuries the mass of debris grew and was covered, except for the two 'Roman towers', by the later city.

Even though the baths continued to be in use during and possibly after the fourth century, they probably came to be superseded by a recently identified much smaller and simpler complex. Below it were the ruins of the Hellenistic and Roman sanctuary of the Thracian Horseman.

No other buildings have been excavated or even securely located. Temples must have been numerous and rich. Pre-Roman cults continued. The Thracian Horseman and the funerary feast are frequently represented on stelai (Pl. 149). By 1964 the number of the latter in the Varna Museum had reached 115 and many more have since been found. Their chronological development between the second and fourth centuries is, as a rule, easily traced in the hair and features of the persons depicted, which follow imperial styles.[7] Inscriptions and coins show that games were held in honour of the Great God, now usually known as 'Darzalas'. Between the reigns of Trajan and Gordian III he or the cult statue in his temple are represented on almost all coins of Odessos, although Roman cults, such as that of Concordia, whose temple also appears on a coin of Gordian, were introduced too. After the reign of Septimius Severus, the growing influence of the settlers from Asia Minor was reflected in the appearance of Cybele, as well as by the syncretisation of Darzalas with Serapis, iconographically apparent on the coins.

At first the city continued to use the old Hellenistic necropolis along the road to Dionysopolis. With the building of the new fortress wall to the south and

PLATE 149 Odessos, Funerary Feast stele, *ht.* 95 cm.

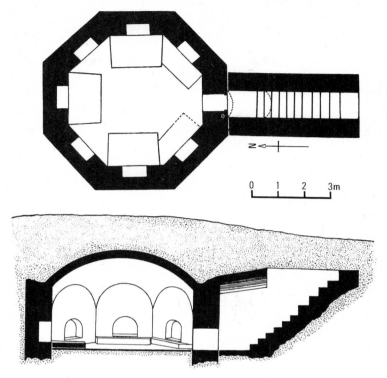

FIG. 54 Odessos, octagonal tomb

west about the middle of the second century, another cemetery grew up along the road to Marcianopolis, and burials were made here until the late fourth century. An interesting monumental tomb near the fortress wall in the older necropolis is dated by situation and skilful construction techniques to the end of the second or beginning of the third century. Cleared by early looters, it is a large underground octagon, approached by a stone staircase and a small barrel-vaulted passage with a tiny opening (Fig. 54). The tomb chamber is oriented north–south and has a domed roof. The walls, of well-cut limestone blocks, bound by red mortar, rise to semicircular curves which, with intervening brick pendentives, support a flat brick dome. In each wall – except the one with the entrance – is a brick-arched niche. There were three podia-beds by the north, east, and west walls and two smaller ones, obviously later, on either side of the entrance.

Another kind of vaulted underground tomb was found about 3 kilometres north-west of the city. Again oriented north–south, it was almost cubical, the dimensions just under 3 metres. Ten steps approached it. The arched walls, of carefully smoothed limestone blocks bound with red mortar, supported the brick-vaulted ceiling, basically cross-groined, except that the centre was occupied by a regular domed apex measuring only 70 by 80 centimetres, in which vertically

PLATE 150 Odessos, balsamarium, *ht.* 9 cm.

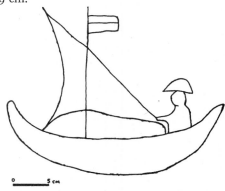

FIG. 55 Odessos, brickwork imitation of dome

FIG. 56 Odessos, tomb graffito

placed tiles were arranged diagonally across the angles (Fig. 55), an interesting attempt to create the illusion of a dome on a square base without either pendentives or squinches. The careful construction and nearby finds – though the tomb was empty – date it to the end of the third century. On either side of the entrance rough graffiti incised in still damp mortar depict an anchor and a sailor sailing his boat, pennant flying from the mast (Fig. 56).

Some scattered graves near the city reflect the culture of partly or almost wholly Hellenised Thracians. On a natural ridge near the 'Vladislas Varnenchik' tumulus three graves were found, one containing a coin of Hadrian. In this small family plot, although all were coffin burials, one was by cremation and the others by inhumation, showing the co-existence of both rites towards the middle of the second century. One burial, with Charon's obol in the shape of a coin of Antoninus Pius, contained, among strigils and clay, glass and other bronze objects, a fine example of a *balsamarium*. This last was probably an import from Alexandria or Asia Minor. Balsamaria were in common use during the first to third centuries, but, as they were used for aromatic substances, they often represented the native inhabitants of the southern or eastern lands from which the spices came or were believed to come, as in the case of a moving portrayal of a young negress which was a chance find in Odessos (Pl. 150).

Finds along the coast, both north and south of Odessos, confirm the continuance of the amicable relationship between Greek and Thracian communities. At Galata, the Hellenistic sanctuary of the Thracian Horseman continued to flourish and a nearby tumulus, $2\frac{1}{2}$ metres high today with a diameter of about 25 metres, contained a single central burial with grave goods including coins of Hadrian and Lucilla. North of Odessos, its fellow Greek colony Dionysopolis, although still remaining of secondary importance, probably shared in the prosperity of its neighbour. Remains of a recently found two-wheeled chariot with the skeletons of three horses (one a saddle horse) from a nearby tumulus are on view in the local museum, but not yet published.

Although the Black Sea colonies survived under Roman rule and Anchialos and Odessos are known to have prospered, their renaissance belongs to the Early Byzantine period.

NOTES

1 Ovid, *Tristia* bk. I,x, trans. Riley, H. T., *The Fasti, Tristia, Pontic Epistles, Ibis, and Halieuticon of Ovid*, London, 1878, 271.
2 Jordanes, *Getica*, 109, trans. Mierow, C. C., *The Gothic History of Jordanes*, Princeton, 1915, 82.
3 NAC 1970, *Arh* XII/3, 1970, 78.
4 Petrov, T. *et al.*, *Antichnata Grobnitsa krai Pomorie*, Bourgas, 1960, 21.
5 Dimitrov, D. P. *et al.*, *Kratka Istoriya na Bulgarskata Arhitektura*, Sofia, 1965, 46.
6 Gerasimov, T., *IVAD* V (XX), 1969, 54 ff.
7 Toncheva, G., *Arh* VI/4, 1964, 37 ff.

PART THREE

Christianity and the Byzantine Withdrawal

10 The End of the *Limes*

I. BYZANTIUM DISPLACES ROME

In the history of European civilisation, few centuries can have seen greater revolutionary changes than the fourth century – between the reigns of Diocletian and Theodosius I. Diocletian's reforms, aimed at consolidating the empire, instead formed the basis of its political division into east and west. This was promoted by Constantine's establishment of 'New Rome' at Constantinople and perpetuated by Theodosius' bequest of the 'Eastern empire' to Arcadius and the 'Western' to Honorius.

Christianity emerged from its last and fiercest persecutions at the beginning of the century to gain official toleration in 311, imperial favour under Constantine, and religious monopoly under Theodosius. Its organisation was based on the civil structure devised by Diocletian and Theodosius. As the state religion, its churches replaced the pagan temples as symbols of both imperial and divine power, which were inextricably associated. Invariably among the most important and so most carefully built structures, the churches are often the main and sometimes, in the more vulnerable areas, the only archaeological evidence of fifth- and sixth-century Byzantine civilisation.

Constantinople succeeded Rome as the political centre of the Eastern empire; but in the field of religion Rome retained its position of *primus inter pares*. Already the doctrinal differences were apparent which were to result in the schism between Catholic and Orthodox. Those harassed by invasions might be distracted by immediate issues of life and death or with eking out an existence oppressed by barbarians and by imperial tax-gatherers. But where men enjoyed sufficient peace to indulge in controversy religion was the burning issue of the time. Even a bishop, Gregory of Nyssa, commented in exasperation that in Constantinople

> all places, lanes, markets, squares, streets, the clothes' merchants, money-changers and grocers are filled with people discussing unintelligible questions. If you ask someone how many obols you have to pay, he philosophises about the begotten and the unbegotten; if I wish to know the price of bread, the salesman answers that the Father is greater than the Son: and when you enquire whether the bath is ready, you are told that the Son was made out of nothing.[1]

II. THE *LIMES* IN THE FIFTH AND SIXTH CENTURIES

For what is now Bulgaria, the defeat and death of Valens in 378 ended an era of relative development and prosperity and the beginning of one of constant attack, insecurity, impoverishment, and changing population. The *limes* was no longer defended by the Romanised provincials who had replaced the Italic legionaries but, in increasing measure, by Gothic *foederati*. The new insecurity and its effects were especially apparent in the area between the Danube and the Stara Planina, which, with the rest of Dacia Ripensis and Moesia Prima, formed the outer defences of the Eastern empire's two wealthiest cities, Constantinople and Thessalonica. The major cities had remained intact, only their fortifications needed repair; generally opus mixtum with uncut stone was used. City-dwellers had suffered but had generally survived. But the countryside had been devastated. Many of the Thracian peasantry had fled their lands, been carried off as slaves, or killed. They were now replaced by defeated Visigoths, who also supplied recruits for the garrisons and the imperial army, in which they quickly rose to the highest posts.

Although during the first 40 years of the fifth century there was a degree of economic revival, the earlier prosperity was wrecked beyond recovery. The finds of fourth- and fifth-century bronze coins in place of gold and silver in the fortresses is indicative of the lower standard of living, even among the army. Taxation was increased to subsidise defence expenditure and this, together with the greed of officialdom during the latter part of the fourth century, had left most of the surviving peasants with little option but to accept the status of *colon*, or serf, on a large estate, to which they were legally bound by an edict of Theodosius I.

In the 440s the Huns struck briefly but disastrously. A far more terrible enemy than the Visigoths, they were now established in Pannonia and undisputed rulers of all trans-Danubia. Not only was the land once more laid waste, but with the help of siege engines, fortified cities, hitherto vulnerable only to treachery, were taken and sacked. Priscus has left a report of the attack on Naissus in 441:

> . . . they brought their engines of war to the circuit wall – first wooden beams mounted on wheels because their approach was easy. Men standing on the beams shot arrows against those defending . . . the battlements, and other men grabbing another projecting beam shoved the wheels ahead on foot. Thus, they drove the engines ahead wherever it was necessary so that it was possible to shoot successfully through the windows made in the screens. In order that the fight might be free of danger for the men on the beams they were protected by willow twigs interwoven with rawhide and leather screens, a defense against other missiles and whatever fire weapons might be sent against them.

> Many engines were in this way brought close to the city wall, so that those on the battlements, on account of the multitude of the missiles, retired, and the so-called rams advanced. The ram is a huge machine. A beam with a metal head is suspended by loose chains from timbers inclined toward each other, and there are screens like those just mentioned for the sake of the safety of those working it. With small ropes from a projecting horn at the back, men forcibly draw it backward from the place which is to receive the blow and then let it go, so that with a swing it crushes every part of the wall which comes in its way. From the walls the defenders hurled down stones by the wagon load which had been collected when the engines had been brought up to the circuit wall, and they smashed some along with the men themselves, but they did not hold out against the vast number of engines. Then the enemy brought up scaling ladders. And so in some places the wall was toppled by the rams, and elsewhere men on the battlements were overpowered by the multitude of siege engines. The city was captured when the barbarians entered

where the circuit wall had been broken by the hammering of the ram and also when by means of the ladders they scaled the part of the wall not yet fallen.[2]

In 443 the Huns made an attack on Ratiaria, but whether it was actually captured is not recorded. Naissus suffered again in 447 and in the following year Priscus passed through and 'found the city destitute of men, since it had been razed by the enemy. In the Christian hostels were found people afflicted by disease'. His party halted 'a short distance from the river – for every place on the bank was full of the bones of those slain in war'.[3]

The castellum of Asemus or Asamus (Musalievo), near the confluence of the Osum (the ancient Asemus) and the Danube, is unexplored. Priscus' account shows that with courage even the Huns could be defied:

> Asemus is a strong fortress . . . adjacent to the Thracian boundary, whose native inhabitants inflicted many terrible deeds on the enemy, not only warding them from the walls but even undertaking battles outside the ditch. They fought against a boundless multitude and generals who had the greatest reputation . . . The Huns, being at a loss, retired slowly from the fortress. Then the Asimuntians rushed out and . . . fell on them by surprise. Though fewer than the Huns opposing them but excelling them in bravery and strength, they made the Hunnish spoils their own . . . killed many Scythians, freed many Romans, and received those who had run away from their enemies . . . [Attila refused to withdraw or make peace] . . . unless the Romans who had escaped to these people should be surrendered, or else ransoms paid for them, and the barbarian prisoners led off by the Asimuntians be given up . . . [The latter request was eventually complied with, but in spite of an order from the Byzantine commander in Thrace to comply also with the former] . . . the Asimuntians . . . swore that the Romans who had fled to them had been sent away free. They swore this even though there were Romans among them; they did not think they had sworn a false oath since it was for the safety of men of their own race.[4]

Such courage is a brave contrast with the general Byzantine policy of attempting to buy off Attila with ever-increasing sums of gold, and the return of deserters and refugees. Even two children, Hun princes and imperial protégés in Constantinople, were ignominiously handed over – to be promptly and publicly crucified.

Even a century and a half later Asemuntian independence and courage remained undimmed. Theophylact Simocattes relates that in 593 the Byzantine general, Peter, brother of the emperor Maurice, was so much inpressed by the spirit of its defenders that he decided to draft them into his own army. The citizens protested strongly, producing an exemption from such service, granted them by Justin I. When Peter was obdurate, the soldiers claimed sanctuary in a church and the bishop refused to expel them from the altar. Peter then sent a captain of infantry with his troop to enforce the orders, but the captain, awed by the sanctity of the church and frightened of sacrilege, refused to obey. Peter deprived him of his rank and on the following day sent another officer into the city to bring the recalcitrant bishop to his camp. The citizens drove the officer

PLATE 151 Cherven

away, shut the gates on him, and stood on the walls, loudly praising Maurice and reviling Peter, who beat an ignominious retreat.

Little more than ten years separated the disintegration of the Huns after Attila's death from the Ostrogothic wars. There is an echo of Ovid's complaints in Jordanes' description of the Danube at about this time.

> . . . when the wintry cold was at hand, the river Danube was frozen over as usual. For a river like this freezes so hard that it will support like a solid rock an army of foot-soldiers and wagons and sledges and whatsoever vehicles there may be – nor is there need of skiffs and boats. So when Thiudimer, king of the Goths, saw that it was frozen, he led his army across . . .[5]

From 481 until 488, Theodoric the Amal, son of Thiudimer, under a treaty with the emperor Zeno, ruled land which had been within the empire for nearly 500 years; his kingdom covered parts of Moesia Secunda and Dacia Ripensis and his capital was Novae, the old home of Legio I Italica.

Towards the end of the fifth century, large numbers of Isaurian rebels from south-east Anatolia were forcibly resettled in Thracia; it is likely that the depopulated north received many of them. Their presence may explain liturgical innovations of oriental origin which are reflected in the architecture of some of the churches of this time.

In the sixth century, the policy of defence in depth was intensified. Many Danube fortresses were strengthened and repaired under Anastasius, Justin I, and Justinian, Procopius giving full credit to the last, but increasingly they became isolated outposts. The rapidly diminishing security they could offer spurred the civilian population to depart, a process already begun in the fifth century, especially since they could no longer support themselves by work beyond the walls or by unwanted luxury crafts within them. On fortified hilltop refuges in the Stara Planina and the Ovche hills round Shoumen, existence could be prolonged in conditions of varying comfort or even luxury. In this way, for example, the inhabitants of Sexaginta Prista are said to have evacuated themselves to the naturally defended site of Cherven on the Cherni Lom river, where below the long-known medieval fortifications, walls of the Early Byzantine period have recently been uncovered (Pl. 151).

Meanwhile, quietly, the Slavs began to fill the deserted northern lands. At first they were probably welcome as a valuable source of agricultural labour and quickly assimilated. Particularly in north-east Bulgaria – at such sites as Nova Cherna, where there was an Early Byzantine fortress, Garvan, and Popina – the many traces of Slav habitation in the sixth century included Christian burials. They were also another source of recruitment; from 530 to 533 a Slav, Hilbud, was a successful commander of the Byzantine forces. But the pressure of numbers became too great to be absorbed and during the second quarter of the century military incursions increased, leading up to a massive invasion in 550 that reached the Aegean coast.

By 586 a new military power, the Avars, described by the Byzantine military historian Michael the Syrian as 'the accursed barbarians with unkempt hair . . . from the extremities of the Orient', were established in Pannonia and only held off by annual tribute from invading the empire. Fleeing from their oppression the Slavs surged across the Danube, the border garrisons depleted by wars in Asia. Following the traditions of Byzantine diplomacy, Tiberius II invited the Avars to attack the Slavs from the rear. The Avars came, but not to waste time on the Slavs, with whom they joined forces. John of Ephesus describes the situation:

> The accursed people, the Slavs, advanced and invaded the whole of Greece, the environs of Thessalonica and the whole of Thrace. They conquered many towns and fortresses, they ravaged, burned, pillaged and dominated the country, which they inhabited as if it were their own land. This lasted four years, as long as the Basileus [emperor] was making war against the Persians; in this way they had a free run of the country until God drove them out. Their devastations reached as far as the outer walls [of Constantinople]. They took away all the imperial flocks and herds. Now [584] they are still quietly settled in the Roman provinces without anxiety or fear, laying waste, murdering and burning. They grow rich, they possess gold and silver, they possess flocks and horses, and many arms. They have learnt to wage war better than the Byzantines.[6]

The last of the Danubian fortresses fell early in the seventh century. By the middle of the century the hilltop refuges had suffered a similar fate and north of the Stara Planina only Odessos is known to have remained in Byzantine hands. South of the range there remained Serdica, Philippopolis, Beroe (lost but later retaken), and Mesambria.

The Slavs were no longer invaders; they were occupiers who had made the country their own. There was no question of evicting or conquering them. The Byzantine strongholds possessed a trade and cultural function, as well as a military one, but their role was merely defensive.

The emphasis on destruction during the fifth and sixth centuries inevitably limits the archaeological record and most of the survivals of the Danube *limes* are Roman rather than Early Byzantine. The latest phase was the first to be demolished, whether by enemy action, decay, or for building materials, and, where reconstruction took place, as often occurred in the medieval period, the Roman remains usually provided the more solid foundation, with the exception of some of the fortifications erected in the first half of the sixth century.

Castra Martis and Ratiaria

Castra Martis was captured by the Huns in 408–9, thereby escaping the terror of Attila, but although it was refortified by the Byzantines in the sixth century and substantial remains exist of the fort at Kula, it seems never to have regained its former prominence. Ratiaria, still a large and rich city in the fifth century, suffered heavily during the Hun invasions. Both cities fell to the Avars.

Bononia

Bononia grew in importance during the fifth and sixth centuries, probably superseding Ratiaria after the Hun invasions. Several sections of the fortress wall of this period, including six towers, have been identified. With four sides of unequal length, they enclosed an area of about 23 hectares. Towers at intervals of about 100 metres were connected by curtain walls with foundations 4·30 metres thick. Bononia suffered heavily from both Huns and Ostrogoths, and Procopius speaks of repairs to its defences. It, too, finally succumbed to the Avars, although there is historical evidence for some limited cultural continuity.

Botevo

Botevo, on the Danube 5 kilometres east of Ratiaria, has archaeological remains indicating a minor settlement or military outpost of the city in the Early Byzantine if not also the Roman period. In 1947 remains were discovered of a small Early Byzantine church of unusual plan – a free cross with arms of slightly unequal length, the eastern terminating in a three-sided apse (Fig. 57). In some places the brick walls were over a metre high; elsewhere only foundations remained. From a west doorway steps led down to a brick floor. Three marble blocks from the altar screen found *in situ* showed that the sanctuary occupied the whole eastern arm of the cross.

The brick construction and the existence in the debris of sixth-century amphora fragments and Slav pottery suggest a date about the turn of the fifth-sixth centuries. Anastasius' resettlement of the Isaurian rebels in Thracia at this time might account for the unusual plan. Analogies with the cruciform churches at Tsurkvishte and Ivanyani (p. 279) suggest the possibility of a funerary function.

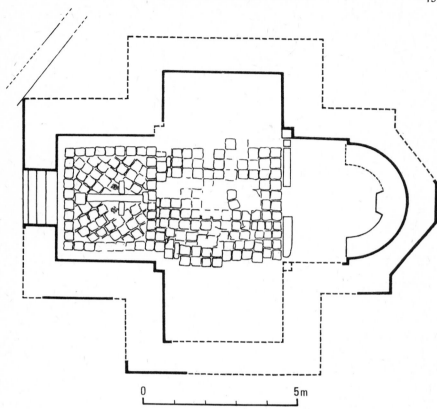

FIG. 57 Botevo, church

Novae

The line of Novae's original north, south, and west curtain walls and the fourth-century east wall seem generally to have been preserved during the Early Byzantine period, although the inferior building techniques of the later repairs and reconstructions can be clearly detected (Pl. 152). On the east there are signs of one or more walls, in some places inside, in others outside, the main wall excavated (Fig. 21). Some repairs were probably needed following the Hun attacks, but Theodoric's residence must have preserved Novae from Ostrogothic devastation, and his departure for Ravenna in 488 left it to resume its role as a frontier outpost. Although Procopius mentions some refortification nearby, the city's defences were apparently sound; no typical sixth-century triangular or pentagonal towers have been uncovered.

In the north-west sector a large building has been partially excavated. It had

PLATE 152 Novae, S.W. angle tower

PLATE 153 Novae, Romano-Byzantine building

a hall with two central piers or columns which led through two narrow rooms to a chamber with two brick-built apses (Pl. 153). The building, its purpose still unclear, was erected during the Roman and reconstructed in the Early Byzantine period.

One church, a much-damaged single-apsed, three-naved basilica, has recently been discovered. Three bishops of Novae, like all others in Moesia Secunda subject to the archbishop of Marcianopolis, are known by name about the mid-fifth century and another, anonymous, is mentioned in 594. The name – and the name only – of one local martyr, St Lupus, has survived through the appearance of Peter, the Byzantine general who fared so ill at Asemus, at Novae on the saint's feast day; Peter accepted a pressing invitation to remain for the two-day celebrations.

Novae survived into the seventh century but only for a few years.

Iatrus

Iatrus, having escaped damage by the Visigoths, was sacked, probably by the Huns, and occupied by the Ostrogoths in the fifth century.

A church (Basilica I) was built inside the walls, probably in the last years of the fourth century or early in the fifth (Fig. 26). Three-naved with a single semicircular apse and a narthex, it was 22 metres long, including the 4½-metre-deep apse, and 12 metres wide. The floor was brick-paved and the walls, nearly a metre thick, of opus mixtum with several courses of brick. A Mithraic altar was re-used as building material.

The apse, surviving only to the height of a few centimetres above the floor, contained what was probably the remains of a *synthronon* – seats round the wall

PLATE 154 Iatrus, superimposed churches

PLATE 155 Durostorum, fortress wall

for the clergy – constructed of stone and faced with tiles. Debris here included fragments of a white marble altar table, its slender columns decorated with stylised acanthus leaves, and a shallow reddish-brown clay dish with a cross stamped in the centre.

Soon after this church was built and before the end of the first quarter of the fifth century, the eastern end of the massive annex in the south-west corner of the fortress wall (p. 134) was demolished to provide space and material for houses. Basilica I was burnt down sometime in the fifth century, as well as the two-storeyed rectangular structure and some remaining parts of the south-west annex, when the castellum was sacked.

The wreckage was used as a quarry by the next inhabitants, perhaps Ostrogoths. Fragments of columns, capitals, and bases were used in fifth- or sixth-century houses. One or more were built on top of the church, their stone foundations using its columns and bases but their walls of mud brick. After a time these, too, perished in flames.

Basilica II, built above the first, was larger and its construction seems to have followed immediately on the destruction of the houses, early in the sixth century. Their debris raised the new floor 1·77 metres above that of the earlier church. Judging by the foundations, which alone remain, the plan was the same as its predecessor's, an interesting exhibition of conservatism on the part of the inhabitants. Just over 30 metres long without the apse, its substantial walls and stylobates suggest a barrel-vaulted roof.

Iatrus is mentioned by Procopius as a fort repaired in the sixth century, but its role seems to have changed from that of a military castellum to a fortified refuge for people in the country round about during raids by Avars and Slavs. Excavation has uncovered a group of small, flimsy, single-roomed houses, employing old masonry and architectural fragments but for the most part built of mud bricks, plastered inside with clay. An unusual feature in some of the outer walls was that at about 1-metre intervals the horizontal rows of mud bricks were intersected by a vertical line of similar bricks, apparently performing the function of upright stakes or beams. Wooden beams – some with decorative carving – were, however, used for roofing, covered with reeds or straw and weighted down with heavy tiles. Household goods and tools were relatively primitive.

About the year 600, these humble dwellings, together with the fortifications and any other buildings, perished at the hands of Slavs or Avars in a final conflagration so fierce that the excavated mud bricks had almost the appearance of having been fired in a kiln.

Durostorum

Modern Silistra has far outgrown Durostorum, which remained a rock against which barbarian waves broke in vain until 584 when it fell to the Avars. An inscription suggests that its bishop, Dulcissimus, sought refuge in Odessos, where he died. One of its sons, Aetius, was the imperial general whose victory over Attila in the battle of the Catalaunian plains, near Châlons-sur-Marne, ended the Hun threat to western Europe.

A recent rescue dig in connection with the construction of a new harbour has uncovered parts of an Early Byzantine fortress wall beneath one of the ninth or tenth century[7] (Pl. 155). Otherwise little if anything is known from the Early Byzantine period, but the city seems to have continued some kind of existence until the Bulgar invasion of 681.

NOTES

1 Migne, J. P., *Patrologia Graeca*, 46, p. 557
2 Priscus, fr. 1b, trans. Gordon, C. D., *The Age of Attila*, Ann Arbor, 1960, 64, 65.
3 Ibid., fr. 8, 74.
4 Ibid., fr. 5, 67, 68.
5 Jordanes, *Getica*, LV,280, trans. Mierow, C. C., *Gothic History of Jordanes*, Princeton, 1915, 132.
6 Tafrali, O., *Thessalonique des origines au XIVe siècle*, Paris, 1919, 98, 99.
7 NAC, *Arh* XII/3, 1970, 81.

11 The Northern Foothills (11)

I. THE CENTRAL SLOPES

Although fortified, the urban centres in the interior of western Moesia Secunda had a fundamentally commercial rather than military function. While they had mainly survived the Visigothic attacks, their economies had been severely disrupted and during and after the Hun and Ostrogothic invasions even survival largely depended on natural defences. If the site was vulnerable, the population, provided they acted in time, moved south to stronger positions in the Stara Planina or beyond.

Nicopolis-ad-Istrum and Veliko Turnovo

Until there are results from the new excavations at Nicopolis-ad-Istrum, the city's existence after the Visigothic wars must remain an enigma. Its fall is not recorded; it is not even listed as a city attacked by the Huns. Procopius mentions the establishment of a fortress of 'Nicopolis' by Justinian, but, as remains of an Early Byzantine fort have recently been reported at Danubian Nikopol,[1] the reference may have been to this site. Bishops of Nicopolis-ad-Istrum are, however, mentioned about 458 and 518. At the time of writing, archaeological evidence is limited to the aerial photograph reproduced in Pl. 94. From this the construction may be deduced of a much smaller fifth-sixth-century fort abutting on to and using part of the south wall, but this reading requires confirmation by excavation.

Sometime after the Visigothic invasions, perhaps gradually, the inhabitants of Nicopolis-ad-Istrum left their city for Veliko Turnovo, where the river Yantra twists and turns through a deep gorge to create a chain of steep-cliffed peninsulas. One of them, the Tsarevets hill, was ideally situated for defence (Fig. 58). Coins of Heraclius and Constantine III show that it survived some fifty years after most of the Moesian fortresses, although it, too, finally perished in flames. Fifth- or sixth-century fortifications have also been found on another Turnovo hill, the Momina Krepost, across the river from the Tsarevets.

The discovery that Turnovo was an important Early Byzantine city and not merely a strongpoint in the sixth and seventh centuries stems from the unexpected find in 1961 of an Early Byzantine church and annexed buildings beneath the medieval palace complex on the Tsarevets hill. Later excavations have shown that the whole hill was inhabited during this period. A plan of a three-naved basilical church with a single semicircular apse, a narthex, and remains of mosaics and wall painting, superimposed above a smaller single-naved basilica, was pubished in 1965 (Fig. 59).[2] Further investigation has now identified as many as four superimposed basilicas on this site close to the north gate and the excavation of other buildings provisionally assigned to the reign of Justinian is in progress.[3] Although the fifth- or sixth-century fortifications were probably levelled to serve as foundations for the medieval walls, a contemporary double gate, the outer portcullis divided by a propugnaculum from the inner swing doors, and a triangular tower nearby have been uncovered.

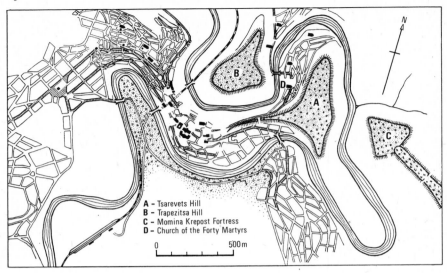

FIG. 58 (*above*) Veliko Turnovo
FIG. 59 (*above right*) Veliko Turnovo, superimposed churches
FIG. 60 (*below right*) Veliko Turnovo, church and cruciform building

Elsewhere below the palace complex was a small single-naved church attached
to a cruciform building with a common portico (Fig. 60). Limestone slabs
paved part of the floors of both buildings, but there were also remains of tiling.
A colonnade on the west of the portico had unequally spaced columns linked by
limestone slabs; one intact column, 2 metres high, was discovered with its base
in situ on beaten earth. A Corinthian capital was also found, similar to one of
several re-used as bases for a wooden portico when the thirteenth-century church
of the Forty Martyrs, below the fortress, was converted into a mosque (Pls.
156–8). The cruciform building has a small two-chambered crypt in its partly
destroyed eastern part. The excavator dates it and its annexed church to the
sixth century and first half of the seventh; he considers it too large for a martyrium, suggesting some connection with other rooms to the south. Nevertheless,
on present evidence it is difficult to see it other than as a shrine, built perhaps to
house threatened relics from further north.

The distance between Nicopolis and Turnovo is only 18 kilometres, close
enough for the population to move without difficulty, given time, and bring
their household goods and chattels. Nicopolis was even used as a quarry. Three
second- and third-century stelai of Hotnitsa limestone, all depicting a Thracian
Horseman, and the base of a statue bearing an inscription from the *boule* and
demos of Nicopolis form part of the socle of a tower of the medieval palace
(Pl. 159). In this proximity may be an explanation for the continued existence of
the bishopric of Nicopolis into the sixth century. The new city may have been
regarded as the official successor of the old, retaining, for a while at least, its
ancient name and, in so far as was possible, its administrative functions.

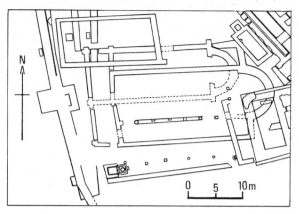

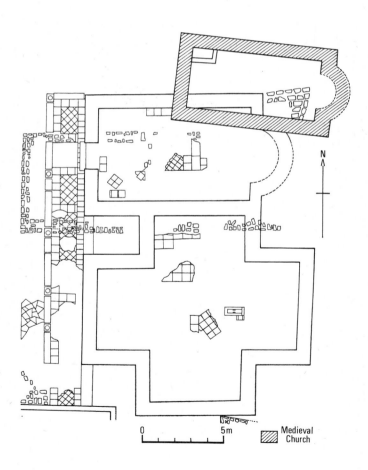

0   5m   ▨ Medieval
                            Church

PLATE 156 V. Turnovo, re-used capital

PLATE 157 V. Turnovo, re-used capital

PLATE 158 V. Turnovo, re-used capital

Discoduratera

The intrinsic importance of Discoduratera as a trading post on the Beroe–Novae highway persisted as long as traffic continued to pass through it. The merchants returned after the Visigothic wars. Flimsier buildings replaced the porticoed house and its contemporaries, but the outer walls were rebuilt and strengthened. Except where eroded on the south-east by the river Yantra they have survived up to about 1 metre high, through the fortunate chance that they have served as boundaries between peasant properties.

The fortifications took good account of natural advantages. A steep bank down to the Yantra on the south-east, a deep valley to the south-west, marshes to the north-east; only the north-west side was easy of access and here traces of a ditch were found. There were four walls of unequal length, the only gate being on the south-west. External round towers defended the three surviving corners and doubtless the fourth, and single external four-sided towers reinforced each wall (Fig. 61). But Roman precision was gone. The angle towers projected to protect only one, not two, walls, almost as if the builder had heard that round towers were right for corners without understanding why. Yet, although irregular in shape and size, like the rectangular towers they were strongly built. The north tower, partly preserved up to a height of 2·20 metres, is topped by two courses of brick, the remains of a bonding layer.

The much-destroyed gate had inner and outer double swing doors. The openings were over 2 metres wide, large enough to take vehicles, and the propugnaculum about $2\frac{1}{2}$ metres deep. An originally square and free-standing watchtower east of the gate was burnt down and replaced by a rectangular one, built against the outer wall.

PLATE 159 V. Turnovo, re-used stelai from Nicopolis-ad-Istrum

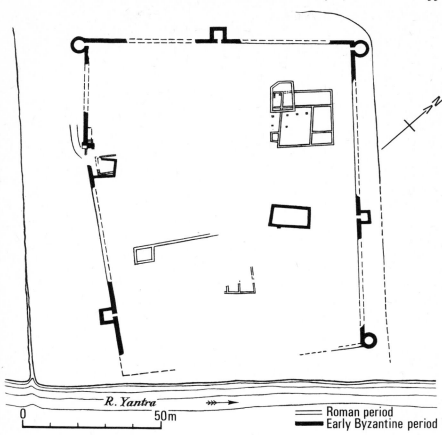

R. Yantra

0   50m

=== Roman period
━━━ Early Byzantine period

FIG. 61 Discoduratera, site plan

Coins of the end of the fourth century and the first quarter of the fifth are much more numerous than those of earlier periods, but also more worn. This points to a decline in local minting and to inflation, due to the general insecurity and impoverishment. The latest coins are of Arcadius and the Western emperor Honorius.

Sixth-century pottery found inside the walls suggests some continuity after the Hun invasion, perhaps even a revival under Justinian, but the emporium – if such it still was – is unlikely to have outlived him and was finally destroyed by fire.

Storgosia

Storgosia (the 'Kailuka' gorge near Pleven) is one of the Roman sites which, though less than 50 kilometres from the Danube, now increased in importance owing to its strong natural defences. Such remnants of fortress walls as can be seen today are medieval, but inside them substantial remains of a large Early Byzantine three-naved church, 45 metres long and 28 metres wide, were discovered in 1909 and have now been conserved and partly restored (Pl. 160).

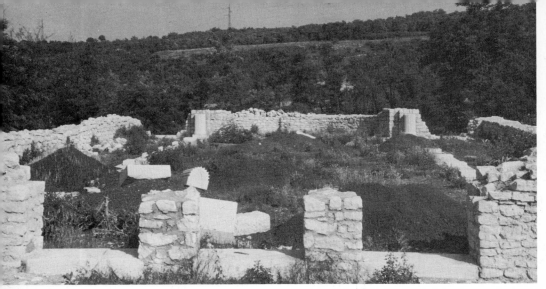

PLATE 160 Storgosia, church

The excavator commented on the unusually wide and thick-walled central apse compared with those terminating the north and south aisles. The impression is given of a single-naved church of the fifth century to which side-apses were later added. A large masonry-lined pit, presumably a pool, of the type found in the sixth-century Episcopal church at Caričin Grad in Serbia, occupied much of the atrium, its edge being so close to the west wall as to preclude entry from this direction (Pl. 161). Not only is this one of the largest Early Byzantine basilicas in Bulgaria, but one with unusual architectural features; it is hoped that the conservation will be followed by new and fuller publication.

A smaller building, thought to be a fourth- or early fifth-century church, was found at the foot of the cliff, partly eroded by the river. It seems to have been oriented towards a southern apse. Remains of a mosaic floor, no longer *in situ*, included intricate geometric designs, fragments of a Latin inscription, and the Constantinian *labarum*, or standard with the sacred monogram of Christ.

A short distance up the little valley, in a building that was possibly a villa of the Roman period, an octagonal structure contained, in addition to some ten human skeletons, 26 bronze coins of Justinian, testifying to Byzantine occupancy until about the middle of the sixth century.

Sadovets

Near Sadovets, south-west of Pleven, the hill-plateau of the Golemanovo Kale overlooks the river Vit in a situation very similar to that of the Kailuka. Inhabited during the Roman period, after destruction in the third or fourth century, it seems to have remained deserted throughout the fifth century and the early part of the sixth.

Coins of Justinian help to date resettlement and the impressive defences (Fig. 62). The southern curve fell vertically from a height of 50 to 70 metres to the river, but the more accessible northern approach was defended by a triple wall. Burnt down once and immediately rebuilt, the fortress survived until its reduction by the Avars about the end of the sixth century, which was followed by permanent abandonment.

PLATE 161 Storgosia, church atrium

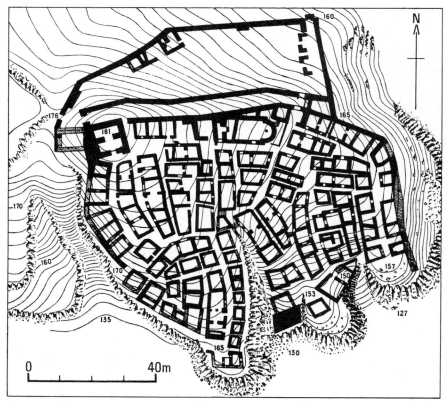

FIG. 62 Sadovets, Golemanovo Kale

The keystone of the defence system was a strongly built tower about 11 metres square which, with a western bastion, occupied the highest, north-western sector. From here three walls, built on a steep slope, itself a deterrent, extended to a fortified section of the east cliff. Entrances, at the eastern and western ends, were only 1·70 metres wide. The walls, with no foundations and 1½ to 2 metres thick, were built of small rough limestone blocks with a filling of rubble and white mortar, the latter also being used to plaster the outer faces. Brick was not used at all.

Behind the triple walls densely packed groups of dwellings, roughly built of limestone bound with mud, were separated by narrow alleys. Many houses had two rooms; one was found with a flimsy upper storey. I. Velkov suggests that one room served as living quarters and the other as a stable or byre, with perhaps a barn overhead for grain or fodder. Elsewhere there were separate rows of individual storerooms. Some people lived on an open terrace below the west wall.

Remains of two churches were found, both single-naved, with rounded apses, one on the terrace, the other in the fortress. The latter was oddly placed, its north-western part against the inner north wall, which cut into it at a slant. It was built on such a steep slope that the interior was on three different levels. The west wall of the church abutted on to an internally projecting tower, so that the main entrance had to be at the west end of the south wall. Much of the altar table was *in situ*; built of stucco-plastered masonry, its hollow interior must have contained relics. The conch of the apse was of unbaked bricks, but the roof is thought to have been a wooden barrel-vault. The building's anomalies suggest that the inconvenient site was particularly hallowed.

Sadovsko Kale, a nearby fortified settlement on the other side of the Vit, possessed similar types of dwellings and a large workshop making agricultural tools which must have served the surrounding countryside. Both settlements show signs of wealth incongruous with the rough, huddled dwellings, although these had glazed windows. Silver ornaments, including Gothic-type fibulae, were found, and a remarkable number of coins. V. Velkov states that Sadovsko Kale holds first place in the whole of northern Bulgaria for coins of the late antique period.[4] Fifth-century gold coins – of Arcadius and Honorius – numbered only nineteen, but finds of sixth-century coins included: in one building, 54 gold and 50 copper coins; in a clay pot, 128 gold coins; by a wall, 12 gold coins; in a living room, 162 copper coins. The coins were in such good condition that they suggest direct official payments which never went into general circulation.

I. Velkov and G. Bersu have put forward the interesting theory that Gothic foederati were settled here by Justinian as part of the defence system as well as a repopulation measure. Other settlements in the area await excavation and may confirm this hypothesis.

Vicus Trullensium

The natural fortress of Vicus Trullensium (near Kunino), guarding the entrance to an Iskur gorge through which ran the Oescus–Serdica road, has not been excavated, but inscriptions have identified it. One, on an altar dedicated to Jove, was found in the local church, turned upside down to serve as the altar. The vicus cannot have survived the third- and fourth-century raids, but the insecurity of the latter half of the fifth century is likely to have increased the importance of so strategic a site. Earlier fortifications were restored and a double wall built to protect the easy, east approach. Perhaps because of a local tradition of stone masonry, defences were not skimped; walls, whether new or repaired, were up to 2 metres thick. Inside them were remains of a sixth-century single-naved church. The vicus was probably finally destroyed by the Avars, although the Slavs seem to have settled for a time in the ruins before abandoning them for the present site of the village of Kunino.

II. THE NORTH-EAST

A number of sites of strategic importance in the fourth century, but more particularly the fifth and sixth centuries, have been found in a shallow crescent-shaped area, roughly centred on Shoumen, in the hilly country about half-way between Abritus and Marcianopolis. Outposts of the latter, these and other fortresses constituted part of the defence in depth protecting the easy routes across the eastern end of the Stara Planina to Constantinople. In several cases, only a few details have been published in archaeological journals; and thus little more than their existence can be recorded. Nevertheless, the various sites are beginning to compose a coherent pattern illuminating the Byzantine defence strategy of the fifth and sixth centuries. Some of these are described below.

Abritus

The fourth-century town house in the centre of Abritus seems to have remained intact until about the end of the sixth, perhaps an indication that Abritus was occupied peacefully by the Ostrogoths under Theodoric. Two Early Byzantine churches have been located. A. Yavashov found the narthex and west end of the nave and two aisles of one, and a recent salvage dig has uncovered its apse, but finds, which include a marble reliquary, have still to be published. The second church, dated to the fifth century, seems originally to have consisted of a single vaulted nave with a round apse and perhaps also a narthex, but to have had later additions.

Procopius mentions Abritus as one of the fortresses restored or strengthened by Justinian. Either at this time or after further damage the north and south gates were walled up (Figs. 30, 31), leaving the battered west gate as the only entrance. The city was burnt by the Avars or Slavs about the close of the sixth century. Probably the inhabitants had had time to remove themselves and their valuables, for the only skeleton found was of a dog, trapped in the town house's peristyled courtyard. Before long a group of Slavs settled among the ruins.

Voivoda

In the late fourth century Voivoda was severely damaged by the Visigoths, Following this, current excavations have shown that the north-west gateway was strengthened by a new wall (Fig. 33). This began at the angle tower and ran outside the western U-shaped tower. It incorporated a new outer gate, with two pivoted wings; in a guardroom to its south small copper coins of Theodosius, Marcian, and Leo I were found. The old outer – and now inner –

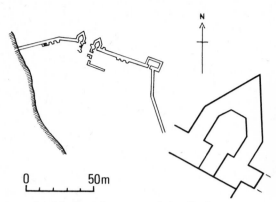

FIG. 63 Madara, fortress and detail of gate tower

gate, which showed signs of a conflagration, was also strengthened, but neither here nor in the walls did the workmanship approach that of the original structure.

Layers of ash and charred material suggest that Voivoda also suffered from many of the later Avar and Slav invasions. The last coins found were of Justin II, indicating its existence into the second half of the sixth century. But finally the fortress was taken and razed. Among the ruins Slav pottery and what the excavators have described as 'early medieval' dugouts have been found, suggesting that it was probably soon reoccupied, but by the invaders.

Pliska

Ten kilometres south of Voivoda, with the crow flying over gently rolling country, is Pliska, the site of the first Bulgarian capital. Much excavated and restored since its first identification by K. Škorpil, this vast settlement with its outer city and its inner palace-citadel has been the subject of considerable controversy. Generally, Bulgarian archaeologists have considered it to have been built on virgin soil and any earlier materials, including some bricks bearing the 'Dules' stamps, to have been brought from Voivoda or elsewhere for re-use in the new city, but some scholars favour a Roman or Byzantine substratum. Resemblances in the plan of the fortifications of the walled inner city to those of the Justinianic period are clear, but this model must have been available for copying all over the Balkans, and in any case the Bulgars probably used Byzantine builders. Controversy centres also around two churches, one the 'Palatine church' inside the walls, the other a huge basilica outside the walled city. Both were certainly used by the Christianised Bulgars; current excavations should decide whether they were also sites of earlier churches.

There can be no doubt that most of the monumental inner complex of Pliska was of eighth–tenth-century construction, but insufficient evidence is available to show whether or not some fifth–sixth-century fort or earlier villa rustica had previously existed there. The site itself, in the middle of a flat, open plain, is more typically Bulgarian or Roman than Early Byzantine and far from fulfilling the usual desideratum in the latter period of a natural defensive position.

PLATE 162 Madara, gateway

Madara

At Madara, about 12 kilometres south of Pliska, the big villa rustica had probably been razed by the Visigoths, but it did not remain deserted. A new complex with five rooms, two exedrae, and heating, all suggesting a baths, was built on the ruins of the wall which had surrounded the pars urbana (Fig. 34). The general plan, the coins, and pottery associated with it date the building to the end of the fourth or the fifth century, but there are signs of habitation until the early sixth, although whether connected with the fort above or with peasants squatting among the ruins is hard to say.

The great cliffs which rise precipitously above the villa are surmounted by a plateau. On its edge, probably in the late fifth or early sixth century, a fortress was constructed (Fig. 63). The sheer cliff on which it stood obviated the need for any walls on the west, and ravines gave some protection on the east and south-east. Only on the north did the open plateau offer no obstruction. This side was defended by a 2·60-metre-thick wall, almost 100 metres long with a projecting rectangular tower at the angle with the east wall. In the centre of the north wall, the fortress gate, flanked by two pentagonal towers (Pl. 162), consisted of an outer portcullis flush with the wall and inner swing doors, with a guard-house inside. There are remains of several staircases against the inside of the wall.

Almost at the foot of the cliffs a great shallow cave, which had previously been a nymphaeum, was now an auxiliary base, linked to the fort by a staircase of some 400 steps cut in the vertical face of the rock, taking advantage where possible of fissures. Erosion has rendered the route impracticable today. Suitably fortified and itself some way above the plain, the cave provided the garrison with food and water and probably also served as a refuge for the local population and their livestock. Close by in a well-built granary were 11 huge clay dolia, each above a man's height. Finds showed the granary was in use during the fifth and sixth centuries. Madara was an early and very important Bulgar centre, but there is no evidence when and how Byzantine occupation ceased.

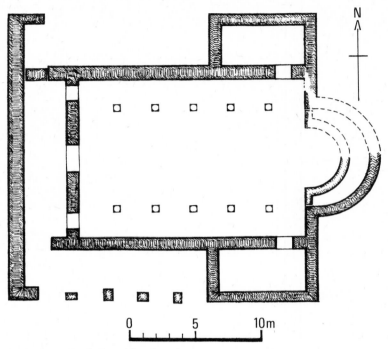

FIG. 64 Preslav, Deli-Doushka church

Shoumen

West of Madara is Shoumen, the administrative centre of the region. On a terrace of the high hills dominating the city on the west and looking east and north towards Madara, Pliska, and Voivoda, excavations of a medieval fortress have uncovered some of its earlier history. The preliminary indications are that triangular towers flanked the main entrance to the fortress and were also found at intervals along the curtain wall above older structures. The second – or Early Bulgar – phase is considered to be a restoration of the fourth- to sixth-century structure. Traces of burning everywhere testify to the stormy life led by this fortress.

Long used as a quarry for later buildings, those of earlier periods are naturally much destroyed. However, a large 'late antique' complex has recently been discovered and to its west at least three superimposed churches. The earliest, with an overall length of only 10 metres, was single-naved, the walls terminating in a semicircular apse. Only foundations of the western half remained; on the east the superstructure indicated a primitive broken-stone and mud construction, the apse being slightly better built. The simple nature of the building suggests a date in the second half of the fourth century.

Preslav

At Preslav, about 20 kilometres south-west of Shoumen, evidence of late antique settlement is obscured by the monumental buildings erected when it was the Bulgar capital in the ninth and tenth centuries, and by their subsequent destruction. K. Škorpil, the first excavator of Preslav, said that most of the Roman coins found in the ruins were of the fourth century and that the Early Byzantine period was chiefly represented by those of Justinian, Justin I, and Anastasius.[5]

An exception exists east of the main site, by the Ticha river, at Deli-Doushka, where a fifth-century basilical church has been excavated (Fig. 64). The walls were of mortared uncut stone, with occasional use of dressed blocks to line the entrances; the roof was probably wooden. The wide central nave was separated by rows of five pillars from side-aisles only 2 metres wide. A large single apse corresponded to the width of the nave and contained remains of a synthronon. At the west end three openings led into a *narthex*, or vestibule possessing liturgical functions. Two rectangular *pastophoria* or side chambers, entered from the east ends of the two aisles, are of special interest as they must have served as the *prothesis* and the *diaconicon*, rooms designed respectively for the preparation of the Eucharist and as a vestry or sacristy in the Eastern Orthodox rite. Coins date the church to the first half of the fifth century, more than a hundred years before the Orthodox rites of oriental, particularly Syrian, origin found official recognition in Constantinople, a fact suggesting strong Eastern influence among the local population, a proportion of whom may have been immigrants.

Preslav is situated where the river Ticha emerges from a gorge into a fertile plain. On a hill commanding the entrance to the gorge, Early Byzantine pot-sherds were found among the ruins of a Bulgar fort which, roughly oval in shape, had one square and one round tower. It was concluded that this site – an obvious choice – had been fortified in the fifth or the first half of the sixth century.

Draganovets

On a tributary of the Ticha river some 15 kilometres south-west of Preslav, a rescue dig recently uncovered a fortress provisionally dated from the mid-third century to the end of the sixth.

Partial excavation of a church dated to the fifth or sixth century showed a long apsed room annexed to the south side of a three-naved, single-apsed basilica. The excavators' suggestion of the possibility of a five-naved basilica must be regarded as tentative until more information is available. Stone and mud walls of an earlier building were found beneath the church and were identified by finds of marble votive reliefs as a sanctuary of the Thracian Horseman. A double furnace for brick-making, dated to the fourth or fifth century, was also excavated.

Krumovo Kale

At the western end of the Preslav hills, near Turgovishte, a fort known as Krumovo Kale defended the northern end of a pass and commanded a wide view towards Abritus. Enclosing an area of about 15–20 dekas, the walls, 2·50 to 2·80 metres thick and still standing up to 3·50 metres high, were built of stones laid in regular courses and a fill of rubble and mortar. Remains of mortar over the stones, with incised vertical and horizontal lines, gave an impression of dressed stonework. The single gate, facing the only easy approach, was 3·70 metres wide and the depth of the curtain wall; it had pivoted wing doors and finds of wedge-shaped bricks show that it was vaulted. U-shaped towers defended the gate, the south one being 6·80 metres wide and projecting perpendicularly 5·30 metres beyond the wall. The northern, almost identical in size, was angled away from the gate towards the saddle on which the access road is still visible. Both towers were constructionally linked to the wall and remains of stairs suggest an original height of about 12 metres.

Excavation showed two building phases, both within the Early Byzantine period. Although the plan remained the same, in the second the stonework was much less skilful; there was no longer an attempt at regular courses and large limestone slabs were re-used in the gateway. The U-shaped towers – inferior in size and construction to those of Abritus and Voivoda – suggest a date about the mid-fifth century for their construction. As the culture layer is very thin, the first destroyers may have been the Ostrogoths. Restoration followed quickly, probably in the first half of the sixth century. Supporting evidence comes from the remains of a three-naved church only 2 – 3 metres inside the walls and closely related to them. The second phase of the church is well dated by coins of Justinian. At this period the church, 28 metres long and almost 16 metres wide, had a single apse, its exterior five-sided and containing a concentric ambulatory behind a synthronon. Columns on stylobates separated the nave and aisles, and the narthex was undivided. Since this church has not been published in any detail, it can only be assumed that, like the walls the second phase was more or less a reconstruction of the first, with a possible remodelling of the apse.

North of the walls fortified outposts served as observation points. Round these a civilian settlement grew up, probably for craftsmen and small traders. It included a single-naved church on the edge of a cliff about 300 metres north of the walls (Fig. 65). The lower parts of its walls were of broken sandstone, the upper of mud brick, probably reinforced by a wooden frame. The sanctuary, an adaptation of the Hellenistic basilica to the Eastern rites which required pastophoria, comprised the apse and 2½ metres of the east end of the nave, partitioned into three and slightly higher than the rest of the church. Because of the steep drop outside, there was no narthex and the entrance was by the west end of the south wall. The church was paved with irregular sandstone blocks in the pastophoria and re-used tiles elsewhere.

Evidence from the walls suggests that this church had also been rebuilt after severe destruction; a chronology according generally with that of the fort seems likely. Coin finds suggest that Krumovo Kale survived well into the second half of the sixth century.

Tsar Krum

Near the village of Tsar Krum, 10 kilometres south-west of Shoumen and on a slight rise 2 kilometres from the river Kamchiya, excavation of a ninth-century Bulgar fortress unexpectedly uncovered three Early Byzantine churches. Two, superimposed, are just inside the north wall of the fortress, the third a short way away to the south-west.

The lower of the superimposed churches, destroyed by fire and much of its material re-used in the one above, was a small basilica only 9 metres long (Fig. 66). The ovoid apse contained a single-stepped synthronon. The nave was flanked by stylobates, each with three pillars, leaving 'aisles' no more than half a metre wide. The narthex, severely damaged, appears to be undivided. Tiles

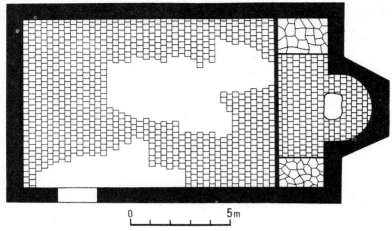

FIG. 65 Krumovo Kale, church

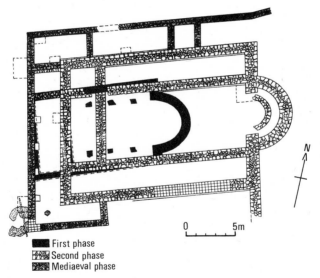

First phase
Second phase
Mediaeval phase

FIG. 66 Tsar Krum, superimposed churches

were found from the roof and the floor was brick. The plan of the church, its relationship with the one above – a depth of 1 metre between the two floor levels – and finds of ceramic and fourth-century bronze coins show this to be one of the earliest churches in Bulgaria. Fragments of wall paintings add to its especial interest.

Most of these fragments, some with three layers of paint, were in the 60-centi-metre-thick debris that covered the floor of nave and apse, but others, apparently parts of panels, were *in situ* at the bases of the walls. Most important were

PLATE 163 Tsar Krum, wall painting   PLATE 164 Tsar Krum, wall painting

fragments of almost life-size human faces, two nearly complete and the fresh colours extraordinarily well preserved. One shows the head, turning slightly to his right, of a man, perhaps in his forties, with brown hair, a drooping moustache, and a short beard. His large eyes and his nose and mouth are firmly modelled with pinkish-orange and brown strokes. The background is blue and an acanthus leaf can be seen behind the right cheek (Pl. 163). The second head is of a younger, beardless man (Pl. 164).

It is hardly possible that more than fifty years divide these paintings from those in the tomb at Durostorum; they may even be contemporary. The colouring is somewhat similar, but spirit and techniques are quite different. The Durostorum figures are portrayed in a realistic, Roman manner. The spiritual quality of the Tsar Krum heads places them unquestionably in the full tradition of Byzantine sacred art. These recently discovered paintings are important examples of an art of which very little survives from this early period. Relationship with the Hellenistic East seems evident; there are certain resemblances with the earliest – fifth- to seventh-century – icons at Mount Sinai.

According to pottery and building remains, this church lasted until the late fourth century, when it may have been a casualty of the Visigothic wars. V. Antonova has tentatively placed its construction within the first half of the fourth century; it can scarcely be later, given the three identified layers of wall painting.

The second church to be built was the one a short distance away, a single-naved basilica without a narthex (Fig. 67). The apse was unusual in that its slightly horseshoe-shaped ends – an Anatolian feature – extend 2 metres within and alongside the walls of the nave, perhaps to buttress the vault of the apse. The base of an altar screen was found at the beginning of the apse but did not extend across it; the stone base of an altar table stood in the centre of the sanctuary. The floor was of old, often broken, tiles, laid directly on the earth. The west wall continued south and then turned eastward at a right angle, a feature also found in the Deli-Doushka church. It suggests a wooden portico and this is made more likely by the presence of a south doorway into the church. The roof was tiled on a wooden framework. The general plan, pottery finds, and coins of Constantius and Honorius assign this church to the late fourth or early fifth century.

The third church was on top of the first, on almost the same axis (Fig. 66). Although much larger, it was similarly planned, with a relatively wide nave in proportion to the aisles. Its semicircular apse contained a single-stepped synthronon. The nave and aisles were divided by stylobates, but all the columns had been removed. The outer walls, preserved in places up to 1·40 metres, were 1·30 metres thick. A southern extension of the east wall may have been needed as a buttress or been the enclosing wall of a portico. A bonding layer of three courses of yellow brick was found above the stone masonry at one point. The narthex was tripartite, corresponding to the nave and aisles. This essentially Hellenistic basilica is elongated compared with the Deli-Doushka church and lacks its side-chambers. Both churches, as well as the one below, reflect the variety of influences in this region in the fifth century, to which this last church must be dated. The contrast with those at Iatrus is strong.

Although damaged, the stout walls of the third church survived the Slav settlement and even incorporation into the fortress of the pagan Bulgar ruler Omurtag. Its cult purpose was either remembered or later recognised, for towards the end of the ninth or in the tenth century it was restored and enlarged by Christians in the first Bulgar state.

Marcianopolis

Marcianopolis withstood the Visigoths, but their devastations of the surrounding countryside caused the city to undergo a period of decline, reflected

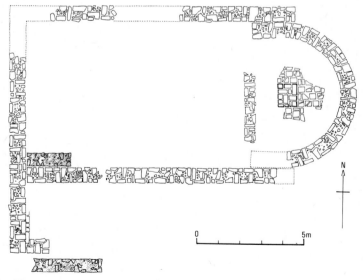

FIG. 67 Tsar Krum, second church

in constructions attributed to the late fourth and fifth centuries. Nevertheless, the state munitions factory is believed to have continued to function until at least the mid-fifth century, and a pottery for making Christian lamps is also dated to this time. The only early – late fourth- or early fifth-century – church so far identified is single-naved with a mosaic floor, although Marcianopolis was an archiepiscopal centre as well as the capital of Moesia Secunda. Two painted tombs from the necropolis with decorations that included garlands and doves may also belong to this period, which came to an end in 447 when the Huns captured and set fire to the city.

The city was to have a brief flowering in the sixth century. According to Procopius, its walls were restored by Justinian, and the remains of four churches have been attributed to this period. One, superimposed on the early single-naved basilica, was three-naved, with a narthex and a rectangular annex, believed to be a baptistery. The nave was separated from the aisles by marble columns, each with a cross carved in relief in the middle, crowned by acanthus capitals, one incorporating an eagle. In the nave, in front of the sanctuary, the mosaic floor was almost completely preserved. Using stone and ceramic tesserae of white, black, brown, orange, and yellow, zones of interlacing flanked geometrically patterned squares in *kilim*-like fashion.

In the arena of the destroyed amphitheatre another three-naved basilica was erected, using much of the old building material. Perhaps this site was chosen in commemoration of martyrs who had earlier met their deaths there.

So Marcianopolis, a strategic bulwark in the defence of Constantinople, enjoyed prosperity until the second half of the sixth century, when it was taken by the Avars, but probably more plundered than destroyed, since it is mentioned in 595 as a military base visited from Odessos by Peter, brother of Maurice.

The last mention of the archbishopric of Marcianopolis was in the seventh century, after which it seems to have been transferred for a short time to Odessos. The title was resurrected a thousand years later, when Pope Urban VII appointed one Marko Bandulević (perhaps a Bosnian) to the archiepiscopate of the Catholics in north-east Bulgaria and some lands beyond the Danube, and gave him the title of archbishop of Marcianopolis.

NOTES

1 NAC 1970, *Arh* XII/3, 81.
2 Miyatev, K., *Arhitekturata v srednovekovna Bulgariya*, Sofia, 1965, fig. 148.
3 *BASEE* I, 1969, 51, 52.
4 Velkov, V., *Gradut v Trakiya i Dakiya prez kusnata antichnost*, Sofia, 1959, 164.
5 Škorpil, K., in *Bulgariya 1000 Godini*, I, Sofia, 1930, 186.

12 Serdica and the West (11)

I. SERDICA AND THE CENTRAL REGION

The fourth-century extension of Serdica's fortifications was probably destroyed by the Visigoths in the last quarter of the same century, and the fall of the city to Attila's Huns in 441–42 put an end to any question of its reconstruction. Serdica was sacked and looted; the destruction was less severe than at Naissus, but at a meeting here in 449 between Byzantine and Hun envoys, the latter could still point to the surrounding devastation to illustrate their master's power.

After Attila's death, Serdica's walls must have been hurriedly repaired – or else the city would have been defenceless during the ensuing Ostrogothic wars – but the original Aurelian plan was readopted and continued during the sixth century. Then or, it has been suggested, as early as the reigns of Marcian I or Leo I, a massive renovation of the city's defences was part of the general refortification programme. A new wall was built along the whole outer face of the old one, the socle of which formed part of its base. Like the old wall, it was 2·15 metres thick, except on the south where it was 2·60 metres. The strength of the walls was thus doubled (Fig. 68). Although earlier rounded towers were incorporated in the new curtain wall, triangular and pentagonal towers were added, especially by the two gates, as can be seen by the east gate in the pedestrian underpass (Pl. 165).

There is no evidence how Serdica fared at the hands of the Avars and Slavs, but it appears to have remained in Byzantine hands, reappearing in history at the beginning of the ninth century, when the Bulgars captured it and dismantled the fortifications before retiring.

The insula east of the St George complex underwent little change. Sometime, what had probably been a pagan shrine in the form of an inscribed octagon was converted to Christianity and given a rounded eastern apse. A small single-naved basilica, also with a rounded apse, was attached to it.

Outside the east gate were two churches, one above the other, a baptistery beside them (Fig. 69). The earlier church, single-naved but with pastophoria-like annexes, an apse almost as wide as the nave, and a narthex where a fragment of geometric mural painting has survived, recalls Deli-Doushka. Dated to the fourth century, it was probably destroyed by the Visigoths. Its successor was an early fifth-century type of basilica with walls of opus mixtum, stylobates carrying colonnades, and a massive rounded apse with a single-stepped synthronon. The two-roomed baptistery, 2½ metres from the earlier church and 5 metres from the later, was not precisely aligned with either. East of the piscina, which had three steps at either end, an apse had been bricked up to form a semicircular basin reaching down to the floor, perhaps some kind of stoup for holy water. Although fourth-century coins were found, the baptistery is considered on a variety of grounds to belong to the later church.[1]

A few hundred metres away along the road to Philippopolis was the city's main Early Byzantine necropolis, marked today by the church of the Holy

FIG. 68 Serdica, reconstruction of Early Byzantine angle tower

PLATE 165 Serdica, east gate

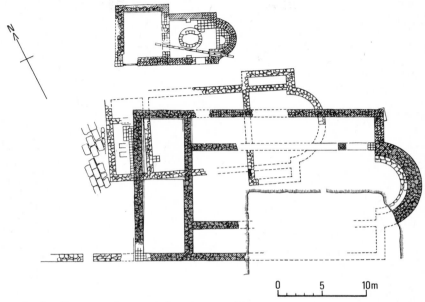

FIG. 69 Serdica, superimposed churches outside east gate

Wisdom (Sophia), the fifth church to occupy the site (Pl. 166). Patched but dignified, this ancient basilica carries its years with a modesty in sharp contrast to the gleaming golden-domed nineteenth-century church of Alexander Nevski standing nearby.

Alongside third-century pagan graves, Christian burials began to take place here in the first half of the fourth century. A concentration, among them tombs with painted vaults, was found under and close to the church of Holy Wisdom, clearly intended to be as near the original church as possible. They are architecturally similar and have the same reddish-orange painted frames round the walls as the contemporary pagan one at Durostorum. Facing birds and tree motifs are common to the paintings of both, but in Serdica the lighted candles flank a labarum. On one vault poppies replace rural scenes.

The finest painted tomb here was found in 1909. Brick built and vaulted with a north–south orientation, it had been looted and was badly damaged by damp. The walls were painted to imitate marble revetment. In the centre of the ceiling a green laurel wreath with white fruit enclosed a Latin cross in yellow ochre, outlined with pearls and with white rays radiating from its centre. Busts of the four archangels, named in Latin, occupied each angle of the long sides of the vault. Three were in a very poor condition and only Uriel was photographed before disintegration (Pl. 167). The excavators dated the paintings on stylistic grounds to the fifth or possibly sixth century, but Latin suggests the fourth, and the orientation of the tomb also argues for an earlier dating.[2]

The first church on the site of Holy Wisdom (Fig. 70), single-naved with a

PLATE 166 Serdica, church of Holy Wisdom

PLATE 167 Serdica, Uriel, tomb painting

PLATE 168 Serdica, Holy Wisdom,
Church I, mosaic floor

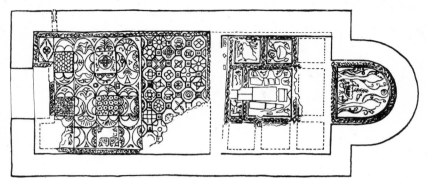

FIG. 70 Serdica, Holy Wisdom, church 1

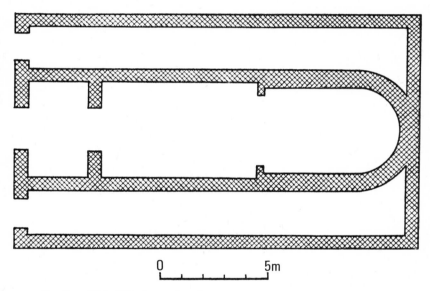

0   5m

FIG. 71 Serdica, Holy Wisdom, church 2

rounded apse, occupied an area about 14 metres long and nearly six metres wide under the east part of the present church. Only mortar foundations of its first pebble mosaic floor remain. The next floor was of multicoloured mosaic tesserae, divided into three zones and probably used during more than one building phase. In the centre of the apse zone, birds perched round a large fluted bowl, plant, and two baskets, were flanked by cypress-like trees and spiralling vines (Pl. 168). The next zone, occupying rather more than the eastern third of the nave, was square, its subdivisions containing such common symbols as the vine, ivy, lambs, and a peacock. Beyond, a single border enclosed the third zone, divided into two parts; the western had complex and luxuriant geometric

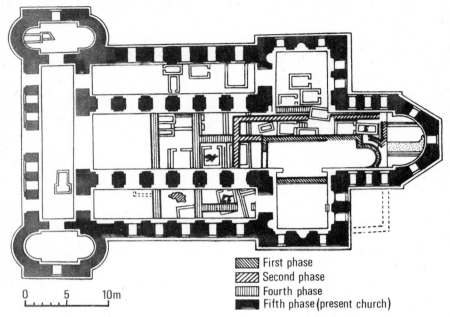

First phase
Second phase
Fourth phase
Fifth phase (present church)

0   5   10m

FIG. 72 Serdica, Holy Wisdom, overall plan of superimposed churches

FIG. 73 Serdica, Holy Wisdom, reconstruction of church 5

patterns, with here and there a vase and once a bird, the more schematic and regular eastern part being considered a later repair.

The nave of the second church was built on the foundations of the first, but with two side-aisles to north and south extending to a new east wall which inscribed the apse, now as wide as the nave. A tripartite narthex was added (Fig. 71). The repaired part of the mosaic floor of the first church may have belonged to its successor or the whole floor may have been common to both buildings.

The third church widened the aisles and narthex of its predecessor; the few remains include new fragments of mosaic, also with geometric designs but using larger tesserae with less skill.

The fourth church (in B. Filov's 1913 excavation report the second) is a puzzle, the first clue being the existence of a floor mosaic above the earlier levels. Including damaged areas, but without borders, which have entirely disappeared, this mosaic covered nearly 144 square metres and paved part of the nave. More was found at the same level in the south-east corner of the south transept. Here was perhaps the beginning of an edge to the floor. In 1913 the plan of the church was impossible to determine. The south aisle of the present building, then in use as a chapel, could not be excavated. Nevertheless, Filov suggested that two parallel north–south walls, running near or under the second and fourth piers (counting from the west), seemed to correspond to the narthex of a single building, and proposed that a similar wall between the north piers supporting the dome might be part of its north wall. The overall plan published after recent conservation (Fig. 72) supports these theories and suggests stylobates along the middle of the present nave and south aisle. Pending fuller publication, no further analysis is possible.

The fifth church, although mutilated by eventful centuries, is in essentials the one standing today. The building has been variously dated between the fifth and twelfth centuries, and described as influenced by Anatolian or Romanesque architecture, or even as having influenced the evolution of the Romanesque, the Crusaders acting as 'carriers' in either direction. Some of these theories may be due to the splendid soaring height of the nave which is a familiar sight to the Western eye.

Much larger and more solidly built than its predecessors, the new church was wholly brick. Beginning from the west, the ground plan consisted of an undivided narthex with north and south extensions, a nave and two aisles, a slightly protruding transept, and finally a short choir and an apse with a three-sided exterior. The total length was 46½ metres, of which the nave and aisles occupied only 21 metres. In spatial terms, the church gives less the impression of a three-naved basilica than of a Latin cross with an architecturally integrated narthex and vaulted and galleried side-aisles.

The high vaulted nave is separated from the aisles by massive arched piers, five on each side, spaced only 1·70 metres apart. The openings from narthex and transept are little wider, establishing a great contrast between these relatively shut-in areas and the broad lofty space formed by the integral and apparently uninterrupted unit of the nave, transept, and choir-apse. Separation of aisles from nave is not at all unusual in fifth- and early sixth-century basilicas; but, where a transept exists, its arms are normally occupied by the prothesis and

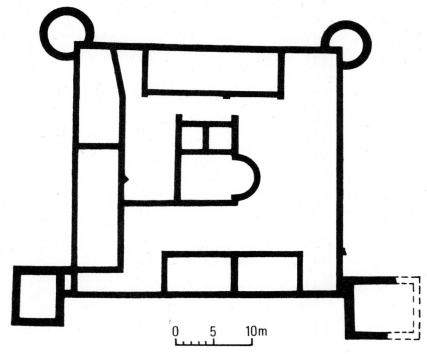

FIG. 74 Orlandovtsi, villa rustica

diaconicon. The plan shows that the transept did not serve this purpose here, consequently the sanctuary consisted of the choir and apse. The funerary church of Holy Wisdom thus provided a suitable position beneath the dome for the deceased during the burial service.

A similar plan was found in another funerary church nearby at Ivanyani. Analogous cruciform churches with a less clearly defined function have been excavated at Tsurkvishte, and at Caričin Grad in Serbia.[3] Possibly Botevo (p. 242) falls within this category. This plan was by no means the sole funerary type; probably of eastern Anatolian origin it occurs in the Balkans only in a relatively small area.

The Holy Wisdom stood, exposed, outside the walls on a site where at least four predecessors had been destroyed within two or three hundred years. There were many graves, perhaps some of martyrs, beneath the floor and the church itself must have contained much of spiritual and material value. Hence its solid construction, calculated to withstand minor raids. Galleries, perhaps for defence as much as for worship, were built above the narthex and transept as well as over the aisles. It is now believed that there was a second storey above the narthex and transept, and that the north and south extensions of the former carried towers (Fig. 83). Cross-groined vaults covered the transept arms and choir, and also formed the ceiling of the nave and aisles. The present dome, supported on four piers, has no drum, but S. Boyadjiev has proposed that originally a dome on an octagonal drum rose in place of the one visible today.[4]

Finds of 23 coins, ranging from Licinius to Arcadius, between the upper and lower mosaic floors give some help in dating the earlier churches. The first may have been built soon after the Edicts of Toleration – not unlikely if martyrs had been buried there. Historically feasible periods of destruction are the reign of Julian the Apostate, the late fourth-century Visigothic war, and the sack of Serdica by the Huns in 441–42. Julian passed by in 361 on the road from Naissus to Constantinople, where he was proclaimed emperor; his supporters might have razed the church to gain favour. It was an easy target for Visigoths and Huns. Added to these possibilities were natural disasters, such as fires, to necessitate rebuilding, as well as a fashion for new and larger churches. All that can be said with reasonable certainty is that the first four churches were built between the first half of the fourth and the middle of the fifth centuries.

The late fifth century, after the Hun and Ostrogoth devastations, was an unpropitious time for building the present church. Such skilful brick construction – especially in an exposed situation – is most unlikely in the late sixth century, yet the influence of Justinian is not evident in the massive, though noble, simplicity of the interior. On the whole, the first quarter of the sixth century seems most probable.

Even if Serdica remained a Byzantine outpost until the ninth century, a church so far outside the walls is unlikely to have been kept in repair. There is some slight epigraphic evidence for restoration in the late tenth or the eleventh century. Yet its fame grew. A charter granted to the monastery of Dragalevtsi in 1382 refers to the 'region of the Holy Sophia' and in the course of time Serdica, after being 'Sredets' to the Slavs, took the name of its most renowned church.

The necropolis had other churches. The foundations of a single-naved basilica with a round apse and a narthex, in all 16 metres long and 5·60 metres wide, were found 12 metres south of Holy Wisdom. Another, only partly excavated, lay to its west.

Orlandovtsi

The environs of Early Byzantine Serdica were not wholly cimiterial. Villae rusticae of the late fourth and fifth centuries have been uncovered, but the open aspect of more peaceful days has gone. An unusually fortified villa was found in 1935 at Orlandovtsi, 4 or 5 kilometres outside the city. The walls, preserved up to a metre high, formed a rectangle measuring 31 by 34 metres (Fig. 74). Two round angle towers projected at the north-west and north-east corners, whilst the south-west and south-east corners were defended by external rectangular towers. Built of local broken stone and mortar, the walls were 65 to 70 centimetres thick, except at the towers, where they approached 1 metre.

The site had been long under the plough so that, although the plan was clearly discernible, there were few finds *in situ* to help determine the interior arrangement. Rooms were annexed to the walls on all sides except the east. The west was completely occupied by a rough construction, divided into two parts, probably farm buildings. On the south were two smaller rooms, probably living quarters; they were better built and contained materials apparently brought from Serdica,

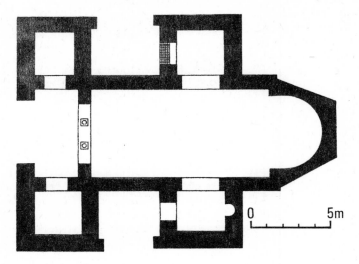

FIG. 75 Ivanyani, church

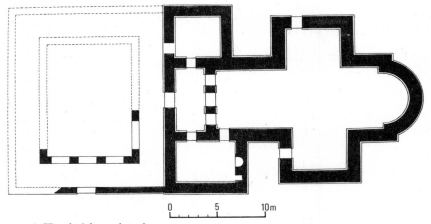

FIG. 76 Tsurkvishte, church

architectural and funerary stele fragments among them. Inside the north wall was a long, undivided room. The largest of a group of three rooms in the centre of the villa had an eastern apse and may have been a chapel.

Few coins were found, the earliest of Maximin Daza (305–13), and more and better-preserved examples from the reigns of Constantine, Constantius, and Theodosius II. On the basis of building techniques, pottery finds, and coins, the excavator dated the villa to about the end of the fourth century, when a chapel would be normal. During this troubled period defence must have been an essential feature in any building plan, but the Huns probably destroyed it when they attacked Serdica. Similarly fortified villas are believed to have existed at Bistritsa, in the Dupnik area, and also at Radomir in the Chirpan region, but neither has been fully excavated; the Orlandovtsi villa is unique in Bulgaria in its unusual combination of round and square towers.

Ivanyani

Near the village of Ivanyani on the outskirts of Sofia, a rescue dig some fifty years ago brought to light a single-naved church with side-chambers flanking the narthex and others projecting from the nave like the arms of a cross (Fig. 75). The line of the nave continued, as in the church of Holy Wisdom, beyond the 'arms' to form a short choir before the apse; indeed the basic plan was very similar except for the lack of side-aisles and the presence of two crypts under the eastern 'arms'. The southern crypt was rectangular and barrel-vaulted, its narrow entrance below the socle of the south wall. The northern crypt was almost identical except that the entrance – also small – descended in a vaulted right-angled curve from the sanctuary. Both had been looted, but the site of its entrance suggests that the northern one probably contained relics – to be brought out on ceremonial occasions – and perhaps a tomb as well. The south crypt may have been the founder's tomb, but there are no finds to support this or any other hypothesis. The church was built in opus mixtum, the crypts of brick; the sculptured architectural fragments were of high quality. Destruction was severe; the church was pulled down and set on fire as well. Like the Holy Wisdom of Sofia, it may be dated to the earlier half of the sixth century.

Tsurkvishte (Klise-Kuoi)

Another cruciform church was found in the region of the upper Topolnitsa valley between the Stara Planina and the north-western slopes of the Sredna Gora. Seven kilometres west of the district centre of Pirdop is the village of Tsurkvishte, known in the Turkish period as Klise-Kuoi, both names enshrining a tradition that a church had existed below the ruins of a mosque. In the early 1900s, according to P. Mutafchiev, who later tried to restore some order out of the ensuing confusion, the villagers decided to dig for it, motivated by a mixture of piety, curiosity, and greed. They uncovered the east and south-west parts of a church and some medieval graves.

The plan established was of a cruciform church with a narthex, two western side-chambers, and a colonnaded atrium (Fig. 76). For such a solid building – with foundations 2·30 metres deep and walls – mainly of brick – 1·25 metres thick, the church, as the plan shows, was extraordinarily asymmetrical. Unlike others in the 'cruciform group', there were two niches in the south-western annex; the larger one was U-shaped with a clay outlet pipe in its floor. The entrances are so placed as to support the suggestion of a baptistery.

Unfortunately little work was possible, since the debris from the mosque – which had preserved most of the interior – also prevented a complete survey. The one early grave found was a brick tomb, roofed with slabs. Only re-excavation can decide if this church had the funerary function its plan suggests (if so, a baptistery would be unusual) and if Mutafchiev's dating to the early fifth century is to be preferred to the sixth.

Pirdop

A few kilometres north-east of Pirdop, the Elenska stream emerges from the Stara Planina and flows past the noble ruins of the Elenska church (the church of the stag) also known as the monastery of St Elia, which looks across the valley to the distant Sredna Gora (Pl. 169). P. Mutafchiev suggests that the two names for this church relate to a legend that at its festival on 20 July – the feast of St Elia, who often replaced pagan mountain gods – it was the custom for a stag to come down from the Stara Planina and offer itself for sacrifice. One year the stag, having travelled a great way, arrived very late and covered with sweat and foam. Since all were impatient and hungry, the exhausted beast was slaughtered at once, leaving no time for it to recover the strength to submit itself voluntarily in the sacrificial rite. Because of this cruel and impious act, the mountain ended its annual tribute. The large quantities of stag bones and antlers found in the site debris are proof only of a popular festival. But the wild and picturesque site, beside a ravine at the foot of the 'Old Mountains', and the towering ruins of splendid brickwork are the stuff from which legends are easily born.

Excavation in 1913 showed these ruins to be those of a large three-naved basilica which had been rebuilt, after very severe damage, on the old foundations and using part of the old walls. A massive rectangular wall with four angle towers enclosed the church (Pl. 170, Fig. 77). As at Tsurkvishte, there is a tendency to irregularity. The side-apses are not exactly symmetrical and although on the outside the solid foundations of all three apses coincide with the superstructure,

PLATE 169 Pirdop, Elenska church from north

inside they project some 35 centimetres below floor level in the form of arcs quite unrelated to the walls. This berm continues, still irregularly, inside the walls of the sanctuary (Fig. 78).

Two massive piers, beginning 2 metres from the central apse, create a triple sanctuary, linked by arched openings, and also form the eastern supports of a central dome. The corresponding western piers, built of large sandstone blocks, are half-way down the colonnades between nave and aisles. There are two brick

PLATE 170 Pirdop, Elenska church from west

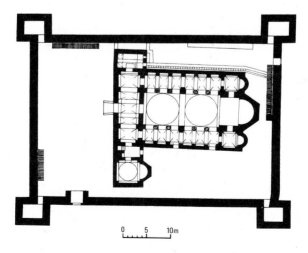

FIG. 77 Pirdop, Elenska church and fortifications

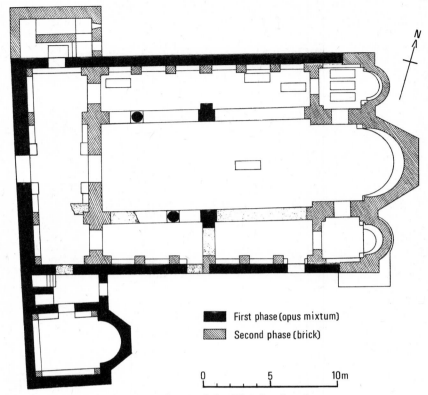

FIG. 78 Pirdop, two building phases of the Elenska church

piers at the western end, but it is debatable whether this half of the nave was domed or barrel-vaulted. The narthex, divided by pilasters suggesting arches corresponding to the colonnades, was half a metre wider at the north end than at the southern. A north annex contained a spiral staircase and a southern, a small rectangular room – also with stairs – had an entrance to a square apsed chamber, perhaps once a baptistery, although with no trace of a piscina. The existence of galleries above the narthex and aisles, implied by the stairs and general solid construction, is confirmed by the remains of brick vaulting at the east end (Pl. 171).

The two building phases are easily distinguishable. One consists of opus mixtum – broken stone and mortar with a bonding layer of three brick courses, the other entirely of carefully laid brick. At a point in the south wall – probably originally a doorway – the dividing-line is very clear. Of the existing structure, the east end, with its piers, the wall between nave and narthex, and the north annex are brick-built. The rest of the walls and the south annex are in opus mixtum (Fig. 78). The brick pilasters against the inner face of the north and south walls, but not constructionally linked, must be later additions. As their materials and construction techniques are identical with the wholly brick-built

PLATE 171 Pirdop, Elenska church, east end

eastern parts of the church, the opus mixtum clearly represents the first building phase and the brick the second.

There had originally been plain monolithic columns, standing on stylobates. *In situ* were two columns of mortared sandstone drums, no doubt re-used fragments. In this provincial context, the few remains of decorative carving could belong to either the fifth or the early sixth century. Mutafchiev dated the earlier phase to the second half of the fifth or the early sixth century, and the later to the reign of Justinian. The sanctuary's resemblance to that of the Episcopal Church at Caričin Grad[5] supports the latter dating; the earlier is more open to question.

The surrounding walls have lent superficial support to the monastic legend, but the angle towers and the 1·60–1·70-metre-thick walls with ramparts are purely defensive. Judging by surviving steps, the height varied from 5·30 to 10 metres, according to the terrain. No trace of other building was found within

PLATE 172 Pautalia Hissarluk, south sector of east wall

PLATE 173 Pautalia Hissarluk, S.E. angle tower

PLATE 174 Pautalia Hissarluk, east triangular tower

the walls, nor was there much space available. But the church itself could provide
a local refuge during a raid, and there was room enough outside it for livestock.
The main entrance, a double gateway, was in the south wall, protected by the
south-west tower. A smaller gate, probably a postern, near the north-east tower,
led down a steep slope to the stream.

II. PAUTALIA AND THE SOUTH-WEST

When Dacia Mediterranea was created, Pautalia ranked after Serdica and
Naissus as the third city of the province. Julian repaired the fortifications, but
the west gate was first narrowed to a postern and later blocked up entirely. In
479, Zeno offered the Pautalia region to Theodoric the Amal and his Ostrogothic
followers. It is possible that the territory had escaped the Hun invasions and
Malchus of Philadelphia quotes the imperial envoy's description of 'abundance
of land beside that which was already inhabited, a fair and fertile territory lacking
cultivators, which his people could till, so providing themselves with all the
necessities of life'.[6] Theodoric, with reason suspicious of Zeno's motives, declined
the offer.

Current excavations, including a large three-naved single-apsed Christian
basilica with a fine mosaic floor,[7] show the city's continuing existence in the fifth
century. Procopius speaks of repairs to the walls, stating that, like those of
Serdica, Naissus, and Germania, they had fallen into disrepair, but he may not
have been referring to the city in the plain, the modern Kyustendil, for a new
fortress had been built some 150 metres above it, on the summit of the Hissarluk.

Unlike those on the Danube *limes*, the citizens of Pautalia had only to climb
to their Hissarluk for refuge. Its flat summit, the shape of a truncated arc roughly
250 metres long, was joined by a narrow saddle to the main Osogovska massif.
The walls of the fortress – a deep re-entrant on the east, a long convex curve on

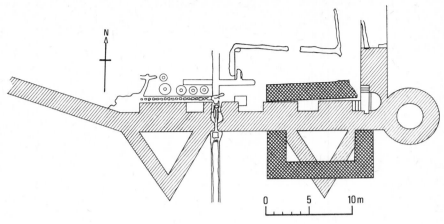

FIG. 79 Pautalia, south-east sector of Hissarluk

the west overlooking the city – were reinforced at the four corners by external
round towers. No others were needed to defend the precipitous north, west,
and south slopes, but two rectangular external towers strengthened the more
exposed east wall, which, incorporating two double gateways, was up to $2\frac{1}{4}$ metres
thick, compared with an average of $1\frac{1}{2}$ metres on the north side, which had only
a postern.[8] The most vulnerable point, the south-east corner, had, in addition
to its round angle tower, an eastern rectangular one with a postern between them
(Pls. 172, 173). Protecting the south side and a conduit bringing water into the
fortress were two substantial triangular towers only $8\frac{1}{2}$ metres apart, the nearest
but $2\frac{1}{2}$ metres from the round tower (Pl. 174). It appears that a semi-projecting
square tower later replaced the triangular one next to the angle (Fig. 79).

Partly on grounds of the building techniques, notably comparisons with
Theodosian walls at Thessalonica, and partly because of 22 fourth-century coins
(the reigns are not stated) and 14 small coins of the second and third centuries
found in the foundations, I. Ivanov dated the walls to the fourth century,
considering them a part of Julian's defence programme for Illyricum. However,
the recently re-excavated south-east angle with the triangular towers must be
fifth- or sixth-century work.

Current conservation work has mainly concentrated on the important south-
east corner. During the 1906–12 excavations, walls of what were probably
barracks or stores were traced by the east wall. On the west side, where the
present Hissarluk hotel stands, part of what were thought to be baths were
found. South of this, overlooking the city below, on the magnificent site earlier
occupied by the pagan temple (Pl. 115), are the fragmentary remains of a large
three-naved single-apsed basilical church, probably of the fifth or sixth century.

Pernik and Germania

The disastrous Visigothic invasions led to a temporary revival in the fortunes
of the middle Struma valley, the speediest route from Macedonia for reinforce-
ments to the Thracian plain, the Dacias, and the lower Danube.

The Krakra stronghold above Pernik continued to be inhabited, which is hardly surprising in view of its almost impregnable position above the Struma. Coins continue until those of Justin II, when there is a gap – no doubt filled by Slavo-Bulgar occupation – until the end of the first Bulgarian state.

Germania was the birthplace of Justinian's great general, Belisarius. Procopius states that Justinian rebuilt its fortifications and a sixth-century wall has recently been identified.

Sandanski

Confirmation that Sandanski shared this brief, strategically motivated prosperity comes, paradoxically, not from military monuments but from the excavation of four churches, three with mosaic floors, and one large baptistery. The last was found by soldiers in 1917; the churches are new discoveries and only one has been published, although a second, three-naved, has been provisionally dated to the fourth century.

Only part of the baptistery, probably attached to an episcopal church, was found (Fig. 80). Inside a circular outer wall, it seems that an ambulatory enclosed another wall in which remained evidence of two shallow niches flanking a doorway, itself enclosed within a wider and yet shallower niche, leading to an octagonal piscina. Here and opposite the doorway three steps led down to the marble floor of the pool. Fragments of slender marble columns, decorated at the top with stripes of red and gold paint, probably surmounted pilasters round the pool to support a ciborium or ornamental canopy. The niches of the inner wall were painted in geometric patterns. Other architectural fragments included a marble column 2 metres long, Ionic impost capitals carved with crosses, birds, ivy and acanthus leaves, and a few small remnants of wall mosaic.

A hundred metres away, in a church now partly preserved within a new museum, a mosaic inscription names a bishop, although not the still unidentified

FIG. 80 Sandanski, baptistery

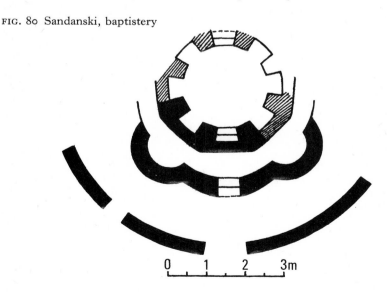

0   1   2   3m

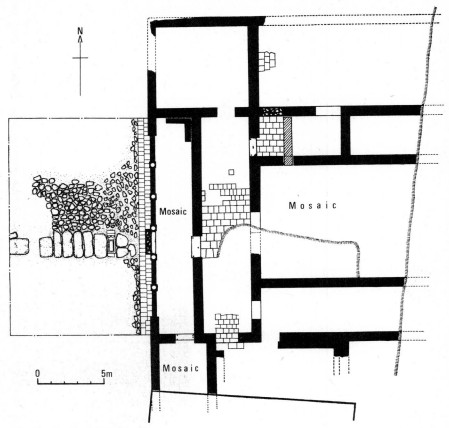

FIG. 81 Sandanski, church

see. The existence of this building, a three-naved basilica with narthex, *exonarthex* (or outer vestibule), and various annexes (Fig. 81), was detected by an alert local history-master during the course of building operations, and work was stopped to allow excavation and conservation. Unfortunately, the eastern half – probably long destroyed – lay under a main road.

The basilica stood on earlier buildings in use until about the middle of the fifth century. In the western part of the dig an open courtyard, possibly an atrium was found, but could not be fully uncovered. A path of granite slabs, including the funerary stele of M. Herennius Rufus (p. 184), crossed the middle of the courtyard to a colonnaded exonarthex, one intact column showing it to have been 2·40 metres high.

The whole exonarthex floor was mosaic, laid in geometric patterns and using a variety of colours. Facing the entrance a meander border framed the Greek inscription (Pl. 175) which may be roughly translated as follows:

+ You desire to know who built this splendid edifice which delights the eye with its beauty. It is John, that wise and humble man who came to take care of the episcopal seat and having as his predecessor the devout man named O . . . . .

The rest of the inscription is lost and Bishop O . . . who, John's expression of humility notwithstanding, may actually have been the founder of the church, remains known only by his initial. On either side of the inscription are identical geometrical patterns consisting of a series of octagons linked by a meander motif and containing a white quatrefoil inscribed in a dark square, the dark areas forming a 'Maltese' cross.

A single entrance led to a brick-paved narthex, with three entrances to the nave and aisles, which were probably separated by colonnades on stylobates. The nave floor was also of mosaic, mostly geometrical in design but incorporating realistic birds, fishes, flowers, and ivy leaves. North and south rooms were attached to each narthex. The southern extended for an unknown distance below the present post office and possessed a mosaic floor resembling the geometric pattern of the exonarthex, but with a border of stylised lotus flowers and fish or birds in the octagons.

Very little sculptural decoration was found, with the interesting exception of fragments of three marble altar tables. One, with an unidentifiable scene carved in low relief, was round; the other two were of the 'sigma' type, one plain with a Latin cross in the centre, the other of the type with 12 rounded divisions.

PLATE 175 Sandanski, mosaic inscription

The excavator compares the plan of the basilica with that of Suvodol in western Macedonia, ascribed to the mid-sixth century, and there are resemblances between the mosaics and those in the Episcopal Church at Caričin Grad. For these reasons and by analogy with other churches in Bulgaria, he suggests the Sandanski basilica belongs to the first half of the sixth century, probably the beginning of Justinian's reign. But until publication of the other churches here has established some chronology for this corner of Macedonia, dating must necessarily be tentative.

The church – and the city – were almost certainly destroyed by the Slavs late in the sixth century in some foray down the Struma to attack Thessalonica.

The Mesta Valley

As in the Roman period, little is known of Nicopolis-ad-Nestum in the Early Byzantine era. Although probably still something of a backwater, it did not entirely escape the Ostrogoths, since the Mesta route was probably used by Theodoric on his way to besiege Philippi in 473. A hoard of gold coins buried at about that time is a sign of approaching danger, but that there was gold to bury shows the relative prosperity of the region compared with others farther north.

Although Nicopolis was the seat of a bishopric, so far only one church has been excavated, in 1903, on a site locally known as the monastery of St Nedelya. A mosaic floor with decorative vegetal motifs was found. A 'double wall' was said to enclose the church, about which no other information is available.

Much more recently, a preliminary survey[9] of a single-apsed church, 23 metres long and 14 metres wide, was made at a site called 'the monastery of St George' near Debren, some 10 kilometres east of Gotse Delchev on a plateau enclosed within a fold of the Rhodopes. Among the finds were fragments of oval marble columns, marble slabs, profiled cornices, and oval impost capitals decorated with volutes and crosses, one having an alpha and omega beneath the arms of an inscribed cross. These last were dated tentatively between the fifth and seventh centuries, but it is thought that the church, with the surrounding settlement, continued to exist throughout the medieval period until its conversion to a mosque, which eventually fell into ruins. Columns were removed to be built into fountains in Debren, but the abandoned site retained what is believed to have been its earlier name, 'the monastery of St George'.

NOTES

1 Stancheva, M., *Serdika I*, 1964, 159 ff.
2 Katsarov, G. and Tachev, H., *IBAD* I, 1910, 23 ff.
3 Hoddinott, R. F., *Early Byzantine Churches in Macedonia and Southern Serbia*, London, 1963, 211–13.
4 Boyadjiev, S., *Izsled Dechev*, 1958, 611 ff.
5 Hoddinott, op. cit., 206–9.
6 Quoted Hodgkin, T., *Theodoric the Goth*, London, 1891, 86.
7 NAC 1970, *Arh* XII/3, 1970, 79.
8 Gocheva points out that the orientation shown on the Hissarluk plan published in *IBAD* VII, Fig. 66, is incorrect; for 'north' read 'west'.
9 Mihailov, S., *Rodopski Sbornik* II, 1969, 169–72.

13 The Thracian Plain (11)

I. PHILIPPOPOLIS

During the Visigothic wars, Valens' strong control over Philippopolis ensured for the city and its environs a higher degree of immunity than was the case in the rest of Thracia. Not until the Hun invasion of 441–42 was it endangered, but then the damage seems to have been severe. No details are known, but substantial repairs were needed to the outer wall and to the Trimontium fortress. During the Ostrogothic wars the city was again under heavy attack. In the sixth century Procopius designates it as one of the especially vulnerable centres requiring refortification.

Except on the south side, the original walls, which were surrounded by a ditch, seem to have been repaired or rebuilt to a thickness of up to 3 metres on their old foundations. On the south the wall was drastically retracted to a new position that almost halved the size of the enclosed area, reducing the walled circuit from about $3\frac{1}{2}$ kilometres to a little over $2\frac{1}{2}$ kilometres.

Remains of one of the inner fortress gates, the 'Hissarkapiya', built in the late fifth or early sixth century, still stand today near the church of SS Constantine and Helena. The gate, now impinged upon by neighbouring buildings, is in the east wall between Djambaz-tepe and Nebet-tepe. It was probably flanked by two square towers, the size of which could not be ascertained. The site of one is occupied by the present Ethnographical Museum and the other by the east end of the church, beneath which was found an entrance to the tower from inside the fortress. In the vicinity of this gate, the curtain wall – of opus mixtum with bands of five brick courses – has been preserved to a height of over 4 metres. It incorporated an externally projecting round brick tower, the lower parts of which survive.

Walls have also been uncovered on the south slopes of Djambaz-tepe and the north-west slopes of Nebet-tepe. They vary in height from 2 to 8 metres and were often built upon Roman and Hellenistic substructures (Pl. 176). From a gate in the north wall of Nebet-tepe a flight of steps, 16 of which remain, descended the steep slope to the outer wall.

These measures enabled at least the inner fortress to survive Avar and Slav attacks and to remain in Byzantine hands until its absorption into the first Bulgarian state. Anna Comnena visited it in the first half of the twelfth century. 'Once upon a time', she wrote, 'Philippopolis must have been a large and beautiful city . . . equipped with an enormous hippodrome and other buildings of note. I myself saw traces of them.'[1]

The fourth-century baths near the foot of Djambaz-tepe were destroyed in the fifth century, probably by the Huns, and rebuilt on a more modest scale. A room from the lower floor, with opus mixtum walls, had four cross-groined vaults, each with three ventilation holes, supported on nine massive brick piers (Pl. 177). This room had originally had hypocausts; in the second phase it was probably part of a heating system using hot water. Avars or Slavs finally destroyed these baths about the end of the sixth century.

PLATE 176 Philippopolis, Nebet-tepe walls   PLATE 177 Philippopolis, baths

By the end of the fourth or early fifth century, a temple to the new imperial religion of Christianity had replaced the shrine of Apollo on Djendem-tepe, recalling the similar transformation at Pautalia. This was a three-naved, single-apsed basilica with a narthex, 35 metres long and 19½ metres wide; it was buttressed by opus mixtum walls on the sloping sides of the hill. A wide apse and relatively wide nave and narrow side-aisles are evidence of an early date. The erection of a church in this situation must have been a symbol of triumph, seized by the Christians as soon as the religious climate made it possible, probably

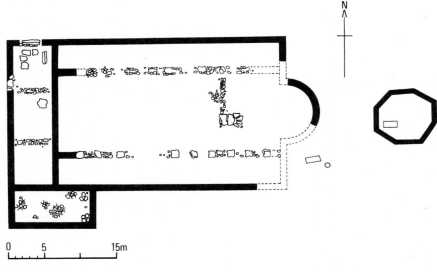

FIG. 82 Komatevo, church

after Theodosius' Edict of 380 had enabled the Christian hierarchy to take over the pagan shrines.

The foundations of an unusually large – probably fifth-century – Christian basilica have been excavated at Komatevo, originally a Thracian settlement 7 kilometres south of Plovdiv. Single-apsed, three-naved, and with a narthex, it had an overall length of 43½ metres (Fig. 82). The width of the nave was almost three times that of the aisles. A rectangular annex on the south-west may have been a baptistery, although no trace of a piscina was found. An octagonal structure had stood 8 metres east of the apse; its plain brick floor covered two Christian graves. The well-cut stone blocks of some earlier building on the site had been used in the church. The size of the basilica may simply be due to its serving a populous area; the remains of small, flimsy two-roomed houses were found, densely packed, in the neighbourhood.

II. PEROUSHTITSA

At Peroushtitsa substantial ruins of a sixth-century church built on an unusually interesting plan stand alone against a background of the Rhodope foothills, an impressive memorial of the prosperity of the Early Byzantine settlement (Pl. 178). Two brick piers on the north side of the church are still nearly 14 metres high; between them an intact arch spans 5½ metres and curves up to 11½ metres above the floor (Pl. 179). Even traces of wall painting are still discernible.

The Red Church – so called from its exceptionally fine all-brick construction, the only stonework being later repairs – was the second church on the site (Fig. 83). Little remains of the first, for there is only a thin layer of soil over solid rock, obviating both need and possibility of deep foundations. From the west, a central entrance in a portico led into an exonarthex and then by a corresponding doorway into a narthex of the same size. A square baptistery

PLATE 178 Peroushtitsa, 'Red Church'

PLATE 179 Peroushtitsa, 'Red Church', north aspect

PLATE 180 Peroushtitsa, 'Red Church', brick vaulting

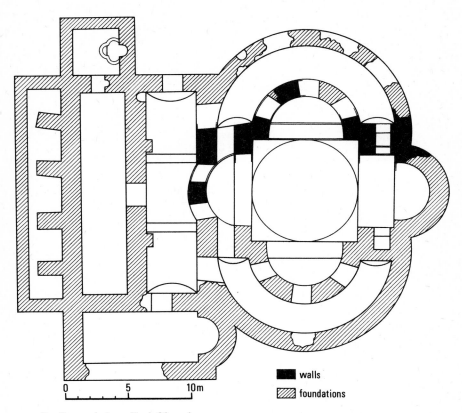

0   5   10m   ■ walls
                    ▨ foundations

FIG. 83 Peroushtitsa, Red Church

with a quatrefoil piscina was reached from the north end of the exonarthex, while
the south end of the narthex opened into a rectangular apsed annex.

The main part of the church, for all its centralised appearance, was essentially
based on a modified basilical plan. Four great piers connected by arches enclosed
a central space 8 metres square with apsidal extensions making it a tetraconch,
the floor of which was probably laid with mosaic. In the north and south walls,
three arched openings, formed by two freestanding piers and the end pilasters,
connected this tetraconchal nave with encircling single-storied north and south
aisles. The eastern apse of the tetraconch was set further back than the rest so
that a barrel-vaulted choir 2·80 metres deep replaced the arched openings of the
other three. Its outside curve projected as part of the outer wall of the church.
On either side of the choir were two small rooms, walled off from the aisles.

Fundamentally, therefore, the Red Church can be considered as a basilica
with a tetraconchal nave, two aisles, a single apse, two small presbyteries
apparently serving as prothesis and diaconicon, a narthex and exonarthex. To

PLATE 181 Peroushtitsa, 'Red Church', wall painting

PLATE 182 Peroushtitsa, 'Red Church', wall painting

this was added a baptistery and a second side-chamber or presbytery which, in view of the relatively small sanctuary, was probably a service room for the priests and deacons and perhaps also a sacristy. The central area of the tetraconch was domed, with supporting half-domes over the apses. The narthex and exonarthex appear to have been barrel-vaulted.

The unusual form has given rise to widely varying theories about date and origin. The association of the tetraconch form of nave with martyria may have been a factor, but perhaps of greater account is the evident attempt to cope with the transition from the basilical to the centralised plan in accordance with contemporary trends in Constantinople. The attempt was, in fact, remarkably successful; only the single apse coupled with the rudimentary prothesis and diaconicon rooms suggest the earlier half of the sixth century rather than the later or even, as has been proposed, the seventh. A very similar plan occurred in a now destroyed church at Hadrianopolis, and another, but with the Western form of sanctuary, in the recently excavated tetraconchal church at Ohrid.[2] Analogies are also to be found in the church in the Stoa of Hadrian in Athens and at Resafa in Syria.

Wall paintings of both the sixth and the thirteenth or fourteenth centuries have suffered severely from exposure. Plate 181, taken in 1964, shows what may have been a representation of the church itself. In the 1920s, five main groups of sixth–seventh-century paintings were identified:[3] on a soffit of the prothesis two angels holding a medallion in which was the Mystic Lamb; on the wall of the north apse three rows of scenes, including the Adoration of the Magi, the Flight into Egypt, and apocryphal subjects; on the vault of the north aisle a scene of martyrdom; on the soffits of the arches between the nave and north aisle three medallions including one showing Moses unfastening his sandal before climbing Mount Horeb (Pl. 182) and another of him receiving the Law; elsewhere on these arches were angels in medallions and scenes which include the fragment of the high domed church.

III. ISPERIHOVO

At Isperihovo, nearly 20 kilometres south of Pazardjik in the Rhodope foothills, an Early Byzantine monastery (Fig. 84) incorporated a small single-naved church with a horseshoe-shaped apse and a deep narthex built of broken stone and red mortar. A contemporary baptistery was annexed on the south, but a north-west annex containing a font was a later addition, following the introduction of infant baptism (p. 325).

The rest of the complex consisted of a series of later rooms, some roughly mortared with mud; they included a cattle shed, a bread oven, and so on. Tools for woodwork and agriculture as well as household pots show that soon after the church was built a group of monks must have settled here and cultivated the land. The complex was not entirely excavated and it is possible that by the sixth century it was surrounded by a wall, of which one entrance led into the narthex of the church and a second into the farm buildings.

It is rare to find monasteries in Bulgaria at all during this period; the two baptisteries and the plan of the sanctuary suggest that the church should be dated to the end of the fourth or the beginning of the fifth century. The horseshoe-shaped apse is usually a sign of Anatolian influence.

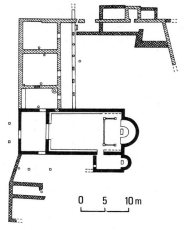

0   5   10 m

FIG. 84 Isperihovo, monastery

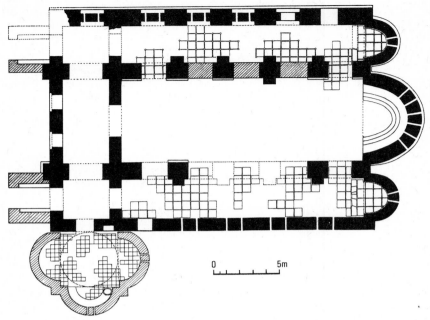

FIG. 85 Golyamo Belovo, church

IV. GOLYAMO BELOVO

Golyamo Belovo is high on a mountain terrace above the western edge of the Thracian plain, 26 kilometres west of Pazardjik. Here the substantial remains – reaching a height of over 7 metres – of an Early Byzantine brick church excavated in the 1920s were recently re-examined. Some of the apparent inconsistencies are now thought to be due to changes of plan made during construction; others occurred later when the building was partly reconstructed.

The church was a three-naved basilica built on bedrock foundations, with three ovoid apses and a narthex (Fig. 85). The central apse was lined with a three-stepped synthronon and parts of what appear to be the base of a sanctuary screen were found *in situ* at the openings of the side-apses, so these latter presumably served as the prothesis and diaconicon. Unusual differences were noted between the north and south outer walls. The former, in effect, consisted of a series of substantial piers, between which narrower sections enclosed large windows and, at the eastern end, a doorway. The southern wall was normally constructed, with a doorway in the western end and four evenly spaced windows.

Four brick piers of the same thickness as those of the north wall separated the nave from the aisles. Although not symmetrical either with the piers of the north wall or with the windowless parts of the south wall, they supported cross-groined vaulting over the aisles. The roofing of the nave is disputed. While the remaining six piers have pilasters on their outer faces, only one has a pilaster projecting into the nave. The opposite pier has not survived, but a dome could not have been supported by the relatively weak piers and walls of the apses. A. Grabar and W. Emerson suggested a barrel vault. After re-examination, S. Boyadjiev detected signs that all the piers originally had inner pilasters, so proposed that the nave, too, had a cross-groined vault.

The trefoil-shaped baptistery, it is now pointed out, was certainly added later. It is also likely that the narthex had no upper storey, as at first thought, but was flanked by two towers. But the proposed siting of the towers as north and south projections of the narthex, rather than above the aisle divisions, is less convincing on the evidence adduced, although it is a common contemporary feature in the central Balkan area. The first phase of the church may have been begun in the late fifth century, but the structure of which part is standing today essentially belongs to the sixth.

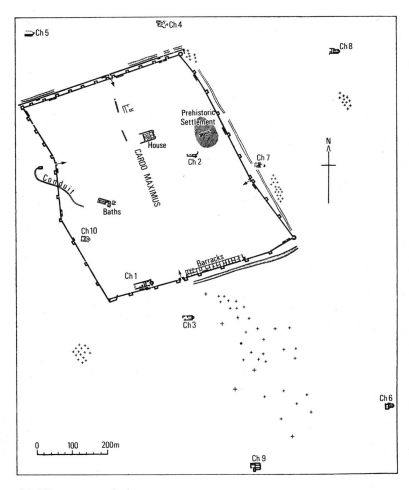

FIG. 86 Hissar, general plan

Golyamo Belovo is only one of several churches, as well as fortresses, built in this part of the Rhodopes during the fifth and sixth centuries. Around Velingrad others have been found at Barata, Beglichka, Rangela, and Rakitovo,[4] and the church at the Tsepina fortress was originally constructed in this period. In spite of the mountainous terrain, it was then a populous area and controlled the strategic routes linking the Thracian plain with the Mesta and Struma valleys.

V. HISSAR

The fourth-century prosperity of Hissar continued, in spite of destruction by the Visigoths – and probably some damage by passing Huns and Ostrogoths – at least to the turn of the sixth and seventh centuries, when Solomon, vicar of Thracia in the reign of Maurice, is recorded as having died there while taking the waters. Even today the surviving walls are a testimony of successful resistance to the Avars – a point in favour of identification with Diocletianopolis, which is said to have fought them off in 587 with the help of strong fortifications. Soundings in the town and pottery finds indicate that Hissar probably came to terms with the surrounding Slavs during the seventh century. It later became a Bulgarian strongpoint in the Thracian plain, thus accounting for a burning layer associated with coins of John Tzimisces, who conquered much of the first Bulgarian state in the late tenth century. Thereafter Hissar appears to have lost its strategic importance and, far enough from the main roads to avoid the march of progress, it continued as a small watering-place in a land abounding with them. It has thus preserved an important archaeological heritage.

The impressive curtain wall (Fig. 86), long stretches of which have been conserved and are visible today to a height of nearly 12 metres, was in opus mixtum with bonding layers of, usually, four courses of brick and between $2\frac{1}{2}$ and 3 metres thick. The quality of materials and high standard of workmanship have been important factors in its survival. The stone facing – of granite and gneiss from nearby quarries – was laid in bands of approximately 1 metre, the outer surface being carefully smoothed, the fill being rubble and mortar. The bricks were well fired and the mortar extremely hard (Pl. 183).

At least 11 double staircases led to the rampart walk; now from 14 to 18 metres wide at the base they were originally slightly larger. Under the arches of two in the inner north wall, small posterns gave access to the outer defences. Five single staircases have also been found. Brick-vaulted channels pierced the wall to expel surplus rainwater.

So far 43 contemporary towers have been located, 12 being on the inner north wall, ten on the west, eight on the south, nine on the east, and four angle towers. All projected and, except for the rounded north-east and south-east angle towers, all were quadrangular. With inner dimensions of about 5 by 5·30 metres, they were probably at least two-storeyed; recesses being visible in some of them for beams to carry a second floor 4·2 metres above the berm. The earlier towers were generally similar, but some did not project so far. Analogies have been drawn with the towers of the east wall at Novae.

The eastern angle towers were planned to withstand battering rams. The south-east one was fan-shaped, as at Abritus and Voivoda. The north-east angle tower is quite different – an irregular octagon built on rounded foundations

PLATE 183 Hissar, south wall, inner face

(Fig. 87).There are two floor levels, one 40 centimetres above the other, with traces of burning between. The round foundation may have been earlier – it was of opus mixtum with one remaining bonding layer of five courses of brick – or else a special base because of the tower's site on the steep bank of a stream. In the final building phase, the entrance, previously apparently open, was given grooves for a door, perhaps in case of a breach in the curtain wall.

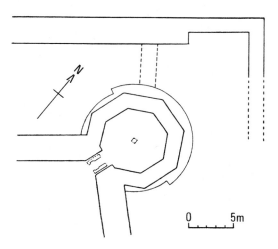

FIG. 87 Hissar, north-east angle tower

PLATE 184 Hissar, south gate

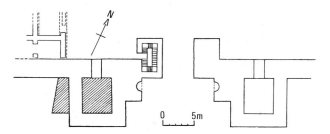

FIG. 88 Hissar, south gate

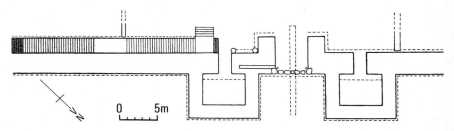

FIG. 89 Hissar, east gate

A gate was more or less centrally situated in each wall. The main gate (popularly called 'The Camels') in the south wall met the road from Philippopolis and had a ceremonial as well as a defensive purpose; it probably replaced a simpler one. It stands $14\frac{1}{2}$ metres high today, an impressive monument in regular use (Pl. 184, Fig. 88), which has acquired the inevitable legend that someone was walled up alive to keep it from collapse. Here a craftsman's wife leading a child is said to have been chosen. She had tucked a sprig of rue into her headscarf and the child was playing with a nut. In the early 1900s the legend was locally claimed to be proven because nut trees and rue, growing high up in the ruin, were always visible and always green.

The ceremonial gateway, projecting beyond the curtain wall and flanked by two projecting rectangular towers, consists of a great outer brick arch $11\frac{1}{2}$ to 12 metres wide. Erosion precludes precise measurement. Above the 12-metre high apex stand the remains of a second arched opening, $2\frac{1}{2}$ metres high. The walls of the lower arch contained a shallow niche on either side, perhaps for statues of emperors or gods or some other ornamental or pious purpose. The rest of the gate projected inside and was aligned with the curtain wall. Its 4-metre-thick walls enclosed a propugnaculum – nothing is left of the doorways – and obviously supported a tower, of which the upper arch formed part.

The west gate, even better preserved and also in daily use, is slightly smaller, than the south gate and without its ceremonial accretions and integrated flanking towers (Pl. 185). The outer face is an arched opening in the curtain wall,

PLATE 185 Hissar, west gate

7·90 metres high and 4·30 metres wide. The 5-metre-deep gateway projects inside the wall, which continues on either side of the gate and uninterruptedly above it to a preserved height of 11·60 metres.

The east gate, on the same general plan but with flanking towers, has survived only to a maximum height of 2·20 metres, but has been fully excavated (Fig. 89). The lower parts consisted of socles of large cut-stone blocks, some re-used. Three floor levels were found in the entrance, the first reconstruction probably following comparatively minor fire damage, but the next after a major razing of the structure. A brick-paved drain, 1·32 metres deep and 60 to 68 centimetres wide, passed under the entrance, narrowing to 25 centimetres just under the threshold, presumably to prevent enemy infiltration. Building phases of the rectangular towers flanking the entrance corresponded to those of the gate.

East of the south gate were three large barrack-like buildings, terminating in a colonnade; finds suggest the rooms included a kitchen, and a store-room with many lower parts of dolia. Other similar buildings were annexed west of the same gate. These were dismantled and replaced by a church, an operation which provides the main evidence for the date of the walls.

Comparatively little of the double north wall now remains above ground (Pl. 186). The inner wall had towers, posterns, and staircases like the others; its gate faced one in the outer wall, which was a separate structure, 3·2 metres wide. Also built in opus mixtum, the stone, from another quarry, was friable compared with that used in the main walls. The construction of its three single staircases was also inferior. The wall extended several metres west of the inner wall, ending

PLATE 186 Hissar, north wall and gateway

in a buttress which also protected a postern linking the two walls. There had been heavy destruction at the eastern end.

The only epigraphic evidence on the fortifications is provided by two dedicatory inscriptions of the reign of Alexander Severus re-used in the facing of the west wall. The main clue to the date of construction is provided by the church known as no. 1. Originally thought to have been fifth- or sixth-century, new thinking assigns the walls to the late fourth or beginning of the fifth century, that is, after Visigothic destruction of the earlier fortifications. The various building phases may be explained by the growing number of attacks in the Early Byzantine period. Pending fuller excavation – difficult in a popular health and holiday resort – this conclusion, generally agreed by archaeologists concerned in recent excavations at Hissar, seems reasonable.

Hissar is also archaeologically important for the number of Early Byzantine churches excavated in and around the town. Unlike the walls, most are no longer visible, and in any case little more than foundations remained, uncovered at different periods over the last 75 years. Their number, counting superimposed churches, totals 11, excluding two in the nearby village of Sindjirli, by no means an extraordinary total for what was almost certainly an episcopal centre in that age of church building and of barbarian destruction; their significance lies in being a group based on a single town, so that even though dates must be tentative, it is possible to trace some kind of chronological evolution in a small area. The churches are numbered in scientific literature according to their order of discovery – a convention followed here and in the plan of the town (Fig. 86).

The approximate order of construction here suggested in general agrees with the dates proposed by the excavators – although a major qualification must be the unscientific nature of some of the early excavations. Nevertheless, it illustrates the architectural response to the evolution of the liturgy, with local ritual requirements – or idiosyncrasies – also playing a part, as did the nature of the terrain. What churches existed together at any given time is impossible to say; demolition was not always due to enemy action. Two demonstrably replaced predecessors, but other replacements were not necessarily erected on old sites. The introduction of the three-sided apse is usually deemed to follow the construction of St John Studios in Constantinople in 463, but, owing to population movements, regional developments and fashions often spread faster in the provinces than in the more conservative capital. The same considerations apply to the introduction of the tripartite narthex and to the subsequent appearance of the tripartite sanctuary – in Constantinople in the reign of Justin II.

Two churches were probably built very soon after the Visigothic war. Church 3A, 100 metres south of the south gate, provided the plan and foundations for church 3B, which, in fact, was probably the simple restoration of a badly damaged building with the substitution of a more 'modern' three-sided apse for the earlier rounded structure (Fig. 90). Church 3A was three-naved with a narthex and an atrium, the nave being precisely three times the width of the aisles. At the east end of the north aisle steps led up to a doorway. The much-destroyed narthex appears to have had no internal division. A flimsy wall, leaving an ambulatory about a metre wide inside the apse, was probably the synthronon of church 3A.

Church 4A (Fig. 91), about a hundred metres north-west of the north-east angle tower, was built on an earlier structure, perhaps a pagan shrine. The church was three-naved, with a disproportionately large and accentuated horse-shoe-shaped apse, 6 metres wide at the chord and 3½ metres deep; a similar flimsy concentric wall or synthronon provided an ambulatory. The stylobates of the nave, each bearing five columns, turned outwards at a right-angle a metre from the east wall and continued parallel to it almost to the side-walls. About a metre from the west end, north and south projections from the stylobates formed a kind of narthex. Two small semicircular walls projecting from the stylobates by the westernmost pillars may have held receptacles for offerings.

There are three other three-naved basilicas with single semicircular apses and undivided narthices. These are no. 2, inside the walls, no. 5 about 200 metres north of the north-west angle tower, and no. 8 at Momina Banya.

Church 2 was relatively large, over 34 metres long and about 24 metres wide. Only the foundations of the south half remained, but it could be seen that the nave was about double the width of the aisles. The south wall continued beyond the east end of the south aisle, possibly to inscribe the apse. The narthex was about 6½ metres wide, about 2 metres more than the aisles. The columns of the nave were made of separate drums of local granite-gneiss.

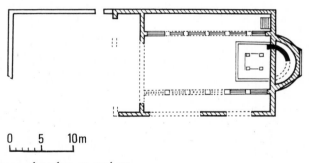

0   5   10m

FIG. 90 Hissar, churches 3A and 3B

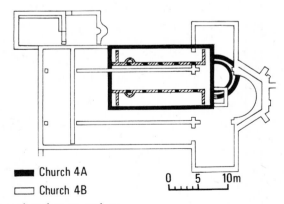

■ Church 4A
☐ Church 4B

0   5   10m

FIG. 91 Hissar, churches 4A and 4B

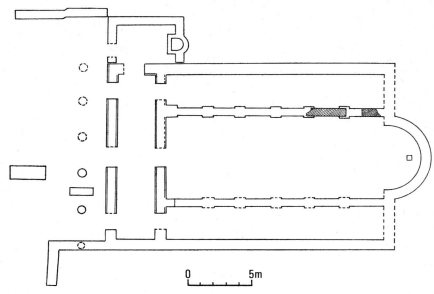

FIG. 92 Hissar, church 8

Church 5, similarly destroyed, was smaller, only 26½ metres long. With a wide apse, the nave was nearly three times the width of the aisles, which were very slightly narrower than the narthex. Bricks laid directly on the ground formed the floor. Remains of two columns showed a construction of quarter-circle brick segments mortared together, a feature of several Hissar churches and a town house.

Church 8 (Fig. 92) at Momina Banya had a narthex, as usual slightly wider than the aisles, opening on to a western portico with two granite bases remaining *in situ*. Possibly here was an atrium, but a modern street prevented further exploration. As a baptistery with a shallow eastern apse and U-shaped piscina was not constructionally linked to the church, it was probably a later addition. The church itself showed signs of having twice been repaired.

These five churches must be dated to the last two decades of the fourth and first half of the fifth centuries. The likelihood that churches 3A and 4A were the earliest does not imply that the others were much later. As both were replaced by churches with three-sided apses, first seen in Bulgaria during the fifth century, the Huns or Ostrogoths may have destroyed the whole group.

Church 7, just outside the east gate, was so mutilated that even the foundations of part of the east end were untraceable (Fig. 93). Unlike the earlier group, the narthex was divided into three rooms, with communicating doorways. In the west wall, three other doorways led to the nave and aisles. Granite-gneiss bases with grooves for intercolumnar slabs stood on stylobates which carried brick pillars like those of church 5. An opening in the north stylobate about 3½ metres from the east wall suggests that the eastern end of the north aisle was used as a prothesis. Unfortunately nothing more of the sanctuary survived. Nevertheless,

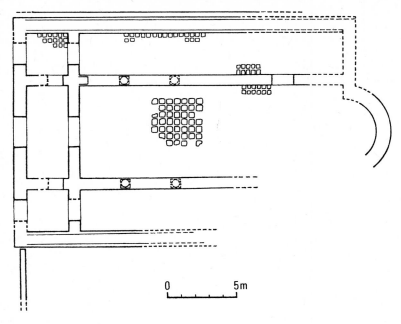

FIG. 93 Hissar, church 7

with a tripartite narthex and possibly a tripartite sanctuary, church 7 begins a new phase in the ecclesiastical architecture of Hissar. It is a question whether this church should be dated shortly before or shortly after the Hun attack.

Church 3B, already described with its predecessor, was built in the second half of the fifth century (Fig. 90), probably retaining the ⊓-shaped sanctuary with a marble ciborium above the altar table. Colonnades of five segmented brick pillars, plastered and painted, on stone bases, lined the nave. The stylobates ended at the second pillar from the east, suggesting a conversion to a tripartite sanctuary. A silver reliquary was found here, and a funerary slab with an inscription, probably of the fifth century, shows the church was dedicated to the 'first martyr', St Stephen.

Church 1, annexed inside the south wall west of the gate, was also a conversion, although its predecessor was possibly a barracks (Fig. 94). Its dating is a key factor for that of the walls. The earlier 'barracks' was a series of intercommunicating rooms parallel to the walls and separated from them by a corridor partly occupied by a double staircase to the rampart-walk, and a tower. North of the rooms another, slightly wider, corridor was bounded by a colonnade. Just east of the tower, a north–south passage between the 'barracks' and another room (or series of rooms) gave access to a postern, underneath which ran a drain.

The church, built above the foundations of these rooms and the colonnade, was two-naved, the south wall using the foundations of the south wall of the barracks, the north wall following the line of the colonnade. A new colonnade separating the nave from the north aisle inside the church did not coincide with the north wall of the barracks, but was just outside it, giving the nave – some 13½ metres long – a width of about 8 metres, three times that of the aisle. The three-sided apse stood above the room east of the passage to the postern; the passage itself appears to have been rebuilt as a tripartite sanctuary and the postern walled up. The west wall of the narthex made use of one of the older walls and an original doorway. Although the wall between the narthex and the nave was new, giving the former a depth of 4 metres, the nave entrance was not opposite the outer door. Another curious asymmetrical feature was a bend in the line of the new colonnade to meet the north pilaster of the apse.

The original excavator, B. Filov, considered this church a three-naved basilica partly demolished by the later construction of the walls, but a re-examination by S. Boyadjiev revealed the precise arrangement of the earlier 'barracks' and the fact that the southern extension of the passage to the postern overlies the socle of the curtain wall. There thus seems little doubt that the curtain walls are earlier than the church, which was always two-naved. The area between the nave and curtain wall could not have served as the south aisle, for the staircase, which occupied most of its space, was needed to provide access to the rampart-walk. One possible explanation for this strange plan is that it was built as a 'garrison chapel'. The relationship between liturgical requirements and ecclesiastical architecture in the early Church has been insufficiently studied, but it is known that catechumens and communicants, and men and women, were separated. If at the time of building it was customary to segregate the sexes into different aisles, one aisle only would suffice for soldiers, whilst the passageway to the walled-up

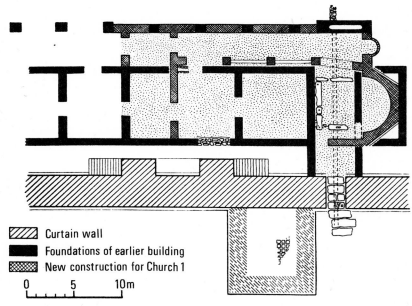

Curtain wall
Foundations of earlier building
New construction for Church 1

0   5   10m

FIG. 94 Hissar, church I (with tower of first building phase)

postern provided a ready-made site for a diaconicon. It is noteworthy that the two churches at Sindjirli, 4 kilometres from Hissar, are a single-naved church with a three-sided apse and a two-naved church with a rounded apse. The latter is the only other example of a two-naved church known in Bulgaria. Taking account of the new evidence, church 1 is dated soon after the middle of the fifth century. Fragments of architectural decoration do not conflict with this date.

Church 4B, although built above 4A, had little structural relationship with its predecessor (Fig. 91). A three-naved basilica with a single three-sided apse, transept, and narthex, it was about 33 metres long with a two-roomed baptistery on the north side. The apse was unusually thick-walled and also buttressed because of its site on the river bank. The narthex contained two square bases attached to its west wall and aligned with the nave colonnades, but no other trace of divisions. No entrances were preserved and no bases of the colonnade pillars were found in situ. The transept, probably separated from the nave and aisles by arched openings, formed a large tripartite sanctuary, in its centre the altar, a substantial rectangular structure open on the long west side, measuring 2·40 by 1·80 metres with walls 55 centimetres thick. A small crypt below it held a lead reliquary. Nothing else remained of the sanctuary arrangements. This church is generally dated to the latter half of the fifth or beginning of the sixth century.

Church 6 (Fig. 95), about half a kilometre south-east of the south-east angle tower, has a basic plan reminiscent of the early group of churches. It had a single semicircular apse, buttressed by a supporting wall because of the nearby river. The narthex was divided into three by arched openings, and a small square room was attached to the south end. West of it a later courtyard contained a row of partly preserved brick pillars and some re-used marble capitals. The contrast with the early group lay principally in the well-defined tripartite sanctuary, 6 metres deep compared with the 14-metre-long nave. Almost in the centre, below the probable site of the altar, a brick vaulted crypt with stone walls, 1·40 metres square and about 1·70 metres high, was approached by five steps on the east side. In the middle of its north, west, and south walls were niches, beginning just over a metre from the floor. The walls were plastered and painted, although only black rectangular frames could be distinguished. Such a deep tripartite sanctuary is unusual, but proximity to the river may have hindered the building of side-apses – buttresses supported even the straight walls – and there may consequently have been practical reasons for creating a deeper prothesis and diaconicon than usual within the body of the church. Despite its single rounded apse, a date in the sixth century seems appropriate.

Church 9 (Fig. 96), about 700 metres south-east of the south-west angle tower, stood in the middle of the largest necropolis. Remains of slim marble columns were found in its strongly developed tripartite sanctuary, and it is the only Early Byzantine church in Hissar to have three apses, all of which were semicircular. The nave is so short as to be almost square, the aisles exactly half as wide. Fragments show that the floor was paved with marble and brick in careful patterns. The narthex was also tripartite; the length of its central and northern divisions was 6 metres, nearly a metre longer than the nave; the south room was shorter but wider. The building is obviously sixth-century; in view of its situation it may have had a funerary purpose.

The discovery of the only secular building of the Early Byzantine period in

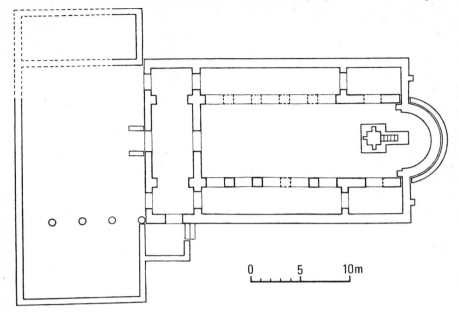

FIG. 95 Hissar, church 6

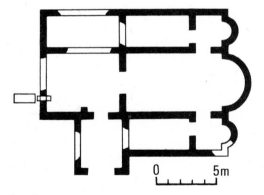

FIG. 96 Hissar, church 9

Hissar was unfortunately made by a bulldozer, which in one day destroyed half the remains of a large town house. Its plan was reconstructed from what was left of the foundations plus a partial dig of the western half. The building occupied an area of about 2,000 square metres and contained over 22 rooms; the superstructure – less than a metre high – was faced with smoothed broken stone and had a rubble and mortar fill. So far as could be ascertained, the western part was occupied by a spacious peristyled courtyard on to which the living quarters opened. The columns of mortared brick segments were like those found in many

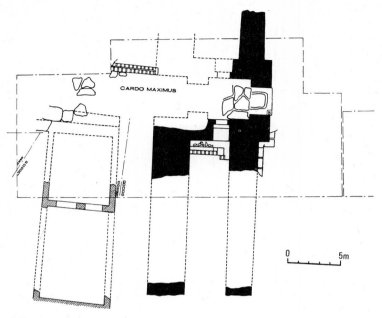

FIG. 97 Beroe, south gate

of the churches; their square brick bases stood directly on the earth. From the
courtyard, two entrances led into what was probably a double, intercommunicating vestibule, with brick-lined entrances and a brick floor. Beyond was the largest
room, no doubt the triclinium. Many fragments are evidence of glazed windows.
It is suggested that eastern apsidal projections were semicircular towers,
constructionally linked with the building, and that a larger rectangular tower
projected from the centre of the east wall. Evidence for the nature of the
superstructure is, however, slight, and complicated by the likelihood of two
building phases, the first in the late fourth or early fifth century.

The walled area of Hissar, comprising some 30 hectares, was 2 hectares larger
than that of Nicopolis-ad-Istrum. The two cities must have formed an interesting contrast in the fourth century, as indeed they do today.

VI. BEROE

Fourth-century Beroe, the 'considerable and rich city' of Ammianus Marcellinus, did not long enjoy this prosperity. The many small coin hoards show
how seriously the Visigothic wars affected its economy, although the city's sack
and destruction was left to the Huns. Beroe is mentioned by Procopius as a city,
like Philippopolis, vulnerable and needing restoration under Justinian's programme, but the work may have already started and taken time to complete. The

refortification and building programme of the end fifth or early sixth century was on a large scale. The second-century wall, already once strengthened, was not only partly rebuilt, but a new wall, some 2 to 4 metres from the old, also surrounded the city. It was $2\frac{1}{2}$ metres thick, constructed in opus mixtum with bands of stone a metre wide between bonding courses of four or five layers of brick.

The most important sector so far studied is the south gate (Fig. 97) discovered in 1962. Modelled on the earlier gate, it consisted of an outer portcullis and inner swing gates, the latter occupying approximately the same site as the second-century portcullis. It is estimated that the tower housing and operating the new portcullis must have been about 12 metres high. Posterns opened from the propugnaculum into the intra-mural corridor and, presumably, to staircases ascending to the rampart-walk. On the western threshold a bronze coin of Anastasius constitutes a *terminus ante quem* for the new defence phase.

The city, temporarily secure behind its double walls, underwent a major rebuilding programme in the sixth century, using the same plan. Owing to a destruction layer formed by the fifth-century sack, the new streets were some 80 centimetres higher. The new surface was gravel, but brick shafts with openings at street level carried sewage down to the original drains. Buildings were repaired or restored, and new ones were built. Pillars, capitals, and other materials were re-used, sometimes very much at random. The floor levels of the sixth-century houses varied. One house had a sixth-century mosaic floor laid 60 centimetres above an older mosaic. A house by the south gate also overlaid an older dwelling (see Fig. 97). Its stone-paved forecourt opened on to the cardo maximus. West of the forecourt, two rooms containing dolia were probably storerooms, with living accommodation on an upper storey. Coins of Alexander Severus were found in the foundations of the earlier phase.

The house with the Constantinian mosaic (p. 201) retained its original floor, exterior walls, and some other parts, but was generally reconstructed (Fig. 98). On the east a series of little rooms, probably shops, had no access to the rest of the complex. Two entrances were on the south, where pilasters projected at regular intervals. One led into the south-west part, where no building remains were found; perhaps it was a yard or garden. East of this, bordering the decumanus, was probably a small working area, consisting of two little rooms built in opus mixtum, a court – also with a southern entrance – with a small open pool faced with marble slabs, a big stone mortar, five or six clay dolia, re-used drums of marble columns, and an altar, as well as stone slabs set about 60 centimetres above the floor, perhaps seats or low working surfaces. The north part of the house, which has not been published in any detail, seems to have been residential, keeping the old dining room and adjoining 'kitchen'. Nearby were two impost capitals, dated to the sixth century. Of fine marble, carved with a cross surrounded by acanthus leaves, one has an eagle between the volutes at the base, the other a grinning face (Pl. 187). These must have been carved for a church.

With its new fortifications, Beroe resisted an Avar attack in 587 to survive until the reign of Tiberius, whose coins were the latest on the sixth-century streets. Eventually the city fell to and was sacked by Avars or Slavs, but was not left entirely deserted. In the centre of the Constantinian mosaic floor a later structure appeared. Of fragments of brick and stone mortared with mud, it had two square

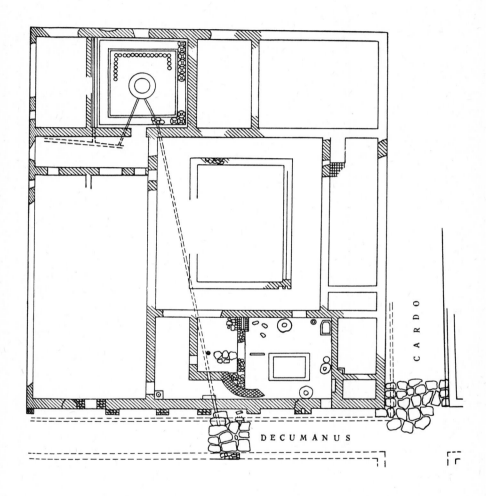

FIG. 98 Beroe, sixth-century phase of town house

PLATE 187 Beroe, impost capital

rooms, without doors, their dimensions 3 and 2 metres. These were identified as *zemlyanki*, or dugouts, which continued to use the mosaic for a floor. As the potsherds in the vicinity are not considered Slav or Bulgar, these are assumed to be dwellings of survivors, but the scale of excavation is too limited for the evidence to be conclusive. Nevertheless, the walls were by no means entirely destroyed, and in 778, when they were restored by the Byzantine empress Irene, the city temporarily assumed the name of Irinopolis. Evidence of this restoration was found at the south gate and in other parts of the wall that have been excavated.

VII. CHATALKA

Outside the south-east corner of the pars urbana of the Chatalka villa a small chapel was built, probably in the third quarter of the fourth century; the site chosen was not that of the earlier sanctuary of the Thracian Horseman. Destroyed, together with all the buildings on the estate, by the Visigoths, the little church was later rebuilt and in the ruins of the villa a modest hamlet grew up. The more distant cemetery continued in use, its burials now Christian. Coins show that this settlement existed until about the middle of the fifth century, so that Hun devastation seems certain.

By the sixth century, it appears that the surviving population had migrated to a naturally defended site on a hill overlooking the abandoned villa – which became its cemetery in the medieval period. This settlement – and similar ones in the area – showed by its thick culture layer and comparative size that it was neither a military fort nor a temporary refuge but a permanent village. In 1965 soundings indicated that an area of about a hectare was inhabited, enclosed by double stone walls between 5 and 10 metres apart, with only one tower, a 6-metre square structure projecting from the inner wall. Inside were the foundations of buildings, a cistern, and a mass of pottery dated from the sixth to the fourteenth centuries, as well as a few coins from the sixth and the tenth-eleventh centuries.

VIII. THE EASTERN RHODOPES

The Haskovo mineral baths, according to coins, continued in use until early in the sixth century. In one complex, the drainage channel yielded coins up to the reign of Anastasius; in that of the large pool, the last coins were of Justin I, but Theodosius II was the most commonly represented. Signs of repair to this pool included the use as building material of two pagan funerary stelai and a fragment of a votive tablet to Herakles. Probably the baths were damaged by the Visigoths about the time of their victory at Hadrianopolis, but, unlike the Armira villa, were restored and enjoyed a new popularity in the first half of the fifth century. Final destruction probably occurred towards the end of the sixth century by Avars or Slavs; it was so thorough that the baths were abandoned and the springs forgotten. The next coins found were nineteenth-century Turkish.

The Sveti Duh fort above the baths was still in use during the Early Byzantine period. Strategic considerations and the need for a refuge appear to have ensured continuity of habitation here, albeit with intermittent periods of destruction and changes of ownership, into the twelfth century. During the reign of Heraclius, Armenians were transported into the area in an effort to counteract the mass settlement of Slavs, but how long the fort remained in Byzantine hands is unknown; there are signs of Bulgarian occupation in the ninth century.

A little medieval church inside the fort, at least up to 1936, was the scene of a moving annual ceremony, when the villagers from the country round about gathered on the eve of Pentecost, the patronal festival, to celebrate a mass for the souls of those who had died in the battle at nearby Klokotnitsa – a great Bulgarian victory over Byzantine invaders – in 1230. It suggests an important medieval role for the fort which current excavations may support.

NOTES

1 Comnena, A., *Alexiad* XIV, viii, *The Alexiad of Anna Comnena*, trans. Sewter, E. R. A., Harmondsworth, 1969, 463.
2 Koco, D., *Godishen Zbornik Filozofski Fakultet* 19, Skopje, 1967, 257 ff.
3 Fortunately a careful examination was carried out and some reproductions of the then existing paintings made. (See under A. Frolow and A. Grabar in site bibliography).
4 Changova, I. and Shopova, A., *Rodopski Sbornik* II, Sofia, 1969, 181 ff.

14 The Black Sea Coast (II)

I. MESAMBRIA AND THE SOUTH

In the south-eastern province of Haemimontus in the Diocese of Thracia, Hierocles put Anchialos as second city to Hadrianopolis. Third came Deultum. Both were episcopal seats. Anchialos was an important centre in the struggle against the Avars, both the city and its mineral baths at Aquae Calidae having been respectively refortified and fortified under Justinian. Procopius especially mentions that

> Emperors of earliest times used to allow this place [the baths] to remain un-walled from ancient times, though such a host of barbarians dwelt nearby; and sick persons used to visit the place, gaining relief at the cost of danger. Therefore the Emperor Justinian made it a walled city, as it now is, and thus made the cure free from danger.[1]

The baths were much frequented during the sixth century and, according to Michael the Syrian, Anastasia, wife of Tiberius II Constantine, took the cure here and presented purple vestments to the church of Anchialos. Several years later, when the Avars were in possession, Theophylact Simocattes refers to the residence here of the khagan's harem; Michael the Syrian writes that the walls were overthrown and that the khagan had flaunted on his own person the vestments of Anastasia. Some of the buildings remained standing until the arrival of Crusaders.

Apollonia was already known by 431 as Sozopolis (city of the Saviour), a neat transition of protectors preserved in the modern name of Sozopol. It is mentioned in the struggles between Anastasius and Vitalian, and, although not among Procopius's list of cities fortified or strengthened, its bishops continue to be recorded after the sixth century. So far only chance-found architectural fragments remain from the Early Byzantine period.

Little is known about Mesambria, also an episcopal centre, but its archaeological monuments demonstrate both prosperity and power of survival. The Hellenistic fortifications, perhaps repaired, probably continued to serve the city during its period of relative obscurity, but a new wall was built during the Late Roman or Early Byzantine period. Although much still survives, as can be seen from the varying methods of construction it was frequently and sometimes extensively restored until its final decay in the late medieval period. Without help from building inscriptions or other written sources, no exact chronology can be established. Sectors of the Romano-Byzantine wall investigated concurrently with the Hellenistic structure showed conclusively that the two ran roughly parallel; the deeper foundations of the earlier wall were not re-used. Publication, although detailed, is admittedly incomplete and the finds have not yet been fully analysed.

The west and only gate, which is still the entrance to modern Nesebur, thus hindering excavation, was flanked by virtually identical pentagonal towers projecting from the curtain wall (Fig. 99). Parts of the north tower are preserved to a height of nearly 6 metres, the south tower up to 3 metres.

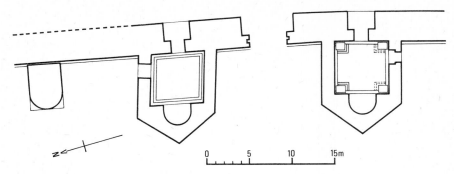

FIG. 99 Mesambria, west gate

The gate is built within the 3·80-metres thickness of the curtain wall. In the outer part, which was faced with large andesite tufa blocks and only 4·40 metres wide, were remains of a portcullis groove. In the inner part, where the opening widened to 6·10 metres, double swing doors were closed by a cross-beam, the holes to contain it being still visible.

Plate 188 shows, viewed from the west, part of the northern gate tower, with its eastern entrance (extreme right) and the north postern, beyond which the curtain wall stretches north to a projecting U-shaped tower. A variety of building methods can be seen – a single layer of the rusticated ashlar above larger, rougher blocks outlining the angle of the pentagonal tower; the stone-walled, brick-vaulted entrances; and, most clearly visible on the U-tower, opus mixtum with bands of three and four courses of brick, thickly mortared. This tower, originally rectangular, stood between the gate and a large projecting circular tower which defended the angle at the sea approach.

A joint between the wall and the circular tower showed the latter to be a separate construction, and excavation of the foundations revealed an originally rectangular plan. The tower, now partly restored, had an overall diameter of 7·15 metres; the walls, 85 centimetres thick, were of opus mixtum and three building phases could be discerned. As in the gate towers, there was an external postern, but no means of communication between the ground floor of the tower and the interior of the fortress could be traced. Remains of a corresponding but much smaller projecting round tower were found at the south angle of the walls, and of a rectangular tower which was a medieval addition between it and the gate.

I. Venedikov has suggested the second half of the fifth or the beginning of the sixth century for the construction of the gate towers and the opus mixtum work to various times between the fifth and tenth centuries. There is no historical evidence that the earlier walls were destroyed by barbarian invasions; earthquakes may have caused damage or the city defences simply needed strengthening. Mesambria was strategically important to the Byzantine empire and both Zeno and Anastasius were zealous builders. The omission of Mesambria by Procopius is an argument for a date well before the reign of Justinian. The powerfully reconstructed fortress seems to have survived the Avar attacks and historians continue to refer to the fortified city of Mesambria during the seventh and

PLATE 188 Mesambria, Early Byzantine fortifications

eighth centuries. During these years inland trading activities were incommoded by the fact that Mesambria and Anchialos frequently served as Byzantine bases in the wars against the new Bulgarian state. The immediate hinterland continued to be rich farming land – it is recorded that the future emperor Leo III gained the favour of Justinian II at Mesambria in 705 by offering his services and a gift of 500 sheep. But as the territory south of the Stara Planina came under Bulgarian rule, the city's traditional skill in accommodating itself to circumstances proved once more of value. After a short-lived occupation by the Bulgarian tsar Krum, the city remained in Byzantine hands until the fourteenth century.

The latest excavations have included an unpublished Early Byzantine three-naved basilica not far from the north round tower. Another, much further along the north coast, was excavated some 50 years ago. Twenty-eight metres long and 18 metres wide, but partly eroded by the sea, it is today preserved to a height of at most some 2 metres (Pl. 189; Fig. 100). The church had three main building phases, only the first within the Early Byzantine period; this is distinguished by careful ashlar construction with occasional layers of brick and tufa.

A three-sided apse terminated the central nave and semicircular ones with triconchal interiors the aisles. The north aisle has mostly been eroded. The sanctuary was tripartite and stone piers separated the nave and south aisle; according to the excavator, the north aisle appears always to have been divided by a wall from the nave. The narthex was originally tripartite, the divisions being later removed, possibly when two rooms were annexed to the west. The few finds include marble architectural fragments and broken bricks bearing the sign of the cross and the name of Justinian. Mesambrian links with Constantinople

PLATE 189 Mesambria, 'Sea Basilica'

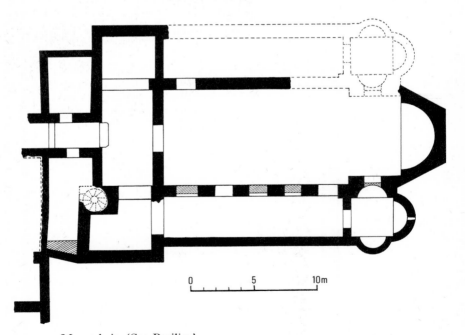

0   5   10m

FIG. 100 Mesambria, 'Sea Basilica'

in the sixth century were close and, bearing this in mind, the church is dated to early in the second half of the sixth century. The second and third reconstructions, using only the south aisle, were separated from the abandonment of the original church by a long period of years. The church, known in archaeological literature as 'the Sea Basilica', may at some stage have been dedicated to the Virgin Eleousa.

In contrast, parts of the church known as the Old Metropolis, in the centre of the little town, are preserved to roof height (Pl. 190). It was a three-naved basilica with a single, three-sided apse, a narthex, and an atrium (Fig. 101). The nave and aisles, separated by five pairs of massive opus mixtum piers, were unusually short in relation to their width, so that, without the narthex, they were almost square. The deep apse contained a synthronon. The narthex was divided into three rooms corresponding to the nave and aisles. Very little of the atrium remains, but part of a north side-chamber has been found and probably there was a similar one on the south. Above the aisles were galleries with arches almost as large as those below. The east end as it is today is clumsily proportioned, the roof line here being clearly the result of a makeshift repair.

Both the original form and date of the Old Metropolis are disputed. The church is thought to have been either a basilica with clerestory lighting and without galleries above the aisles, or else a 'barn church' with side-galleries and covered by a single roof. Dating ranges from the fifth to the eleventh centuries.

A recent survey with particular attention to the masonry throws fresh light on both problems.[2] Several building phases have been identified which resulted in drastic alteration of the original conception yet little change to the ground plan.

PLATE 190 Mesambria, Old Metropolis

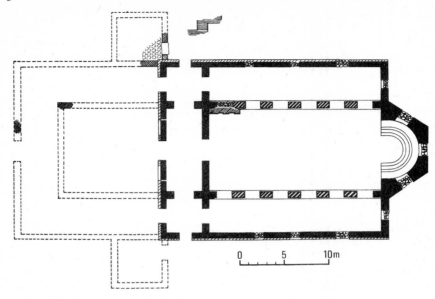

FIG. 101 Mesambria, Old Metropolis

FIG. 102 Mesambria, reconstruction of Old Metropolis

According to this analysis, the first restoration followed a razing of the original church to, at most, little more than a metre above the ground, a level where a band of five courses of brick ran above a wall of dressed stone. The new walls incorporated the remains of this band. The arched piers today separating nave and aisles date from this second period, similarly the squat arch and semi-dome of the apse.

As the plan closely resembles that of St John Studios in Constantinople, it is suggested that in the Old Metropolis, too, the nave and aisles were originally separated by pillars on low stylobates. There would have been galleries above the aisles and the narthex, with clerestory windows above to provide more light for the nave. The height of the apse would have corresponded to that of the galleries (Fig. 102). Although there is no supporting archaeological evidence, this is a feasible explanation of many puzzling anomalies. The ground plan is appropriate to a church of the fifth or first half of the sixth century in a city closely linked with the capital and for Mesambria to have copied the famous church of St John Studios would not be surprising. The latter being dated to about 463, a little later in the fifth century is reasonable for the Old Metropolis.

The thorough destruction of the original building argues deliberate demolition rather than accident, and the disappearance of any pillars and sculptural ornament that existed suggests that rebuilding was not immediate. It is proposed that the destruction occurred in the sixth century and the rebuilding in the seventh or eighth, the grounds being the construction technique, and that by the ninth century the basilica had been replaced by the inscribed cross plan in Byzantine church architecture. However, in Constantinople the Hellenistic basilica was already obsolete in the sixth century, the latter part of which also saw the general acceptance of the triple apse. There would surely have been a triple apse and tripartite sanctuary in a seventh- or eighth-century rebuilding.

It is more likely that the first church was destroyed during an unrecorded raid or other disaster soon after its construction in the latter part of the fifth century and rebuilt at the end of the century or early in the sixth. A rebuilding during this period – perhaps coinciding with the new fortifications – would account for the single-apsed basilical form, and haste due to the insecurity of the times for the clumsiness of the reconstruction.

II. ODESSOS AND THE NORTH

Odessos, which had regained its earlier importance as a base for Valens' operations against the Visigoths, continued as a busy commercial and diplomatic centre throughout the fifth century. In 442, a mission from Theodosius II to Attila encountered another embassy in Odessos. During the sixth century, as well as being a base for campaigns against the Slavs and Avars, the latest that of 595 led by Maurice's brother Peter, it increasingly became a centre for refugees from the lost or endangered cities along the Danube. There is little doubt that the fortifications, mentioned by Procopius, were kept in good order.

Administratively, Odessos reached its peak in 536 when Justinian made it the military and administrative centre (*quaestura exercitus*) of a union of Moesia Secunda, Cyprus, the Cyclades, and Caria. Sea communications appear to have been the only common basis for this geographically widely separated region.

Fifteen months later, after a stream of pleas from inhabitants of Rhodes and Cyprus against the necessity for voyaging to distant Odessos, with the attendant risk of barbarian attack, to lay a case before the *quaestor*, the emperor agreed to move the judicial function to Constantinople. But the other functions remained.

The 65th *novella* of Justinian, concerned with Tomi and Odessos, is illuminating evidence of the wealth of the Church, accumulated through official 'inheritance' of the lands and goods of the older religions and gifts from pious and expiating Christians. The lands included vast vineyards, wine now being a major local export. The novella permitted the sale of uneconomic property, for example a vineyard incapable of bearing a good annual grape-harvest or land laid waste by enemy attack, provided that the money obtained was applied as a Christian donor had specified or, in other cases, for appropriate Christian purposes, such as hospitals, orphanages, the general welfare of the poor, and for the ransom of captives, in which the Church took a leading part. It appears there had been forbidden dealings in land to the profit of both laymen and clerics.

Funerary monuments show the continuance of immigration from the eastern provinces. Traders and shipbuilders came from Asia Minor to settle, and the fifth and sixth centuries saw a remarkable growth in the Syrian colony, whose attested occupations included furriers, sellers of linen, and soapmakers.

Within the actual city limits of Odessos, architectural and mosaic fragments have proved the existence of at least four fifth- or sixth-century churches. Although their full-scale excavation proved impossible, K. Škorpil collected and studied the finds for a monograph on the churches in the Varna district. Unfortunately, his work – in manuscript and with the full documentation – was despatched abroad for publication but appears to have been lost.[3] One must hope for its reappearance, for at present it is hard even to identify the find-spots of many important items in the Varna archaeological museum.

However, three early churches near the city – at Galata, Djanavar-tepe, and Pirinch-tepe – have been fully excavated and two of them published. The Galata church was built on top of the old sanctuary of the Thracian Horseman (p. 51). There can have been no appreciable time gap between the latter's destruction, probably towards the end of the fourth century, and its obviously deliberate Christian replacement. Votive reliefs dedicated to the Horseman were first defaced by hammering – in front of the sanctuary, where many tiny fragments were discovered – and then re-used, face downwards, to pave the south aisle.

The church was a three-naved basilica with a single semicircular apse (Fig. 103). The nave, 17·20 metres long and 6·30 metres wide, was separated from the aisles by rows of six limestone bases standing directly on the earth. All but one of the bases were *in situ* and fragments of marble columns were in the debris. West of the north aisle and extending alongside the narthex to the entrance of the nave was a baptistery with a square, brick-built piscina. The general absence of tiles and the finding of many nails and remains of beams point to a wooden roof. Fragments of flat thick glass probably came from windows.

As well as a piscina, there was a clay font, its foundations *in situ* north of the entrance from the narthex into the church. The rest was found, broken and dug into the earth, but has been reassembled (Pl. 191). The pedestal has a double wall, the outer heavily decorated by cut-out geometric patterns and the inner

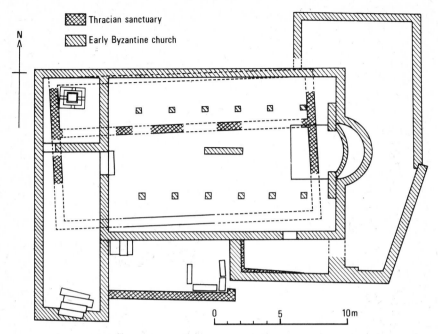

FIG. 103 Odessos, Galata, church superimposed on pagan sanctuary

with openings corresponding to those in the outer wall. The top is a wide
shallow bowl, 69 centimetres in diameter, with an elaborately ornamented rim.
There was an opening for emptying water from the bottom of the bowl, and space
between the walls of the round base for a fire to warm it; at the time of discovery
ash and embers still remained. Discussing this unusual font, J. Lafontaine-
Dosogne points out stylistic parallels in Constantinopolitan sculpture and recalls
that in the early fifth century the baptism of infants was encouraged by, among
others, St Augustine and probably St John Chrysostom.[4] The early fifth-century
date ascribed to the font is also applicable to the church, which probably continued in use until about the end of the sixth century, when it was destroyed by
fire.

The site of Djanavar-tepe is a flat-topped hill 4 kilometres south of Varna.
The church was excavated by K. Škorpil, but the documentation was among the
lost papers. The church was a single-naved basilica with projecting north and
south rooms inscribing both apse and narthex (Fig. 104; Pl. 192). A ⌐¬-shaped
sanctuary occupied the east end of the nave and the apse was lined by a synthronon. One of the narthex annexes was a baptistery, containing a cross-shaped
piscina. A large *ambo*, or pulpit, stood over a brick tomb in the centre of the
mosaic floor of the nave. The base of the marble sanctuary screen was found
in situ and fragments of its marble pillars stand nearby round the grave of
Škorpil. In a small crypt below the sanctuary a valuable triple reliquary was
discovered.

PLATE 191 Galata, font, *ht.* 99 cm.

The remains of the massive opus mixtum walls, between 2 and 2½ metres thick, are particularly striking. Stairs from the eastern side-chambers led to an upper storey and the nave was almost certainly vaulted. The powerful walls and towered projecting rooms suggest a defensive purpose, probably a refuge for the local population, although it is strange that the towers project only to the north and south, and not even to the west to protect the entrance.

As D. P. Dimitrov points out, the resemblance between Djanavar-tepe and such churches as Ivanyani and Tsurkvishte is superficial.[5] Yet, with the ⌐-shaped sanctuary, it is open to doubt whether the sanctuary is tripartite, and the projecting rooms the prothesis and diaconicon. The combination would be an

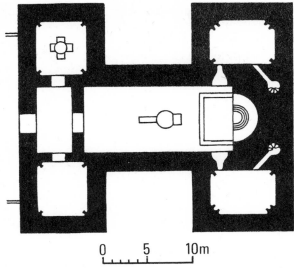

FIG. 104 Odessos, Djanavar-tepe church

unusual liturgical compromise. Djanavar-tepe is usually dated to the fifth century; in the circumstances it is hard to be more precise about a church that is so much out of the ordinary as well as, despite being levelled almost to the ground, so impressive.

Pirinch-tepe, discovered and excavated by K. Škorpil during the construction of a shipyard, and published in 1910, had two building phases, the later over-laying and using the earlier foundations (Fig. 105). Both were three-naved basilicas with a single apse and a narthex. The earlier apse was probably semi-circular and the narthex undivided. The nave was separated from the aisles by colonnades.

PLATE 192 Odessos, Djanavar-tepe

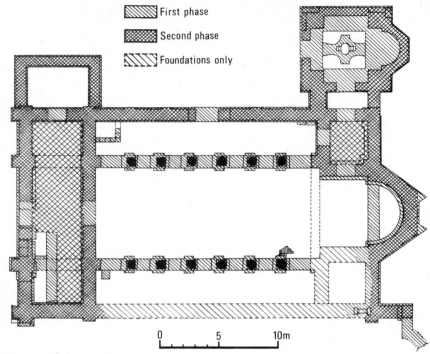

FIG. 105 Odessos, Pirinch-tepe church

PLATE 193 Odessos, Djanavar-tepe reliquary, *l*. 6.5 cm.

The rebuilt church had a new floor and a three-sided apse. The nave was shortened by converting its east end and those of the aisles into a tripartite sanctuary. Square limestone blocks carried re-used column bases on brick stylobates. One Ionic impost capital was found in the debris, with a few other fragments and pieces of window glass. Later additions also included a rectangular room north of the narthex and a baptistery, with a three-sided apse and a piscina, linked by a small vestibule to the prothesis.

On the basis of coin finds, Škorpil dated the first church to the reign of Constantine the Great, the second to that of Justinian. The possibility, here and elsewhere, that Constantinian coins had an especial sanctity in relation to church building cannot be dismissed, but in any case a fourth-century date is likely for the first phase. The main rebuilding may be Justinianic or a little earlier.

The gold reliquary of Djanavar-tepe (Pl. 193), which had been placed in a silver box which, in turn, was in a miniature alabaster sarcophagus, symbolises the wealth of the Early Byzantine Church of Odessos, perhaps especially of its Syrian community. Contemporaneous with the church, it miraculously remained hidden. The lid has a square emerald in the centre and a sapphire at each corner. The sides, each inset with a larger sapphire, are bordered, top and bottom, by a wide cloisonné band of gold swastikas against a garnet background. The reliquary may have been made by an Odessitan goldsmith but could equally well have come from Constantinople or some other leading city. There are not enough objects of proven origin to reach any definite conclusion.

The sacred treasure of Djanavar-tepe is matched by a collection of Early Byzantine jewellery found by chance in Odessos just outside the fortress wall in an early Roman necropolis where isolated later burials also took place. Although less unusual than the reliquary, the jewellery, nine objects weighing a total of 417 grams and of almost pure gold, over 22 carats, is also magnificent. D. I. Dimitrov ascribes the collection to the sixth century; although clearly the work of more than one goldsmith, this need not involve differences of date or provenance. The two bracelets (one shown in Pl. 194) have a hinged clasp of a type usually thought to have been invented in the late fourth or early fifth century. The main motif is the familiar symbol of the vine, the bunches of grapes consisting of large, re-used pearls with the intervening 'leaves' of light green glass.

Perhaps the finest work is in the diadem (Pl. 195), the plain gold band with its delicate poinçonné geometric pattern contrasting with the rich central ornament inset with five round pearls. A Greek cross central pattern, probably originally formed by five flat opals of which only two remain, supported the topmost pearl between two oval plaques of dark emerald green glass.

Completely different in style are a pendant and two belt appliqués. The former is a cross inset with garnet and malachite to form a 'tree of life' pattern against a dark red background, a round garnet in the centre (Pl. 196). The belt appliqués have plant motifs using the same materials and technique.

Different again are necklace fragments; one is a medley of irregularly shaped pearls, transparent stones, and pieces of coloured glass, hanging from rounded inset stones or glass, themselves hanging on golden hooks and alternating with granulated gold triangles from which hang smaller pearls or other roundels (Pl. 197). This barbaric, although skilful, splendour is representative of

PLATE 194 Odessos, bracelet, *ht.* 3·4 cm.

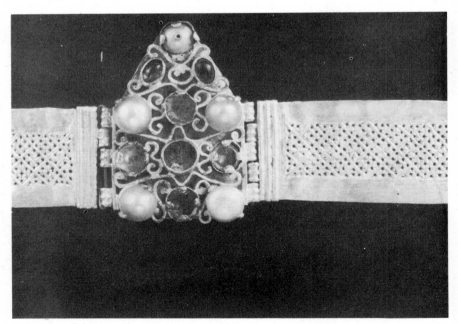

PLATE 195 Odessos, diadem detail, *max. ht.* 2·5 cm.

PLATE 196 Odessos, pendant, *ht.* 7·3 cm.

PLATE 197 Odessos, necklace, width *c.* 4–4·5 cm.

PLATE 198 Odessos, candlestick, *ht.* 20·4 cm.

sixth-seventh-century Byzantine jewellery, a demonstration of the deep penetration of Gothic influence, even in Constantinople.

Barbaric elements are even more apparent in a specimen of – probably – local sculpture. The candlestick (Pl. 198) of greyish marble, found somewhere in Varna, portrays a male head. Dated by hair style and a distant stylistic relationship to works such as the statue of Heraclius at Barletta, it probably belongs to the end of the sixth or beginning of the seventh century, a period when, although military links with Constantinople still existed, Odessos had entered a state of cultural decline.

North of Odessos, little from the Roman or Early Byzantine period has been found either at Dionysopolis or at Bizone, the latter abandoned after an earthquake in the first century A.D., when the population no doubt moved to nearby Cape Charakman. Here Early Byzantine remains include a wall of dressed limestone and a gate defending the neck of the cape at a point only 12 metres wide, and the foundations of a three-naved basilica with a single, semicircular apse and narrow narthex. The comparatively wide nave and narrow aisles, 5·65 and 2 metres respectively, and wide apse suggest a fifth-century date, probably before 450, for this church. It was destroyed towards the end of the seventh century, but life seems to have continued in the settlement for several centuries.

Twenty kilometres beyond Bizone is the long narrow rocky cape of Kaliakra, probably to be identified with Strabo's Tirizis. Projecting over 2 kilometres into the Black Sea, Kaliakra closes the northern end of the wide bay at the south of which lies Varna. Easily defended at a neck only a few metres across and with steep cliffs on all sides, Kaliakra has only recently been excavated. Early Byzantine Kaliakra was the headquarters of Vitalian, the Romanised son of a Goth, born at nearby Zaldapa (Pobeda), who led a popular revolt against Anastasius in the first quarter of the sixth century. Vitalian succeeded in capturing Odessos and Apollonia and made a series of attacks on Constantinople.

Three defence walls have been found. The first, faced by small dressed blocks,

PLATE 199 Kaliakra, fortress gate

PLATE 200 Naulochos, capital   PLATE 201 Naulochos, capital

is dated to the fourth or fifth century. It was 2·90 metres wide and had square and
U-shaped projecting towers and bastions which also flanked the single entrance
(Pl. 199). The second, similar in construction, is attributed to about the sixth
century, so may have been due to Vitalian or part of the later Byzantine fortification programme. The third wall was medieval.

South of Odessos, Erite or Ereta (Dolni Bliznyak) at the mouth of the Kamchiya river (ancient Panysos) is marked in the *Tabula Peutingeriana* as the first
station south of Odessos on the road to Constantinople. The site was identified
by K. Škorpil at the end of the last century, when he described it as a triangular
fortress, built of cut stone, on a high peak above the left bank protecting a bridge
across the river of which the remains were still visible. Excavations in 1939
brought to light – in spite of quarrying and erosion – the remains of a three-
naved church. At least 30 metres long and 20 metres wide, the nave and aisle
were divided by white marble columns with Corinthian capitals, their bases
standing on square limestone blocks as in the second phase of Pirinch-tepe, which
it also resembled in construction and materials. Coins of Justinian and Maurice
found in and near the church suggest it was built in the reign of the former and
that the settlement continued to exist into the seventh century.

Farther south, just before the last spur of the Stara Planina reaches the sea,
was Naulochos (Roman Templum Iovis – modern Obzor), where a few architectural fragments, lying in the public gardens, are forlorn evidence of Early
Byzantine prosperity. They include capitals which must once have crowned the
columns of some not particularly humble church (Pls. 200, 201). Also from this
locality comes a remarkable life-size sandstone portrait head (Pl. 202). The left
side is broken off and the left eye much damaged. D. P. Dimitrov suggests that

PLATE 202 Naulochos, portrait head, *ht.* 26 cm.

traces of the sculptor's hammer on the hair over the right ear show it to be un-finished, local work. The head, despite strong stylisation, especially in the hair, retains something of Roman art, but the impressive frontal gaze with deliberately exaggerated eyes proclaims it a rare example of Byzantine portrait sculpture. Dated between the mid-fifth and the mid-sixth centuries, this battered fragment records the vitality of the civilisation which, in spite of barbarian pressures, survived in the cities of the Black Sea coast.

In the interior it was very different. Theophylact Simocattes relates that, having defeated the Avars at Viminacium (Kostolac, in Yugoslavia) in 601, the Byzantine general Comentiolus halted on his way back at Novae and asked the inhabitants for a guide to take him along the so-called Trajan's Road over the Stara Planina. He was told that there was only one man, aged 112, living 12 miles away, who knew the road. When the old man was found, he refused to act as guide, saying that the road had not been used for ninety years and was in any case unlikely to be practicable in winter. Comentiolus succeeded in reaching Philippopolis, crossing the mountains by either the Shipka or the Troyan pass, but only after great hardship and many losses. Only a few years after his journey almost all the cities created by Rome had fallen and, in what is now Bulgaria, in many ways the wheel had turned full circle to the situation which had prevailed when the Greeks first settled their colonies along the coast.

NOTES

1 Procopius, *De Aed.* III, vii, 19–23, trans. Dewing, H. B., *Procopius, VII, Buildings*, London, 1940, 219.
2 Boyadjiev, S., *Byzantino-Bulgarica* I, 1962, 321 ff.
3 Dimitrov, D. I., *IBAI* XXX, 1967, 42, n. 11.
4 Lafontaine-Dosogne, J., *CA* XVII, 1967, 45 ff.
5 Dimitrov, D. P., *Kratka Istoriya na Bulgarskata Arhitektura*, Sofia, 1965, 55.

Historical Outline

PART ONE

Sixth century B.C.

By 600 Apollonia Pontica was already established. Odessos followed about 585 or 570 and Dionysopolis later.

In 513 Darius' Scythian expedition included the Persian conquest of Thrace, parts of which remained under Persian domination until the 460s.

Fifth century B.C.

By 493, possibly earlier, Mesambria was founded.

About 465 the Persian withdrawal was completed and was followed by the rise of the Thracian Odrysian state, under Teres, incorporating non-Odrysian tribes and based in south-east Thrace. Although said at its peak to have stretched from the Danube to the Aegean, it probably never subjected the Bessi, Getai, or tribes of the west. In 429, Teres' son and successor Sitalkes' invasion of Macedonia with a large army, of independent as well as subject tribes, failed through lack of unity and discipline. In 424, Sitalkes was killed fighting the Triballi. After the death of Seuthes, the Odrysian kingdom was split among three successors. Xenophon was in Thrace at the turn of the century.

Fourth century B.C.

In 376, the Triballi, probably pressed by the Celts, invaded southern Thrace, reaching Abdera.

In 352–51, Philip II of Macedonia subdued Thrace south of the Danube and in 341–40 annexed the territory. Certain Thracian centres, including Philippopolis, were settled with Macedonians and created cities.

In 336, Philip was succeeded by Alexander the Great, who quickly crushed Thracian revolts. During his Asian expedition, the Getai rose and routed a punitive force. An Odrysian rising, led by another Seuthes, was suppressed by Antipater.

In 323, Lysimachos became ruler of Thrace. His firm measures and installation of garrisons in the Black Sea cities aroused resentment among both Greeks and Thracians, and led to several revolts. His relations with Seuthes, initially hostile, are later obscure. About 320–10, the latter founded Seuthopolis.

Third century B.C.

At the beginning, Lysimachos was temporarily captured by the Getic king Dromichaites, but peaceful relations were established. Thereafter, until Lysimachos' death in 281, his main preoccupations were with the Celts, the Paeonians, and his rival Seleukos.

In 279, his successor, Ptolemaios Keraunos, died fighting the Celts. From 278 to c. 218 a Celtic group formed a kingdom in Thrace, probably based in the south-east, which was finally overthrown by a Thracian revolt. The main beneficiary of this new situation was Philip V of Macedonia, who involved Thrace as a pawn in his intrigues against the rising power of Rome.

Second century B.C.

During the first half, the conflicting ambitions of Philip V and Rome encouraged tribal aggression and disunity. In 183, Philip invaded Thrace and temporarily occupied Philippopolis. In 179, the Bastarnae raided down the Black Sea coastal strip and reached Macedonia. In 163, Rome conquered Macedonia and thus obtained a frontier with Thrace.

The second half of the century was studded by Thracian raids and Roman punitive expeditions.

First century B.C.

During the first half, aggression by the Maidi and Dentheletai, and general tribal unrest, led to increased Roman intervention, since Thrace occupied a strategically important position in the wars between Rome and Mithridates of Pontos. In 72, a major Roman expedition reached the Black Sea coast, subjugating the southern cities.

In 73–71, Spartakos, a Thracian slave-gladiator, led a revolt of 70,000 slaves in Italy.

C. 50 B.C., trans-Danubian Daco-Getic tribes, led by Burebista, invaded Thrace and reached Apollonia. A full-scale Daco-Roman confrontation was averted only by the contemporaneous assassinations of Julius Caesar and Burebista.

Augustus 27 B.C. – A.D. 14

In 27, Rome established vassal kingdoms south of the Danube, thus confining resistance to guerrilla warfare, mainly by the Bessi. But the tempo of raids and invasions from north of the Danube by Dacians, Sarmatians, and Bastarnae increased.

During 14–12, Roman detachments were established along the south bank of the Danube as far as the river Yantra.

PART TWO

First century A.D.

Tiberius 14–37	*Caligula* 37–41	*Claudius* 41–54	*Nero* 54–68
Galba 68–69	*Vespasian* 69–79	*Domitian* 81–96	*Trajan* 98–117

Mainly due to the Dacian and Bastarnae threat, the Roman province of Moesia was constituted by A.D. 6. Subjected to intensive Romanisation, it was essentially a military zone, occupying the south bank of the Danube east of Pannonia, the Dobroudja, and the Black Sea coast, with legionary headquarters at Oescus, Novae, and Durostorum. Only the established Greek cities retained their civic autonomy.

The interior remained under the rule of vassal kings until 46, when it was transformed into the province of Thracia, extending from the north slopes of the Stara Planina to the Aegean. Although detribalised, it retained Greek as its official language and its Thraco-Hellenistic culture. Romanisation was not attempted. Roads were built for military purposes, including the 'Diagonal' from Naissus across the Western uplands and the Thracian plain to the Bosphorus, the Danube road, and others running north-south. But the countryside was neglected, being regarded only as a source of food and conscripts – and potential unrest.

Sarmatian and Dacian raids increased, especially during the latter half of the century. To meet the Dacian threat, Moesia was reorganised by Domitian into Moesia Inferior and Moesia Superior, the border being the Tsibritsa river.

Second century A.D.

Trajan 98–117   *Hadrian* 117–38   *Antoninus Pius* 138–61
Marcus Aurelius 161–80   *Commodus* 180–93   *Septimius Severus* 193–211
Rome was victorious in the First Dacian war (101–02), but Moesia Inferior was subsequently invaded by Dacians, Sarmatians, and Bastarnae. The Second Dacian war (105–06) and the Roman annexation of Dacia began a period of peace and prosperity for Moesia and Thracia, reflected in the expansion of existing cities and garrison towns and new strategic foundations by Trajan in Thracia, always on Hellenistic lines with immigration from Asia Minor encouraged. The rural economy was assisted by the development of emporia.

The Costoboki invasion of 170–71 resulted in the fortification of hitherto open cities and in a general strengthening of defences. Depopulation by plague may have led to much resettlement of territories by defeated invaders.

Third century A.D.

Septimius Severus 193–211   *Caracalla* 211–17   *Elagabalus* 218–22
Alexander Severus 222–35   *Maximinus Thrax* 235–38   *Gordian III* 238–44
Philip the Arab 244–49   *Decius* 249–51   *Valerianus* 253–60
Gallienus 253–68   *Claudius II Gothicus* 268–70   *Aurelian* 270–75
Probus 276–82   *Diocletian* 284–305
During the first half, both Moesias and Thracia reached their peak of prosperity under Rome, although in 238 Karps, Goths, and Sarmatians invaded the northeast. Under Septimius Severus, Moesia Inferior gained Nicopolis-ad-Istrum. The further promotion of emporia and increased local recruiting with opportunities for military promotion encouraged the growth of rural prosperity. A Thracian soldier, Maximinus Thrax, rose from the ranks to the imperial throne after the murder of Alexander Severus – to meet the same fate at the hands of his own troops.

Gothic invasions, already begun in the reigns of Gordian and Philip, reached a climax in 250–51, when Philippopolis was sacked and Decius defeated and killed near Abritus. Twenty years' devastation of the countryside followed, only the fortified cities remaining secure, until in 269–70 the Goths were decisively vanquished by Claudius.

Aurelian's planned withdrawal from Dacia between 271 and 275 was followed by the reinforcement of the Danube *limes*. Dacian Roman or Romanised refugees were resettled, mainly in two newly constituted provinces south of the Danube – Dacia Ripensis, administered from Ratiaria and having, approximately, the Iskur-Vit watershed as its boundary with Moesia Inferior (renamed Moesia Secunda), and Dacia Mediterranea, administered from Serdica and including the territory of Naissus. Another Gothic invasion in 278 was followed by the settlement in depopulated Moesia Secunda of Gothic, Sarmatian, and Saracen prisoners to promote agricultural production. By the end of the century the

Visigoths, firmly established north of the Danube and separated from the Ostrogoths in south Russia, had replaced the original Gothic group as the main trans-Danubian danger.

The beginnings of the division of the empire into East and West appeared with Diocletian's administrative reorganisation, which separated the Prefecture of Illyricum (including the Dioceses of Illyricum, Macedonia, and Dacia and their component provinces) from the Prefecture of the East. The latter included the Diocese of Thracia, composed of the provinces of Scythia, Moesia Secunda, and, south of the Stara Planina, Thracia, Rhodope, Haemimontus, and Europa. (To avoid confusion, henceforth the term 'Thracia' is used in this book to denote the diocese, not the new province.) The border between the two Prefectures lay along the Iskur-Vit watershed, the Succi-Ihtiman pass, and the Mesta valley.

Fourth century A.D.

Diocletian 284–305   Constantine 306–37   Constantine and Licinius 311–24
Constantine sole emperor 324–37   Constantius II 337–61   Julian 361–63
Valens 364–78   Theodosius I 379–95   Arcadius 395–408

Galerius, Caesar of Illyricum and Thracia from 293 to 311, and Constantine were engaged during the early part of the century in repelling Visigothic attacks (which continued intermittently during subsequent reigns) and with the re-fortification of the *limes*.

Christianity, after a final persecution, developed as a major factor of imperial policy. In 325, Constantine's presence at the Council of Nicaea established a permanent link between Church and state, their administration jointly based on Diocletian's reorganisation. The work of the Council included the condemnation of the Eastern monotheistic doctrine of Arianism.

Thracia increased in strategic importance when Constantine established Constantinople as his imperial capital in 330. His heirs again followed Diocletian's reorganisation in dividing the empire, with Thracia in the Eastern and Illyricum in the Western half.

In 343, the Council of Serdica's disastrous attempt to resolve the Arian controversy widened the religious gap between East and West.

In 376, Valens' agreement to the settlement of Visigoths in Moesia Secunda was wrecked by the rapacity of local officials, leading to full-scale warfare. In 378, Valens was defeated and killed near Hadrianopolis. Rural Thracia again suffered devastation. In 382, peace was concluded and the Visigoths settled as *foederati* in Moesia Secunda.

PART THREE

In 380, the Edict of Thessalonica confirmed Christianity as the only legal religion in the empire. In 382, eastern Illyricum was ceded to the Eastern empire, joining the two Dacian provinces and Macedonia to the Diocese of Thracia.

Permanent division of the empire followed Theodosius's death, Honorius taking the West and Arcadius the East.

In 400, the Visigoths left Moesia for Italy.

Fifth century A.D.

Arcadius 395–408   *Theodosius II* 408–50   *Marcian* 450–57
Leo I 457–74   *Zeno* 474–75   *Basiliscus* 475–76   *Zeno (again)* 476–91
Anastasius I 491–518

The first half was shadowed by the growing menace of the Huns, although their first invasion in 408, which captured Castra Martis, was repulsed. A quarter-century of relative peace bought by heavy annual tribute permitted refortification of the *limes* and a degree of economic recovery. Byzantine acceptance of new, humiliating terms in 435 failed to prevent major invasions between 441 and 451. For the first time many fortified centres fell to the enemy and heavy damage was inflicted on most major cities.

After Attila's death in 453, the Ostrogoths succeeded the Huns as the main trans-Danubian power, invading Thracia from 463 onwards and pursuing inter-necine strife on Thracian and Macedonian soil. Zeno's intrigues and grant to Theodoric the Amal of a realm based on Novae did not prevent an invasion in 486 which reached the walls of Constantinople. In 488, Theodoric and his Ostrogoths left for Italy, and towards the end of the century, a major programme of general refortification of the *limes* and the rest of Thracia began under Anastasius. At the turn of the century the future rulers of the land, the Bulgars, made their first unsuccessful raids.

Sixth century A.D.

Anastasius I 491–518   *Justin I* 518–27   *Justinian* 527–65
Justin II 565–78   *Tiberius II Constantine* 578–82
Maurice 582–602

The refortification programme, accompanied by a great expansion of church building, was continued under Justin I and Justinian. To help the land recover, Thracia's normal responsibility to provide grain for cities and troops was re-mitted, but this did not prevent a serious revolt, motivated also by religious questions, of peasants and Gothic *foederati*, led by Vitalian in 513–18.

Bulgar raids decreased, but Slav pressure and infiltration in increasing num-bers from early in the century gradually developed from a source of labour and recruitment into one of danger, forcing the civil population of Moesia to leave the lowlands for hill fortresses. By mid-century the Slav invasions had become more numerous and aggressive and had reached the Thracian plain. A Byzantine invitation to the Avars, now the major power north of the Danube, to attack the Slavs in 580 merely resulted in an Avaro-Slav coalition and the Avar capture and destruction of most northern cities, although at the end of the century many fortresses still remained in Byzantine hands.

Seventh century A.D.

Maurice 582–602   *Phocas* 602–10   *Heraclius* 610–41
Constans II 641–68   *Constantine IV* 668–85   *Justinian II* 625–95

During the anarchy of Phocas' reign the Avars and Slavs overthrew most of the surviving fortresses and the Slavs completed the settlement of the countryside unopposed. All but the major coastal cities, such fortresses as Philippopolis and Serdica on the 'Diagonal', and possibly some in remote, impregnable situations elsewhere, succumbed during the next fifty years.

Heraclius, preoccupied with the Persian danger, could not concentrate his resources against the Avars, but a mighty Avaro-Slav attempt by land and sea to take Constantinople was decisively defeated in 626 and the Avar power finally broken.

The Slav occupation and settlement of the Balkans was such that the military reconquest of Thracia had ceased to be a practical proposition. Any possibility of peaceful absorption of the Slavs into the Byzantine empire was destroyed by the reappearance of the Bulgars in 681.

Select Bibliography

I. Publications and Bulgarian journals which are the main sources for an archaeological study of Bulgaria during this period. The former have been selected with some preference for recent work and relative availability; the latter are almost the only sources for excavation reports.

II. A site bibliography listing the main publications giving fuller information on archaeological sites; the omission of some sites indicates the absence of a special report or that no information additional to that published here was available to the author at the time of going to press.

Notes

1. Publications with especially useful bibliographies are marked by an asterisk.
2. The footnotes in many cases supplement the bibliography by references to publication of individual finds, to primary historical sources where quoted, and to a few general works of reference.

I. PUBLICATIONS

Angelov, D., *Obrazouvane na Bulgarskata Narodnost*, Sofia, 1971.

Blavatskaya, T. V., *Zapadnopontyskie goroda v VII–I vekakh do n.e.*, Moscow, 1952.

Beševliev, V., 'Les cités antiques en Mésie et en Thrace et leur sort à l'époque du haut moyen âge', *Etudes Balkaniques V*, 1966, 207 ff.

Casson, S., *Macedonia, Thrace and Illyria*, Oxford, 1926.

Danov, H., 'Iz drevnata ikonomicheska istoriya na Zapadnoto Chernomorie do oustanovyaneto na rimskoto vladichestvo, *IBAI* XII, 1938, 185 ff.

——, *Drevna Trakia*,* Sofia, n.d. (*c.* 1969).

Dimitrov, D. P., *Bulgaria, Land of Ancient Civilisations*, Sofia, 1961.

Dimitrov, D. P., *et al.*, *Kratka Istoriya na Bulgarskata Arhitektura*, Sofia, 1965.

Fol, A., *Demografska i sotsialna struktura na drevna Trakiya prez I hil. pr. n.e.*, Sofia, 1970.

Georgieva, S., and Velkov, V., *Bibliografiya na Bulgarskata Arheologiya* (1879–1955),* Sofia, 1957.

Gerov, B., *Prouchvaniya vurhu Zapadnotrakiskite Zemi prez Rimsko vreme*,* Sofia, 1961 (previously published in 3 parts of the GSU).

——, *Romanizmut mejdu Dounava i Balkana ot Avgoust do Konstantin Veliki*,* Sofia, 1954 (previously published in 3 parts of the GSU).

Ivanova, V., *Stari Tsurkvi i Monastiri v Bulgarskite Zemi*, GNM IV, 1922–25, 429 ff.

Jones, A. H. M., *The Cities of the Eastern Roman Provinces*, 2nd edn., Oxford, 1971.

Kazarow, G. I., *Die Denkmäler des Thrakischen Reitergottes in Bulgarien*, Budapest, 1938.

Mihailov, G., *Inscriptiones Graecae in Bulgaria repertae*,* I (2nd edn.), II-V, Sofia, 1958–70.

Strong, D. E., *Greek and Roman Gold and Silver Plate*, London, 1966.

Velkov, V., 'La construction en Thrace à l'époque du Bas-Empire (d'après les écrits)', *Archeologia* X, Warsaw, 1958, 124 ff.

——, *Gradut v Trakiya i Dakiya prez Kusnata Antichnost (IV-VI vv),** Sofia, 1959.

Venedikov, I., 'Predahemenidski Iran i Trakiya', *IBAI* XXXI, 1969, 5 ff.

——, *Bulgaria's Treasures from the Past*, Sofia, 1965.

Wiesner, J., *Die Thraker,** Stuttgart, 1963.

Acta Antiqua Philippopolitana: Studia Archaeologica et *Studia Historica et Philologica* (VI Mejdunarodna konferentsiya po klasicheski studi), 2 vols, Sofia, 1963.

Actes de Ier Congrès international des études balkaniques et sud-est européennes, II,* Sofia, 1969.

*Antike und Mittelalter in Bulgarien,** ed. Beshevliev, V. and Irmscher, J. Berlin, 1960.

Izsledvaniya v chest na Akad. D. Dechev (Studia in honorem Acad. D. Dechev), Sofia, 1958.

Izsledvaniya v pamet na Karel Shkorpil (Studia in memoriam Karel Škorpil), Sofia, 1961.

*Kunstschätze in bulgarien Museen und Klöstern,** Essen, 1964.

Pauly-Wissowa, *Real-Encyclopädie der classischen Altertumswissenschaft.**

Razkopki i Prouchvaniya (Fouilles et Recherches), I–IV, Sofia, 1948–1950.

Sbornik Arheologicheski otkritiya v Bulgaria, Sofia, 1957.

Sbornik Gavril Katsarov II (published as *IBAI* XIX), Sofia, 1955.

Thracia: Primus Congressus Studiorum Thracicorum, I, Sofia, 1972.

II. BULGARIAN JOURNALS

Sofia

Arheologiya I, 1959– .

Godishnik na Narodniya Arheologicheski Muzei v Sofia (Annuaire du Musée Archéologique de Sofia) I, 1920, – VII, 1942.

Izvestiya na Bulgarskiya Arheologicheski Institut (Bulletin de l'Institut Archéologique Bulgare) later entitled *Izvestiya na Arheologicheski Institut (Bulletin de l'Institut Archéologique)* I, 1921– .

Izvestiya na Bulgarskoto Arheologichesko Drujestvo (Bulletin de la Société archéologique bulgare), I, 1910, – VII, 1919–20.

Muzei i Pametnitsi na Kultura (Museums and Monuments) I, 1961– .

Godishnik na Sofiskiya Universitet (Annuaire de l'Université de Sofia), I, 1904– , published in parts by, *inter alia*, the faculties of history, philology, and philosophy, also contains archaeological reports.

Bourgas

Izvestiya na Narodniya Muzei Bourgas (Bulletin du Musée National de Bourgas), Sofia, I, 1950; II, 1965.

Plovdiv

Godishnik na Narodnata biblioteka v Plovdiv, 1907-08–1927.

Godishnik na Narodnata biblioteka i Muzei v Plovdiv, 1928-29–1940-41.
Godishnik na Narodniya Arheologicheski Muzei v Plovdiv (Annuaire du Musée National Archéologique de Plovdiv) I, 1948– .

(Some issues of the above journals were published in Sofia, the rest in Plovdiv; only the last series is numbered.)

Godishnik na Muzeite v Plovdivski Okrug, I, 1954– .

Shoumen

Izvestiya na Narodniya Muzei Kolarovgrad (Bulletin du Musée National de Kolarovgrad), Varna, I, 1960, – III, 1965; from IV, 1967, onwards, with the town's resumption of its earlier name of Shoumen, the journal was renamed: *Izvestiya na Narodniya Muzei Shoumen (Mitteilungen des Volksmuseums Schumen)*.

Turnovo

Izvestiya na Okrujniya Muzei Turnovo (Mitteilungen des Bezirksmuseums Tirnovo), Varna, I, 1962– .

Varna

Izvestiya na Varnenskoto Arheologichesko Drujestvo (Bulletin de la Société archéologique de Varna) I, 1908, – XV, 1963; VIII, 1951, and IX, 1953, appeared when the city was temporarily named 'Stalin' and the journal accordingly.
Izvestiya na Narodniya Muzei Varna (Bulletin du Musée National à Varna), I (XVI), 1964– .

Site Bibliography

Abritus (*Razgrad*)
Ivanov, T., *Abritus: vodach za antichni grad pri Razgrad*,* Sofia, 1965.
——, *Arh* VIII/4, 1966, 18 ff.
——, *AAP* (*A*), 88 ff.

Anchialos (*Pomorie*)
tomb: Petrov, T. *et al.*, *Antichnata grobnitsa krai Pomorie*, Bourgas, 1960.

Apollonia (*Sozopol*)
Arheologicheski Muzei Bourgas,* Sofia, 1967.
Venedikov, I., *Sbornik Arheologicheski otkritiya v Bulgaria*, Sofia, 1957, 95 ff.
necropolis: various, 'Apoloniya na Cherno more', *RP* II, Sofia, 1948; Venedikov, I. (ed.), *Apoloniya: razkopkite v nekropola na Apoloniya prez 1947–1949*, Sofia, 1963.

Armira
Mladenova, Ya., *Arh* VII/2, 1965, 20 ff.
——, *Izkoustvo*, Sofia, kn. 4, 1965, 20 ff.
——, *Actes Ist BC*, 527 ff.
——, *IBAI* XXXII, 1970, 129 ff.

Augusta Trajana – see *Beroe–Augusta Trajana*.

Batkoun
Zontchew, D., *Le sanctuaire thrace près du village de Batkoun*, Sofia, 1941.

Beroe – **Augusta Trajana** (*Stara Zagora*)
Okrujen Naroden Muzei Stara Zagora: staro izkoustvo,* Sofia, 1965.
Nikolov, D., *Arh* VII/3, 1965, 11 ff.; *Arh* IX/4, 1967, 30 ff.
town house: Nikolov, D., *Arh* I/1–2, 1959, 59 ff.
Starazagorski Mineralni Bani: Nikolov, D., *Arh* X/1, 1968, 43 ff.; Tsonchev, D., *IBAI* XII, 1938, 350 ff.
Mogilovo chariot burial: Venedikov, I., *Trakiskata kolesnitsa*, Sofia, 1960, 34 ff.
Trite Mogili chariot burials: Nikolov, D., *Arh* III/3, 1961, 8 ff.

Bizone (*Kavarna*)
Mirchev, M. *et al.*, *Iz Varna* XIII, 1962, 21 ff.

Botevo
Stanchev, S., *Arh* I/3–4, 1959, 70 ff.

Branichevo
Dremsizova, Ts., *IBAI* XXV, 1962, 165 ff.

Burdapa (*Ognyanovo*, formerly *Saladinovo*)
Dobrusky, V., *BCH* XXI, 1897, 119 ff.

Butovo (? **Emporium Piretensium**)
Sultov, B., *Actes Ist BC*, 479 ff.; *Arh* IV/4, 1962, 30 ff.

Chatalka
villa rustica: Nikolov, D., *Actes Ist BC*, 513 ff.
burials: Nikolov, D. and Buyukliev, H., *Arh* IX/1, 1967, 19 ff.; *Arh* IX/3, 1967, 10 ff.

Chertigrad
Velkov, V. and Gocheva, Z., *Arh* XIII/4, 1971, 52 ff.; *Thracia* I, 1972, 121 ff.

Dionysopolis (*Balchik*)
Škorpil, K., *IBAI* VI, 1930-31, 57 ff.

Discoduratera (*Gostilitsa*)
Sultov, B., *Iz Turnovo* III 1966, 25 ff.

Dolno Sahrane
Getov, L., *IBAI* XXVIII, 1965, 201 ff.

Douvanli
Filow, B., *Die Grabhügelnekropole bei Duvanlij*, Sofia, 1934.
Strong, D. E., *Greek and Roman Gold and Silver Plate*, London, 1966.
Koukouva tumulus: Dyakovich, B., *IBAI* III, 1925, 111 ff.; Filov, B., *IBAI* IV, 1926–27, 27 ff.
Bashova and Moushovitsa tumuli: Velkov, I., *IBAI* VI, 1930–31, 1 ff.
Golyama, Lozarska, and Arabadjiska tumuli: Filov, B., *IBAI* VII, 1932–33, 218 ff.

Durostorum (*Silistra*)
painted tomb: Dimitrov, D. P., *Arh* III/1, 1961, 10 ff.; *CA* XII, 1962, 35 ff.; Frova, A., *Pittura romana in Bulgaria*, Rome, 1943.

Erite (*Dolni Bliznyak*)
Pokrovsky, S., *IBAI* XIII, 1940–42, 252 ff.

Germania (*Sapareva Banya*)
Ivanov, T., *IBAI* XXI, 1957, 211 ff.

Golyamo Belovo
Boyadjiev, S., *Arh* XI/3, 1969, 10 ff.
Grabar, A. and Emerson, W., *Bull. Byz. Inst.* I, 1946, 43 ff.

Haskovo Mineralni Bani
Tsonchev, D., *God Plovdiv*, 1937–39, 94 ff.

Hissar
Boyadjiev, S., *IBAI* XXX, 1967, 101 ff.
Filov, B., *IBAD* II/1, 1912, 99 ff.
Madjarov, K., *IBAI* XXX, 1967, 113 ff.
Tsonchev, D., *Hisarskite Bani*, Plovdiv, 1937.
churches: Ivanova, V., *IBAI* XI, 1937, 214 ff.; Madjarov, K., *Arh* XIII/3, 1971, 34 ff. (The general works listed are also concerned with the churches.)
mausoleum: Djambov, H., *God Plovdiv* V, 1963, 117 ff.
town house: Madjarov, K., *Arh* IX/1, 1967, 50 ff.

Hotnitsa
Sultov, B., *Arh* XI/4, 1969, 12 ff.

Iatrus (*Krivina*)
Ivanov, T., *Arh* III/3, 1961, 18 ff.; *Arh* V/4, 1963, 10 ff.; *Vorträge des VI Internationalen Limes Kongress in Süddeutschland*, Cologne-Graz, 1967, 154 ff.; Ivanov, T. *et al.*, *Klio*, XLVII, 1966.

Isperihovo
Djambov, H., *Godishnik na Muzeite v Plovdivski Okrug*, II, 1956, 174 ff.

Ivanyani
Ivanova, V., *IBAI* VIII, 1935, 220 ff.

Kaliakra
Djingov, J., *Kaliakra*, Sofia, 1970.

Kasnakovo
Venedikov, I., *IBAI* XVII, 1950, 105 ff.

Kazanluk
domed painted tomb: Mikov, V., *Antichnata grobnitsa pri Kazanluk*, Sofia, 1954; Tsanova, G. and Getov, L., *Trakiskata grobnitsa pri Kazanluk*, Sofia, 1970; Vasiliev, A., *Kazanlushkata grobnitsa*, Sofia, 1958; Verdiani, C., *AJA* XLIV, 1945, 402 ff.

Krumovo Kale
Ovcharov, D., *Arh* XII/3, 1970, 16 ff.; *Arh* XIII/4, 1971, 18 ff.

Krun
Tabakova, G., *IBAI* XXII, 1959, 97 ff.

Madara
Madara: Razkopki i Prouchvaniya I and II, Sofia, 1934, 1936.
Dremsizova, Ts., *Madara: vodach na pametnitsi i muzeya*, Sofia, 1967.
villa rustica: Antonova, V., *Iz Shoumen* I, 1960, 25 ff.; *Iz Shoumen* II, 1963, 25ff.; Dremsizova, Ts., *AAP(A)*, 111 ff.

Marcianopolis (*Reka Devnya*)
Mirchev, M. and Toncheva, G., *Istoricheski Pregled* XII/6, 1956, 69 ff.
Toncheva, G., *Drevniyat Martsianopol*, Varna, n.d.

Mesambria (*Nesebur*)
Arheologicheski Muzei Bourgas,* Sofia, 1967.
Gulubov, I., *Nesebur i negovite pametnitsi*, Sofia, 1960; *Antike und Mittelalter in Bulgarien*, Berlin, 1960, 306ff.
Ognenova, L., *BCH* LXXIV, 1960, 221 ff.
general and fortifications: Venedikov, I. (ed.), *Nessèbre*, tom I, Sofia, 1966.
churches: Rashenov, A., *Mesemvriski tsurkvi*, Sofia, 1932.
'Sea Basilica': Velkov, I., *L'Art byzantin chez les Slaves* (recueil Uspenskij), Vol. I, Paris, 1930, 75 ff.; *Bull. Byz. Inst.* I, 1946, 61 ff.
Old Metropolis: Boyadjiev, S., *Byzantino-Bulgarica* I, 1962, 321 ff.
tombs: Chimbuleva, J., *Arh* VI/4, 1964, 57 ff.; Gulubov, I., *IBAI* XIX, 1955, 129 ff.

Mezek
Filov, B., *Antiquity* XI, 1937, 300 ff.; *IBAI* XI, 1937, 1 ff.
Velkov, I., *IBAI* XI, 1937, 117 ff.

Mogilovo – see *Beroe–Augusta Trajana*

Montana (*Mihailovgrad*)
Aleksandrov, G., *Arh* XII/3, 1970, 43 ff.
Filov, B., *IBAD* V, 1915, 216, 217.

Nicopolis-ad-Istrum (*near Nikyup*)
Bobchev, S. N., *IBAI* V, 1928–29, 56 ff.
Ivanov, T., *IBAI* XVIII, 1952, 215 ff.; *Antike und Mittelalter in Bulgarien*, Berlin, 1960, 279 ff.

Novae (*Stuklen, near Svishtov*)
Dimitrov, D. P. *et al.*, *IBAI* XXVI, 1963, and subsequent issues.
Majewski, K. *et al.*, *IBAI* XXVI, 1963, and subsequent issues.
Majewski, K. *et al.*, *Archeologia*, Warsaw, XII, 1961, and subsequent issues.
Pres, L. and Chichikova, M., *Arh* V/2, 1963, 59 ff.

Odessos (*Varna*)
Arheologicheski Muzei Varna*, Sofia, 1964.
baths: Mirchev, M., *Actes Ist BC*, 455 ff.
Pirinch-tepe: Shkorpil, K., *Iz Varna* III, 1910, 15 ff.
tombs: Mirchev, M., *Izsled Dechev*, 569 ff.; *Iz Varna* V (XX), 1969, 223 ff.
early Byzantine jewellery: Dimitrov, D. I., *Iz Varna* XIV, 1963, 65 ff.
terracottas: Mirchev, M., *Iz Varna* X, 1955, 1 ff.
Galata church and sanctuary: Mirchev, M., *Iz Varna* IX, 1952, 1 ff.; Toncheva, G., *Iz Varna* IV (XIX), 1968, 17 ff.
Galata tumuli: Toncheva, G., *Iz Varna* VIII, 1951, 49 ff.

Oescus (*Gigen*)
Frova, A., *IBAI* XVII, 1950, 34 ff.
Ivanov, T., *Arheologicheski otkritiya v Bulgaria*, 1957, 113 ff.
——, *Rimska mosaika ot Ulpiya Eskus*, Sofia, 1954.
Kreta Mithraeum: Velkov, I., *IBAI* VIII, 1934, 82 ff.

Orlandovtsi – see *Serdica*

Panagyurishte
gold treasure: Venedikov, I., *The Panagyurishte Gold Treasure*, Sofia. 1961; Strong, D. E., *Greek and Roman Gold and Silver Plate*, London, 1966; Botou-sharova, L., *God Plovdiv* III, 1960, 357–9*; Toteva, P., *God Plovdiv* VII, 1971, 159 ff*.

Pautalia (*Kyustendil*)
Ivanov, I., *IBAD* VII, 1920, 66 ff.
Hissarluk fortress; Gocheva, Z., *Izvestiya na Bulgarskoto istorichesko drujestvo* XXVII, 1970, 233 ff. (see also Ivanov, *IBAD* VII)
baths: Kuzmanov, G., *MP* 4, 1972, 11 ff.; Ruseva-Slokoska, L., *Arh* VI/1, 1964, 33 ff.

chariot burial: Slokoska, L., MP 4, 1970, 7 ff.
coins: Ruzicka, L., *IBAI* VII, 1932-33, 1 ff.
Kadin Most: Ivanov, I., *IBAD* I, 1910, 163 ff.
Kopilovtsi: Katsarov, G., *IBAD* IV, 1914, 80 ff.

Peroushtitsa
Tsonchev, D., *IBAI* XVII, 1950, 237 ff.
Red Church: Frolow, A., *Bull. Byz. Inst.* I, 1946, 15 ff.; Grabar, A., *La peinture religieuse en Bulgarie*, Paris, 1928, 22 ff., Pls. I, II.; Panaiotova, D., *Chervenata tsurkva pri Peroushtitsa*, Sofia, 1956.

Philippopolis (*Plovdiv*)
Arheologicheski Muzei Plovdiv*, Sofia, 1964.
Djambov, H. (ed.), *Arheologicheski prouchvaniya za istoriyata na Plovdiv i Plovdivski krai*,* Plovdiv, 1966.
fortifications: Botousharova, L., *AAP(A)*, 105 ff.; Botousharova, L., *God Plovdiv* V, 1963, 77 ff.; Botousharova, L. and Kolarova, V., *God Plovdiv* VII, 1971, 75 ff.; Djambov, H., *God Plovdiv* III, 1959, 165 ff.; Kolev, K., *God Plovdiv* VII, 1971, 99 ff.
baths: Tsonchev, D., *God Plovdiv*, 1937–39, 129 ff.; *God Plovdiv* II, 1950, 137 ff.
stadium: Mateev, M., *God Plovdiv* VII, 1971, 135 ff.
tombs: Botousharova, L. and Kolarova, V., *Izsled Shkorpil*, 279 ff.; Botousharova, L., *AAP(A)*, 105 ff.
Komatevo church: Djambov, H., *God Plovdiv* III, 1959, 115 ff.

Pirdop
Elenska church: Mutafchiev, P., *IBAD* V, 1915, 20 ff.

Pliska
Mihailov, S., *Starinar* XX, 1969, 213 ff.
Stančev, S., *Antike und Mittelalter in Bulgarien*,* Berlin, 1960, 219 ff.

Preslav (See also entries under *Pliska*)
Deli-Doushka church: Ivanova, V., *RP* III, 1949, 5 ff.
fort: Djingov, G., *Arh* IV/4, 1962, 16 ff.

Prisovo
Sultov, B., *Iz Turnovo* II, 1964, 49 ff.

Ratiaria (*Archar*)
Hošek, R., and Velkov, V., *Listy Filologicke* VI (LXXXI), 1958, 32 ff.
Velkov, V., *Eirene* V, 1966, 155 ff.

Sadovets
Golemanovo Kale: Bersu, G., *Antiquity* XII, 1938, 31 ff.
Sadovsko Kale: Welkow, I., *Germania* XIX, 1935, 149 ff.

Sandanski (*formerly Sveti Vrach*)
Ivanov, T. *et al.*, *IBAI* XXXI, 1969, 105 ff.
Ivanova, V., *GNM* IV, 1922–25, 549–51.

Serdica (*Sofia*)
Serdika I, Sofia, 1964.
Gerov, B., *Prouchvaniya*.
fortifications: Boyadjiev, S., *Arh* I/3–4, 1959, 35 ff. (but see also the two general works above).
Mithraeum: Bobchev, S., *IBAI* XIX, 1955, 208 ff.
'St. George complex': Karasimeonov, P., *GNM* VII, 1942, 188 ff. (See also *Serdika I*.)
church of Holy Wisdom: Boyadjiev, S., *Izsled Dechev*, 1958, 611 ff.; [Boyadjiev, S.], *Sofiskata tsurkva Sv. Sofiya*, Sofia, 1967; Filov, B., *Sofiskata tsurkva Sv. Sofiya*, Sofia, 1913.
tombs: Katsarov, G. and Tachev, H., *IBAD* I, 1910, 23 ff.; Miyatev, K., *Dekorativna Jivopis na Sofiskata nekropol*, Sofia, 1925.
villa rustica, Gara Iskur: Velkov, I. *IBAI* XII, 1938, 408.
villa rustica, Orlandovtsi: ibid., 409.

Seuthopolis
Chichikova, M., *Seuthopolis*,* Sofia, 1970; *IBAI* XXI, 1957, 129 ff.
Dimitrov, D. P., *Sovetskaya Arheologiya* 1957, kn.1, 199 ff.; *Antiquity* XXXV, 1961, 91 ff.
Getov, L. and Tsanova, G., *Naroden Muzei Kazanluk: staro izkoustvo*, Sofia, 1967.
Koprinka necropolis: Juglev, K., GSUFIF XLVII/2, 1952, 217 ff.; GSUFIF XLIX/2, 1955–56, 35 ff.; Getov, L., *Arh* III/4, 1961, 58 ff.

Shoumen
Antonova, V., *Iz Shoumen* V, 1970, 3 ff.

Starazagorski Mineralni Bani – see *Beroe–Augusta Trajana*.

Storgosia (*Kailuka, near Pleven*)
Vulev, K., *IBAD* I, 1910, 203 ff.

Sveti Duh
Aladjov, D., *Rodopski Sbornik* II, 1969, 249 ff.

Transmarisca (*Toutrakan*)
Zmeev, R., *Arh* XI/4*, 1969, 45 ff.

Trite Mogili – see *Beroe–Augusta Trajana*

Tsar Krum
churches: Antonova, V., *Arh* X/4, 1968, 52 ff.; Antonova, V. and Dremsizova, Ts., *Arh* II/2, 1960, 28 ff.

Tsurkvishte (*formerly Klise-Kuoi*)
Mutafchiev, P., *IBAD* V, 1915, 85 ff.

Veliko Turnovo
Okrujen Naroden Muzei Turnovo: vodach, Sofia, 1957.
Angelov, N., *Iz Turnovo* III, 1966, 1 ff.; *Arh* IV/4, 1962, 20 ff.

Vicus Trullensium (*near Kunino*)
Velkov, I., *Izsled Dechev*, 557 ff.

Voivoda
Dremsizova, Ts. and Antonova, V., *Arh* IX/3, 1967, 30 ff.
Milchev, A., and Damyanov, S., *IBAI* XXXIII, 1972, 263 ff.

Vratsa
Nikolov, B., *Okrujen Istoricheski Muzei, Vratsa: staro izkoustvo,** Sofia, 1968;
    Arh IX/1, 1967, 11 ff.
Venedikov, I., *Arh* VIII/1, 1966, 7 ff.; *Etudes Balkaniques* V, 1966, 243 ff.

Note on Pronunciation

Bulgarian is written in Cyrillic characters and has been transliterated when used in this book. The system followed has not been entirely logical or consistent. For example, 'Sofiya' is the capital of 'Bulgariya', but the common usage of 'Sofia' and 'Bulgaria' has been followed in the text. In Bulgarian all letters are given their full sound value and terminal vowels are pronounced. Many letters are pronounced in the same way as English, but the following notes on the rough sound values of others may be helpful.

Transliterated letters	Sound value
A	bath
E	den
G	get
H	hut
I	marine
J	like 's' in 'measure'
O	got
OU	tour
S	sat
SHT	fishtail
TS	huts
U	but
V	vote (but like FF as in 'off' at the end of a word)
YA	yahoo
YU	yule

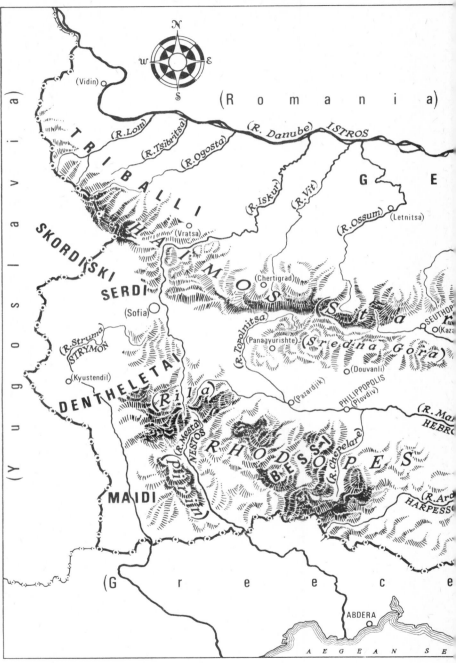

Map 1 Bulgaria: sixth to first centuries B.C.

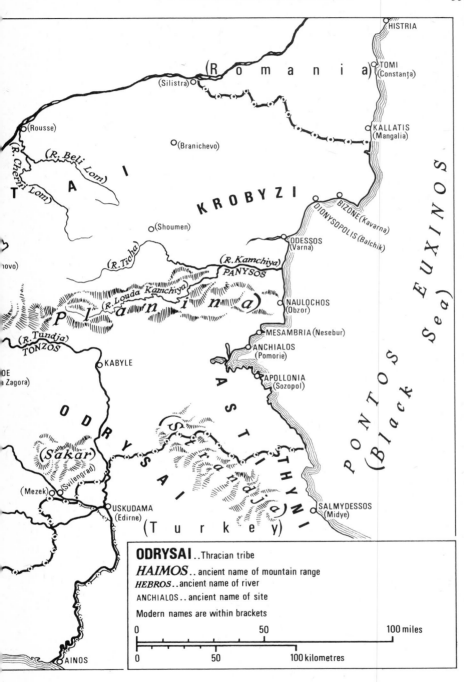

HISTRIA

TOMI
(Constanţa)

(R o m a n i a)
(Silistra)

KALLATIS
(Mangalia)

(Rousse)

(R. Beli Lom)
T A I
(Branichevo)

(R. Cherni Lom)

K R O B Y Z I

BIZONE (Kavarna)
DIONYSOPOLIS (Balchik)

(Shoumen)

ODESSOS
(Varna)

EUXINOS

(R. Ticha)
(R. Kamchiya)
PANYSOS
ovo)

(R. Louda Kamchiya)
(P l a n i n a)

NAULOCHOS
(Obzor)

PONTOS

(Black Sea)

(R. Tundja)
TONZOS

MESAMBRIA (Nesebur)

ANCHIALOS
(Pomorie)

KABYLE

OE
a Zagora)

APOLLONIA
(Sozopol)

O D R Y S A I

S t r a n d j a

A S T I T H Y N I

(Sakar)

(Svilengrad)

(Mezek)

USKUDAMA
(Edirne)

SALMYDESSOS
(Midye)

(T u r k e y)

ODRYSAI .. Thracian tribe
HAIMOS .. ancient name of mountain range
HEBROS .. ancient name of river
ANCHIALOS .. ancient name of site

Modern names are within brackets

0   50   100 miles

0   50   100 kilometres

AINOS

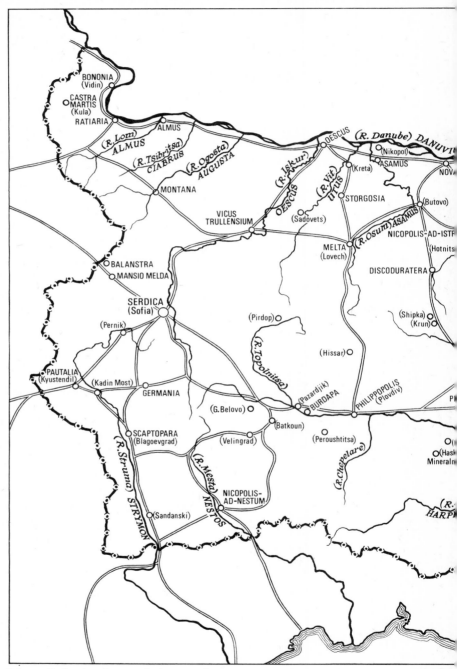

Map 2 Bulgaria: first to sixth centuries A.D.

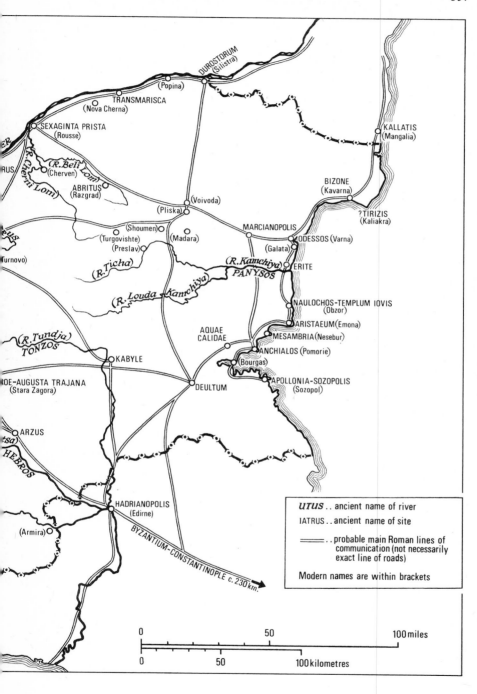

UTUS .. ancient name of river

IATRUS .. ancient name of site

═════ .. probable main Roman lines of communication (not necessarily exact line of roads)

Modern names are within brackets

Index

Principal references to ancient names of sites and geographical features in present-day Bulgaria appear in bold type. Main pages on archaeological sites are similarly shown. Text figures are indicated by the use of italic. Modern towns in Bulgaria near archaeological sites have been included for convenience of identification, although for reasons of clarity they are not all in the maps.

Printed in Great Britain by
The Garden City Press Limited
Letchworth, Hertfordshire SG6 1JS